Digital Asset Management

Digital Asset Management

David Austerberry

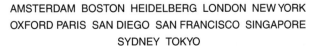
AMSTERDAM BOSTON HEIDELBERG LONDON NEW YORK
OXFORD PARIS SAN DIEGO SAN FRANCISCO SINGAPORE
SYDNEY TOKYO

Focal Press is an imprint of Elsevier

Focal Press
An imprint of Elsevier Ltd
Linacre House, Jordan Hill, Oxford OX2 8DP
200 Wheeler Road, Burlington, MA 01803

First published 2004

British Library Cataloguing in Publication Data
Austerberry, David
    Digital asset management
    1.   Broadcast data systems – Management   2.   Digital communications
    I.   Title
    621.3'82

ISBN 0 2405 1924 8

For information on all Elsevier Focus Press publications visit our website at
www.focalpress.com

Typeset by Charon Tec Pvt. Ltd, Chennai, India
Printed and bound in The Netherlands

Contents

Preface

My interest in this subject started when I joined the broadcast equipment manufacturer, Chyron. For a few years I was the product manager for their playout automation and asset management product lines. These were one of the first applications that gave television broadcasters the means to manage the ingest, storage, archiving, and play-out of programmes and commercials using the video servers that had just been introduced. The use of video compression, and the availability of high capacity disk drives, meant that the server had become a viable replacement for videotape.

Before that time, television programming had been broadcast from a combination of automated videocassette libraries (usually referred to as cart machines) and manually operated videotape recorders. The cart machines had sophisticated control systems to manage playlists and even make backup tapes for commercial breaks. As the broadcasters migrated to disk storage they demanded a similar functionality. The asset management system needed to handle multiple copies of a television commercial or programme, whether a tape or a file. The complete system had to be highly available and to fail-over gracefully–a spoilt commercial slot is a revenue opportunity lost forever. I must thank Spencer Rodd, now of Pharos Communications, for introducing me to the many issues involved in television channel playout from video servers.

Since those days, transmission from servers rather than tape has become the norm. The old methods for managing tapes, little different from a public lending library, have been replaced with digital asset management to control the ingest and playout of files.

I then moved to an industry working with much smaller video files–streaming media. I joined a team that was planning the system architecture for an application service provider that was to offer media encoding, archiving and distribution. Part of my role was to evaluate the leading digital asset management systems. That knowledge gained was the starting point for this book.

As I looked through the collateral from the vendors, they promised object-oriented software architectures with XML interfaces. The storage products offered helical or linear tape transports, NAS or SAN? The list went on and on. I had to sift through all the information and decide whether the claimed product benefits really gave a clear advantage in managing the content workflow, or would deliver a better return on investment. The problem was that the products covered many disciplines, from software engineering to video technology (for me familiar ground). Furthermore, no deployment can be successful without a deep understanding of the processes and workflows of content creation and publishing.

As video asset management evolved, the document and web sectors were progressing along parallel paths. This was a consequence of business information migrating to the digital domain. Once an asset becomes a file, it does not matter whether it is a text document, a web page, a music track or a video clip. Obviously there are differences in file size and data transfer rates–compare the data required for high-definition television with a simple text file–but the underlying principles are similar. The convergence of solutions for different sectors into a unified enterprise content management has been aided by the ever-decreasing costs of disk storage, and the ever-increasing processing power of the desktop PC.

One barrier to the adoption of asset management has been the number of closed systems. Even now, many content files are in proprietary formats. The emergence of internationally agreed standards has greatly eased the task of interfacing a digital asset management solution to the other business applications, and to the content that comprises those assets. The XML family of standards has proved ubiquitous. In the audio/video arena, the new AAF/MXF standards promise to enable the trouble-free interchange of assets across different hardware and software platforms.

Through the research for this title I have called upon some old friends, and have also received great assistance from some new acquaintances. In no particular order I would like to acknowledge the people who have helped with background information on the many aspects of asset management, both as vendors and as users.

During the research I interviewed many asset management vendors. All gave me valuable insights into their own product lines. First off, I would like to mention all the folks at Artesia, Convera and eMotion who first introduced me to enterprise scale asset management. Nigel Booth and David Cox showed me around the Leitch video servers, and Brian Smith helped me out with all the Leitch product shots. Neil McLaren described the products from Arkemedia Technologies. Many others at Documentum, Virage and Autonomy gave invaluable help. Numerous people supplied me with marketing collateral including Tammy Feinreich at MediaBin and Amy Lee at Virage

A special mention is due for my old friends at blue order, Jeremy Bancroft, Peter Gallen, and Serena Brinkman, who all spared me time to discuss their product line in great detail.

For more general background information I have had many chats with Neil Maycock at Pro-Bel about developments in the field of media asset management, and David Stebbings pointed me towards some very useful reports on the real world issues of digital rights management.

For the case studies I had great help from Andre McGarrigle at the Guardian Newspaper, who explained the background behind their choice of content management system and Danny Sofer at KitSite for his continuing interest and support. At Pathe, Peter Fydler, as well as Paul McKonkey and Tony Blake at Cambridge Imaging Systems. I would also like to thank Gordon Castle very much for giving me background information on the Archive Project at CNN, along with Dave Trumbo, David Farrell and Jeff Stromberg at IBM.

And finally, during my research the Global Society for Asset Management (G-SAM) was formed to promote the development and adoption of DAM technologies. The society is not just for the media business, but is to reflect the potential for asset management across the full spectrum of business. Their website at www.g-sam.org gives more details.

Throughout the text I have listed a number of links to further information on the Web. In this fast-changing field, vendors come and go, and sources of information change. For regularly updated information and links you can visit the supporting website for this book at www.davidausterberry.com/dam.html.

1 Introduction to digital asset management

Introduction

This chapter introduces the concepts of asset management. First it answers the question 'what are assets?'. Then some of the related solutions are described—document management, content management and media management, and finally, 'why is digital asset management (DAM) useful for any enterprise, not just publishing and media industries?'.

DAM has proved quite a technical challenge. It was not until the end of the twentieth century that affordable systems became available. The fall in the price of processing and disk storage has been the primary enabling factor, along with the ever-increasing bandwidths of computer networks, both within a local area and over long distances. Many of the products that are designed to manage the very large repositories can automate labour-intensive and repetitive tasks. These include cataloguing and indexing the content, then the powerful search engines that we use to discover and find content.

The product developers have leveraged research into the understanding of speech, character recognition and conceptual analysis to index and catalogue digital assets. The widespread application of these ideas requires considerable processing power to provide real time ingest of content—essential in many audio-video applications. The introduction of the low-cost and powerful computer workstations that today we take for granted now makes such technology commercially viable.

The modern business creates media content in many guises. Table 1.1 shows typical departments in a corporate enterprise, and the content that they each produce (see Figure 1.1). Traditionally each department would manage its own media content, usually with some formalized filing structure. Global brand management demands the enterprise-wide sharing of content if the corporation is not to descend into chaos, with the wrong logos, out-of-date corporate images, and link-rot on the website.

Content is now being delivered over a myriad of different channels. There are the electronic channels: television, iTV (interactive television), Internet and webcasting, cellular phones, and wireless personal digital assistants (PDAs). To this add the conventional print-based media: catalogues, brochures, direct mail, and display advertising. Re-purposing the content to offer compelling viewing for these different channels presents an enormous challenge to content publishers and aggregators. The project-based methods familiar to the brochure designer or video producer are replaced with a cooperative web of talent, each contributing to an organic process. The potential for mistakes is ripe, with the large number of files, and the disparate formats.

Table 1.1 Corporate media content

Department	Content	Formats	Distribution channel
Corporate communications and public relations	Press releases	HTML, PDF	Web
		MS Word	Mail
Investor relations	Annual reports	QuarkXPress (MS Word, JPG, AI*)	Print
	Quarterly earnings call	Windows Media and Real	Webcast
Marketing communications	Brand management		
	Brochures	QuarkXPress (MS Word, JPG, and AI)	Print
	Web pages	HTML	Web
	Exhibitions and shows	TIFF	Graphic panels
	Advertising	Audio, video, and TIFF	Television, radio, and print
Sales	Presentations	MS PowerPoint	PC and projection
	Responses to RFP and RFQ	MS Word	Mail
	e-commerce	ColdFusion	Web
Product management	Guides and handbooks	QuarkXPress	Shipped with product
	White papers	MS Word, PDF	Mail, Web
Training	Audio-visual	MPEG, DV, and QuickTime	CD-ROM
	e-learning	Windows Media, Real, MS PowerPoint	Web
	Manuals	QuarkXPress	Print

*AI, Adobe Illustrator

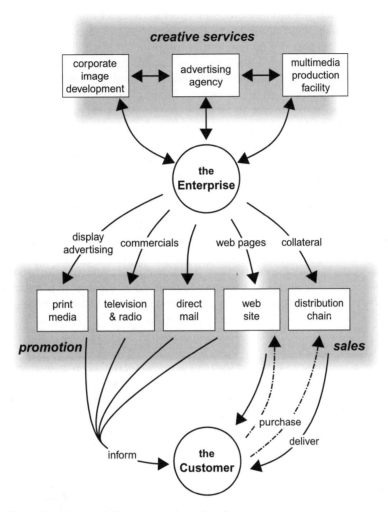

Figure 1.1 Content exchange in the corporate enterprise.

Content and media asset management (MAM) are already core back-office applica-tions for the print and broadcasting industries. These systems are ideally suited to the control and management of the large content repositories that publish via the diversity of new technologies.

This book examines some of the potentials for applying asset management systems to the creation of content and its publishing, and presents the benefits that can stem from increased efficiency and the lowering of costs.

Digital Asset Management (DAM)

Document management has already proved its worth in the traditional print industries. Content management has enabled the efficient deployment of large web sites. As the number of distribution platforms increases, the needs of brand management and the desire to control costs, lead naturally to a convergence of the creative and production processes. A large corporation can no longer run print, web, and multimedia production in isolation. Rich media is a term that has been applied to this converged content.

For some enterprises, this convergence may only apply to content creation. It can also extend to the management of marketing collateral and corporate communications. As an example, a show booth set up by the marketing department should have a common look to the CD-ROM produced by the training department.

The corporation that communicates directly with the consumer may want an iTV commercial to link through to the company web site. The customer can then view web pages or request further information. All these different media must exhibit a seamless brand image.

The same principles used for content management can be used as the basis of systems for managing rich media assets. The complexity of rich media means that DAM is becoming vital to improve operational efficiency and to control costs.

Rich media production may start with conventional audio and video materials, and be enhanced later with synchronised graphic and text elements. The production workflow will have more parallel processes than the traditional linear flow of television production using different creative talents. The pressure to drive down the cost of production is paramount, yet the market is demanding the publication of content in a plethora of formats.

What are assets?

A quick look at a dictionary will tell us that the word *asset* usually relates to property. The same association with property also applies to digital media content. If you have the intellectual property rights to content, then that content can represent an asset. So intellectual property management and protection (IPMP), and digital rights management (DRM), should form an integral part of an asset management framework.

Content without the usage rights is not an asset (Figure 1.2).

content   rights   asset

Figure 1.2 An asset is content with the right to use.

Using metadata, DAM enables the linking of content with the rights information. The same systems that protect property rights can also be used to guard confidential information; so DAM can also be used for the internal distribution of commercially sensitive information.

Asset management is much more than rights management—forms a small, but vital, part of the total solution. Perhaps, the most important feature is that DAM provides a framework for the successful monetisation of media assets.

There are potential drawbacks. If the system is to be dropped onto a mature corporation, there will be a vast legacy of existing content. What are the costs of indexing and cataloguing the archive? These costs may well outweigh any potential advantages of the online access to the older material. The deployment of DAM, like any other major business decision, should involve a cost–benefit analysis.

It may be that compromises can be made to reach a halfway house of partial digitisation, rather than an across-the-board incorporation of every piece of content in the archive. As an example, one criterion could be the last-accessed date. Just because you have the rights to content, its value may well be negligible, so it could well remain in the vault. If the storage cost is high, you could even dispose of it.

What gives an asset value? If it can be resold, then the value is obvious. However, it can also represent a monetary asset, if it can be cost-effectively re-purposed and then incorporated into new material. To cite just one example, a new advertising campaign can build on the lessons and experience of the past through access to the media archive. This can save a corporation with both time and resources in such research projects.

What is asset management?

Asset management covers a wide field. A search for asset management in a trade shows that catalogue will include shelving systems for tape cassettes, fancy file management software, hardware vendors of disk arrays, and robotic data tape silos; as well as end-to-end software solutions that can index, search, and manage a wide variety of audio and video contents. This book does not cover all of these products but focuses on the software solutions and their associated hardware platforms.

To be more specific, DAM provides for the sensible exploitation and administration of a large asset repository. An asset management system provides a complete toolbox to the author, publisher, and the end users of the media to efficiently utilise the assets.

Media assets can be in a number of different formats: audio and video clips, graphic images, photographs, and text documents. There may be links and associations between the assets. The files may be shared across an enterprise-scale organisation. The media may be traded; it can be syndicated, rented, or sold.

The system architecture must be flexible to provide for all these requirements. These are some of the features and facilities that may be found in a DAM system:

- Co-authoring
- Storage management
- Archiving
- Multiple formats
- Version control
- Workflow
- Search tools
- Publishing tools
- Wide-area distribution.

Asset management can be extended through web-based access. This opens up the opportunity to preview and author at the desktop, remote from the content. This access can be within the enterprise, from any dial-up location, or over the Internet.

Why use asset management?

Even the best-designed filing scheme has limitations. This is particularly evident when material is shared across a large enterprise in many formats. The optimum scheme for one user may not suit another. Support of multiple file formats on different platforms further complicates the scheme; files may be on Windows or UNIX servers, on dedicated video servers, or videotape and CD-ROM.

The user may not know the file name. To help locate wanted material, the filing scheme will require a catalogue. Imagine a request like 'find me a happy-looking child wearing a red dress on a crowded beach'. Asset management provides the answer to such questions.

What is rich media?

The twentieth century saw rapidly accelerating change in the electronic media. First, radio acquired pictures, and then became television. In the last quarter of the century, video became accepted as one of the primary vehicles for corporate communication. In the final decade with the adoption of hypertext markup language (HTML), the web evolved from a means of document exchange for the scientific community into a universally adopted medium. Television now has a back-channel giving interactivity. Combine all these and we have rich media—a synchronised presentation of text, graphics, and audio and video (Figure 1.3). To this is added user interaction, for navigation or to conduct a dialogue.

The strength comes from interactivity and the dynamic links. These two allow the viewer to search and navigate the presentation in a non-linear fashion.

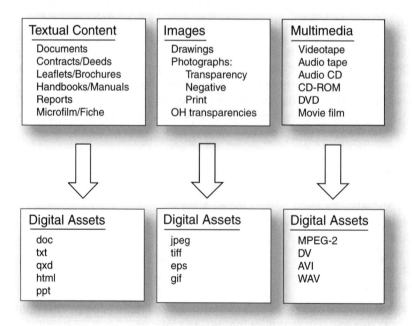

Figure 1.3 Media content becomes digital files.

Rich media is now used by a wider community for corporate communications, marketing, and training. The one-time linear flow traditionally used in content creation has not proved cost-effective for the wider application of rich media across a corporation. To leverage the cost of producing content, it can be re-used. This process is called re-purposing. This is not necessarily in the original form, but re-edited with other content, and with new material. Rich media has early adopters with training and distance learning. Sales departments are finding numerous applications for more compelling presentations.

Rich media is not new to the enterprise. Training and marketing departments have long used audio and video contents, from the 16 mm film, through the U-matic and VHS, to the CD-ROM. The latest additions are streaming media and the DVD.

The need to re-purpose exposed the shortcomings of the legacy production methods. Content management in linear program production is relatively easy. A good file system will solve most of the potential problems. Most of the video content was probably to be found on the avid system. This meant that it was easy to find. The presence of a close-knit team also meant that the wanted content could be easily located.

The content provider who wants to re-purpose existing material is in a different position. What content is available? Where is it? Who knows about it? Have they left the corporation? Are there rights issues?

How do you manage the authoring and editing? How can you publish to all the different communications channels in an efficient, cost-effective manner? One solution is to look at document management—a tool long used by the printing and publishing industry.

Streaming media

Streaming media is an important tool for DAM. As we shall see later, streaming offers the ideal vehicle for previewing material remote from the content repository. It can be used to create compact proxies of audio and video contents. Streaming allows the, typically very large, audio and video files to be played across a network or the Internet and to be viewed immediately without having to wait for the content to download completely from the server. Normal file transfer forces the user to wait until the entire file has arrived.

Libraries and vaults

Audio and video contents have traditionally been stored on tape. The tape cassettes are treated much like books, stored on library shelves (the vault) and loaned out. This is fine for a linear production process, but it makes sharing during production difficult. There can only be one master, so most staff can only view dubs of the master. Any editing or re-purposing requires that the master be passed around like a baton in a race. Rich media production demands much more parallel processes, allowing several people, maybe with different creative skills, to work together on the master. Digital, disk-based production enables this parallel working. This sharing of the master assets can only sensibly be managed with careful role-based permissions, with file locking and with version control of the editing process. This may sound familiar—they are standard features offered by enterprise-scale database engines.

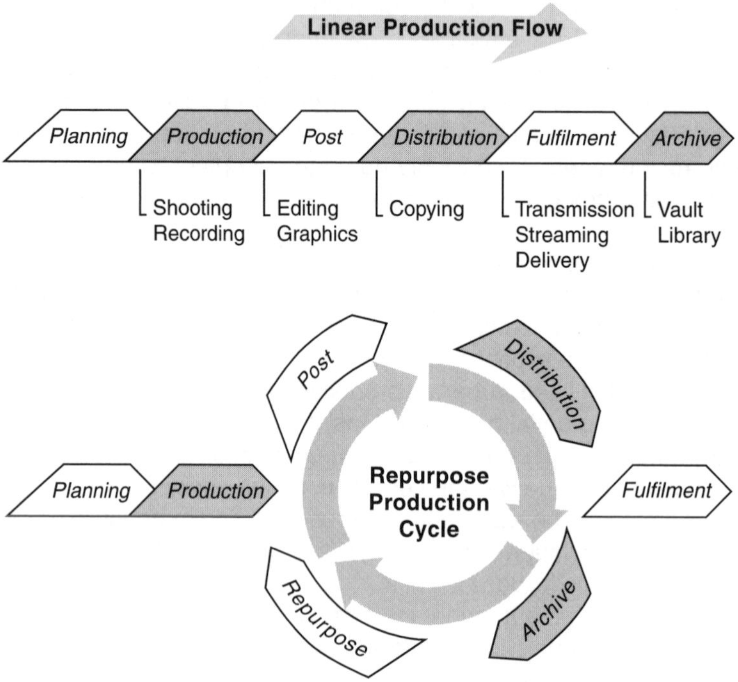

Linear Production Flow

Figure 1.4 Linear flow versus re-purposing cycle.

Re-purposing assets

Rather than consigning media content to the trash or filing it into the archive, re-purposing leverages, the value of a media asset by re-using it in a fresh production (Figure 1.4). In many organisations, the departmental structures and systems negate content sharing, even if there were the desire to re-use material. It often ends up being quicker and easier to re-create new material rather than finding existing material that would fit the requirements.

To successfully re-purpose material, the potential user has to be able to search the media library, identify that the content is the correct material, and then request delivery in the appropriate format. These functions form part of the total offering of DAM.

Three-letter abbreviations

Content and asset management vendors use a number of three-letter abbreviations for the product lines. DAM, DMM, MAM, WCM, DCM, ECM—what are they, and how do they differ?

- DAM Digital Asset Management
- DCM Digital Content Management
- ECM Enterprise Content Management
- DMM Digital Media Management
- MAM Media Asset Management
- WCM Web Cotent Management.

Media Assets

Videotapes	Optical discs	Digital Video File
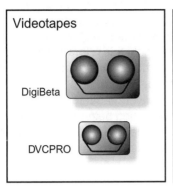 DigiBeta / DVCPRO	 CD-ROM DVD	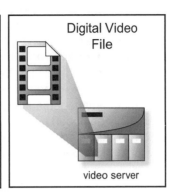 video server

Figure 1.5 Media assets: (a) videotapes, (b) optical discs, and (c) digital video file.

Content management

This is often called WCM or DCM. The term is usually applied to products designed to manage the assets used for the construction of large web sites. The content includes the basic HTML page templates, plus the images and animations embedded in the pages. The complex cross-linking and frequent update typical of web sites can make the management of content much more difficult than publishing traditional printed documents. Content management also allows staff to change information on pages without the need to use web developers.

The second function for content management is to control interactive sites. This is where the content is generated on the fly from information stored in a database and loaded into the page templates. Such sites are typically used for e-commerce. For example, the price of an item is stored in the database rather than hard coded into an HTML page.

Media Asset Management (MAM)

The advent of the video server created the need for MAM. When video was stored on tape, the tape cassettes could be managed by library software similar to that used for documents or books. Bar codes can be used to check-in and check-out the documents to individual users. Once the server was adopted for production and transmission, the media asset became a file. It could not be managed in the same way as a physical asset.

A programme will exist as a master tape, a security copy, and working copies. These copies may exist in several tape formats, Digital Betacam for transmission, and VHS for preview. Assets can be digital or analogue, even 35 mm film (Figure 1.5).

The video server originally had a limited storage capacity, so content was usually rotated with only the recently used material stored online. MAM systems incorporate hierarchical storage management (HSM) to control the purging of unwanted material and the restoration of wanted material from offline storage (usually tape or optical storage). The offline storage may well be on data tapes, rather than videotape.

The MAM maintains the associations between the many copies, whether as files or tapes. The user can thus retrieve or locate the desired program material in the appropriate format.

MAM usually offers basic search facilities. Each media file is given a unique reference number, and has a title and date of creation. This reference number may well be the same as the master tape number. To recall a file from a server, only this reference is required, not the actual file name used by the server operating system. A simple database can store other information, like program title, against the reference number.

Many media management systems offer facilities to deliver media to remote sites, or fulfilment. This has been a key component in the central casting being adopted by many television broadcasters. This allows content creation to be deployed at a single location, usually the headquarters, and pushed out to the regional stations.

Digital Asset Management (DAM)

Content in digital form can be manipulated in the same way as any computer file. It can be distributed over networks, copied, and automatically backed a RAID storage sub-system. This ability to network media assets means that anyone authorised to view or use material can potentially access material from a workstation attached to the computer network. Early DAM systems emerged around 1990, but were initially limited to the storage of graphics and still images. Perhaps the online picture library is the best example of the early deployments. The drive to include video files was delayed until the development of efficient compression architectures to allow sensible-sized files for media preview. Another enabling factor was the ever-lowering cost of digital storage, an important consideration for the very large video files.

This ability to share content files has great appeal to those who wish to re-purpose media assets. Unfortunately, the basic search facilities of a MAM system limit the recall of files to those who know the filename are even aware that such material exists.

Most of us are used to the Internet search engines like Google that can index and locate references to HTML content on the web. The potential re-purposer of media assets needs something similar—a powerful search engine. The search engines that we are familiar with from the Internet are text based, but video material in its raw form has no text to search. Several vendors have addressed this major shortcoming. They have developed new search engines that are specifically oriented to the searching of video assets. The key to the products is the generation of an index that can be used to build a catalogue of the assets.

Convergence

The convergence of discrete content management systems into a single enterprise-wide content management system brings many benefits (Figure 1.6). It becomes easier to manage brands if television and radio advertising, the company web site, and printed collateral, can all be accessed through a single information portal.

The external appearance from the portal of a seamless, unified system does have to mean a single-vendor solution. It is perfectly possible to integrate a number of best-of-breed solutions. For specialist applications like video logging or the search engine, it pays to go to a vendor that has developed a high-performance product for that single

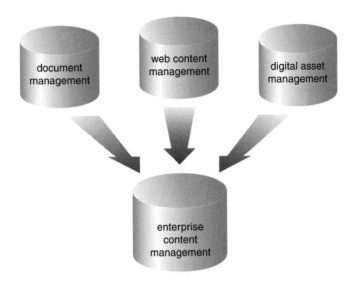

Figure 1.6 The convergence of systems.

application. Integration has been much simplified by the universal adoption of extensible markup language (XML) for data exchange.

Asset management systems

Content owners have each evolved ways to store content. Broadcasters have library systems for the storage of videotapes, and more general media management applications. The book, magazine, and web-publishing industries have developed systems to solve the storage and management problems associated with handling very large numbers of files. These are usually referred to as document management systems. Web developers use content management. All three of these have much to offer the rich media publisher.

The database

A database can serve as the kernel of an asset management system. A database is a repository of textual information like the metadata and documents. To handle audio and video assets in an efficient manner, the asset management system will require additional services. This means that pointers (or resource locators) stored in the database can act as references to media assets that are stored either as files in server farms or as raw video on tape cassettes.

The multi-tier architecture

Many rich media production tools have developed as unitary applications, running on a powerful graphics workstation. It may sound simple to deploy, but in practice, there are many problems with this approach. In a large enterprise, there are the issues related to

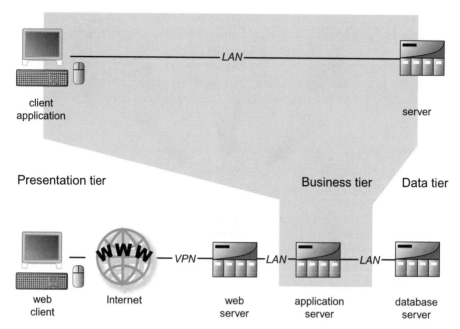

Figure 1.7 The multi-tier architecture.

sharing work, plus the maintenance of such systems requires skilled information technology (IT) resources.

Most products use a multi-tier architecture (Figure 1.7). This concentrates the processing into a centrally administered location that can allow the desktop client to be as thin as a web browser. This may sound like a return to the mainframe—but for the workgroup sharing the creative processes, to have a central core of services performing the business logic, it gives a far more manageable system.

The multi-tier architecture has evolved from the needs of large enterprises, and now enables the use of complex applications across the organisation in a scalable and highly available way.

The key feature of the multi-tier model is that the presentation layer (the look and feel), the business logic, and the data layer are separate. The favoured presentation layer is a web server; this allows a standard web browser to be used on the client workstation. To view video content, a media player plug-in is also required.

System features

Co-authoring

The authoring and production of rich media content will probably involve a number of different people, possibly from different departments, or maybe from different companies. There may be a video production team, an author for the presentation, and an editor for a series.

The asset management system recognises both single users and groups of users and gives role-based access. Each user is allocated rights to create, edit, or view material. This also provides security to prevent unauthorised access to confidential information or content with monetary value.

The security may also be enhanced with a DRM system. This encrypts the media files, so that access is only possible with a suitable key.

Storage management and archiving

A small number of files can be stored on a single hard drive, possibly with regular backup to a streaming tape. Once a company has acquired a large number of files, a hierarchy of storage sub-systems will allow access time to be traded for cost. RAID systems can be used for immediate online access, with lower-cost magneto-optical or tape storage used for offline archive. The long-term storage medium may be mounted in a storage robot (like a jukebox) for rapid retrieval or simply stored on shelves.

These many storage solutions are controlled by a HSM system. The HSM controller will automatically migrate little-used content to lower-cost storage, and restore the files on demand. The HSM system will be integrated transparently with the asset management system, so that the user will have no need to know the physical location of a file.

Although much rich media content is ephemeral, with a brief lifespan, legislation by national governments may oblige publishers to store some forms of content for many years. Some rich media content aggregate from several sources—a typical example is with desktop publishing, with a core text document, and separate image files. Providing this linked archive is no trivial undertaking.

A key component of the storage management relates to the withdrawal and purging of obsolete content. The ever-changing and evolving nature of rich media, together with the interlinking of content, means that a single edition of a site is rarely published in the way that a television programme episode or magazine is released.

Multiple formats and versions

Content exists in so many file formats. Consider a photographic image. There may be a multi-layered Adobe Photoshop original. There could be a flattened TIFF for print and a JPEG for the web.

Video content will exist in at least three formats: the master videotape, the encoded file, and the streaming file. There may be many versions of the files:

- Different videotape formats (Digital Betacam, VHS, and DV)
- Different video compression formats (DV, MPEG-1, MPEG-2, and MPEG-4)
- Multiple streaming formats (Windows Media/Real/QuickTime)
- Different program edits (English version, Spanish version, and airline edit).

Similarly, audio can be encoded in different formats like MP3 and WAV.

The catalogue and its index

The catalogue of media assets uses the database to store information or *metadata* about the media. Metadata can be user information (like title, artist, and duration) or control information used by the asset management system.

Metadata is parsed to generate an *index* to make the catalogue searchable. The index is one of the key features of the asset management; without an index, media can only be found by filename.

Searching

One of the most powerful features of asset management from the user's perspective is the ability to search for a file using minimal information. Basic searching uses Boolean logical expressions: AND, OR, and NOT. Such a search looks for matching character strings.

Two key parameters apply to the search:

- *Recall*—does the engine find the relevant files?
- *Precision*—does the engine return relevant results?

To improve the search performance, other criteria are used beyond Boolean matching of text strings, typically conceptual and natural language searches.

The index

The search engine uses the index to locate files. The index is generated automatically during the ingest or capture processes. It can later be edited manually, for example, to correct errors or to add attributes that may be difficult to generate automatically.

A basic search on a personal computer may be limited to file names. To improve the ability to search a catalogue an associated index has to be used. The index can be generated in many ways, but typically keywords are extracted from the content. In the case of video, this could be from a transcript of the soundtrack.

Material can then be located by a search of the catalogue. If the file name is known, the catalogue entry can be located immediately—if not, a search is made. This could use keywords or other attributes and properties of the file or metadata. These are some examples of metadata: title, artist, author, bit rate, copyright, and duration.

The keywords may be entered by the author, generated automatically from the content, or may be entered by the archivist. An image asset may need emotional characteristics to aid searching: 'happy, sad'. Clearly, these have to be entered manually.

Video and images can also be searched by attributes. The image analysis engine can index content by colour, shape, texture, brightness structure, and colour structure. Audio can also be analysed. Speech-to-text conversion can automatically create a transcript of the soundtrack.

Unique identifiers

With an asset management system, the user can be freed from the need to have a systematic file-naming scheme. Many archives may have been created under different regimes. It would not be feasible to rename everything to fit with the current taxonomy. A DAM system can automatically assign a unique identifier (UID) when content is ingested. The item could possibly be catalogued to fit the taxonomy after it has been indexed.

Result sets

If you make a search of an asset archive, the result set may be 10 or 100 possible assets that meet the search criteria. To further narrow the search, the user of the asset management application can present the searcher with a hierarchy of proxies of the asset. This will be a text description with keywords, and maybe a summary. A thumbnail picture can portray a video or image file. A video clip can also be portrayed by a storyboard of thumbnails. This sequence of images represents the scenes and it can be used to quickly locate a specific scene within the clip.

Key-frame extraction

A video analysis engine is used to generate the thumbnails or key frames for the storyboard. The engine will detect the cuts, fades, and dissolves that indicate a scene change, and a time-referenced index entry is placed in the database.

Audio transcription

Speech analysis software can be used to decode speech on the soundtrack into a textual file. This information can be used to generate index information. If the original video material has closed captions or subtitles, then these can also be used to provide a synchronised transcript of the associated audio soundtrack. Unfortunately, only broadcast material has captions, and then only the final release, unused original footage will not carry closed captions. Although captions are simple to use, speech analysis is a more general approach for the automatic creation of a transcript.

Keywords

To satisfy a query, the search engine uses index keywords to locate the clips. Editorial personnel can add manual entries to the automatically generated indices. These may include emotional characteristics that are not extracted from the transcript—for example, happy or sad expressions.

Ingest

New media assets have to be registered with the asset database. This may also apply to legacy assets from the content archives. They may also be encoded to a convenient format for editorial processing. For video content, this could be a mid-bandwidth MPEG-2 (25 Mbit/s) or DV format. After encoding, the video files can also be indexed to generate index metadata for the asset management catalogue. Film can be scanned, with still images converted to TIFF files. Paper documents can also be scanned and, via optical character recognition, converted to text files. Many text formats are proprietary, but they can be converted to SGML or XML.

Publishing and fulfilment

Once all the editorial processing is complete, the finished content is published. The material can be physically delivered on transportable media—CD-ROM, DVD or videotape, or alternatively by file transfer over a wide-area network—a process called fulfilment.

Content may be delivered on demand from a web site. A low-resolution preview can be delivered as a media stream or a thumbnail. The audio or video media files will be delivered to the client from a separate server dedicated to streaming. A link embedded in the host web page will direct the customer's media player (Windows Media, Real, and QuickTime) to this server. The streaming server is a proprietary application that provides intelligent flow control of the video file across an IP network to the client.

Higher-resolution video files (MPEG-2 or DV) can be delivered by FTP. Long-form material may prove expensive to transmit, but electronic transfer is ideally suited to short clips like commercials or news items. Documents can be delivered using portable document format (PDF). This can be encoded in a number of resolutions ranging from e-books to read on a screen, to high resolution for an imagesetter and final printing. This multiple-resolution fulfilment to different delivery channels is often called cross-media publishing.

Data links

The business logic of the application server offers new opportunities to link the asset management with the back-office systems of the enterprise. Typical links could be to the accounts department and rights management. If content is to be sold or syndicated, seamless links to the e-commerce systems would also be a necessity.

Scalability

Early asset management systems may have been limited to departmental access over a local area network (LAN). A central file server provided facilities for the department, with client workstations for each operator.

Providing the same facilities across a corporate enterprise, possibly across geographically dispersed sites, is much more challenging. Careful planning is essential to ensure optimum use of the wide-area telecommunications capacity. To an enterprise that is used to communicating by e-mail messages of perhaps 2 or 3 kByte, or transmitting electronic documents and spreadsheets of 50 kByte, the transfer of video files of several gigabytes could severely stress the network.

In traditional video media companies, the video files live in the technical areas—the edit bays. Opening up access to the computer desktop may ease the task of the creative personnel, but adds greatly to the loading on technical resources. To ease this load, a hierarchy of images is used to give the creative personnel preview facilities.

A search for media will initially return text descriptions; further 'drill-down' will return thumbnail images forming a storyboard of a video sequence. Once the required file is identified, a low-resolution proxy of the video image can be viewed. This will be a highly compressed version of the primary file delivered at data rates below 56 kbit/s. Such resolutions are often sufficient for rough-cut editing or training material, where the soundtrack carries most of the information.

A high-resolution image can then be ordered as videotape, or if sufficient network bandwidths exist, by file transfer.

Remote access

Many staff, especially in sales, would like remote dial-up access to the asset management system while travelling. Creative staff may prefer to work on location or from home. The advantage of a web-enabled multi-tier architecture is that remote access can be via the public Internet, and does not require special circuits to be set up. If confidentiality is an issue, secure circuits can be set up using a virtual private network (VPN) with technologies like secure Internet protocol (IPSec).

Remote access is also an enabler for e-commerce systems. Media assets may be sold to the public, or syndicated to resellers. Sub-sets of the asset catalogue can be made available to e-commerce systems.

Rights management

Rights management means different things to different people. To the program distributor it refers to contract management of his rights to use the content, to the program reseller it signifies the means of enforcing copyright protection against unauthorised access or use—piracy, and to the database administrator it means controlling the rights to read, write, and edit information within the database. All three protect the opportunities to earn revenue from content.

Contracts management

Several products have long been used to provide a range of services to manage the contracts related to artists and intellectual property owners. It is of great benefit if such systems can have data links with the asset management.

Anti-piracy measures

If content is to be delivered as a file, or streamed over a network, then encryption may be necessary to protect that content against unauthorised viewing or copying.

Such measures are known as DRM. Systems typically encrypt the content, then wrap that file with the business rules to open the content. Embedded in the content header will be links to sites to download the DRM client, plus details of any clearing house that may be hosting the financial transactions.

The business rules support normal trading scenarios, with a publisher, a distributor, a reseller, a retailer, and a customer. Most systems allow customers to forward content to friends, for them also to purchase content—that is viral marketing. To aid the tracing of fraud, the media can also be watermarked—identifying the origin.

Web client access rights

The asset management business logic will have a sophisticated hierarchy of role-based permissions to view, edit, and publish content. Role-based permissions allow a group, such as system administrators, to be allocated the appropriate rights according to position and responsibility in the enterprise and in relation to a particular project.

DAM systems

Typical DAM systems are built in multi-tiered architecture (Figure 1.8). Underlying the system is the repository of the metadata. This is a relational database, such as Oracle. Layered over that is the business logic running on the application server. This forms the heart of the asset management. Technologies like CORBA and EJB often feature in this tier. Above that is the presentation layer, where the information is formatted into web pages and served to the end users.

Although databases can store large binary objects, the media content is normally stored in dedicated fileservers. This is more efficient; media files are very large and can be simply referenced by fields in the primary database.

Note that there are two media servers, the main content repository, and the media proxy server. To manage network utilisation, the media is previewed at a lower resolution than the final file delivered to the user—this is the proxy file. Typically, it uses one of the popular streaming media formats.

What are the advantages of deploying asset management?

As a corporation grows, the media assets grow with it in a topsy-turvy manner. Each department, possibly each user, may have private filing systems. Some content may be filed in an archive, some may be sitting unused on a file server, and some may even be lost.

To leverage the value of content as an asset, it has to be shared around the corporation. To do this, several questions have to be answered:

- What content exists?
- Where is it?
- What format is it in?
- Who has the rights to use it?
- Is it company confidential or in the public domain?

An enterprise-wide DAM system provides a framework for the solution to these questions. The indexing and cataloguing process identifies the content available within the corporation, its location, and the storage format. Any contracts related to the rights could be stored in the legal or copyright department.

Once the information has been logged to the database (not a trivial undertaking), the way is open for departments to share up-to-the-minute information on content. The hours of time frequently spent tracking down a video clip for a customer presentation is

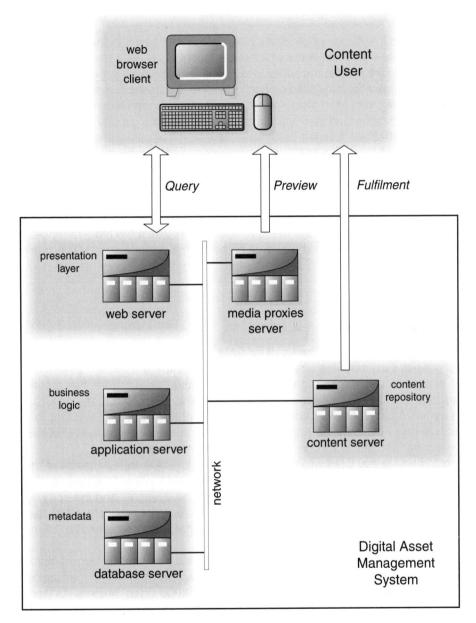

Figure 1.8 The basic system architecture.

compressed to minutes. The partner requesting the latest logo in a specific format can be satisfied in seconds.

Many enterprises today either waste time finding content, or, in desperation re-create the same content. The return on investment for DAM should take into account these many savings, plus the advantages of the instant access to wanted material.

The thin client

Although computer software applications have given great power to the user in a desktop PC, the enterprise-wide maintenance of thousands of PCs is not a trivial task. Fault fixing and software upgrades consume human resources and downtime impacts on productivity. The fewer the applications installed on each machine, the easier is the maintenance task. A basic office suite, with word processing and spreadsheets, and a communications package with a web browser and mail application will suffice for the general user.

Many media files are created using specialised craft application software that is not generally found on the office PC. These include Adobe Photoshop for image manipulation and Illustrator for graphics; QuarkXPress for desktop publishing; Macromedia Flash and Director for web animations; and Avid, Media 100, or Adobe Premier for video editing.

To view all these different files from a thin client PC, the most widespread method is to use a standard web browser, Internet Explorer, or Safari, with a few plug-ins. A web server can then deliver suitably formatted proxies of the original content in an HTML compatible format.

Early adopters

One of the first groups to see the need for DAM was the television news industry. A fast-breaking news story requires almost instant access to the archive. An essential part of many news reports is a backgrounder using material drawn from the archives—or re-purposed. If it takes two weeks in the library finding the material, the opportunity for the story has passed. Another important issue is that the journalists wanting to access the archive may have only minimal search criteria; it is extremely unlikely that they have a tape number and the time code of the scene that they require.

It could be said that CNN wrote the original RFP for DAM. Indeed, some of the earliest products, like the Informix Media 360, were developed to meet their needs. The real-time nature of news demanded robust and easy to use systems, and the early systems set a great benchmark in performance and design for later products. CNN has since extended pilot systems to a massive digital archive that can store over 120,000 hours of news footage.

Another early adopter was not a broadcaster, but the world's largest automobile manufacturer—General Motors (GM). In 100 years, the corporation had amassed a vast library of motion pictures, with 2000 films and 10,000 video masters. As well as the moving image, they had 3 million still images in their central library. This archive was a visual record of the development of the GM products, their production, and promotion. As part of their brand management processes, GM needed online access to this library to view everything from earlier television commercials to marketing materials like logos and product brochures for potential re-purposing across multiple media delivery channels.

The Artesia DAM system deployed by GM allows stakeholders, within the corporation, and the external suppliers and partners, to get access to all the legacy material. This may be for the production of entertainment or information related to cars, or it could be a company manufacturing toy cars. Not only does the archive contain the basic video or still images, but also the metadata that is used to keep track of copyright and trademark information, providing GM with the potential additional revenue streams from licensing.

Summary

A comprehensive DAM system can form the kernel of a corporate-wide brand management system. The asset management is used to index and catalogue content. This can free talent to innovate and share content across the diverse platforms. The concept of 'produce once, use many times' can solve many of the problems of creating compelling content with efficient use of creative resources.

The users of DAM have several different requirements from the system. The first is the management of a large library or archive in many different formats, so that value can be leveraged from media assets.

Stemming partly from the different formats, and from the demands of different fulfilment channels, there is the need to provide a unitary production environment with efficient workflows across departments and partners.

There is the need for secure and controlled access to assets in a central library from remote locations. These may be branch offices, agents and distributors, or creative partners like advertising agencies.

The unifying nature of DAM binds together the content creators and consumers across the enterprise in a free-flowing and networked environment, where digital content can be shared to the mutual advantage of all stakeholders.

2 Document and content management

Introduction

Many of the roots of digital asset management lie with document and web content management applications. These systems are digital asset repositories, with modules for the ingest, archive, and publishing of content. The products include workflow automation to manage the collaboration between the different parties creating and using the assets. At ingest, content may well be classified to enable the efficient searching for content.

Document management has arisen from the propensity of bureaucracies to generate paperwork. The advent of the desktop computer has released the serried ranks of the typing pool to alternative employment in the customer call centre. Before every knowledge worker used their own word processor, the typing pool imposed limits on the volume of paperwork that could be generated. Now that anyone can create documents, paperwork has mushroomed.

The document template allows everyone in an enterprise to write documents in the corporate style. You only have to look at the growth of the memo. In 1970, the average office worker might get two a day, now they can receive 200 e-mails. Luckily you do not need asset management to deal with the majority, the trashcan is just fine.

Some professions are obliged to document all their work. The legal profession has long generated important documents that have to be stored for many decades. They include the contracts that regulate our lives, from house purchase to business contracts. They were carefully transcribed onto archival paper, neatly tied with ribbons, and then filed away.

As governments regulate more businesses to protect public safety, and to control accounting practices, there is now an obligation to store more and more information on write-once media. A typical example would be the development of a new drug. The drug company has to place all the documents relating to the application to market a drug, maybe running into millions of files, into a long-term archive.

What happens when you place millions of documents into a repository? Who knows what is there, and how to find it? Document management brings order to this potential chaos.

Unstructured information

As the data-processing industry developed during the last half of the twentieth century, governments and businesses grew accustomed to storing information in databases.

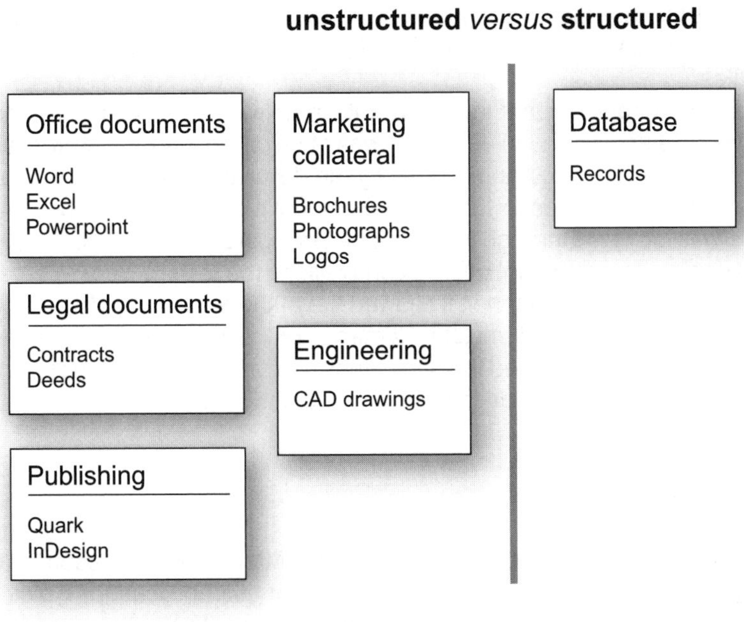

unstructured *versus* structured

Figure 2.1 *Unstructured versus structured documents.*

This information could be records of transactions, payroll, and inventories—all maintained in databases as columns and records. This information was stored online on disk arrays, and backed up and archived to data tapes.

As the word processor was introduced to the office, vast numbers of unstructured documents started to mushroom throughout businesses (Figure 2.1). Many held important information, but did not lend themselves to storage in the rigid table structures of a database. Similarly, engineering companies produced large numbers of CAD drawings. Many have to be archived for the service life of the product. Then lawyers have deeds and contracts.

The marketing department has a wide range of collateral. It may be printed brochures and white papers, through to logos kept as film or image files. The department often has a photographic library with corporate images, portraits of senior executives, and product shots.

Companies grew accustomed to the order that the database brought to their structured data. Why could not electronic documents be subject to similar disciplines?

Around 1980, the first document management products started to emerge. Many of the ideas came from the established practices of librarians that had been developed long before computers. To manage documents, some form of structure has to be imposed. A librarian will categorise a document before filing and log the basic metadata into an index. This includes title, author, publisher, date, and keywords describing the content. The category is also added to this metadata. Document management adds access control for each document allocating a set of permissions to authorise the users or groups of users that can view or edit the document.

Web content management has grown out of a similar explosion of content. Rather than rolls of parchment or filing cabinet full of paper documents, the problem has been with digital files.

Another issue that rapidly came to the fore with large web sites was the human resource problem. A webmaster, as the web developer was often called, puts the early sites together. Every page had to be formatted and laid out by the developer. As site grew to hundreds of pages, and required daily updates, the initial workflow was not going to be cost effective. Every update was funnelled through the developer, in most cases creating a logjam of information. Web content management offered corporations the tools to deploy large web sites in a controlled and affordable manner. It allowed the authors of content the ability to create and update pages using simple templates. It managed the lifecycle of web pages and their associated graphics, and it enabled the deployment of dynamic sites. Therefore, the logjam was removed, allowing parallel working across the entire site.

Document management

What is a document? Originally, a document was a written or printed record of ownership or an agreement and also a means of providing proof of identification. Typically, it could be a contract drawn up by a lawyer, or an identity card issued by a government. The original Latin meaning of *proof* became lost with the introduction of the computer. The term 'document' became applied to any writing that conveyed information. Therefore, it could be a text file or a spreadsheet, a slide presentation, or a CAD drawing. Therefore, to the lawyer a document is a specific proof or evidence, whereas within the average business a document is synonymous with a computer file. The file extension for a Microsoft Word file, *.DOC*, reinforces this association.

The document is a subset of a computer file. We would not think of an Adobe Photoshop file or a database as documents. The concept of document management is not the same as file management, but is specifically the management of files containing unstructured written information, although the inclusion of CAD file blurs the distinction between the written and the drawn. Before the age of the computer, the document was any form of office paperwork, written, drawn, or typed.

The first document management was little more than a filing cabinet and a card index (Figure 2.2). If access control was needed, the filing cabinet was locked.

Each new document was categorised, and put in the appropriate drawer and folder, so that it could be easily found again. The location may well have been recorded in a card index. So there was already the means to search the repository.

This system, though, has many obvious drawbacks. The first being that only those physically near to the office can get immediate access to the files. The need to collaborate and share documents throughout a geographically dispersed enterprise drove the search for systems with remote and concurrent access (Figure 2.3).

Storage

The first moves to document management were the development of compact and organised storage systems. Businesses could not afford to devote more and more valuable

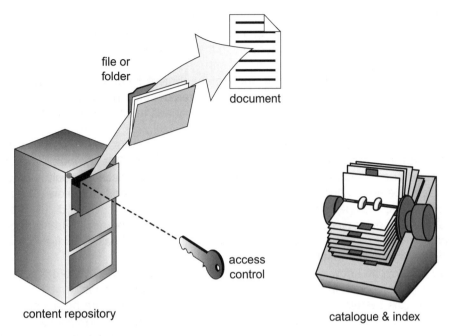

Figure 2.2 Early document management.

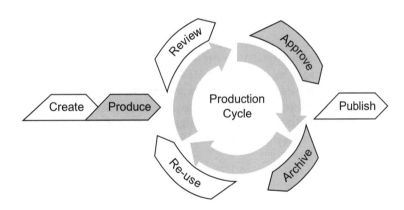

Figure 2.3 The document lifecycle.

office floor space to ranks of filing cabinets. The first systems could store information in a fraction of the volume by the use of optical media.

Microfilm

The early document storage products were based around microfilm. The principle was invented in 1839, but it did not come into common use for storing government archives, libraries, and banking records until the 1930s. Other businesses adopted the microfilm in the 1950s, as the cost of storing paperwork mushroomed. As part of the microfilming process, the documents were categorised. In that way, one film could be used for documents with some commonality.

Microfilm went as a part way to document management. It certainly revolutionised the storage. Vast numbers of documents could be stored on a few reels of film. But the system was no more than storage. It still relied on librarians to categorise the documents, and to maintain the indices to the microfilms.

The desire to share documents needed information technology. A paper document could be scanned into a digital format, and the files from an office computer application could be placed in a common repository. Other users on the network could then share these files. The application software allowed users to create, edit, and view (or publish) the documents. The operating system allowed the user to copy, move, or delete the files. The ability to move objects was key to the sharing and collaboration. Rather than the sneakernet, anyone on a corporate network could gain access. The files could be backed up or archived to alternative storage.

How did anyone know what was there, and what it was called? Who controlled the copying and deletion of files? What protected confidential information?

To make the system useful, the users need a formal file structure or taxonomy, and an index. Therefore, the first document management systems needed an application to categorise or index, and a search engine—together with the advances in shared storage technologies and workflow management that emerged as a complete document management solution.

Data storage

Microfilm is an analogue system with a long storage life, and cannot be rewritten. When digital systems were introduced, permanence was important. Many of the files were important legal documents and it is a requirement that the document cannot be altered at a later date. A medium that can be written to only once is essential. The write once-read many (WORM) optical disk meets this requirement, but data tapes, which can be overwritten, are more generally used for the bulk of corporate information.

Security

The document management system should support the authorisation and authentication of users. To control access to documents, first the user should be authenticated; are they who they say they are? This can be by a user name and associated password or by more sophisticated systems like smart cards. Once authenticated, then a user can be authorised to view a subset of the repository. The system's administrator sets the rules for access.

If content is highly confidential it can be encrypted. Even if access is gained fraudulently, then the file cannot be easily read. This can be used, not only within the file repository, but also when the document is checked out for editing. For example, if a confidential document resides temporarily on a laptop computer, the possibility of the computer being stolen can be quite high, and encryption will protect against these risks. Modern operating systems can natively support an encrypted file system.

Access control is often set up in a hierarchy: by department, roles, and user. This is possibly overlaid with a cross-departmental workgroup. Many companies have existing access control policies that can be adopted by the document management.

There are many different ways to implement access control, but many rely on the network security provided by the operating system, and by the database management system (DBMS) underlying the document management.

Ingest

Once the principles of digital storage were adopted, there was the problem of the legacy paper documents. Basic optical character recognition (OCR) had been used by industries like banking, but it could only read a limited number of specially designed typefaces. Once again, research into artificial intelligence produced solutions for smart systems that could not only read a wide range of typeset information but could also decipher good handwriting. These systems are a vital part of any enterprise document management system, avoiding the wasteful processes of retyping whole documents.

The ingest of electronic documents is much easier. They may well be left in their original format if they are Word, Excel, or PowerPoint. There is a move now to convert information into extensible markup language (XML) for easy exchange between applications. Ingest is also the stage at which documents are categorised, and the metadata for the search index is generated.

Document scanning

Microfilm proved to be very useful in reducing the size of document repositories. But microfilm is just a miniature analogue representation of the original document. The information did not lend itself to integration with data-processing systems. If access to information was required across a large enterprise, the microfilm had to be copied by conventional photographic processes and distributed by some form of sneakernet.

By the 1980s, the word processor was becoming generally available, so documents were beginning to be stored as computer files. In spite of this new technology, there was a mountain of legacy documents that only existed as paper. Many documents had entered a business as faxes or letters. What was needed was a way for a computer to read the paper documents and automatically generate a text file.

From the 1950s, scientists had worked on the development of reading machines, starting with the Sheppard's GISMO. By the 1960s, the machines could read a very limited number of fonts. They were used for specialised tasks like reading cheques. A special font called OCR was even developed especially for scanning. These early scanners used a set of rules to recognise the small set of character outlines. Although they met the requirements of task-specific readers, they were of no use for general office documents. Another problem to be overcome was the poor quality of some office documents. A facsimile is often distorted with blurred characters and general noise. The photocopier also degrades the quality of documents; the characters bleed into one another as unwanted ligatures.

It was the application of neural networks in the 1980s that led to the development of OCR systems that could read a wide mixture of fonts and cope with degraded copies.

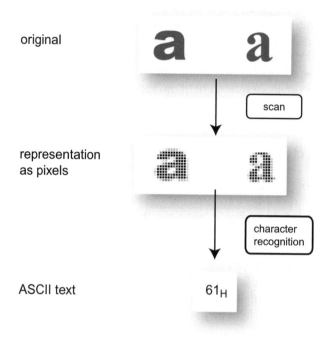

original

scan

representation
as pixels

character
recognition

ASCII text 61_H

Figure 2.4 OCR.

The OCRs have libraries of font templates to use as a basis for the recognition. Fonts can also be decoded by analysing their structural components: by strokes, holes, and other attributes. Many characters cannot be matched to a template, this may be because a single character has been decoded as two separate characters, or alternatively two characters interpreted as one. One big advance was to recognise characters in context. Letters could be decoded in frequently occurring groups. This requires the use of Bayesian statistical techniques. Imperfectly decoded characters could be statistically matched as groups. This gave a big improvement in the quality of character recognition.

A document scanner comprises three components:

- Optical scanner
- Character recognition
- Output interface.

The scanner is usually some form of charge coupled device (CCD) imager. A sheet feed mechanism can deliver paper at high speed to the platen, not unlike a photocopier. Automatic gain controls will optimise the signals to give the best contrast for the images. The cleaned-up images are presented as bitmaps to the OCR software. The output of the OCR should be an ASCII file (Figure 2.4). This is then converted by the output interface to a formal document file format like rich text format (RTF). Most systems are able to recover features from the original document like columns and sections, as well as a character formatting like italics and embolden.

Categorisation and indexing

Before you can search for a document, unless you know the file name and its path, it has to be categorised and indexed. This is covered in more detail in a later chapter. To classify a document the content is analysed, and a best match is found within the corporate taxonomy or categories. This can be performed by human operators, but this has several drawbacks. The first is that it is labour intensive, and requires skilled staff who can understand the content. Another drawback is that, being human, the classification can end up being subjective. There are also systems that will automatically categorise content, and at the same time generate aliases to cross reference from other categories. The algorithms used to understand the content are improving all the time, so the technology should be frequently revisited, rather than being permanently dismissed if it does not meet your needs.

The index can be based on keywords, or in more complex (and expensive) systems, based on concepts. The requirements from the search engine depend upon many parameters—the size of the file repository, the skills of the user, and the type of content. Scoping the search facilities and capabilities is an important part of requirement specification for the document management system.

Workflow automation

Once the customers had become accustomed to storing documents in a digital repository, the vendors of the document management applications saw the opportunity to add more intelligence to their products. Early on, access control was added. Just like a database, the users could be given permission to access a subset of the documents. This could be controlled by their name or by their role—author, editor, or manager.

The next step was to aid the business process. The concept of workflow automation was introduced. This term is often cited as a panacea for the inefficient business. The Workflow Management Coalition (WfMC) defines workflow as follows:

> The automation of a business process, in whole or part, during which documents, information, or tasks are passed from one participant to another for action, according to a set of procedural rules.

Take an example from the newspaper publishing industry. Just as a journalist passes a story to the copy or sub-editor, workflow automation manages the flow of documents through the organisation from creator to end user (Figure 2.5). So once the author has finished a document, it is placed in the virtual in-tray of the next participant in the flow. An e-mail alert may also be generated automatically. The next participant may want to review or approve the document. Ideally, the e-mail facilities should have a flexible set of configurable rules. Once a reviewer has approved a document, the reviewer may want to notify both the author and the next person in the workflow. Alternatively, the reviewer may have to reject the document, and return it to the author to make any necessary revisions. In a workgroup, all members of a project team may want notification of the document's progress. The workflow automation may need to track the lifecycle of a document against a publication deadline, and to notify stakeholders of possible late delivery. The workflow automation is replacing manual progress chasing.

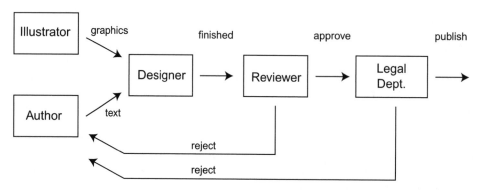

Figure 2.5 The document workflow.

A database uses a controlled transaction when a record is changed; the record is locked during the transaction, so that only one person can update a record at any one time. Similar control has to be exerted in a document management system. If several people are collaborating on a report, they may be making simultaneous changes without each other's knowledge. The document is now split into two or more different versions. To prevent more than one person accessing the document at the same time, the file is checked out, used (in this case edited), and checked back in. To aid the collaboration process, the earlier edits are stored as versions. An audit trail means that each person who has made edits can be identified, and the document can be rolled back to an earlier version if mistakes have been made or if the changes are deemed inappropriate.

The routing should be role based. That way, the flow of a document does not rely on any one person. If they are travelling or on leave, there is often no reason why another person in the same role could not pick up a document and process it.

The workflow may need to handle process exceptions, like workarounds, to overcome unexpected events. If the workflow is too rigid, then it may hinder rather than help the timely publishing of content. Any such constraints may also create hostility from the staff towards the document management system. The system should automate, not dictate.

The workflow is not fixed; it should be an iterative design. Once a satisfactory design that models your business has been built, it should be constantly monitored and reviewed. In this way, the workflow can be optimised to utilise knowledge workers in the most productive manner.

Metadata

Additional information is attached or linked to each file in order to track and control the documents. This data about the file is called metadata. Here the information controlling the workflow, access permissions, and versions is recorded. As documents are approved and reviewed, appropriate flags can be set.

Document management features

To summarise, these are some of the facilities that should be found in a document management system (Figure 2.6).

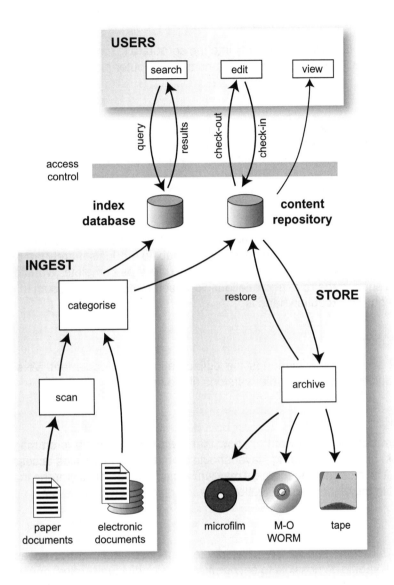

Figure 2.6 Document management system.

Multiple format ingest

Many documents may already be computer files, so seamless integration is important with popular authoring tools like Microsoft Office. Other documents may exist on paper or film. Scanners, and possibly OCR, may be used to ingest such documents. You do not need to purchase all the equipment and software. Many specialist document-scanning companies can provide this facility as a service. Obviously, there may be confidentiality or security concerns, so you may have to do all the work house.

Categorisation

Categorisation places the documents into the corporate taxonomy. This may be by subject or by project. The process can be manual or computer aided.

Search

A good search engine lets the users easily find relevant documents. The facilities may range from a basic keyword search to a sophisticated contextual search. More sophisticated engines can suggest material that is relevant to the user, but the user is unaware of their existence.

Workflow automation

Workflow manages the documents according to the business process. The term is often misused in vendors collateral. Some workflow-enabled products merely fire off an e-mail each time a member of a workgroup flags a document as complete. Workflow automation should support the role- and relationship-based routing of the documents. Finally, it must have proper exception handling.

Collaboration

Check-out and check-in manages the collaboration on a document. Version control keeps an audited history of earlier versions of the document.

Storage management

The system user does not want to know that a wanted document is on magnetic disk, optical disk, or tape. The storage layer should be hidden, and the files accessed by project or job. The storage management may well include hierarchical storage management to control file migration and restoration between different storage devices.

Security

A flexible structure should be provided to authorise and control access to files. Generally, it should be possible to set permissions to individuals, roles, and workgroups. It could well be based on existing policies that apply to corporate database access.

Web content management

Document and content management have much in common. The systems provide control over workflow and the lifecycle of content. They provide a storage repository for the assets, with security against unauthorised access, and facilities for backup and archive. There are important differences. Document management leaves the content pretty much as a unitary file. A document is ingested and stored, it can be recalled, and viewed or copied at will.

Web content management differs in that it treats a web page as a collection of objects. The text and images are stored separately. Images can be easily re-used in thousands of different pages. The web content management provides facilities to aggregate the objects and publish them as pages. This can be done at the time of content authoring, to create a static web page, or can be performed at run time by the server when requested by the user from their browser. This dynamic page can be used to personalise a site or to deliver information from a database.

Just as document management grew out of the need for workers across the enterprise to collaborate, as the first corporate web site grew larger, the same need arose. What may have started as a storefront put up by the marketing department could initially be maintained by a handful of people. When you add e-commerce, corporate communications, product information, and customer relations, now every area of the enterprise is contributing information to the site.

A typical corporate web site may have between ten and 20,000 pages. Quite clearly, this could not sensibly be maintained by expensive technical staff. Although they are required to design the architecture and the page templates, then to administer the site, the task of creating and publishing the content must fall to non-technical staff. They may be the business managers: marketing and product managers, and subject matter experts. They will be aided by specialist artists: the illustrators, writers, and photographers who will be creating the elements of the pages.

Just as document management is used to efficiently organise unstructured paperwork, content management enables the control and organisation of a web site. This is not just the original design of the site, but its day-to-day running. It is about creating new pages, updating existing pages, and retiring out-of-date information. The content management system has to integrate with non-technical staff, so that any knowledge worker can update content without specialist web design tools.

So far, the needs could be much the same as document management: the library functions and storage management. The publishing of web content needs more than simple file sharing and an asset repository. If one department pulls a page because the information is out of date, any links in other pages will be broken. As a site grows, the web page becomes a bottleneck. By using a template to store the boilerplate design of the web page, in theory, anyone in the corporation could drop text into the template. All the page design elements that need coding and thorough testing—the navigation and menus—could reside with the template. By adding a review and approval process, a page could then be checked before staging.

The content management has to address a number of needs. The content creator and the site owner each have a different set of requirements. A successful site will satisfy the end user by presenting accurate information that is up to date. For a site that is used frequently, the user may also desire personalised content. That way they can find what they need quickly without the need to see pages that are irrelevant to them. This may be just as important for an intranet as a public web site.

For the corporate management, their concern is return on investment (ROI). They want to utilise their staff resource more efficiently. They want to know that it is legal and accurate. Litigation is expensive and can impact on the corporate image. Also relating to the image, does the site have a consistent branding? Logos are updated so frequently that it is common for departments to inadvertently use out-of-date artwork. Much corporate content is expensive to produce, whether it is reports, photography, or video productions. Can this be used repeatedly, and can it be readily repurposed? The final concern relates to the IT facilities, does the content management require special client software or is the access from a browser?

The content creator will have a different set of needs—does it integrate with their familiar tools: Microsoft Word and Adobe Photoshop? They may want to integrate the site with an e-commerce system. A very important factor is usability, and does it aid collaboration with a workgroup?

The IT department will also have a view; after all, they have to deploy and maintain the system. Will they need specialist staff to support the application servers? There are security aspects—does the content management have powerful and flexible security, and can it upset the integrity of the main web site?

Web design tools

The first webmasters wrote the HTML code for the pages using a simple text editor. The early pages were little more than text with headings, tables, and links to other documents. Gradually, more graphics were embedded. They could be logos or photographs and drawings. As the web was adopted as a communication tool by businesses, it became apparent that the basic pages used by academics would not stand up against the high quality of the rest of the marketing collateral produced by a corporation. Businesses demanded better navigation and forms for interaction with customers and users.

The addition of graphics led to the development of 'what you see is what you get' (WYSIWYG) editors. The editors were part of fully fledged site design tools. They also offered support for the client side scripting that enabled the improved navigation. The drop-down and fly-out menus that help find our way around big sites all use scripts that run within the browser, usually JavaScript, or the standardised form—ECMAScript. These products hid the user from the foibles of HTML, and together with the scripting, immediately led to improvements to the look and usability of corporate sites.

There are several web design tools available: Dreamweaver, FrontPage, and GoLive are three popular products. Could these be used for content management? Yes and no. If you were operating a small web site, they could probably provide everything that you need. The designers of these products are always extending their capabilities, so that the boundaries between a content management system and the web design products have become blurred. They provide tools for a workgroup to collaborate. They provide shared access to a content repository. Dreamweaver has a partner product called Contribute. Using this client application, any content author can add or change text and images without the need to know any HTML. Macromedia's Contribute includes check-in and check-out, version control and for workflow, and an e-mail alert to a reviewer. The site manager has full control of permissions to authorise the users.

These products still need trained web developers or designers to use them. They should be used by skilled staff to design templates for use by the rest of the enterprise. They do not meet the goal of allowing anybody in the corporation to be able to add or edit content.

Many products have little in the way of facilities for collaboration over a wide area. Most use a thick client model, whereas enterprise-wide applications usually demand a simpler web interface for ease of deployment.

Publishing

The operation of publishing assembles web page templates, scripts, images, style sheets, and data-driven content into a unified document that can be served out to the end user. There the client device can render the file for viewing.

Dynamic pages

Dynamic web pages let the content creator embed structured data into a web page. This is typically information from a relational database for a web catalogue shopping site or it may be to create pages with personalised content. Dynamic pages have become the norm for all but the smallest sites. The information on a web page can be generated on the fly from a corporate database, then encoded and served as regular HTML to the browser.

As the dynamic page gives so much flexibility, why it is not used as a matter of course? Speed of download is all important with the web, as the users are notoriously impatient. As broadband access becomes the norm, if a page does not appear within seconds, the user is off elsewhere in the web. A static page serves much faster than a dynamic page; it is a very simple process. To get around this, many sites keep the home page and key navigation pages as static pages, even if they are rebuilt on a daily basis. Dynamic pages are reserved for personalised or interactive information where a longer wait will be accepted.

WebDAV

The Web-based distributed authoring and versioning or WebDAV server is a simple way to control collaboration and is supported by leading vendors like Adobe and Microsoft. The first release had three main features:

- File locking
- Metadata
- Namespace manipulation.

The versioning component was still in development in 2002. WebDAV is an extension to hypertext transfer protocol (HTTP). The first release supported distributed authoring. One author can check-out a copy of a file, locking the original, so that others can view but not check-out the file. Once the original author has finished editing the file, it can be checked in. The lock is removed and the original file overwritten. This is often called concurrency control. WebDAV also supports shared locking, where more than one author may work on a file in parallel.

Summary

There are two systems that are similar to digital asset management: document and content management. Document management is essentially a file manager that is integrated with the creative and business processes. Content management is usually taken to be web content management. The introduction of other user terminals, like the third generation cellular phones, means that content management is adapting to serve different content formats. Although both systems can be used with multimedia content, the primary focus has been on written information (for document management), and web site development (for content management).

Businesses are moving to a more integrated paradigm. Knowledge and information publishing is becoming multi-channel. The same content may be delivered as a white paper or brochure, as a web page, or formatted for wireless devices like the cellular phone or the Blackberry, or even through interactive television. The divisions between document and content management products are disappearing. By combining the two with digital asset management, a new and more flexible way to manage corporate information will emerge.

One key parameter cited by customers is usability. As the creative processes become so dependent upon the software, ease of use is paramount to ensuring that the promised productivity gains are actually achieved. Traditional document management often integrates very well with Quark, while web products have good interoperability with tools like Macromedia Dreamweaver. An integrated product must offer the tight integration with tools from other disciplines in order to be useful.

3 Media management

Introduction

Media management is a term that different people understand according to the context. This partly stems from the word 'media'. The word even has several meanings within the concept of asset management. As the plural of medium, it can refer to the way something is communicated as in the medium of sound or the medium of television. From this we have the 'mass media' meaning newspapers, magazines, radio, and television. Another meaning is as a substrate for content, as in tape media. This usage has its roots in such use as the artist's medium; the water or oil that carry the pigments are used for painting. Exploiting these many uses, the American television comedian, Ernie Kovacs, once said: 'Television: a medium. So called because it is neither rare nor well done'.

It is a truism that the media store their content on media. Media management is about the latter, the physical medium that stores the content assets. In the case of video, this means videotape, but it includes film, data tape, CD-ROMs, and the DVD. Media management underlies the digital asset management in much the same way as the database management system (DBMS) that used to store persistent data for the control of the content (Figure 3.1).

Media management is not limited to digital assets. Much of the media may be from analogue archives, like movie film, photographs, or paper documents.

Much of this chapter describes the development of media management in television broadcasting. Although many industry sectors have media to manage, the broadcaster had special issues relating to the very large file size. A movie-length file of uncompressed standard-definition video is around 150 GByte; that is over 30 standard DVDs. Not unsurprisingly, broadcasters have stuck with 35-mm film and videotape except in certain limited areas. It is only recently that we see the emergence of digital cinematography. The main areas where television has used conventional computer disk storage have been in post-production and in the publishing area—master control and transmission. That is now changing, as the use of video files is pervading the entire content chain.

Broadcasters long ago developed workflows to manage the scheduling and transmission of programmes and commercials. They made extensive use of software to manage the traffic and sales processes relating to television commercials. Meanwhile, video recording technology was evolving, from open reel tapes to the videocassette,

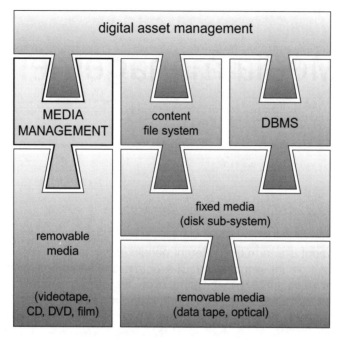

Figure 3.1 Media management supports digital asset management.

and then the broadcast video server emerged. The tape medium required frequent operator intervention and regular maintenance. The operation of master control leaned heavily on printed lists of tapes and playout schedules. If the video server and the traffic software could be integrated, there was the possibility of automating the station. The solution is media asset management.

Up until the 1990s, the television broadcaster considered asset management to be a well-run tape library. The introduction of video servers in mainstream production demanded completely new systems to manage their programme content and workflows. Rather than the physical videocassette, the broadcaster now had to deal with the more ephemeral computer file.

Several basic operations can be performed on a content item:

- Store
- Move
- Copy
- View.

Typically, content can be taken out of storage (the library) and viewed. You could then copy it, and return the original to the store. Alternatively, you could move the content, it could be despatched to another place, where it probably ends up in a different store. Media management has to control these operations in a formal process. That way content always can be located, the copying and distribution can possibly be automated, and access control can be exerted over the content.

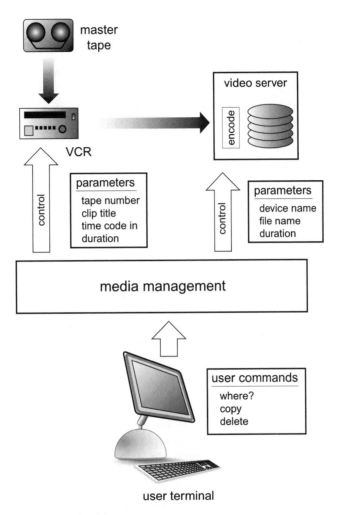

Figure 3.2 Basic tape encode to video server.

Issues in media management

Tape could be managed with basic library software. It lives on a shelf, it is checked out and checked in. Once digital copies can be made by tracking, the content becomes more diffuse. Consider the basic operation of encoding a videotape to a server (Figure 3.2).

The master tape will be identified by a label that carries the unique tape number, the title of the clip, and the start time code. The media management ingest operation can control the tape deck and server, and automatically dub the video clip onto the server as a video file. The operator will set up this operation by marking the in and out points of the clip using time code values. The file name of the server clip in itself is not very useful. Instead, the media management can store the association between the file name and the original tape data: the tape number and the item title. Now the server file can be used by reference to the original tape number.

A remote user terminal can interrogate the media management database, to find material, search on title, and find which clips are on the server. The operator can also initiate the copying and deletion of materials on the server.

The system can be made a whole lot smarter. If the tape carries a bar code, it could be identified immediately, without the need for the operator to type in the tape number. The bar code data may well be stored in a tape library database.

So far, this is all a pretty basic stuff. Broadcasting is much more complex. To cover equipment failure, the servers are often run as mirrored pairs. There may be a whole cluster of servers to feed many playout ports. These ports may be feeding, editing workstations, or be playing finished material to air.

Typically, server groups are linked with a high-speed interconnection like a fibre channel fabric. Files can be rapidly copied and moved between servers. The media management must control all these operations.

Historical perspective

Broadcasting workflows divide loosely into two groups, one to handle programmes and a second for commercial spots. The differences between the two also affect the way that the media is handled. Programmes are long, 30 min or more, and are normally aired once or twice. Commercials are short, around 30 s, and aired hundreds of times. Traditionally, commercials were aired from tape cart machines, and the programmes either live or from videotape recorders (VTRs).

Cart machines

The nature of commercial playback, with a rapid sequence of back-to-back spots, and the demands for random access to each spot, demanded some sort of automated machine. As commercials represent the revenue source for a station, reliability was vital in any design. Originally, commercials were pre-recorded as spot reels, a tape compilation for each break. Ampex introduced the first cart machine, the ACR-25, in 1970. The machine used the same principles as the 2-in. transverse scan recorder that was used for long-form material. The ACR-25 could hold 24 spot cartridges. It is a great complement to the robust construction of the machine that television stations used the machine up to the 1990s.

The advent of the videocassette (as opposed to the open reels of the 2-in. machines) opened the way to a new generation of cart machines. A tape cassette does not have to be manually laced. It can be easily moved by a robotic arm from storage to the tape deck. This time there would no longer be the limited playback duration of the spot cartridge; any standard cassette could be used (Figure 3.3). In 1986, Sony launched a range of products that were to dominate channel playout for 15 years. The LMS (Library Management System) was produced in two versions, one for Betacam tapes and one for the D-2 format (digital composite). Ampex later released the ACR-225 for digital tapes, and Panasonic produced the MARC (which used the MII tape format).

The cart machine revolutionised playout. The machines could handle long programme tapes as well as the short spot reels. The LMS had a powerful automation application

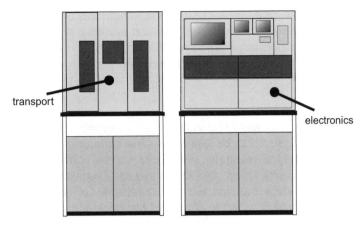

transport

electronics

Ampex ACR-25

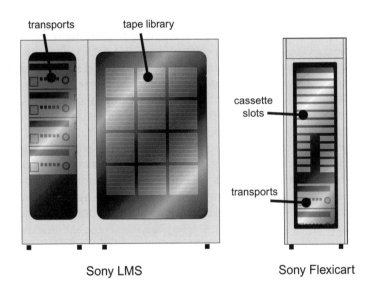

transports   tape library

cassette
slots

transports

Sony LMS   Sony Flexicart

Figure 3.3 Robotic video cartridge machines.

that could run an entire day of tapes, both spots and programmes, all from a playlist. The onus on the operator was just to load and unload tapes, and to monitor the operation; otherwise, it could run virtually unattended.

So far broadcasting still relied on videotape, in the form of the videocassette. Although all these machines have delivered sterling service, and have demonstrated very high levels of reliability, they still suffered from the high maintenance costs of the conventional VTR transport that lies at the heart of each machine. The broadcaster could look with envy at the data-processing industry, where frequently accessed data could be stored on low-cost disk drives. One of the main requirements was the need to ensure perfect playback of commercials. For a station to receive full payment for a spot, the playout had to be free of errors. These could be the result of tape dropouts or head clogs. The usual way to cope with this eventuality was to run two cart systems in parallel. This is expensive, so the alternative was to run a precompiled commercial break on a separate VTR. Each has drawbacks; one is cost, the other complexity.

The video server

The video editing community were first to adopt the magnetic disk drive to store digital video, but many obstacles had to be overcome. The computer drives available in the mid-1980s (the time the LMS was released) could not read out at the sustained rates needed for broadcast-quality video real-time playback. Gradually, products emerged. The Abekas A-62 and A-64 transformed the capabilities of commercial production. These disk recorders could be used to store and playback short sequences that could be composited to form a final image with hundreds of layers. Previous analogue tape-based editing was limited to around six generations (and that includes the distribution copies), so it was just not possible to make multiple generation effects (Figure 3.4). Although these early machines could only store 60 s or so, they were mainly used for the production of commercials or effects, both materials of short duration.

Soon the digital-disk recorder was emerging as a viable technology, but it was still not suited to the task of replacing the tape cart machine for playing spots to air. The storage time was very limited, a few minutes. The solution was partly to use video compression, which allowed a longer clip duration to be stored on a given capacity disk, and partly the ever-falling cost and ever-increasing capacity of disk storage sub-systems.

Hewlett-Packard and Grass Valley both developed video disk stores that could be used on air (the Hewlett-Packard product division was later sold to Pinnacle Systems). These were true file servers that could store finished programmes and commercials.

The way was now clear to play spots to air from disk rather than tape. This was the point when the need for media management became clear. A videotape was a physical entity. You can pick it up and read the label. To preview the content you can load it into

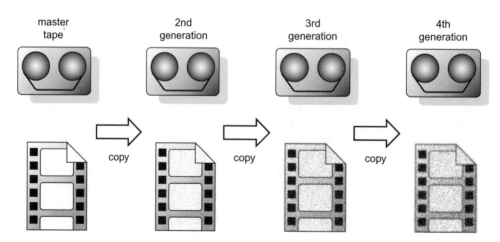

Figure 3.4 Quality degrades with analogue tape copies.

a VTR. If you wanted to play out from a different building, a courier delivered the tape to that site.

The file server was different. The video content could only be located by querying the video-server's internal database. Access to the files was limited to the handful of video ports available. If they were used for playout, they could not be used for preview. Broadcasters were used to control computers of the cart machines. These could run playlists and compile protect tapes to backup commercial breaks. If a tape was no longer required for transmission, it could be unloaded and returned to the tape vault. These functions had to be replicated if the server was ever to replace the cart machine (Figure 3.5).

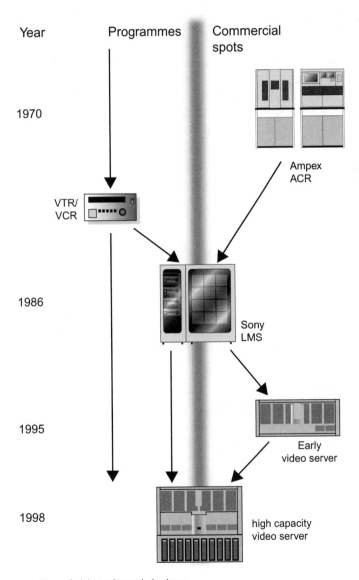

Figure 3.5 The evolution of video playout devices.

Videotape—content or storage media?

When analogue tape was the norm, the video recording and the master tape were intimately linked. Therefore, the tape was the content. Copies could be made, for editing, distribution, and backup. But the original master tape always represented the primary asset (Figure 3.6).

Contrast this with a file on a disk. The actual disk where the file is stored and the specific sectors of that disk are of no interest to the user. The operating system manages all the details. Therefore, the content and the storage media now have an ephemeral linkage. The same principles apply to data tapes.

A video asset could now be considered as a metadata record describing the content with links to logical file names (Figure 3.7). These logical files are then mapped to the physical instances of that content. These could be removable storage media like videotape (in which case the logical file name is replaced with time code values). To view or edit the asset, the storage instances are then rendered by a device into natural video.

The asset is now an abstract concept, you cannot see *it* per se; you can only view an instance of it. This separation of the video content and the storage medium requires a control system to manage the associations between the content and medium. This system is media asset management.

Digital videotape

The digital videotape sits in-between, it is not analogue but it is not a file. It is a stream of data that is written and read in real time. Each time a tape is copied, the video signal

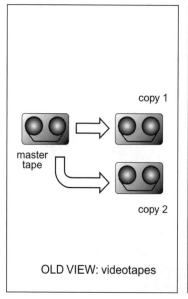
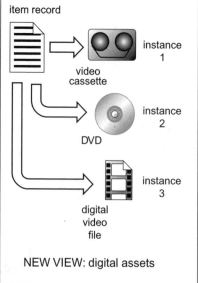

Figure 3.6 Videotapes versus digital assets.

can degrade. Error masking and concealment are used, so many more generations of copies can be made than with an analogue tape, but it is not a perfect copy. Over tens of generations, artefacts from the error concealment will start to become visible. These high-quality copies are often called clones.

Conventional data storage can make essentially error-free copies. The write process can be verified, and blocks re-written if errors occur. Videotape read and write is real time, so there is no possibility to cope with errors by rewriting the data, hence the use of masking and concealment instead.

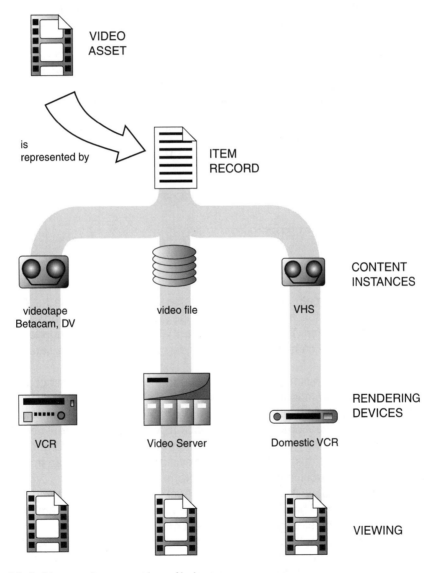

Figure 3.7 A video assets as a number of instances.

Storage & Distribution Media

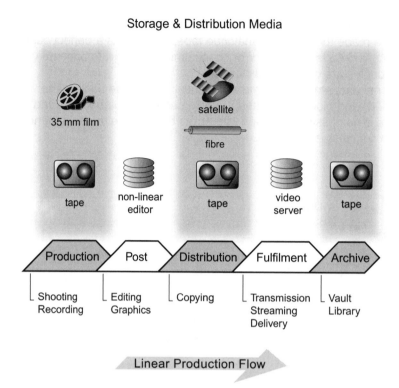

Figure 3.8 The media of storage and distribution.

Media workflow

Until the end of the twentieth century the television workflow comprised a number of digital islands, linked by the medium of videotape. The two main islands were post-production and transmission. To pass programme material from one stage to another it was transferred as a tape cassette or as a live video stream, often by a satellite link or fibre circuit (Figure 3.8).

Material is often shot on film, particularly prime-time programming and commercials. Using a telecine machine, it is transferred to videotape for downstream distribution. In post-production the material is ingested to a disk array and cut on a non-linear editor. The resulting file is conventionally recorded back to videotape as a real-time transfer and placed in the tape library or vault. Once a programme is ready for transmission, a copy can be dubbed and despatched to the television station. After transmission, the tapes can be sent to an archive for long-term storage (Figure 3.9).

Throughout this workflow, the tape is being checked in and out of storage, and it is moved around the station. The aim of media management is to have an umbrella application that can control the storage and movement of the tapes.

Digital asset management can help the migration to a wholly digital workflow, with attendant efficiency savings. Digital asset management can automate many of the repetitive tasks, freeing valuable knowledge workers for more creative tasks.

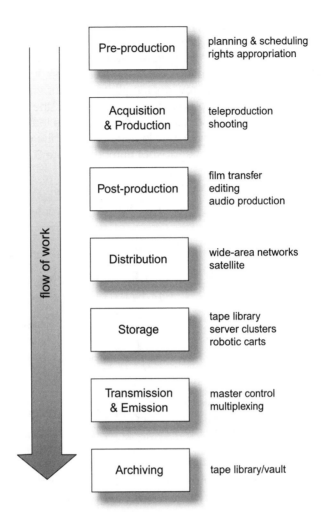

Figure 3.9 Detail of television workflow.

Television transmission: master control

The introduction of the video server changed the operation of master control. From being a tape handling exercise, it became a file management issue. In master control, the programme material is played to air according to a playlist (schedule) from the traffic department. A programme is schedule for transmission at a specified time, but the scheduler is not concerned whether it is played from disk or tape. In other words, the scheduler wants to be abstracted from the media layer.

The first video-server systems used a traditional name space with a hierarchical file system, much like a conventional file server. The file name alone is not very useful for identifying content, as any user of a word processor will know. At least a tape box may contain a dope sheet with information about the content on the tape.

The videotape had a tape number, and a time code reference for the first frame of the programme. Tapes can hold many programme items, so the tape number does not uniquely identify the programme; the time code reference is used. Tapes are scheduled by the tape number and the in time code point—the start of the programme.

The media management service provides the abstraction for the scheduler. The programme can be designated in the playlist as an item record; the media management automatically chooses a suitable instance of the item to air, be that tape or server. Note that the scheduler never needs to know the file name used by the disks, but can schedule using a unique programme identifier or spot number (Figure 3.10).

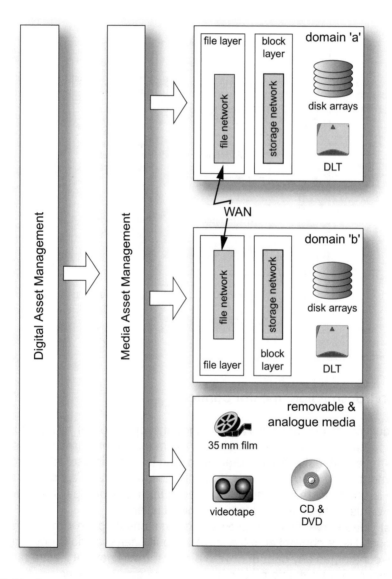

Figure 3.10 Media management links digital domains and the analogue world.

Integrating tape and servers

The simplest media management application could comprise a video server and a VTR to load the server from videotape. The application is based on a database, where the associations between the instances of a content item can be stored.

The basic system shown in Figure 3.11 is just about adequate for a small television station to play a few commercials. The system comprises a number of workstations, all connected to a central media management database. The video flow is from the tape

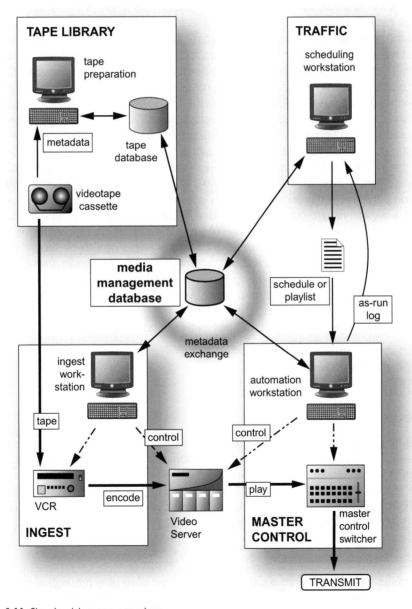

Figure 3.11 Simple video-server system.

library, to the video cassette recorder (VCR) then to the video server. The playout is from the server to the master control switcher then out to the transmitter.

The metadata has a different, more complex, flow. The tape librarian logs new tape into the library database. Most librarians already have systems for bar coding tapes. The tape handling robots in old cart machine use the bar codes to uniquely identify each cassette.

Typical data would be in and out time codes, title, and tape number. Programme tapes usually carry a single item; commercial tapes often carry 10 or more spots.

The ingest workstation is used to control the recording of the tape to the video server. The workstation is linked to the media management database. The operator can interrogate the tape bar code with a handheld reader. That will query the database and retrieve information for that tape. This will include the time code in and out points for the clip, these are used to set up the ingest operation. Once the tape is loaded, the application will cue the tape to the in point, roll the server into record, and then play the tape. A further exchange of metadata will place a new record in the database referencing the newly created clip file on the video server.

Meanwhile in the traffic department, the scheduler can check the programme or spot in the database, then schedule the item in the playlist to be played to air.

In master control, the playout automation system processes the day's schedule. Each event in the list has unique identifier for each video clip. Querying the database will return the correct filename used by the video server. At the scheduled time, the server is cued and played to air through the master control switcher.

That is a basic system, but more is needed before it could be considered as a serious replacement for a tape cart machine. As commercial spots represent the primary revenue stream for a television station, the playout system has to be highly available. Most stations have a target for successful transmission of commercials that allows for a loss of less than 1min per year, barring fire and earthquake. To achieve this, mirrored systems are used with extensive redundancy. As a last resort, an operator is also able to take control and play tapes manually.

A more resilient system with high capacity would add a number of facilities:

- Multi-channel ingest with robotic tape handling
- Server cluster for redundancy
- Near-offline data tape backup.

Tape robots

Clearly feeding tapes manually into tape decks is an inefficient way to ingest content to the servers. The alternative is to use the tape robots that were formerly used for transmission of videotape to air. The tape librarian can load the cart with 30 or so tapes, then leave the media management system to control the ingest. Many stations have retired their carts from the gruelling on-air use, and redeployed them for this ingest operation. The low-duty cycle will lower the maintenance costs.

Server clusters

A cluster gives more capacity to a server pool, and can also give protection against failure of a single server. Servers have a limited number of ports. This limit ensures that the processing capacity of the server is never exceeded. A video server must always have sufficient resources available to play and record in real time, there can be no resource sharing like a conventional file server. In a large video facility, the port limit is soon reached. To add more ports you have to add more servers.

Data tape silos

The encoded files on the server can be stored as data files rather than video on videotape. This has several advantages:

- The encoded files are usually compressed, so occupy less storage.
- The encoded files have been quality checked, so they can be copied back and forth as data in an error-free environment.
- The data can be transferred at high speed, usually faster than real time.

Wide-area transfer

A primary component of media management is the transfer of content from one site to another. This could be the transfer of programmes from a network to affiliate stations, or for the distribution of television commercials. This process was carried out by couriers moving tapes, or by video transmission if the circuits were available. Satellite transmission has also proved popular. The commercials are transmitted at a pre-arranged time, and each station starts a VTR to record the feed at the scheduled time. This cuts out the costs of courier, and the risk of damage in transit. The drawback is that it is an open-loop system. There is no mechanism to ensure error-free delivery.

The system is real time, so it is not possible to have the retransmission that data protocols like TCP/IP or FTP can use. If the need for real time is abandoned, then the content can be moved by file transfer between two video servers. It could be termed 'store and forward'. Such systems can easily be integrated with a media management, so that the entire content distribution can be automated. It can also be made more flexible, so that content can be pulled as well as the more usual push of content out from the centre. As an example, the advertising traffic department could make a list of commercials that are required for broadcast. Then just those spots could be requested for transfer, rather than wasting valuable circuit capacity by downloading all the new commercials.

Examples of media management

This section looks at a number of applications of media management, mainly in television-master control.

Server-based master control

Master control has to be designed for very reliable operation. To achieve this, extensive redundancy is used. Typically, twin video servers are used in a mirrored configuration. The original videotapes are stacked in a robotic cart machine, like the Sony Flexicart.

The media management system has an ingest controller to manage the transfer from tape to server. Typically, a record list is loaded from the traffic department. The material should ideally be acquired in order of first to air. The encoded server can also take in live video feeds, although this will require some form of external control, either a manual start, or by triggers from the live video source. One problem that can arise during automated ingest is that faults may develop in the tape playback. This could be a head clog or tape damage. Important material like commercials will need a quality control check once they have been ingested into the server domain. If necessary, the media management could prevent transmission until this check has been made.

The automation workstation loads a day's schedule. This queries the media management, and all the wanted files are moved and duplicated to the two air servers. The location of material, and the progress of transfers, can be viewed at any time from a media management workstation. The operator can also be warned of any missing material, and take suitable action—maybe a call to the tape vault.

The system in Figure 3.12 would have a small capacity, with only three servers. In most systems, a cluster of servers means that you can store many hundreds of hours of programmes. The servers are linked by a high-speed bus or network, usually a fibre channel fabric. These networks can be duplicated to provide fault tolerance. Again, the media management system controls the copying and moving of content from one server to another. The system will also delete old material to free up disk space. This will require the use of an algorithm to ensure that wanted material is not removed, as this would necessitate a re-ingest from the original tape. The media management will use a separate Ethernet control network. Note that mirrored servers are still required, even if RAID storage sub-systems are used. The mirrored servers provide protection against faults with power supplies, decoder cards (that convert the compressed files to an uncompressed video stream), and other essential components.

There is always a limit, usually financial, to the number of servers, so if you need increased capacity the alternative is to store the compressed files as data on tape (Figure 3.13). One advantage of this is that the compressed and quality checked file is stored on tape, and a perfect copy can be restored to the servers. A re-ingest from video tape requires another quality check. High-performance data libraries can restore a video clip in faster than real time.

A server running a special data storage management application connects to the tape library. Under control of commands from the media management, this data mover can archive files from disk to tape, and restore those files on demand. The data storage management application provides storage virtualisation of the tape library.

A real system could include all these facilities. That is automated ingest of videotape, clustered servers, and near-line storage on an automated data tape library.

Television commercial lifecycle

This is an area of television production that has benefited from digital technologies. Between the commissioning of a commercial and the final airing to the public, there is a long chain of collaboration between several different parties.

Once the client has issued the brief to the advertising agency, the agency will work up a concept. This will involve a storyboard to show the visual ideas, and a script. After

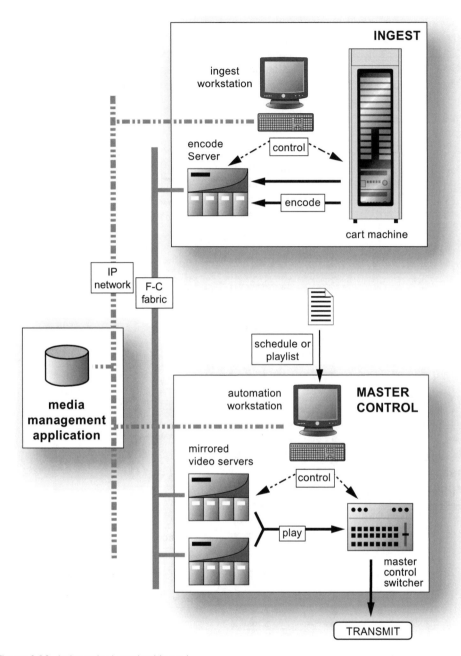

Figure 3.12 Automated content ingest.

an iterative process, with exchanges of e-mails and many meetings and possibly even videoconferences, the concept can be taken to production. During the shooting, several parties from the producer to the client may want to see dailies from the laboratory. Once in the can, the film goes into post-production for the editing, special effects, graphics,

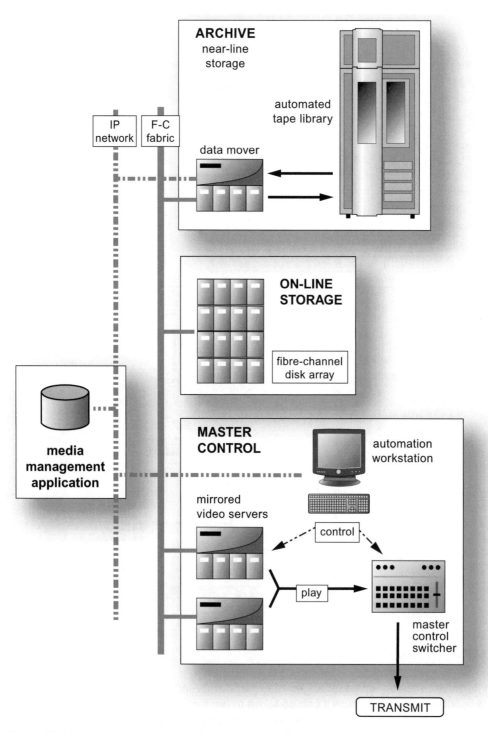

Figure 3.13 Near-line data storage for increased capacity.

and sound design. Again, many parties will want to be involved in the progress, possibly approving creative decisions. Finally, a finished commercial emerges that satisfies the producer and the client.

After client's approval, the commercial still has another hurdle to jump before it can be aired. The network will want to view and approve the commercial for transmission. Their lawyers will check that it conforms to legislation, and hopefully give clearance.

The first issue is geographic dispersal. The client's headquarters could be anywhere. The advertising agency could be in New York. The production could be shot on location anywhere in the world. The post may take place in Los Angeles or London. The network could be in New York. All the parties in the different locations will want to view video material at some stage in the production process. Traditionally, VHS copies were distributed by courier, with the attendant delays and cost.

Finally, once approved and cleared, the commercial has to be delivered to the television stations. Again the tapes, this time of broadcast quality, were distributed by courier.

Media management can provide effective solutions that leverage standard telecom circuits could circulate the material quickly to all interested parties. Media management can ensure simple secure and reliable exchange of material between the parties.

Telestream has made the wide-area transfer of video material as easy as sending an e-mail. It could be rushes and dailies for preview, or to distribute the finished commercials (Figure 3.14).

Figure 3.14 Digital media delivery by ClipMail Pro ©Telestream Inc.

Many wide-area system are closed. They take real-time video in, and transfer it to a remote terminal, where you can get video out. Most video-server manufacturers also support the transfer of files between servers over IP networks. Again, this may be proprietary. There have been moves by the AAF Association to make the transfer of files as easy as exchanging live video, in that there is an agreed common specification for the file formats. The AAF is based on Microsoft's Structured Storage. Once content is in such a format, then wide-area transfer can be made by a storage network controller, without the need for the media management.

Media management in post-production

A video production projects usually starts with a stack of videotapes, possibly Digital Betacam or a DV format. The material is encoded to disk as uncompressed video or DV.

The production process involves much collaboration. The offline editing or the rough-cut may use a highly compressed proxy of the source material. Any complex layering or animation may be laid off to a special effects house and will be uncompressed. Once all the elements have been prepared, the final assembly can take place.

The source material, effect sequences and graphics can be composited online to produce the finished video. Meanwhile, similar operations are happening as part of the sound design. In all these processes, material has to be moved between different companies, it has to be converted between formats, and it all has to be tracked to maintain correct version history and synchronisation between elements.

The media management allows the creative personnel to concentrate on the creative processes and to be abstracted from these underlying mechanisms.

Typical media management systems integrate file-based content with the removable media. Conventional file systems do not meet the needs of production workflows. Editors like to categorise files by projects and bins. They need to search from comprehensive metadata, not just the file name. The move to high-definition production adds yet more formats to manage.

Central casting

This new term is a contraction of centralised broadcasting. For a long time, broadcasters have used satellite to distribute programmes from network headquarters out to remote affiliates. The affiliate then inserts their local programmes and news. A similar process is used for advertisement distribution, where the local station records and stores the commercials, ready for insertion. Programmes that are not distributed in real time can be delivered on tape. The emergence of lower-cost fibre networks, with sufficient capacity for video, provides an alternative to satellite and tape delivery. The bi-directional nature of these circuits opens the way for new models of operation.

The group stations and network affiliates traditionally duplicate much of the processes carried on at headquarters. If wide-area networks are used to distribute the DV files prepared at the headquarters, then much of this duplication of resource can be avoided.

Many stations have a graphics department to produce interstitials, bumpers, and stings to identify the station and promote upcoming programmes. The station will have a small traffic department to manage the advertising sales and scheduling. If all these processes are centralised, then there is a potential for efficiency saving and better utilisation of plant.

There are several models for central casting, representing various shades between two opposites: centralised playout and distributed playout. Centralised playout adopts a similar design to a multi-channel satellite operator. The on-air presentation is assembled in parallel-master control suites. The finished channel, complete with the local commercials, is then distributed in real time by the fibre circuit to the affiliate. The local station has basic facilities to insert local news and other live content and usually operate in a pass-through mode, just like a cable head end. This station no longer needs any facilities for satellite network feeds or for commercial insertion. The savings can extend to engineering staff. To monitor the output, telemetry from the tower can be transmitted back to the central control. This can even include a low-bandwidth video stream from a monitoring receiver.

The alternative model is distributed playback. The graphics and spots are still packaged centrally, but master control still takes place at the affiliate station. The pre-packaged media is distributed by file transfer rather than the real-time streaming. This store and forward can use lower-cost circuits than those required for the central-master control model.

Central casting, whichever model is used, is heavily based on server technologies rather than videotape. Multiple feed to different regions can share the same files, and the servers offer time shifting at no cost—just play out the file later. To control all the servers, and to manage the transfer of files out to affiliates, some form of media management is mandatory if the potential efficiency savings are to be realised.

The viability of central casting relies very much on the cost of the fibre circuits. In many areas, there is not sufficient saving to warrant a move to this new model. The best guess is that ATM links will get cheaper, and labour costs will rise, so in the long run more groups will adopt central casting.

Summary

Media management allows removable storage media, both analogue and digital, to be integrated with a digital asset management solution. Media management moves, converts, and stores. It could be a programme in post-production being moved from the edit bay to the vault, or a finished programme being delivered from the production company to the television station. Media management can also provide new facilities for still images. Images can be dynamically converted from one format to another, without user intervention. This abstracts the user from the image formats, so they can concentrate on the content.

Data tapes do not generally need a separate media management application. The control systems are integrated with storage network systems that manage the disk arrays and tape backup.

Media management provides an all-encompassing service beyond the shared storage systems used for the purely digital files. It unifies tape and disk, videotape and data tape, analogue and digital. It forms an essential part of the digital asset management system.

In many ways, a media management system is analogous to a storage network controller. Media management is not limited to a domain of computer files, but can include content stored on any media substrate, analogue, or digital.

4 The case for digital asset management

Introduction

The case for digital asset management, like most business decisions, hinges around return on investment. The primary gains from asset management are that the time to search for content will be dramatically reduced, the precision and recall of the search will be improved, and the preparation time of content for distribution will be reduced. These three will lead to cost savings and improved efficiencies.

Before making a case for digital asset management, you must qualify the scope of the deployment. Asset management systems can range from a single user installation for image filing with a cost of $50, through to a multi-million dollar installation for hundreds or even thousands of users. The type of asset will make a big difference, as will the number of assets. The assets come in many formats. They can be structured data or unstructured text files, photographic image and illustrations, or multimedia files: audio, video, and animation. As the number of assets increases, so does the complexity of the management. A large asset repository requires tools that would represent a complete overkill for a small library. Although a large library may have economies of scale, it will require more complex management applications to fully realise the advantages of digital asset management. The relationship between the size of the library and the cost is not necessarily linear.

Asset management is often equated to the digitisation of analogue archives: paper, film, and videotape. Although *digital assets* must by their very name be digital, they do not have to be managed *per se*. The advantage of assets being in a digital format is that they *can* be managed, and this management can leverage the availability of affordable information technology. In the past, especially with video assets, special hardware was required to provide the functionality that we now expect from asset management.

Digital asset management covers a very wide field. From documents to video, there has been a gradual migration to these new systems. The acceptance has varied between industry sectors. Who would attempt to run a mid- to large web site without a content management application? Enterprises that use text documents as a key part of their business processes have long ago recognised the value of asset management—the law and drug research being two good examples. Image libraries use digital asset management to enable online trading. They can offer their full catalogue without expensive printing, duplication and distribution overheads, and give their customers instant electronic delivery.

The last sector to adopt asset management has been the media business with audio-visual assets. Until the late 1990s, the cost of hosting these assets wholly in the digital domain had been prohibitive. Most sectors have long understood the value of asset management, the problem has been realising a return on the original investment. There are many potential vendors willing to sell you such systems, but most have only a handful of customers. Many vendors have had to scale back and retrench; some have closed down. They have been fighting over the same small pool of potential customers. So why is this? Everyone understands the advantages, but nobody wants to buy.

A fully featured digital asset management system for an audio-visual library requires massive amounts of storage. Such storage silos were once only found in the systems used by government agencies with deep pockets. The systems also require powerful processing hardware to handle video in real time and to provide the platforms for the artificial intelligence used to catalogue, index, and search the content. Now that the most modest personal computer has a clock rate of over 1 GHz, and disk drives have broken the 100 GB mark, the storage and processing power required is becoming affordable. The system vendors have known how to manage digital assets for 10 years; the problem has been the price point. We have now reached the position where low-cost, high-performance computer products can deliver a return on the investment in digital asset management in a reasonably short period of time.

The pace of business is ever increasing. There is no time for mistakes, or for inefficient processes. The need to stay competitive, and to drive down costs, demands ever more automation of business processes. The media business that wants to survive and stay profitable cannot continue with the old, more relaxed procedures for creating and publishing content. These were often very labour-intensive craft processes.

Some areas like newspaper publishing have readily adopted new techniques and workflows. But many creative businesses are still diverted by time-consuming processes. Staff waste time finding files, backing up work, and converting documents between different formats. Meanwhile, their historical archives are deteriorating.

Many businesses initially view digital asset management as an expensive overhead that will have only minor impact on costs. Since an enterprise scale system can cost from 1 to 5 million dollars to get up and keep running, it represents a substantial investment for a software application.

Many businesses have researched the implications of purchasing asset management as part of their strategic planning. The first two questions are 'what is the investment required?' and 'what will be the return?'. The alternative to an outright purchase was a home brewed combination of shrink-wrap products, some bespoke software coding, and the efforts of the IT department. Many video production facilities have just such systems. With a ready pool of software talent to call on, they were able to build their own systems. Perhaps, the largest is that used by Disney for the production of animation features.

In the case of Disney, they badly needed a system to manage the millions of cells that go to make up a feature-length animation. Not only that, but the artists worked at three sites across the globe. The production workflows demand close collaboration between the three groups. At the time, there were no commercial products that met their requirements, so they had no option but to design and build their own.

Few other companies have asset problems on quite the numeric scale of Disney, but the same issues of collaboration come up over and over again. Many companies that did develop a small in-house solution have come up against common issues. Often the labour costs are hidden, as existing staff write the code in spare time. The product may be poorly documented. If the system architect leaves the company, it may prove difficult or even impossible to maintain.

Early adopters

Businesses that have taken up asset management, find that it frees up valuable human resource for more creative work. The time wasted searching for information is much reduced. Asset management overcomes all the problems of finding content. Once it becomes easy to exploit the archive, then new production opportunities arise. By re-purposing existing assets, low-cost content can be distributed to new delivery channels, where the costs of original production could not be justified.

Cost of operation

There is no doubt that asset management can enable more efficient workflows. But there are costs beyond the hardware and operational costs of the software systems. One question that is often raised is 'who pays for the ongoing metadata entry and collection?'. Metadata is essential to realise the full benefits of asset management. Ultimately, it will be the consumer that pays. Does it save costs downstream? Yes, it usually does. The commercial issue is that the downstream beneficiary may be a different organisation from the upstream company that has to record the metadata. In a competitive world the metadata costs cannot be passed on directly.

There are other cost implications beyond the operation of the asset management system. Do analogue assets have to be digitised? The cost of scanning or ingesting analogue media is largely for the human labour. It is time consuming and boring, repetitive work. Closely allied to this is the generation of the original metadata for each piece of content. Much of this may have to be entered by hand.

The advantages of asset management are best realised when the other information systems can access and share the content metadata. This implies interfaces—they are often expensive.

Who needs asset management?

Any modern business has digital assets, even if it is only word processor files and spreadsheets. Early adopters of enterprise asset management include auto manufacturers, print publishers, and television news broadcasters. What do they have in common? They all use documents and images, and two of them use video.

One niche business that relies on asset management as the cornerstone of their offering is the image library. At least one popular digital asset management product started out as an application for managing pictures. Image repositories have always had a problem with the index. A document can be retrieved by a text search. Images have usually been located by viewing printed catalogues. To index a picture, it can be allocated keywords, but there is no simple way to automate this process. It is an essentially manual process—view the picture and then describe it in 20 words.

The first electronic picture libraries developed many of the features now considered essential to the efficient storage and retrieval of thousands, or even millions of image files. These include keyword searching, dynamic thumbnail previews, and online fulfilment.

Drop by any marketing communications office and you will find a big stack of image library catalogues. The libraries like Allsport and Stone publish catalogues, each with about a 1000 image thumbnails. Clearly, even 10 catalogues represent only a small choice on one particular topic. This leads to the same images appearing repeatedly in print. This may be great for the photographer's royalties, but tends to give corporate collateral that 'stock photo' look.

The move to digital asset management has transformed this business by offering a much wider choice of images. Now the customer can search and view a catalogue that is virtually unlimited in size. The purchase can be made online, and the high-resolution image downloaded for immediate use. The price of rights-managed images has been simplified, so what once required a long phone call, is now all built into the e-commerce system.

Before digital assets, duplicate transparencies were despatched by mail or courier. They then had to be scanned by the customer. There was always the possibility of dust and scratches impairing the image, leading to labour-intensive retouching. With the deliver of an image file, all these will go away.

Clearly, this business has been transformed by the online digital asset management system. For the library, the overheads are capped and many of the simple repetitive tasks have been eliminated. For the customer, they have more choice and immediate delivery.

For other businesses, the case is not so clear cut. The digital asset management may not be key to the product or service offering, but is an aid to improving the efficiency of internal workflows (Figure 4.1).

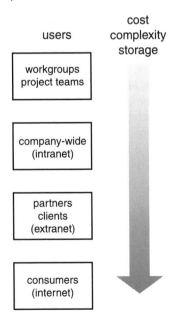

Figure 4.1 The range of asset management.

As the number of users increase from a small project team up to a public e-commerce site, then the cost, complexity, and storage requirements all increase.

What do you want from asset management?

One approach to the planning of an asset management is to make it all-encompassing. Every piece of 'analogue' content is digitised and indexed. Every employee can get instant access to all the corporate content that they are authorised to view. Such a policy may work, but for most businesses, a compromise will more likely achieve a better return on investment.

There may be other reasons to digitise the archive, which are not related to asset management. As an example, magnetic tape deteriorates and, after 20 or 30 years, the content must be dubbed to fresh tape. Colour film fades as the dyes age, again after a few decades. The restoration may well involve colour correction to get back the original colours.

Is the archive an asset? It is often difficult to assess the worth of aged content. Ultimately, it is a matter of judgement, mistakes will be made, but that is the advantage of hindsight. Few businesses can afford to store everything. It requires expensive climate-controlled warehouses with special fire protection and year-round security.

One approach to planning is to analyse which staff would most benefit from access to asset management. Some assets belong to projects; they will only be used by members of the project team. Other assets are used companywide. As an example, the team making a television entertainment series would work with a finite pool of assets. The finished programmes may be made available to a wider group to sell or syndicate the programmes. In contrast, television news is cooperative. It relies on all the journalists and producers having access to the archive.

The bounded asset management for a project-based workgroup is going to be much simpler than unbounded asset management with general access. Are the assets to be made available to external partners or consumers as well as staff? The asset management project can initially be restricted to those staff in workgroups. It can always be rolled out later to the rest of the organisation once the systems are proven.

One big cost saver is to use a simple search facility. Sophisticated search needs comprehensive metadata generation at the ingest stage, a cost in time and effort. In general, the smaller the asset repository, the simpler the search can be.

Many products only support one type of content. As an example, they may manage images, but have limited support for documents or audio–video content. The big advantage of these products is their low price. It may well be that several of these products, when used together, may serve the needs of the users, without the need for an overarching asset management system.

To give examples of asset management, I am going to take two scenarios.

Scenario 1: The lost file

Consider this scenario about a photograph. The marketing communications departments are producing a product brochure. They have a suitable product shot in their library. It is a 5 × 4 transparency. It was taken just before the corporate logo changed, but that can be fixed. A courier delivers the transparency to the design shop. They scan the transparency, and a Photoshop artist drops in the current corporate logo to replace the old one. The brochure is produced; everyone is satisfied.

Time passes, the owners of the design shop fall out, and they go their separate ways. Meanwhile, the web designer working on the company's web site wants a product image, and she sees just the right picture in the product brochure. She calls marketing communications, and they say they can send the original transparency right over. But the web designer just needs the image file from the brochure; she does not want to rescan the image. Unfortunately, the design shop did not keep the scan file, so the brochure is now orphaned from the original images. Therefore, the web designer must rescan the transparency. The file is dropped into the web page, and goes for review. The reviewer notices that the image has the old logo so the page is rejected. The web designer calls up the marketing communications department and asks what has happened. It transpires that the Photoshop touch-up was lost. It has to be done all over again.

How much time and effort was wasted? If the transparency had been scanned at high resolution before storage, it could have been checked out to the design shop by FTP, rather than using a courier. The Photoshop edit could be checked back into the corporate digital asset repository. Then the web designer could have browsed the digital asset management system for a suitable shot of the product, and, in a matter of minutes, call up a low-resolution version of the image with the correct logo.

Scenario 2: Exploiting the value of corporate audio-visual assets

This scenario looks at a multi-national corporation. This is a general trading business rather than a media company. Most such businesses will have a number of audio-visual assets:

- Television commercials
- Training films
- Corporate promotional films
- Product promotional films
- Corporate record (CEOs' addresses, AGMs, and earnings calls)
- Still images for press relations
- Still images used in marketing communications: corporate and product.

This example corporation has an existing multimedia library containing the following:

- 5000 film cans, some dating from pre-WW2
- 10,000 master videotapes in 1-in., U-matic, Betacam SP, and Digital Betacam formats
- 100,000 photographs: negative, transparency, and prints.

Part of the library is recorded on a card index, and some recent photographic material is recorded onto a simple relational database. Such a library presents a number of problems:

1. Tapes are decaying
2. The catalogue is poor; it relies upon the knowledge of a handful of librarians who are coming up for retirement; this is a bottleneck, which limits use of the library

3. Supplying copies to users is labour intensive
4. It is difficult to exploit assets in the library; most staff within the corporation have no idea what is in the library, or how to find out.

The corporation would like to utilise the library as assets. The investment that is required to maintain and preserve the content can be amortised by making it easier to access and distribute material, and by the introduction of more efficient operational practices.

The library is to be made available through the corporate intranet. In the past, some documentary material has been sold to external organisations. To continue with this business, and to possibly increase the sales, a subset of the archive will be made available for sale to partners, broadcasters, and educational institutions via the Internet. Some material is company confidential, so the digital asset management should support proper authentication and authorisation of users.

The project has two facets. One is the preservation of the material by digitisation; the other is the management of the assets in digital form. The digitisation operation is a one-time dubbing operation. The material may also need some clean up, noise reduction, and colour grading.

Once digitised, the content can be ingested into a digital asset management system and then catalogued. This is a process of gathering any information that exists as dope sheets in film cans and tape boxes, and also transferring the library record cards and legacy database to the asset management application. Once everything is in one place, the librarians are in a good position to edit and add to the metadata.

Fulfilment was traditionally a matter of withdrawing the original from the vault, copying it, then despatching to the user. If 10 users want the same film over a period of years, the whole operation is repeated 10 times. Like any multi-national, the offices in different countries will produce marketing collateral for their local marketplace. Much of the video production and photography will be commissioned locally. Without a distributed digital asset management system, it is not easy to share this valuable content with other offices around the world. The usual way is via a courier, but this assumes that you even know that an office the other side of the world has a photo that you could use. With no simple way to search for the content, it might as well not exist.

Digitisation

The digitisation operation is as much a rescue operation as anything else. Aging and decaying analogue formats can be copied onto current formats that should last another 20 or 30 years. Once the assets are digitised, they can be abstracted from the media, and cloned as files to fresh media when it is deemed appropriate.

Film and video

The current favourite for video storage is Sony's Digital Betacam. It is very widely used, a promise to be around for a number of years. It offers a good compromise between compression quality and storage cost and volume requirements. Although Digital Betacam represents a good master format, most distribution can be on DVD or CD-ROM. This means that during the digitisation stage, MPEG-2 (for the DVD) and MPEG-1 (for CD-ROM) can be encoded. The preview proxies can be any highly compressed format, but Windows Media is a favourite for the typical corporate user.

Images

A 10 × 8 still image with a resolution of 300 ppi has a file size of around 21 MByte. This is sufficient for most reproduction purposes, excluding a full-page or double-page spreads, and can be used as a digital master. A typical JPEG version for electronic distribution, with light compression, would be about 2 MByte.

Still images are often used for corporate presentations. A smaller image size can be used in PowerPoint, perhaps 6 × 4 in. at 72 ppi. The file size in an uncompressed bitmap format would be a few hundred kilobytes.

Fulfilment

Traditional fulfilment has been a very manual process. A tape is withdrawn from the library. It is transported to the duplication house. It is copied, then returned to the library and reshelved. The copy, tape or disk, is then packed and dispatched. Such an operation is slow and labour intensive. Once a video file sits on a server as MPEG-2, it is much easier to deliver it immediately by file transfer. A similar process can be used for JPEG image files. Low-resolution video can be delivered by streaming using MPEG-4 or one of the proprietary formats.

Advantages of digital asset management

Although some may view asset management as a fancy archive for old content, it is much more than that. Digital asset management is a productivity tool. It brings just-in-time processes to content retrieval; it frees knowledge workers to concentrate on content creation, editing, and re-purposing.

These are some of the functions that you would expect from asset management:

- Management of the archive catalogue
- Lifecycle management for the archive
- Support for re-purposing and re-use of the archive
- Support for copyright and trademark information, and the tracking of intellectual property use
- Workflow management for content creation
- Search and discovery of content
- Electronic fulfilment.

Implementing asset management

Asset management means different things to different users. Some are all-encompassing products aimed at enterprise content management, with a corresponding price tag. At the other extreme, there are products wrapped with an operating system. A desktop computer like the Apple Mac comes packaged with an image library called iPhoto. This has facilities to ingest, catalogue, and archive digital photo files. To many users, iPhoto may be their first view of asset management. It offers many useful features for the consumer or one-man photographic business to manage their library. There are several very affordable products that started out as image catalogues, but have now been developed further to handle audio and video content.

To support workgroups, and a number of different file formats, something more sophisticated is needed. The wide range of available products makes it all the more likely that a system can be found to meet every budget.

Before purchasing a large asset management system, it may seem like a good idea to set up a small-scale pilot project. The drawback with this approach is that the pace of change is so fast that the hardware and software will be obsolete by the time the pilot has been installed and evaluated. Therefore, the purchasing decision made at the time of the pilot may no longer be relevant. The worst case is that the primary vendor may have changed direction or even ceased trading. The alternative is to start with a small workgroup, and gradually roll out the system to the rest of the enterprise.

Summary

Many businesses move material into an archive immediately after first use. This historical archive is often solely a cost overhead. There are three elements: storage, media maintenance, and content movement.

The content is stored at some expense in a secure and climate-controlled environment. As media ages, there may be costs to dub assets to new media. As an example, nitrate film can be copied to safety stock, and old analogue videotape (like quad and 1 in.) can be dubbed to a digital format. Apart from these long-term maintenance costs, if content is retrieved, there may well be a charge to pull a film can or tape from the library, plus the courier costs.

Digital asset management can rationalise these storage costs by reducing the space needed to store assets, and lowering the handling costs, by both librarians and couriers. As well as these basic cost savings, there are efficiency savings. To balance against the savings is the outlay on the digital asset management installation and the ongoing licence and operational costs for the system.

These straight sums alone can often justify the deployment of asset management. As a bonus, there are potential revenue opportunities once the archive is opened up to the casual browser. The content can be syndicated, sold as it stands, or re-purposed for cross-media publishing.

A case for digital asset management revolves around the return on the original investment. There are two main business scenarios. One is the existing business looking for cost savings through increased efficiency. The other is for new e-businesses. Such a business may want to sell content online. In this latter case, the digital asset management is core to the offering. Making the case for investment for the former scenario is going to be a lot tougher.

In order to realise efficiency improvements, you may need to take a fresh look at workflows. The decision to invest in asset management becomes a very human issue.

Many creative personnel are resistant to new technologies, especially if they believe they are to be marshalled into the corporate business philosophy. The benefits of asset management to the knowledge worker are clear; it can automate repetitive tasks, freeing time for more creative work. It needs to be diplomatically explained and introduced.

The early asset management systems proved to be very expensive, and the majority of potential users could not make a robust business case for purchase. One of the problems was the large element of customisation required to interface with the media hardware and management information systems. This customisation required a heavy spend on professional services, pushing the total budget way up above the baseline hardware and out-of-the-box software costs.

Early adopters of enterprise-sized systems have typically covered the costs of a system after 2 years of operation. It is not a quick win, but certainly not a long-term investment. The main gains have been improved productivity and lower distribution costs. If the asset management is web enabled, then it allows a distributed workforce to cooperate on projects. It can eliminate the tape and CD duplication, and the courier costs that were formerly necessary to support a distributed working environment.

Few media businesses could justify a fully automated digital archive. The hybrid approach will be around for a while. Analogue assets will remain, filed on shelves in climate-controlled warehouses. This implies that the potential savings on storage costs may not be achieved. With digital asset management, it can prove possible to cut down access. This means that the archive can be moved some distance away, to a low-rent area.

Newly created assets will be indexed and catalogued as a matter of course. Depended on their value as assets, they may sit in an automated tape library, or they may be stored on removable media. The advantage of digital asset management is that the index is accessible by all interested parties. Users of the archive can find the assets without resort to the services of an archivist. They can be retrieved relatively easily if they are needed. The same could not be said for the analogue libraries. The difficulties of finding and accessing the content are a big barrier to the use of the asset; it was often simpler to recreate content from scratch. This means that archived content had become a wasted asset.

Asset management can have subtle benefits: turnaround time on projects is reduced; the workflow management can cut down the level of errors in content; staff become better informed through easier access to information; and management get better reporting on content utilisation.

Digital asset management has already proved its worth with document and web content management. The falling costs of computer hardware and new software design philosophies are opening out the advantages to multimedia asset libraries.

5 Asset formats

Introduction

Digital content has taken over in most areas of commerce and entertainment. We take it for granted that documents, still images and video can be transmitted instantly to the other side of the world. This was not the case even 20 years ago. Back then the electronic transfer of content was limited to a few specialised applications. Radio and television could deliver live audio and video. The wireline photo had been in use since 1935, and the fax machine existed but was not in common use until international standards were developed. Financial data was transmitted by telex. The telegram was used for brief text messages.

This digital revolution has by no means replaced the earlier physical content. How many offices could be described as paperless? Any enterprise deploying digital asset management system will have large archives of physical content. The picture library will have filing cabinets full of transparencies; the television station may have climate-controlled warehouses full of analogue tapes and movie film. Pharmaceutical companies have to maintain thousands of documents relating to the approval of drugs. Every company will have contracts, maybe even sealed and tied with ribbons.

Physical content is usually found on four storage media: paper, photographic film, optical disk, and magnetic tape. Film includes photographs, movies, and microfilmed documents. In principal, all four formats can be easily ingested into a digital environment. Paper and film can be scanned. Tape and disk can be played back and converted to a digital stream. The potential problem with tape is that the recording formats become obsolete. There are very few of the original Ampex 2-in videotape recorders left running. So eventually, it will not be possible to recover some tape-based content. Many old analogue archives are being 'digitised'. That is they are being dubbed to a digital tape format, like Digital Betacam. No doubt in another decade or so they will be dubbed again to some yet to be developed format. Standards bodies, including the Society of Motion Picture and Television Engineers (SMPTE), are working to establish representations of content that are independent of the storage format, so that this dubbing to fresh media becomes a background task for the digital archive.

Why should we want the content in digital form? There are many reasons, but for the asset management system, one advantage is that content in digital form can be stored or distributed by conventional data processing systems and networks.

Content

Many of the words used to describe video and audio material can have several meanings. Take the word 'media', this can be the radio, television, and newspaper industries, or it can be the CD-ROM used to store video data. Therefore, a qualifier is often a necessity, *news* media, or *storage* media. When Digital Audio–Visual Council (DAVIC) was developing their specifications, to get around these issues they adopted a structure and a terminology for audio and video material. These definitions were subsequently adopted by the SMPTE/EBU (European Broadcasting Union) taskforce that were looking at the many issues related to the exchange of programme material as bitstreams.

Since the DAVIC and SMPTE/EBU groups were specifically focused on television, they chose the programme as a starting point. A programme is taken to be a concatenation of one or more events under the control of a broadcaster. For example, a news broadcast will consist of a number of video clips with intermediate live inserts from a local anchor, or from a remote correspondent.

Digital assets cover far more than just programmes, but the principles are the same. A product, for example an interactive training session, may replace the programme. The common denominator is that a digital asset is a collection of related video, audio, and data content along with related information—the metadata.

An asset has to have value; content alone does not necessarily represent an asset. The owner of the content has to have the right to use the material before it can be called an asset. Content plus rights equals an asset.

Essence and metadata

Content is made up of two elements: essence and metadata. Essence is the essential data that is delivered to the viewer: the video, audio, and any data that is rendered as graphics (subtitles, captions, and Teletext). All other data is called metadata. This may describe or control the essence.

Document formats

In this chapter, I am going to take a document to mean a file containing written information, possibly with embedded graphics. In the chapter on document management, I laid out the formal definition as 'a written or printed record that provided proof of identification, an agreement or ownership'. Typically, it could be a contract drawn up by a lawyer, or an identity card issued by a government. The original Latin meaning of *proof* became lost with the introduction of the computer. The term 'document' was applied to any writing that conveyed information. It could be a text file or a spreadsheet, a slide presentation or a CAD drawing. To the lawyer, a document is a specific proof or evidence, whereas to the average business a document is synonymous with a computer file. The file extension for a Word file, *.DOC*, reinforces this association.

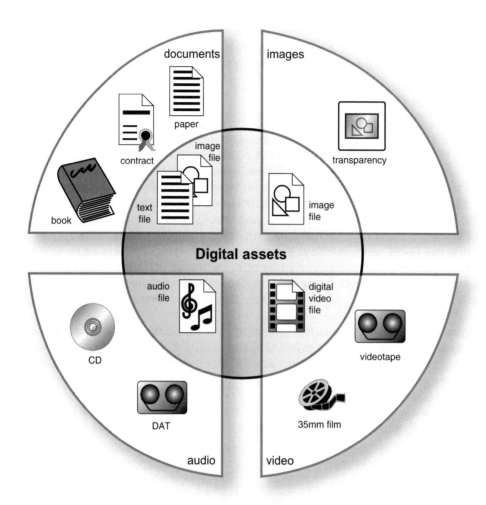

Figure 5.1 Asset formats.

A document file is a subset of a computer file (Figure 5.1). We would not think of a Photoshop file as a document, nor a database. A document is unstructured written information, although the CAD file blurs the distinction between the written and the drawn. Before the age of the computer, the document was any form of office paperwork, written, drawn, or typed.

In the context of digital asset management documents are files, so physical documents must be scanned into a digital format. The document can either be stored as an image, or via optical character recognition, stored as a text file.

Markup

Textual files fall into two main groups: the basic text file and files with markup. Text file are really only used for short notes. Most of the documents stored in a digital asset repository will be in some form of markup language. Anything in a document that is not content is

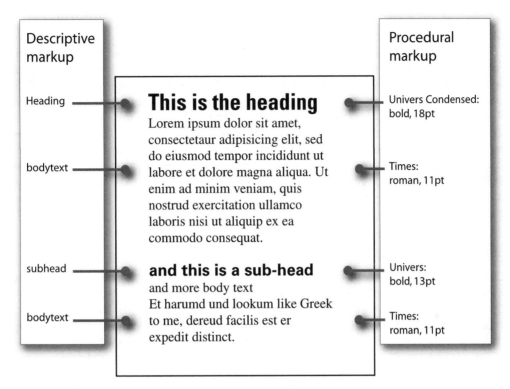

Figure 5.2 Procedural and descriptive markup.

called markup. It can be used to define the structure and the presentation of the document. This could be character formatting—boldface or small capitals—or paragraph formatting to define the document layout: bodytext, heading, subheading, or bulleted list.

This markup can be split into two groups: procedural and descriptive. The descriptive markup includes instructions about the layout of a document, so the author will indicate headings, footnotes, and sidebars—anything that is not body text. Procedural markup was once the domain of the designer, and defines the appearance of the document. It includes the typeface and font (Figure 5.2).

With the introduction of word processor, much of the typesetting markup information can be embedded within the document. The word processor allows the author to freely mix descriptive and procedural markup. A style template is often used to define the purpose of text, if it is a heading or a body text. Character and paragraph formatting are then used for procedural markup. However, each style will also have descriptive markup. The two are intertwined. This is not an issue as long as the file is never used outside the host application.

Office applications

There can be few knowledge workers who do not use a suite of office software applications. These generally cover word processing, spreadsheets, and slide presentation. This is a market dominated by Microsoft Office: Word, Excel, and PowerPoint, but there are several other solutions: Lotus SmartSuite from IBM, Corel WordPerfect Office, and Microsoft Works.

Office files generally use a compound file structure, where files can be embedded in other files. A typical example would be the use of graphics, charts, and spreadsheets within a Word file. Presentation files can even contain embedded audio-visual files. This compound file can be stored as a single entity, a process known as structured storage. This concept appears later in this chapter as a core technology in the Advanced Authoring Format (AAF). Although structured storage has many advantages for keeping all the elements together, it can make the compound files very large. As an example, a compound file will be in binary format, and will contain a number of streams comprising linked lists of file blocks. The streams could be text content data, structural data, and embedded graphics and images. The summary metadata is another stream. Each stream can be read separately, so the summary can be read without the need to open all the other streams.

Desktop processing

QuarkXPress dominates the desktop publishing (DTP) market, and has become a *de facto* standard. DTP applications take a different route to the storage of documents. Rather than embedding graphic elements, the file contains a link to the source file of the graphic. A low-resolution preview is used for layout. This means that the final document is a group of associated files. The graphics files are often very large, compared with those used in office applications. By storing them separately, the demands on the workstation processor and memory are much reduced, allowing the operator to work fast, and not be constrained by equipment limitations. The linked files have always caused problems when work is despatched as a 'job jacket' to another party, for example an imagesetter who is to create the printing plates. Files are often left out of the package. The solution is called the 'pre-flight check'; a process that checks whether all the links have the associated files present.

This same issue will arise with an asset management system. If a file containing links is to be archived, then all the linked files should also be archived if the document is ever to be re-used.

Page description languages

Page description languages are special documents that are formatted for the transmission of page layouts to a printer. At the printer, a raster image processor (RIP) converts the data into a raster or bitmap format that will be output as dots of toner or ink. PostScript is the most popular page description language.

'Standard' documents

All the document formats mentioned so far have been proprietary. If a document were to be stored in an archive, would it not be better to store in a standard format? Although it is hard to find a personal computer that cannot read a Word document, there are other issues. The pagination of a document will be printer dependent unless PostScript is being used for output. For anyone laying out documents for international distribution, there is the problem of two standard paper sizes. Virtually all countries with the exception of the US use A4 for general applications (the US uses $8\frac{1}{2} \times 11$ in). Although these sizes are very close, if a document is laid out for one size, then printed on the other, it will still upset the pagination. There can also be issues with missing fonts. The end user may not have a licence to use the typeface that the original author used. Usually a close font is substituted, but again this will upset the typesetting, and disrupt the pagination.

One method that has been around for some years is to use standardised generalised markup language (SGML) for document content. It has gained broad acceptance by publishers but is being eclipsed by its simpler subset, extensible markup language (XML). The use of XML with associated stylesheets offers a more standard way to publish a document.

Adobe PDF

One *de facto* standard that is very widely used is Adobe's portable document format (PDF). A PDF document is encoded in a manner that is device independent. It is encoded at a target resolution, ranging from web to print, but can be rendered by any reader, albeit, not at the optimum resolution. This means that in principle the same file can be displayed on a 72 ppi computer display, or sent to a high-resolution digital printing press or imagesetter. The PDF is based on the PostScript page description language, but has a more structured format.

Continuous-tone images are stored within the document using JPEG compression. At the time of document encoding, the level of compression must be specified. A high level of compression can produce a compact file for web distribution, but when printed at high resolution it will exhibit artefacts. Therefore, the level of compression that you use will depend upon the end use. Herein lies the usual archive dilemma. Should you archive at the highest resolution, so in the future the document can be viewed at high resolution, or should the demand for storage space be minimised?

A PDF file can also carry links to aid navigation and annotations. Fonts are usually embedded to ensure that the final output does not have to substitute fonts. Documents can be encrypted so that only authorised users can access the file. There are several PDF formats with the current version at 1.6 that allows embedded multimedia and supports JPEG2000 compression.

Documents and XML

The latest standard document format, which is based upon internationally agreed standard, is the use of XML along with a type definition (document type definition, DTD) or schema and a stylesheet. Most vendors of document processing applications are now integrating XML interfaces into their products. This is going to dramatically improve the ease with which document archives can be integrated into a seamless enterprise-wide workflow (Figure 5.3).

Document storage

There are many questions related to the archiving of documents. Do you store the original objects used to create a composite document, or do you store the 'flattened' final

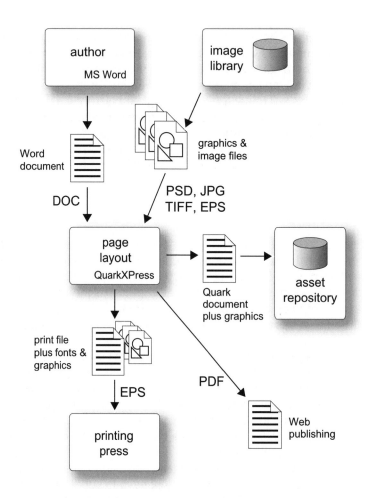

Figure 5.3 Document file formats in the workflow.

version of the document? A flattened document cannot easily be re-purposed for other applications. How much compression should be used for the images? These same questions come up later, with regard to images and video content.

Still images

The ubiquitous format for still picture interchange and storage is the JPEG. But around a hundred others exist, but many are proprietary to specific products. An enterprise-wide asset management system will have the need to store many different file formats. In the interests of simplicity and efficiency, it will pay dividends to restrict the system to a handful of formats. Any other formats can be converted at the ingest point. A few formats have become the most popular: JPEG, TIFF, EPS, and GIF. Restricting the asset repository to just these few formats is not going to place great limitations on the later

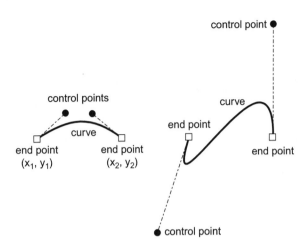

Figure 5.4 Bézier curves.

distribution or re-use of the content. Image files can be classified into two main groups: bitmap or vector.

Vectors and bitmaps

Image assets are created either as a bitmap or in vector format. Each has its advantages; it depends on the type of image to be created. Bitmaps, also called raster graphics, represent an image as a regular grid of pixels. Each pixel is given a colour value. Bitmaps are used for continuous-tone images like photographs. A bitmap has a fixed number of pixels, so a fixed resolution. If the image is rescaled, the value of each pixel has to be recalculated. If a bitmapped image is scaled up in size, the image quality will degrade.

Vector graphics use mathematical equations to describe an image as lines and curves. A compact way of representing a curve is to use a cubic equation. In 1962, Paul Bézier developed this mathematics for use in car body design. He was able to express curved shapes as numbers. The curve is described by the x/y coordinates of the end points of the curve segment, and by the coordinates of two control points (Figure 5.4). Since then, this has become a generally accepted method for expressing text and line art. Vector graphics can be rescaled with any detrimental effect on image quality.

Vectors are more suited to the representation of line artwork, clipart, or cartoons, whereas bitmaps are used for continuous-tone objects, like natural video and photographs. Vector-graphic images are resolution independent. To display vector graphics, they are rendered to a bitmap by the graphics adaptor. Similarly, an RIP in a printer will convert the image to a regular grid of dots.

Colour

Images can be reproduced in monochrome, either bi-level—as black and white—or as a grey scale able to reproduce a continuous-tonal range. Although this is satisfactory for the photocopier, newspapers, and novels, many image applications benefit from additional colour information.

There are two main systems or colour reproduction: RGB (Red, Green, and Blue) and CMYK (Cyan, Magenta, Yellow, and Black). The former is called additive colour, and is the underlying mechanism of human colour vision. The retina has two types of sensor; the rods, sensitive to light across the visible spectrum, and the cones, sensitive to light within three spectral bands—RGB. A similar system using RGB spectral bands is used for colour television. Other forms of reproduction, like printing, use subtractive reproduction, CMYK.

Computer colour displays and television use the additive system to reproduce colour. The light emitted by RGB pixels add to give the wanted colour. All three together are perceived by the eye as white light. Contrast this with subtractive systems, like colour printing. Here the ink or pigment subtracts or absorbs part of the visible spectrum to give the desired colour. The pigments are the secondary colours: cyan, yellow, and magenta. At maximum pigment density, the three subtract or absorb all incident light, so appears black. Although in principle only three colours (cyan, magenta, and yellow) could be used, due to dye deficiencies a satisfactory reproduction of black cannot be obtained. So a fourth, black, ink is used.

Colour space conversion

Often you may need to store an image in both formats: an RGB version as the original and for use in web pages, and a CMYK version for print (Table 5.1).

The hue, saturation, and brightness (HSB) model is used by artists and designers to describe a colour as a hue, then a tint (the brightness) and the saturation of the colour.

The L*a*b model was developed by the Commission Internationale d'Eclairage (CIE) to describe colours as a luminance component and two colour-related components.

Resolution

Picture sizes can vary by vast amounts. A small image to place on a web page may be 100 × 100 pixels. As a GIF, the file size would be less than 10 kByte. Contrast this with an image that is to be used as a double-page spread in an A4-size magazine. A typical

Table 5.1 Representations of colour spaces

Designation	Name	Notes
RGB	Red, green, and blue	The main colour bands of normal colour vision
CMYK	Cyan, magenta, yellow, and black	For colour printing
HSB	Hue, saturation, and brightness	Related to the way artists describe colours
L*a*b	Luminance, a (green to red), and b (blue to yellow)	The CIE model

resolution would be 300 pixels/in. Assuming the image has to bleed off the spread, the image size has to be about 5100 × 3700 pixels. This amounts to a file size of 56 MB as RGB, and 75 MB as CMYK. That is nearly 7000 times larger than the web thumbnail image. When saving an image, you should give due consideration to the end use. In this way, you can minimise the storage requirements.

Tagged Image File Format (TIFF)

One of the most popular image data formats is TIFF. It is designed for the encoding of raster images, often called bitmaps. It uses byte-oriented binary encoding. The format is very flexible, and it is device independent, so can be used with any operating system or file system. TIFF can be used to encode bi-level images (black and white), and limited palette or indexed colour. Continuous-tone images can be stored as grey scale or in full colour in RGB, CMYK, YCbCr (BT 601 video sampling), or the CIE L*a*b colour spaces. A TIFF image can also include alpha channels and paths, but is usually stored without these. TIFF images can be encoded uncompressed, run-length encoded, or compressed using the JPEG standard. Note that a JPEG compressed image can be formatted as a TIFF file (*.TIF extension) or a JPEG file interchange format (JFIF) file (*.JPG extension). The TIFF would be a favoured format for the archiving of images.

Photoshop format (PSD)

Adobe Photoshop has a native file format that has become the *de facto* standard for image files. It is similar to TIFF, but includes many additional features. A Photoshop file comprises a number of image layers, plus layers that store parameter adjustments for underlying layers. Each layer can also have alpha channels or masks. The file may include vector-based paths that can be used for defining the clipping of an image when wrapping text in a page layout application. All this information takes up additional storage space, so the image can be 'flattened' into a composite image for storage with a smaller file size. The advantage of storing in layered Photoshop format (PSD) is that it can be re-purposed or manipulated more easily if the original layer structure is preserved (Figure 5.5).

One common use for layers is to store different versions of text overlays, perhaps in different languages. All but one of the alternatives is turned off for normal use of the image. If the image is previewed, the other layers are not visible. Some asset management products are able to open the file, then read and store thumbnails of each layer. This can be very useful for quickly viewing the different versions of an image all stored within the file, without the need to open the original file in Photoshop (Figure 5.6).

Acquisition formats for digital still cameras

Digital cameras usually use sensors with around 12 bits per colour. To minimise the file sizes for storage on the media cards, the image is rounded to 8 bits per colour then compressed to a JPEG format. For high-quality reproduction the original data can be stored in a RAW format with the original bit depth, although the image file size will be much larger.

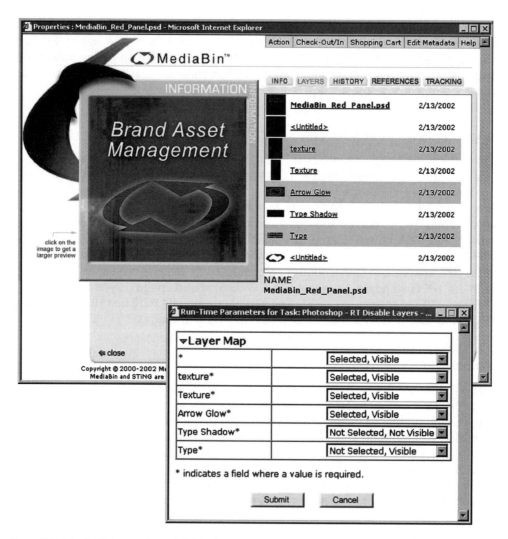

Figure 5.5 MediaBin layered asset. © MediaBin Inc.

As an example, the Nikon D1X digital camera uses a 3008 × 1960 pixel sensor with 12-bit depth per colour channel. The RAW file, with lossless compression is around 8 MByte per image. An uncompressed RGB, 8 bits, TIFF is 20 MByte. There are several JPEG compression settings, but at the normal with 8:1 compression, the file size reduces to around 1.6 MByte. With the standard 96 MByte flash memory card, this means by that storing TIFF images with, only five exposures can be stored. By using modest JPEG compression, nearly 60 images can be stored. Compare the 36 exposures of a film cassette.

The RAW files are proprietary to the camera manufacturer, but generally embed the data in a TIFF file structure. To use the files, the camera manufacturers supply a software application that can be used on a desktop computer back at base. The curves and

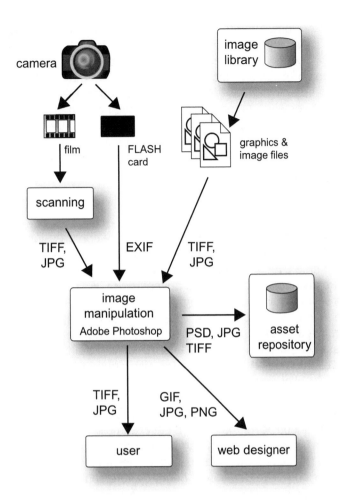

Figure 5.6 File formats in image workflow.

levels of the RAW image can be adjusted, and then the image stored in a conventional format like 8-bit TIFF.

Many cameras use the exchangeable image file format (EXIF). This wraps TIFF or JPEG data in a standard file format that can be read by photo printers.

Film scanners perform similar dynamic range compression from the sensor signal, with around 12 bits per colour, to give the final image file format with 8 bits per colour. For the general digitisation of an archive, this loss of bit depth will not matter. If images are to be processed at a later date, then the original bit depth may be needed. As an example if the input/output transfer characteristic is adjusted to alter the contrast or to modify high- and low-light densities, then the resultant image will exhibit posterisation from missing colour levels. Most users of Photoshop will be familiar with the comb-like appearance of the levels adjustment. The end results that a continuous-tone image will not be using all possible 256 values. If the starting point is 12 bits, then more processing can be undertaken while retaining all 256 levels in the output channel when the sample value is truncated to 8 bits. The storage requirements will be bigger, but if an image is destined for high-quality reproduction, then discarded information could result in visible artefacts.

This is a common problem with archives. How much information should be discarded in the interest of affordable storage? Will the compressed image be of a suitable quality for later use, or is it not worth storing unless in its original format? Our expectations of image quality increase with the passage of time. Just compare the reproduction quality of a colour magazine of the 1960s with one of today. Similarly, 1960 television compared with high definition television today. Therefore, what may seem like a reasonable decision today may look penny pinching in 20 years time.

Compression

The usual way to reduce the file size of the image is by compression. The newspaper business demanded a way to transmit pictures around the world that would not need a long transmission time over low-bandwidth circuits. The JPEG format has become the ubiquitous picture distribution format. One advantage of JPEG is that the level of compression can be set at the time of encoding. The artefacts of compression can be traded against file size. For a news picture printed at a low quality, high compression can be used. For general storage of images, you can use a less aggressive compression.

JPEG is a lossy compression algorithm. Information is discarded from the picture. The algorithm removes information that is perceptually redundant by exploiting the mechanisms of human visual processing. For archive storage, it makes more sense to preserve all the original information. Instead of discarding picture information, and generating the attendant artefacts, you can use a lossless compression algorithm. These are usually based on run-length encoding, or the ZIP and LZW (Lemple–Zif–Welch) algorithms. Many pictures have areas of flat colour. This can be encoded as the colour of a single pixel, then a count for the number of repeated pixels with the same colour value. Obviously, the degree of compression will be dependent on the picture content.

Another way to reduce the storage demands of an image is to flatten it. Many pictures are composed in layers, possibly 100 or so. The final image in print is a flattened version of these layers, so if the image is not going to be manipulated in the future, you can discard the layers and store the flattened version.

JPEG

The JPEG developed this extremely popular format for lossy compression of raster images. It has also proved to be the forerunner for the techniques of MPEG video compression. JPEG compression is used for continuous-tone images, like photographs, both grey scale and colour.

JPEG compresses the file size by selectively discarding picture data. This is called lossy compression. The final picture is a representation of the original, but the original can never be restored from the JPEG file. The standard also supports a lossless compression with about a 3:1 reduction in data; but it is more usually used in the lossy mode with ratios of 20:1 or greater. JPEG compression is based on a technique called the discrete cosine transform (DCT).

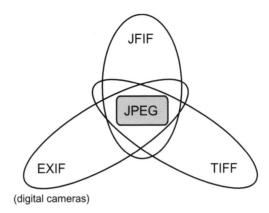

Figure 5.7 JPEG file formats.

A lower compression ratio results in less data being discarded, but the JPEG compression algorithm will degrade any fine detail in an image. As the compression is increased, more artefacts become apparent. Wave-like patterns and blocky areas become visible, and there is ringing on sharp edges. The levels of artefacts that are considered acceptable depend upon the application. A picture reproduced in a magazine should have no visible artefacts, whereas minor distortions are to be expected with a thumbnail on a web page. It is more important to have a small file size with a short download time.

Progressive JPEG

When a web browser is used with a low-bandwidth connection, a large JPEG image embedded in a web page can take some time to download. JPEG image can be encoded in with progressive rather than sequential encoding. The picture is scanned more than once, first a coarse scan, then a more detailed scan. The viewer sees a hazy view of the picture initially, and then the detail builds up to give the final crisp picture.

JPEG files

JPEG is an image compression algorithm. For distribution, the image data has to be wrapped as a file. The usual format is the JPEG File Interchange Format (JFIF). This has the extension .jpg, and is usually just called JPEG (Figure 5.7). JPEG data is found embedded in many other file formats, for example the TIFF and EXIF (used by digital still cameras).

Web graphics

A basic web browser will render hypertext markup language (HTML) files into a screen image. Text is sent as a straight ACSII-like format, the font properties are sent separately as tags and rendered by the browser to give the appropriate display. Text formatting codes give positional information for the text, and enables the author to use other devices like tables and forms.

Table 5.2 Web graphic formats

	Line art	Photos	Colours	Transparency	Compression	Animation
GIF	Y		8 bit	Y	Lossless	Y
PNG	Y		24 bit	Y	Lossless	N
JPEG JFIF		Y	24 bit	N	Lossy	N

To add graphics, the source files for bitmapped images are potentially very large, which leads to long download times—unpopular with users. There are two ways around this. Line art can be sent as the very compact GIF and continuous-tone images can be compressed using the JPEG standard. With a browser plug-in, a few other formats have also gained wide acceptance. For bitmaps, there is the portable network graphics (PNG), and two vector-graphic formats: Macromedia Flash and scalable vector graphics (SVG) (Table 5.2).

Graphic Interchange Format (GIF)

CompuServe released the original GIF format in 1987 as a means of encoding raster graphic images into a compact file. It is normally used for the placement of line art on web pages. It is not suitable for continuous-tone images. In 1989, the format was extended to include support for transparency and interlace (GIF89a). GIFs allowed web designer to liven up the rather dull text-only pages with graphic elements. The GIF format supports indexed colour images with a maximum of 256 different colours. It uses the LZW algorithm for lossless compression.

Portable Network Graphics (PNG)

GIF is a copyright of CompuServe (AOL) and distributed under a royalty free licence for general use across the web. PNG was developed as an alternative open format, but with additional features. It had limited support from the earlier browsers, so had a slow acceptance by web designers. It uses lossless compression, and can encode grey scale or colour images, up to 24 bits per pixel. It carries an alpha channel to define the transparency.

Animated graphics

There are many file formats for storing and delivering animated graphics, both 2-D and 3-D. It is a subject in itself, although such files may well be stored in an asset management system, I am not going into further detail beyond mentioning the leading animation format used on web pages, Macromedia's Flash.

Flash

Flash is an animated vector-graphic format that offers the advantages of dynamic images, without requiring the large file sizes of true video. It requires a plug-in to a web browser in order to view the files. It can be used for user interaction, and short- to medium-length animation clips. Long-form animation is usually composed with the sister product, Shockwave. Somewhat confusingly, Flash content is delivered in Shockwave file format (extension .SWF). Shockwave content is specifically authored with Macromedia Director, whereas Flash files can be created by many applications, with Macromedia's Flash MX being the most popular.

Video formats

Although we live in digital world, there is still much legacy analogue equipment in use in video production. We must not forget that the majority of television viewers still watch an analogue transmission, and the changeover to digital reception may not happen until 2010, varying from country to country. The pioneers in digital transmission have been the satellite operators, where the driving force for the deployment of digital transmission (using the MPEG-2 standard) has allowed the emission of four to six times the number of channels within a given transponder bandwidth. Therefore, any overview has to start in the analogue domain.

Essentially television is the reproduction of a moving 2-D image by the transmission of a regular sequence of colour values or samples (in a digital system). Television started as a monochrome system, with colour added later. The colour information was interleaved into the luminance channel without requiring any additional bandwidth. How this was achieved is a pre-cursor to modern compression techniques.

Analogue television uses several techniques to lower the bandwidth requirements without causing unacceptable visual artefacts. Some of these artefacts may today be considered as obvious distortions, but it must be remembered that the engineering compromises were made half a century ago, and were implemented with a handful of vacuum tubes. The methods used include scan interlace, colour space conversion, and chrominance band limiting. This is called composite video.

Digital component coding

Most video is now recorded in a component colour format. A number of proprietary digital formats evolved for special effects and computer graphics equipment. These early developers established some of the ground rules that could support realistic pictures:

- Three-colour channels or luminance and two-colour channels
- 8 bits per channel
- Around 700 pixels per television line.

601

The standard, ITU-R BT601 to give its full designation, has proved to be a solid foundation for much of the later developments in digital video technology. The 601 standard was intended to be used for programme production, so offered a high picture quality, with sufficient resolution to be used for special effects. One specific example is chroma keying or matting. This is where the talent is shot in front of a blue or green screen. Later in post-production, the coloured screen is replaced with another picture. Much loved by weathermen, it also has many applications for the corporate and training productions.

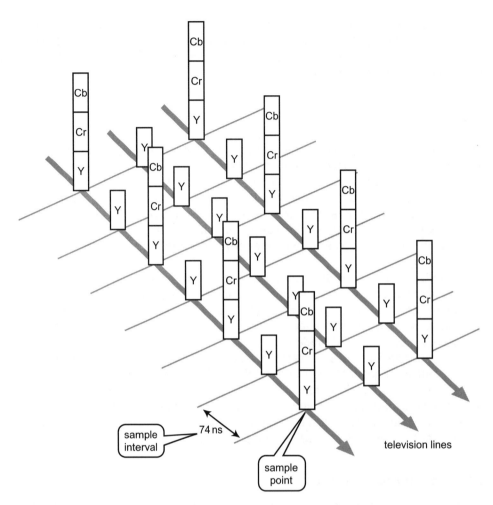

Figure 5.8 4:2:0 sampling.

Sampling

Much as the original NTSC analogue standard uses band limiting for the I and Q colour components, the 601 standard also exploits the feature that colour is perceived at a lower acuity by the human eye. The colour information is sampled at a lower spatial resolution than the luminance. There are several schemes, but the 601 standard uses half the sampling frequency. Early composite digital systems used four times the colour subcarrier frequency as the sampling rate. In digital component coding, the sampling rate used for the luminance signal is twice that of the chrominance channels and is 27 MHz. The nomenclature for the YUV sample as '4:2:2' reflect these ratios. The vertical resolution for luminance and chrominance is the same, whereas the horizontal resolution for colour is half that of the luminance. If chrominance is sampled every other line, then the chroma resolution is one-half the luminance both horizontally and vertically.

This is called 4:2:0 sampling (Figure 5.8), and was adopted for one of the MPEG-2 formats, the main profile @ main level (MP@ML) used for DVD encoding and standard

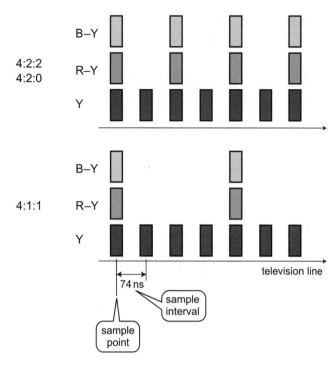

Figure 5.9 Different sampling schemes.

definition (SD) digital television. The alternative is to sample colour at one-quarter the luminance rate, 4:1:1. This has been adopted for the 525-line DV format. The colour resolution is still as good as analogue composite, but is not suitable for high-quality chroma key matting operations (Figure 5.9).

Coding range

Computer video uses the full gamut of codes to specify colours. So black has a value of zero, white is 255 (8-bit coding). Video uses a restricted range, giving headroom above white level and below black. If the original source is analogue, this headroom avoids clipping of the video signal (in the case of dc offsets or analogue-to-digital converter misalignment). So the actual range is from 16 to 235, a range of 220 values, as oppose to the 256 values of computer graphics. You can convert from one range to the other, but this will introduce rounding errors at each conversion. The total number of conversions should be controlled during the workflow to avoid the aggregation of errors.

The 8 and 10 bits

The 601 standard originally specified 8-bit sample values. This proved insufficient for extensive video processing. For example, keying processes could cause visible banded on graduated tones. To ease this problem the standard was extended to support 10-bit samples, although some equipment only supports 8-bit processing. The two least significant bits (of the 10) are truncated or rounded.

Table 5.3 Digital picture resolutions

	Active picture area (pixels)		Total including sync interval (pixels)		Frame rate (Hz)
	Width	*Height*	*Width*	*Height*	
525/60	720	486	864	525	29.96
625/50	720	576	864	625	25

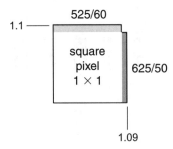

Figure 5.10 Pixel aspect ratios.

Gamma

If you are used to computer video, you may well be familiar with the display of gamma, 2.2 for Windows and 1.8 for Macintosh. Television coding assumes a fixed gamma.

Scanning resolutions

There are two scanning formats for SD television, one the 525/60 system used in North America (used for NTSC), and 625/50 system used in Europe and Asia PAL and SECAM (Table 5.3).

Square and rectangular pixels

Computer paint programs that use bitmap encoding (rather than vector graphics) all use square pixels. That means a circle of 10 pixels high is also 10 pixels wide. Not all digital television standards use square pixels. The horizontal resolution is chosen to have a sensible mathematical relationship to sampling frequencies, line rate and frame rate in the original analogue standards. Simple geometry was not an overriding concern for analogue systems on which the digital sampling is based. The television pixels for systems derived from analogue standards depart from a square by about 10 per cent, 525-line pixels are higher than wide by 11/10, 625-line pixels are wider than high by 59/54 (Figure 5.10).

Videotape formats

The newcomer to video recording might well ask 'why are there so many formats, and which should I use?' Over time, videotape formats seemed to grow with a geometric progression. This development has finally slowed as the magnetic or optical disks, and RAM cards, are all offering alternative means of storage.

Videotape transport designs were originally developed as all-encompassing formats, but are now optimised for specific applications. Formats may be developed for the highest quality—for studio recording and high definition work, or for the low-cost, lightweight demands of newsgathering and consumer camcorders. There have been about 100 formats developed over the last 50 years, but less than 20 have been successful in the marketplace. The SMPTE has standardised many of the tape formats, using letters for analogue formats (type 'C') and numbers for the digital formats (D-1, D-2, D-3, etc.).

Many formats have evolved to give backwards compatibility with legacy formats (Figure 5.11). This allows broadcasters to use the same deck to play back new digital recordings and archive analogue recordings on the same deck, thus saving cost and space (that several decks would occupy).

The enabling development for videotape recording was the flying head. This gave a fast enough writing speed to record the high frequencies of the video waveform, while retaining a low linear tape speed. This flying head was first seen in the transverse-scan quadruplex format by Ampex. That was soon followed by the helical scan system that VTRs still use today. A similar design has also been adopted by some data recording formats like Exabyte and the Sony products.

Analogue formats

There have been many analogue formats, but few achieved any great popularity. The most notable are the 2-in quadraplex and 1-in C-format for reel-to-reel decks. In the cassette formats, the Sony Betacam family for professional use, and VHS for consumer use have dominated the market.

Digital formats

Digital recording has so many advantages that it has largely replaced analogue recording. Digital formats split into composite and component.

Digital composite

Digital composite was a bridge between analogue composite—PAL and NTSC—and the new digital world. The D-2 digital composite format was developed as a replacement for analogue recording formats. It could also replace the ageing robotic cart machines that for 20 years had played out television commercials 24 h a day. Being a cassette format, it was easily handled by machinery rather than a human tape jockey. The digital format meant that tapes could be cloned as repeated plays caused tape wear. D-2 was also used as a general-purpose replacement for the C-format open reel machine. Although a digital format, the recorder was usually used with analogue plant with PAL or NTSC analogue inputs and outputs.

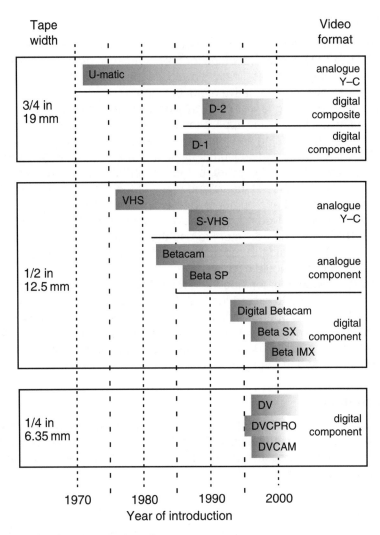

Figure 5.11 Evolution of videotape formats.

D-3 was a Panasonic product, using ½-in tape. It was used in a similar way to D-2, with analogue composite interconnections. Digital composite had been largely replaced by component VTRs, giving the user the many advantages of component processing.

Digital component

The first digital component VTR was D-1 and was launched in 1987. It was much loved for film transfer and high-end commercial production. It did not use compression, and was designed around the then recently developed BT601 sampling format (formerly CCIR 601). It uses 19 mm tape with 8-bit words per colour channel. Panasonic later developed the D-5 format, using ½-in tape, similar to the D-3 machines. It offered

10-bit recording of 270 Mbit/s video, or 8-bit for the little-used 16:9 aspect-ratio 360 Mbit/s format.

Most component formats now use ½- or ¼-in tape. The basic choice is between the Betacam derivates (½ in) or the DV format (¼ in) although there are several other formats. Sony manufactures three 1/2-in formats, Digital Betacam, Betacam SX, and IMX.

The DV family is a group of different professional and consumer camcorder formats, all based on the DV ¼-in format cassette. The format specifies two tape cassette sizes, the standard for VTRs and the miniDV for camcorders. The compact size lends it to the implementation of very small camcorders, the so-called palmcorders. The DV format samples video at 4:1:1 (525/60) or 4:2:0 (625/50), then uses DCT intraframe coding with a 5:1 reduction in data, this gives a final data rate of 25 Mbit/s for SD pictures. It is often referred to as DV25 compression. It has two digital stereo audio channels. The normal tape stock is metal evaporated.

When broadcasters expressed interest in these compact and lightweight DV camcorders, Panasonic and Sony developed two new formats based on the DV tape, but achieving a better performance (the DVCPRO and the DVCAM, respectively). Panasonic also offers an enhanced professional formats also offering 50 Mbit/s recording (DVCPRO-50). This uses 4:2:2 sampling and milder compression (3:3:1).

Most video cassette recorder (VCR) manufacturers have adopted the IEEE 1394 interface as the general video interchange port on their products. This is to download the DV files to the video editing system in their native compressed format, as an alternative to regular video interconnections.

Video compression

The compression used in Digital Betacam is a closed system, optimised for recording on tape. The DV compression format is more general purpose. Data can be interchanged between units in the native format; this avoids unnecessary decompression and recompression stages that would degrade the signal. The SX and IMX formats have adopted MPEG-2 compression.

The compressed formats can often be copied between devices at higher than real time, typically four times. This can be very useful for cutting down the ingest time from tape to disk storage systems.

DV and MPEG I-frame

MPEG-2 at MP@ML is ideal for programme distribution, satellite DTH and DVB transmissions. But the long group of pictures does not easily lend the format to editing. The ideal for editing is to be able to cut to the frame. DV does not use interframe coding, so meets the requirements for editing. The alternative for MPEG-2 is to adopt a profile that does not use interframe coding, or 'I-frame only'. It does not use the B- or P-frames (bi-directional and predictive). The drawback of avoiding interframe coding is that, for a given video quality, the data rate is much higher than regular MPEG-2 (MP@ML). ENG users have adopted 24 or 25 Mbit/s, and for studio use 50 Mbit/s has been adopted. Compare this with the maximum rate used by MP@ML of 15 Mbit/s. DV and

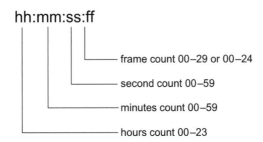

Figure 5.12 Time code format.

MPEG-2, I-frame only, deliver a similar level of video quality for a given bit rate, yet still give the freedom to edit at random frames.

High definition

Everything in this chapter so far relates to SD television. Although SD is great for small- and mid-sized displays, once the screen diagonal gets above 750 mm, the scan lines become very visible for the close viewer. Projection receivers and home theatre systems demand higher resolution to equal to that seen when watching 35 mm film.

The Advanced Television Systems Committee (ATSC) set about defining a new standard for the transmission of high definition television. The result could support a family of possible scanning formats, leaving the broadcaster to make the choice. Both progressive and interlaced scanning is supported.

At the same time, studios were using digital processing for special effects sequences in movies. Often using 4000 × 4000 pixels per frame, such sequences can be seamlessly composited with the film stock. There had long been a demand to shoot productions on videotape rather than using film—electronic cinematography. Rather than shoot at 30 frames per second the same rate as film is used, 24 frames per second.

Time code

Computers usually count time in 'x' millisecond increments for a certain date. Television uses a system more suited to reading by humans. Since program tapes rarely exceed 3 h in length, the time code only needs to count up to a maximum duration of 1 day or 24 h. The resolution needs to be to one frame. The SMPTE/EBU have a standard used throughout the television industry, that counts each frame in frames, seconds, minutes, and hours (Figure 5.12).

Time code can be used as a relative reference to an arbitrary start point, or an absolute reference to the time of day. General recordings to tape often start at 10:00:00:00 h, whereas server files may start at 00:00:00:00. Camcorders can use time of day perhaps from a global positioning system (GPS) receiver to record the actual time of shooting.

Interfacing time code

There are two ways of recording time code. It can be embedded in the video as vertical interval time code (VITC) or recorded as a longitudinal time code (LTC) on an audio track.

Each has advantages and disadvantages. VITC can be read if the tape is stationary. LTC can be read during fast shuttle, but it does use up an audio track that may be required for surround sound or for multiple language tracks. The VTR will use both, if available, and output the best information. Professional VTRs make this signal available at the transport remote control port.

Drop-frame time code

The NTSC standard further complicates the problem, with relation to program durations. The line and frame frequencies are derived from colour subcarrier, rather than the arbitrary line and field rate values chosen for PAL. The new line scanning frequency was defined as 2/455 times the subcarrier (3.579545 MHz) or 15,734.26 Hz, while the frame rate was defined as 1/525 times the line frequency or 29.97 Hz.

With this frame rate of 29.97 Hz (rather than exactly 30 Hz), 30 frames last 1.001 seconds rather than precisely 1 seconds. This means the time code registering the frame count is not the same as the studio clock (probably locked to GPS). If the duration of a clip is calculated from the time codes, over 30 minutes or so this error will accumulate. This can be ignored for short clips like commercial spots, but for a 2-hour movie, the error amounts to a 7 second overrun. This may not sound much, but with the tight scheduling of television commercials 7 seconds of potential revenue. To get around this, the SMPTE standard specifies an algorithm for dropping certain time code values. This drops the first two frames (00 and 01) of every minute, except every 10th minute. This amounts to dropping 108 frames per hour. This is 3.6 seconds, which effectively corrects the error.

You will notice that most editing equipment has configuration settings for time code, to select drop frame or non-drop frame. Note that this setting is not required for PAL (625/50), as the frame rate is exactly 25 Hz.

Film edge numbers

Film does not carry time code, but it does carry an alternative that can be used to reference individual frames. At the time of manufacture, a regular incrementing number and a bar code is burnt on to the edge of the film as a latent image, so that when the film is developed it will be visible. The numbering identifies every 16 frames for 4-perf 35 mm film. Intermediate frames are counted from the edge code location. This latent edge code is usually called key code. It carries other valuable metadata: film stock, year of manufacturer, and roll number. When the film is transferred to video the telecine produces a key code log of this metadata.

Audio formats

Many asset repositories may have audio stored as a video soundtrack, but it can also be a stand-alone asset. It may be music or it could be archive recordings of speeches. Even in a digital world, there is a vast legacy of analogue recordings. Just as video recording has spawned many different formats, audio content is also found in many forms. Analogue audio has always been much simpler than video, using either the vinyl disk or reel-to-reel magnetic tapes.

Table 5.4 AES data rates

Sample rate (kHz)	Data rate (MHz)	Upper frequency limit (kHz)	
32	3.072	15	Broadcast
44.1	2.822	20	Consumer (CD)
48	2.048	20	Professional

Digital audio is usually based on the digital audio standards specified by the Audio Engineering Society (AES). The analogue waveform is represented by 16-bit samples at a rate of 48 kHz (or 44.1 for CDs), with two channels to give stereo reproduction. This signal can be stored as a file recorded onto an optical medium (CD) or on tape, perhaps the most used being the digital audio tape (DAT) format. Audio is also stored in compressed formats like the minidisk.

AES-3

This is the international standard digital audio interface. To give it the full title: 'Serial transmission format for two-channel linearly represented digital audio data'. That means it is stereo and uncompressed. It was a joint development by the AES and the EBU. The standard is based on balanced, shielded twisted pair cable, and for transmission distances up to 100 m. The usual connector is the three-pin XLR.

The AES standard supports three sample rates: 32, 44.1, and 48 kHz (Table 5.4). The usual rate that you will encounter is 48 kHz, the standard rate for professional equipment. Unfortunately, if you want to ingest material from CDs, a different sample rate is used (44.1 kHz). To mix the two, the sample rate of the signal from the CD has to be converted to 48 kHz. This can be performed in software or in real time by hardware.

The 48 kHz rate is well above the Nyquist criteria for sampling audio with a frequency-response extending to 20 kHz, but allows for variable speed operation without losing the upper register. Most professional audio equipment uses this standard for interconnections. Note that the AES format represents a continuous real-time stream, and is not a file format.

Mono, stereo, and multi-channel

Audio can be transmitted and stored as a single channel for monophonic reproduction, or in a multi-channel format where spatial information adds to the listening experience (5.1 being a popular format). Stereo is very popular, most PC audio systems use two loudspeakers for reproduction. Although the original assets may be multi-channel audio, for the search proxies mono will most likely be adequate. It minimises disk space and saves valuable streaming bandwidth for dial-up users.

Audio compression

Lossless audio codecs offer limited opportunity to radically lower the data rates. To achieve the rates demanded by streaming applications, developers have moved to lossy codecs.

A lossy codec throws away data that can never be recovered. There are two ways this can be achieved. The first takes advantage of statistical redundancy in the data; the second exploits our knowledge of psychoacoustics to remove information that is perceived as irrelevant to the hearing process. Of course, there are levels of judgment involved in this. What is considered irrelevant to a narrow band speech circuit is not going to be redundant for high-quality music reproduction.

Perceptual compression

This uses knowledge derived from the study psychoacoustics of human hearing. Redundant information that can be called perceptually irrelevant is removed from the sample data.

Compression schemes split between those developed specifically for speech using very low bit rates (sometimes referred to as vocoders or voice coder), and the more general purpose or waveform codecs that can be used for any material—especially music. The success of a speech codec is measured by how natural and intelligible it sounds.

General audio codecs

Compressing general audio is far more complex than speech. A speech codec is processing a single voice, and can use the human voice-tract model to represent that voice. A general audio codec has to reproduce a wide gamut of sounds. Consider musical instruments; these range from the almost sinusoidal toes of the flute, through to the complex spectrum produced by percussive instruments. This could be a harpsichord, castanets, or bells. Then there are the many non-musical sounds: explosions, audience applause, and the wind. Some have harmonic relationships; others are completely atonal. A general codecs should perform reasonably with any such source.

The input to a codecs is a time-varying voltage, represented by a regular series of discrete samples. Perceptual codecs generally sample a finite-length frame of samples, and then perform a time-frequency analysis of that frame. Frames are typically a few milliseconds long. A coarse time frame is optimum for long pure notes; a fine resolution is more efficient for percussive transients.

Sub-band coding

The designer of the waveform codec does not have the luxury of the model for speech generation used in the vocoder. Instead, he looks to the perceptual irrelevancies identified in by the study of psychoacoustics. The core for general audio coding is the masking effect—a consequence of the critical bands of human hearing.

Sub-band coding is the basis of most general audio codecs. The audio spectrum is split into a number of sub-bands that approximate to the critical bands. Within each sub-band, information that is masked by louder components can be discarded. Although this is a lossy compression, if suitable algorithms are used, the final listener will be unaware of the missing information.

The filter banks have to meet a number of criteria, not the least being a fast processing algorithm. Desirable characteristics are perfect reconstruction (in the decoder), good stop-band attenuation, and constant group delay.

The filter banks convert the frequency spectrum of input waveform into time-indexed coefficients representing the frequency-localised power within each of the sub-bands.

The pseudo-quadrature mirror filter (PQMF) was adopted for the MPEG-1 algorithms. Later code designs have used the modified discrete cosine transform (MDCT) to decompose the frequency components into the sub-bands.

Audio codecs

Although an audio archive is most likely to be stored in an uncompressed form or a Dolby multi-channel format, the proxies used while searching for content may need to be heavily compressed. AES audio can be used in closed environments that have wide-band networks, like television news production, but for general corporate asset management applications, compression is the norm.

The codecs used for compression fall into three groups: those defined by internationally agreed standards, proprietary systems, and open-source. Each has their proponents and supporters. If you are trying to decide which route to take, many factors have to be considered beyond the obvious one of audio quality. Different codecs will have different licensing costs; there is interoperability to think about, and then the level of support offered by the vendor. Most asset management products have adopted one or more of the three proprietary architectures: Apple QuickTime, Microsoft Windows Media, and RealAudio. It may be that MPEG-4 appears in future products.

Codec standards, MPEG

MPEG (from the Moving Picture Experts Group) is the international standard for multimedia. It incorporates both audio and video encoding at a range of data rates. MPEG audio and video are the standard formats used for digital television (along with Dolby audio) (Table 5.5).

MPEG-1

The work undertaken to develop the MPEG-1 audio compression standards forms the foundation stone for the technology of streaming audio. The ubiquitous MP3 standard set the benchmark for good-quality music encoding at low bit rates.

Table 5.5 Summary of MPEG audio

	Bit rate range (Kbit/s)	Target bit rate (Kbit/s)	Typical compression ratio
Layer-1	32–448	192 (mono)	1:4
Layer-2	32–384	128 (mono)	1:6–1:8
Layer-3 (MP3)	32–320	64 (mono) 128 (stereo)	1:10–1:12

MPEG-2

MPEG-2 provides broadcast-quality audio and video at higher data delivery rates. MPEG-2 standard is added to the original work on MPEG-1 to provide a high-quality audio format for digital television. In some applications, Dolby AC-3 has been used as an alternative to accompany an MPEG-2 video stream. The original MPEG-2 standard ISO/IEC 13838-3) supports a low sampling frequencies extension (LSF 16, 22, and 24 kHz) and multi-channel audio (MPEG-1 is mono or stereo). The original standards were backwards compatible with MPEG-1. To take advantage of newer coding algorithms, backwards compatility was abandoned. This led to the definition of the Advanced Audio Coding (AAC) scheme, ISO/IEC13838-7.

Advanced Audio Coding (AAC)

The original goal was to produce a coder that could compress CD format audio (44.1 kHz sampling, 16-bit sample, more than 2 Mbit/s) to less than 384 kbit/s, yet be indistinguishable from the original. This represents about 3 bits per sample. AAC was based on MPEG layers 1, 2, and 3, but introduced several new tools including filter bank window shape adaptation, spectral coefficient prediction, bandwidth and bit rate scaling, and noiseless coding.

MPEG-4 scalable audio profile

The MPEG-4 standard departs from the simple structure of the MPEG-1 and MPEG-2 audio coding. The MPEG team wanted to give a much wider flexibility. MPEG-4 was designed for use in a much wider range of applications than the focused remits of MPEG-1 and MPEG-2. Rather than adopting a number of levels, each more complex than the layer below, MPEG-4 offers a number of profiles.

The first departure is that two groups of codecs are used, one or general audio coding, or waveform audio, and the others for speech. The speech coding is based on the vocoders developed for secure voice communication by the military. The general audio is based more on the previous work of the MPEG-2 team.

Encoding multimedia proxies

One of the common features of a digital asset management system is that the original content is viewed as a proxy at a lower resolution. This means that a compact version of an asset can be stored online on a disk sub-system, whereas the real file is stored in a lower cost archive and retrieved on demand.

Three popular multimedia compression architectures are used for the asset proxies:

- Apple QuickTime
- RealNetworks
- Windows Media

Some asset management vendors offer you the choice of codec, other supports just one. For the viewing of proxies, there is not a lot of difference between the products. Unless you want to squeeze the ultimate quality over a dial-up modem connection, the minor performance differences are not going to matter, after all they are just proxies. The issue is becoming blurred. As an example, Windows Media can support high definition television. Microsoft marketed the format as an alternative to MPEG-2 for the primary asset storage. I guess that in the future we may see more of a continuum with the same formats being used for preview and fulfilment.

Audio file formats

There used to be a large number of audio file formats before the drive to standardisation (Table 5.6). Sun, SGI, IRCAM, SoundBlaster, and Amiga all spawned different file formats. Most were developed to support computer-based music creation and editing systems, rather than for general audio sampling. The move now is to limit use to audio interchange file format (AIFF) for Mac and WAV for PC. In professional circles an enhanced version of WAV is also found, the broadcast WAVE format (BWF).

Most of the formats carry the device parameters and encoding in the header—these are called self-describing. Some older 'raw' formats use fixed parameters that define a single encoding; these are headerless formats. An example of a headerless format is the G.711 μ-law encoding.

Audio Interchange File Format (AIFF)

This format was developed in the late 1980s by musical developers. It conforms to the Electronic Arts Standard for Interchange Format Files, EA-IFF 85. The file has a number

Table 5.6 Some popular audio file formats

	Extension		WM player	Real player	QuickTime player
Audio streaming formats					
MPEG-1					
layers 1, 2, and 3	.mpa		Y	Y	Y
	.mp2		Y		
	.mp3		Y	Y	
	.mpg			Y	
Qdesign					Y
Real Audio	.ra			Y	
Windows Media Audio	.wma		Y		
Non-streaming (local playback) audio formats					
AIFF	.aif, .aiff	Apple, SGI	Y	Y	Y
AIFF, compressed	.aifc	Apple, SGI	Y	Y	Y
Sound file	.snd	NeXT	Y		Y
UNIX audio	.au	Sun	Y	Y	Y
Waveform audio	.wav	Microsoft	Y	Y	Y

of chunks, three are obligatory: the header, common, and sound data. A number of optional chunks can be added as required. The format supports mono, stereo, three channel, quad, four channel, and six channel (5.1). The bit depth can range from 1 to 32 bits per sample.

Microsoft waveform audio (WAVE)

This Microsoft format is derived from the MS/IBM resource interchange file format (RIFF). There are three data chunks:

- RIFF chunk (file format 'WAVE' and file size)
- Format chunk (mono/stereo, sample rate, bits/sample; 8 or 16)
- Data chunk (audio samples)

   The format originally supported 8- and 16-bit mono or stereo. It has been extended to support many more formats, as the audio industry demands multi-channels, greater bit depth, and higher sampling rates. These include MPEG-1, A-law, μ-law, and Dolby AC3. Encrypted content found in Windows Media digital rights management is specifically supported.

EBU Broadcast Wave Format (BWF)

The EBU has developed a file format to meet the special needs of broadcasters. Their requirement was for seamless interchange of files between equipment from different manufacturers, and for program exchange between broadcasters. It is based on the Microsoft WAVE format. It adds a broadcast audio extension with essential metadata, plus a unique material identifier (UMID) to reference the audio content. The broadcast extension is analogous to the text chunks in the AIFF; the extension carries information about the audio program originator plus a date/time reference. Linear PCM and MPEG-1 formats are supported.

Ingesting audio to the asset repository

Audio capture is the process of acquiring the live audio stream and converting it to a computer file format. This process is essentially very simple. The files are composed of a number of chunks. The header chunk describes the file format and the number of samples. The data chunk contains the audio samples as frames, much like the AES standard. The file formatter adds a header chunk with all the necessary data to read the audio samples. To encode audio you do not really need to understand the file formats (Figure 5.13). Usually the configuration consists of just selecting the relevant format from a drop-down box on the user interface.

   There are two common file formats: AIFF and WAVE. The AIFF is used by Apple Mac and UNIX platforms. The other, WAVE, is a proprietary Microsoft format and is the common format for PC applications. Therefore, the decision as to which file format to use is simple.

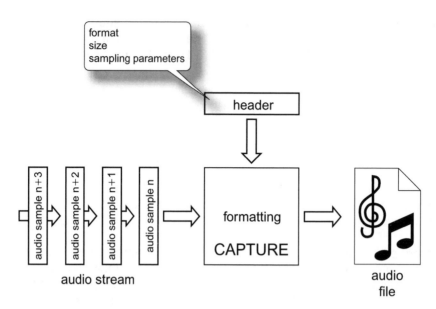

Figure 5.13 File formatting.

Wrappers and containers, Advanced Authoring Format and Media Exchange Format

One of the problems with managing multimedia assets is that a finished programme will have an assortment of associated unstructured information. Consider a video production. There are the source tapes, audio CDs with incidental music, graphics files, production notes, the edit decision list, a possibly numerous documents relating to research, and scripts.

It would be of great advantage to an efficient workflow if all these separate objects and files could be grouped into single package. This is the aim of the AAF model. Closely linked is the Media eXchange Format (MXF), a subset of the AAF, for optimised exchange of finished programmes with associated metadata.

Advanced Authoring Format (AAF)

The AAF is the fruition of broad-based trade association with members from the film, television, and video post-production industries.

Digital media is defined by the SMPTE to comprise two types of data: *essence* and *metadata*. Essence is the manifestation of the content that we perceive: the video, audio, and images. The metadata is data about the essence data.

Some examples of metadata include a tape label, an edit decision list and time code. The AAF is a container that wraps essence and its metadata as an object. We have two basic definitions:

1. Asset = Content + Rights to use
2. Content = Essence + Metadata.

The SMPTE/EBU 'Task Force for Harmonised Standards for Exchange of Programme Material as Bitstreams' identified the need to develop a common wrapper for inter-changing content between multimedia authoring tools. Most products used a proprietary file format for internal processing and storage. Even when a common compression for-mat was used, Motion-JPEG, it was not a standard. So usually the only way to exchange content was to decode to regular video, PAL, NTSC, 601, transfer the material, then re-encode into another format. Not only is this inefficient, but it can only take place in real time. So a 10 min news clip for editing takes 10 min to transfer from server to server, even if the network bandwidth could support a four times transfer rate (2.5 min). Any associated metadata was even more proprietary, although there are *ad hoc* standards for information like the edit decision list.

The SMPTE task force defined a content structure. The first was the division between essence and metadata. Essence is the material that is delivered to the media consumer. It is the video, audio, graphics, plus data essence; this can be data rendered as graph-ics by the receiver, subtitles, and captions.

The basic unit of content is the content element. This is essence of a single type, plus any essential metadata. This could be a video sequence, a piece of music or a caption. Elements can be collected together as items and packages.

Content item

A content item is a collection of one or more content elements, for example a video clip comprises a video element, plus one or more audio elements (soundtrack) and associ-ated metadata like time code.

Content package

A package is a collection of items and elements plus metadata. An example of a pack-age is a finished programme. The items would be all the clips used to make the finished programme, plus elements like subtitles and programme descriptions for an electronic programme guide (EPG).

A complex content package can contain compositional metadata, like edit decision lists, plus references to the source tapes and film reels. The packages and items are gathered together into a wrapper (Figure 5.14).

Wrapper

The wrapper links together the physical media used to store the essence and meta-data, files on disks, or physical media like tapes and CDs. When material is transferred between origination devices, post-production and final distribution to the consumer, it is called a streaming wrapper. One implementation of this is the MXF.

The AAF file uses these same concepts to wrap the essence, and metadata, along with a metadata dictionary and identification. The metadata dictionary used is the SMPTE dictionary. This file represents all the information that has been used to edit together content elements to make a finished programme. Content is either stored as a source file or as external physical media. The content storage metadata references both exter-nal media, via a physical source object, and source files.

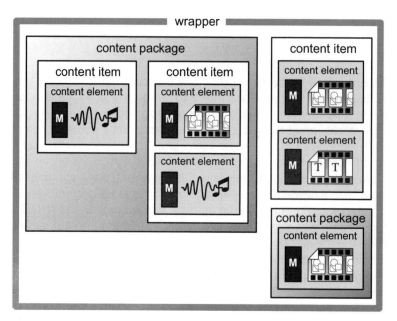

Figure 5.14 SMPTE/EBU content package.

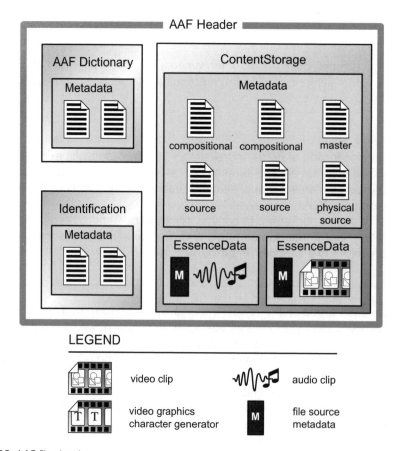

Figure 5.15 AAF file structure.

The AAF file is a compound file (Figure 5.15), in that it encapsulates other files. This concept has long been part of Microsoft's Object Linking and Embedding (OLE). The AAF decided to adopt Microsoft Structured Storage as the storage architecture.

Microsoft Structured Storage

Structured storage is based upon Microsoft's Component Object Model (COM). Instead of storing separate objects as flat files, it allows files to be stored within files—compound files. There are two types of entity within a file: storage objects and stream objects. A storage object is akin to the directory of a conventional file system. A directory contains other directories and individual in a hierarchy. This is the familiar tree structure. A stream object is like a traditional file, and stored a consecutive sequence of bytes on disk.

COM compound files are independent of the underlying operating system; so structural storage can be implemented on Windows, Mac, or UNIX operating systems. One of the most familiar compound files is a Word document. All the embedded graphics and images are stored as stream objects. The main text content can be split into a number of streams. This allows incremental 'fast' saves, rather than having to write the entire document afresh to disk for each save. This leads to another advantage; one stream can be modified and saved to disk, without the need to load the entire storage object to memory and rewritten back to disk. So, if one graphic is edited, that stream alone is written to disk.

With multimedia objects, and their very large disk files, there are obvious efficiencies to this object-based structured storage.

MXF

Originally, video material was distributed and exchanged as tape reels or cassettes. Now editing is performed at computer workstations, and television transmission makes great use of servers. So a file format was needed that could take the place of tape. It had to be self-contained, and an open standard that could be used across different production platforms. Many of the original server-based applications used proprietary formats for internal processing. For interchange, the material was streamed out to a VTR.

The ProMPEG Forum is a group of broadcasters, equipment vendors, and programme makers. Together they formulated the MXF as an open standard for the exchange of programme material between servers, videotape, and archives. Video is normally transmitted as a stream. It is viewed as it is transferred. It is point to point, with a fixed propagation delay. Network resources a reserved, so that transmission is continuous and uninterrupted. Contrast this with file transfers. They often use TCP/IP over normal computer networks. Error-free transmission is maintained, but transmission latencies are variable, and file transfer rates depend upon the available bandwidth. They can be faster than real time or much, much slower. A file cannot be viewed as it is being transferred. Streaming and file transfer each have advantages; it depends upon the application.

The MXF supports streaming and file transfers. Video exists in many forms throughout the production chain. It can be uncompressed; or it can be in MPEG-2 or DV format. MXF is agnostic as to the video format; it wraps the content in a standard header. MXF also carries metadata about the programme material. The MXF developers wanted a flexible file format that could handle short metadata records, and very large video files. The format had to be efficient, to minimise bandwidth for the file exchange. The method adopted was to use variable-length files to the SMPTE KLV (key–length–value) guidelines.

Key-Length-Value (KLV)

The SMPTE had laid down a standard for the wrapping of data. The data has a value, and a key to identify the type of data. This unique 16-byte key identifies items within a file. This is followed by a field indicating the length of the file item, then the variable length value, carrying the data in binary form. The receiver of a file needs only to read the key, and if it is not recognised the data is discarded. So if an MPEG-2 device receives DV-compressed data it can be ignored. Therefore, the same file format can carry yet to be thought of compression schemes—it is extensible. The key is defined as a SMPTE universal label. The SMPTE maintains a register of dictionaries defining the keys.

Traditionally video transfers between devices carried only the essence, video and audio, and one piece of metadata, the time code. If information like programme title and scene number were required, they were carried in vision as a few frames of slate (clapperboard) at the start of a clip. Some limited data is carried on the tape label, notably a bar code that can be used to associate the cassette with a record in a tape library database. What was novel for the MXF was the support of general metadata transport along with the essence.

AAF, MXF, and the production workflow

AAF and MXF are complementary formats for managing audio-visual material through the workflows of programme production. AAF is an authoring format. For the exchange of finished programmes most of the metadata is irrelevant, as is most of the source essence. All that is needed is the composited audio–video and a subset of the metadata. The MXF was developed for just such applications. It is a file transfer format in contrast to AAF, which is primarily for storage. MXF is self-contained, whereas AAF can reference external content in tape or film vaults.

AAF retains the master metadata; MXF has a subset, just sufficient for the needs of programme exchange. If you are adopting the AAF as part of your production processes, the digital asset management that you choose should support the AAF.

Format conversion

Standard file wrappers like MXF greatly ease the interchange of content. But if the content is compressed in one format, and routed to a decoder for a different format, then the interchange cannot take place. So there is still the need for codecs to translate between uncompressed and compressed formats, and for transcoding between different compression schemes.

The Tower of Babel

Most software applications use proprietary file formats. This may be for efficiency, or to support special features of the product. Consequently, there are hundreds of file formats supporting images, audio, and video. Most digital asset management systems use a web interface, which supports a mere handful of formats. Few system administrators will want to supply large numbers of browser plug-ins for viewing different formats. So it is usual to convert files at ingest to the asset repository to a limited number of formats. This process has traditionally been a time-consuming manual process that uses valuable human resources. If you have to make conversions on a small scale, then it is simple to write scripts to automate the conversion.

If you have large numbers of files to convert, then an alternative is to use a product designed for unattended and automated processing.

Images

One of the commonest ways to convert images is to open them in Adobe Photoshop, and then save them in the required format. It may be just to change colour space (RGB/CMYK) or the colour profile (ICC). It may be to change file format (like TIFF to JPEG) or it could be to rescale a large image for web publishing.

The same engine that performs as all the maths can also run in an automated environment as part of the Adobe Graphic Server 2. This can be hooked into asset management systems for the automated conversion of images as a background operation. The graphic server is controlled by simple XML messages from the asset management application.

Another vendor is Venetica with its content bridges, part of the Venice Bridge product suite. Files can be converted on the fly to other formats so that, as an example, they can be viewed from a web browser.

Video and audio format conversion

Video and audio content has just the same problems as images: different file formats and different resolutions. Since the asset management archive usually stores the content at a high resolution, if a smaller file is needed for distribution or fulfilment, then it has to be converted.

Several vendors have products that can be used to convert video to lower resolution proxies including Anystream and Telestream's ClipMail pro.

Summary

Over the years new software applications spawned new file formats for images and video. However, users demand interoperability and standardisation. So a handful of formats have emerged for the interchange and archiving of digital assets. Some are a proprietary, but have become *de facto* standards, other are approved by International standards bodies like the ISO/IEC. Since the turn of the century, there has been a real impetus to improve interoperability across the board. The penalties for the use of closed, proprietary formats are financial. Knowledge workers should be free to concentrate on authoring original material and the production of finished content. Manipulating content into myriad formats for interchange is a waste of valuable time.

The digital asset management system can automate the underlying processes of file interchange. New standards that wrap essence and metadata ease the processes and workflow. Metadata is essential to digital asset management. The AAF provides a framework for the preservation of metadata in a form that can be used on any platform by any compatible application.

For textual material, XML—along with the DTD and XML schema—offers solutions to the problems of re-purposing content for different distribution channels. By separating style from format, the production of printed information and web pages can share common content.

Video formats have evolved from the SD colour format developed by the NTSC in the early 1950s. This standard established the interlaced scan and the composite colour encoding. Later VTRs were developed. The pace of new formats has quickened, but by the year 2000, the DV family has proved very popular for video production.

Analogue television is being replaced by digital formats, although analogue composite is still the most used delivery format for the terrestrial receiver. The defining standard is BT 601; this set the rules for the sampling structure that we see in MPEG compression.

Domestic television formats are moving to higher definition standards, up to 1080 lines. Electronic cinematography is adopting a frame rate of 24 to be compatible with film. There is an ever-increasing diversity in standards and in tape formats.

A digital asset management system should be extensible to cater for all the different contact formats that the enterprise may be using. In many cases, it may prove more efficient to limit the number of formats, and convert legacy assets to the chosen formats. The high number of proprietary formats created in the past is showing signs of ending. The latest software applications are now tending towards support of internationally agreed formats. We see this exemplified by the AAF/MXF standards that have been developed by the video industry.

6 The system components

Introduction

A digital asset management system uses a suite of applications linked together to provide a seamless experience to the user. It is not just a piece of shrink-wrap software that can be used straight out of the box. Rather it is a collection of many components that have been carefully selected to meet the needs and budgets of the enterprise. The system should also have links to existing software applications: accounts, customer records, and planning systems. To maximise the operational benefits, it is advantageous for these applications to exchange data with the digital asset management. Like any enterprise-wide deployment of software, much of the installation costs will be for the professional services. These are usually required to merge the many stand-alone applications into a seamless operating environment, and to customise the business logic to suit the needs of the customer.

This list details some of the components in a typical installation:

- Content repository
- Digital asset management application
- Databases
- Search engine
- Indexing workstations
- Rights management application
- Web portal.

The complete digital asset management system is rarely the product of a single vendor. Most partner with specialists for services like the search engine, video logging, speech recognition, and the underlying database management system (DBMS). The core digital asset management acts like a glue. It binds all these functions together using the business rules. The users see a unitary view of all the systems assembled at the presentation layer.

This modular approach allows the best-of-breed solutions to be used, and should retain flexibility for the customer to stick with their favoured databases and operating platforms. Clearly, with all these different products, a system's integrator will be required to act as a prime contractor to ensure that the final solution operates satisfactorily as a whole and meets the original agreed requirements.

I shall now take a number of views of the system architecture. One view is the software system architecture, usually a multi-tiered system, with presentation, business, and data layers. Another view is content centric, with the system in shells around the core assets, modifying the view the user sees.

One of the key functions of any digital asset management is to relieve the users of the need to perform repetitive tasks. This frees them to concentrate on the more creative side of media creation and publishing. The design of the user interface is the key to the success of the product. The other issue of great importance to the user is the way that the system fits with the existing corporate processes. If too many changes are made to the ways of working, then the users will feel alienated from the asset management. Limited scale trials are very useful for the shakedown of workflow issues. The goal is for the users to feel excited with the opportunities that the system presents, not to resent what is viewed as an imposed system that is designed to reduce manning levels. The goal is a win–win for the corporate management and the knowledge workers.

Mainframes to multi-tier

Looking back through the history of enterprise computing (Figure 6.1), it all started with the mainframe and simple clients based upon the video terminal or visual display unit (VDU). Smaller mainframes (the minicomputer) were developed to suit the needs of medium-size businesses, and then IBM launched the personal computer (PC). This allowed even the smallest business to produce professional-looking correspondence and to run accounts software.

As the power of the PC increased, it became feasible to run graphics-rich programs. Although the PCs had clunky text interfaces with box-like graphics, the way was pioneered by the early Apples for more fluid interfaces using mouse-driven windows. These led to the WYSIWYG (what you see is what you get) user interface that we all demand today.

As the costs of the desktop PC dropped to little more than the desks they sat on, business users demanded the same user interface as the PC. A good example is the word processor. The first products used the mainframe computer to run the application. To see the final layout, you had to make a printout. To produce a complex layout was an iterative process involving many intermediate printouts. The WYSIWYG word processor application did away with this, dramatically improving productivity.

After the replacement of the video terminals with PCs, the minicomputer that ran the word processing became redundant. It was replaced by a central file server.

Client–server

This new architecture was the client–server configuration (Figure 6.2). The user now had the power of the new office application suites. This combination of word processing, spreadsheets, and basic drawing facilities meets most of the needs of the average office worker. Alongside this, the old mainframe systems still ran the company databases for online transaction processing, the sales order processing, inventory control, and manufacturing resource planning—everything that makes the enterprise tick.

MAINFRAME

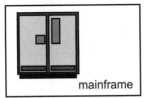

mainframe

transaction processing
word processing

video
terminal

CLIENT/SERVER

transaction processing
word processing

WORKSTATION

graphics compositing
3-D modelling
video graphics

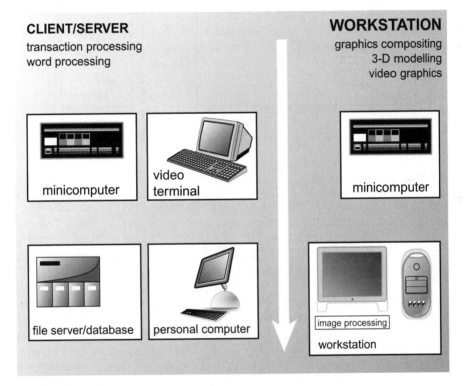

minicomputer

video
terminal

minicomputer

file server/database

personal computer

image processing

workstation

MULTI-TIER COMPUTING

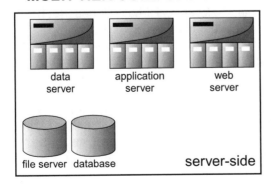

data
server

application
server

web
server

file server   database

server-side

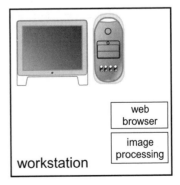

workstation

web
browser

image
processing

Figure 6.1 The evolution of multi-tier computing.

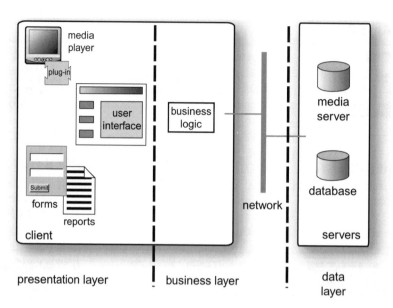

Figure 6.2 The client–server model.

Some asset management products adopted the client–server approach. The client includes the business logic and a presentation layer for the user interface. The server is essentially just a relational database. The clients interact with each other through the DBMS using stored procedures and triggers. Client–server is fine for small systems, but in practice, it does not scale well beyond around 100 clients.

Initially everybody was happy with the wonders of modern computers throughout the business. However, it soon became apparent that running thousands of PCs with thousands of instances of the applications was very expensive. First there were the costs for the per seat licensing. Then there were the costs involved in updating machines when new software releases came out (all too frequently). But the real killer was the ease with which the average office worker could reduce his or her own computer to a state of malfunction. Either by misconfiguring the applications, or by illicitly loading unofficial software, the machine would grind to a halt, ready for rescue by the information technology (IT) department.

The cost of all this downtime, and the staffing levels required in IT, began to be of great concern to senior management. There had to be better ways.

One approach was to use the 'network' PC. This had no removable storage, no CD or floppy drives, so it was difficult to load unauthorised software. Modern operating systems allow remote access by a system administrator, so that software updates could be performed from a central point over the corporate network. This is great in a controlled world, but what about the marketing communications department? How do they exchange files with external designers? How do personnel staff make backups of confidential information? Most enterprises accept that distributed applications are not going away. The network PC has a place, but it is not the answer for the typical distributed asset management application.

IT professionals have taken two paths to counteract these problems. One is to retain the advantages of the client–server environment. The solution is to use a desktop management system. This allows the IT managers to have complete control over software distribution to the clients. The operating system access is configured to forbid local software installation and configuration. Applications, patches, and updates are all loaded from a central point. The systems also offer remote troubleshooting, and can usually self-heal local software faults. Such a system removes most of the problematic maintenance issues that have dogged client–server and distributed installations.

The thin client

The other route is the thin client. This is a return to the simple terminal of the old mainframes. Today's user has many expectations from a user interface that the VT100 style terminals could not offer. Perhaps the most important are support for graphics and mouse-driven user interaction.

The current implementation of a thin client is to use a web browser on a standard PC. One option is to add additional functionality to the web environment by adding a Java virtual machine. This supports applets to run small programmes on the client. The business logic is then transferred from the client to a third tier, the application server.

The two paths are best suited to different applications. The client–server is ideal for office applications, where the work is file based. The user loads a file from a central server, edits it locally, and then saves back to the server. The user has all the advantages of a powerful application running locally. Imagine the latencies of using a spell checker while you type, if the word processor were running on a remote server.

Data-record-oriented applications are more suited to the central data server. Information is viewed and updated from the client, but the data resides on the central server.

Digital asset management has elements of both. There is much data processing, relating to metadata queries and updates. There is also file processing, the creative processes applied to the content: editing, format conversion, and compositing.

The outcome is a hybrid approach. Many of the productivity tools run locally on the client machines. They can be centrally maintained using a desktop management system. These include Word, Excel, Quark, and Photoshop. The craft-oriented applications, like the non-linear editor may still run a stand-alone application, maintained locally at the workstation. The database intensive applications, with workflow management and peer-to-peer collaboration, can use a web browser to view a presentation layer in the application server.

Three tier

The complex business logic of asset management leads naturally to a central application server. This can support the collaborative workflow and communications between the client workstations with central business logic to manage communication between the clients. This logic forms a third layer between the database and the client (Figure 6.3).

Many enterprises planning to purchase digital asset management will want to minimise the cost of each client. Many users only want to search, then preview files. Such an application does not warrant to cost of a fully featured client running a local application. The enterprise may well want to share asset information with suppliers and customers.

The requirement to minimise cost dictates a thin client, especially for remote users. Suppliers of creative services may well use Apple Macs. Other partners may use Linux.

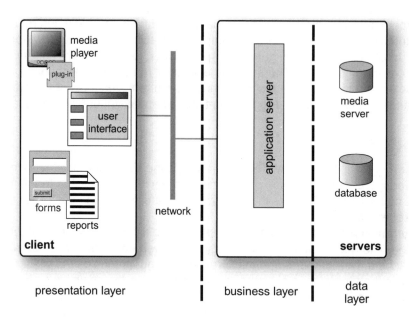

Figure 6.3 The three-tier model.

Your own enterprise may use Windows for office applications and UNIX for transaction processing. All this demands a client that is agnostic to operating system, and that can use widely available communications protocols. Well, there is one such client—the web browser.

Rather than running the two tiers of the client–server model, the web browser requires at least three tiers with a web server generating the presentation.

Multi-tier

The multiple or *n*-tiered approach to computing splits an application into manageable chunks (Figure 6.4). Typically, there is a data layer, a presentation layer, and a layer of business logic linking the two. This has many advantages for the IT department. The data layer can be a standard relational database: DB2, Oracle, or SQL Server, it does not matter. These are mature products, with predictable behaviour, and formal maintenance procedures. The presentation layer is just a web server, again no great problem to operate and maintain. With this architecture the digital asset management can be broken away into a separate box called the business logic. Here the rules for manipulating the data and the connections to third-party applications can all reside on a separate application server that runs the core asset management software.

The central server has now become fragmented into functional blocks: data server, web server, and application server.

Application server

The business logic runs on the application server. This provides the services and framework to run the software objects that implement the business logic. The framework has

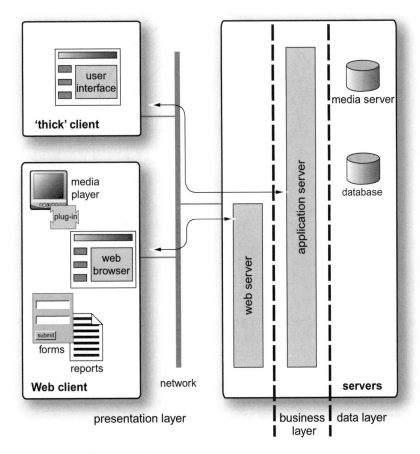

Figure 6.4 Multiple or n-*tier computing.*

two sub-systems. One is to implement the rules of the business logic, the processes like the workflow and categorisation. The second is the transaction management for updating metadata records in the database.

The data tier

The data tier is usually a relational database, although this is for administrative convenience rather than elegance of design. It could alternatively be an object database. The database has a management system, DBMS, to control the connections and for the general maintenance of the database (Figure 6.5). The application server is a client to the database. The DBMS manages the transactions to enter and update data, and the information retrieval to generate views and reports of the data. The database administrator (DBA) will have a number of tools to maintain the database.

Originally, each database product required different driver for the applications to perform operations on the data. Microsoft developed the language-independent open database connectivity (ODBC) interface that rationalised the database connections into a single

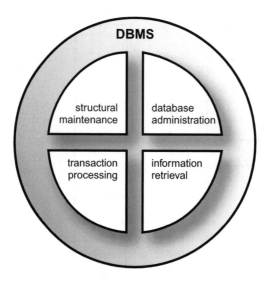

Figure 6.5 Elements of the database management.

standard. This was later joined by Java database connectivity (JDBC), which exposes a Java application program interface to the database drivers. These technologies have much simplified the connection between the business logic and the database. There are limitations to ODBC; it was designed to use SQL for access to relational databases. There are now many data sources that are not relational, mail systems, object databases, and file servers. There have been newer and more efficient components that can provide a more universal data access than ODBC.

Limitations of the web tier

Some clients need more functionality than can be provided by the basic web browser. For example, media ingest requires PCs equipped with specialist video encoding cards and extra processing power for the speech analysis. Many digital asset management products use a hybrid approach. Simple search and retrieve operations can be made from a web browser, but more complex ingest and editing operations use a full client application.

So far, I have been describing closed systems, a corporate network. Most collaboration in asset management extends outside the enterprise. Customers and partners will need controlled access to the asset management. Again, the web browser provides a simple option. The remote user needs no special software application; the technology is familiar and ubiquitous.

The content model

The Society of Motion Picture and Television Engineers/European Broadcasting Union (SMPTE/EBU) Task Force on Harmonised Standards in 1998 developed a system model to

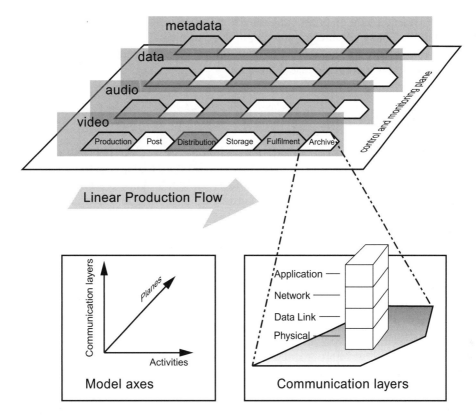

Figure 6.6 System model for television production.

represent the relationships between signals, processes, and control systems (Figure 6.6). This report has become a very popular starting point for building object models of content.

The model has three orthogonal axes: activities, content planes, and communication layers. The communication layers represent the intercommunication between peer entities. The layers are similar to the International Standards Organisation (ISO) open systems interface: application, network, data link, and physical. A control and monitoring plane lies under the activities and content planes.

This model focused on television content, so splits content into audio, video and data (all classed as essence), and metadata but the principle could be applied to other forms of content. Essence is the raw content that represents the pictures, sound, and text that are delivered to the user. Data essence can be graphics, animation, text files, and still images. An example of data essence is the closed caption.

The activities are those typical of the processes in the workflow of television production. The production phase represents planning and shooting. Post is the post-production, where the original footage is edited into a final programme, the graphics added and the sound design implemented. Distribution is the dissemination of the finished programme to the publishers. These could be broadcasters or DVD distributors. The storage operation is optional, as the product may be aired immediately. Fulfilment is the delivery to the consumer. This could be as broadcast television transmission, or as sell-through media: DVD and VHS. Finally, the programme is archived to a vault.

This flow is linear, but many programmes return from the vault to the post-stage for re-purposing and re-use in a cyclical process.

The asset management

The asset management can be looked at as a number of blocks. This view is somewhat flexible, what is content, what is data? In this view content that is stored in a file system like the network file system (NFS) is called data, content that is stored as video on tape or in special video servers is treated separately as content and managed through the media management component.

Most products are modular, and sit like a hub at the centre of media operations and processes. The core asset management should offer a number of different functions:

- Indexing and categorisation
- Search
- Content editing
- Workflow management
- Task and project management
- Resource management
- User management
- Storage management.

The asset management functions will be supported by a number of services:

- Load balancing and fault tolerance
- Access control
- Security
- Configuration.

Indexing and categorisation

The index module uses metadata generated at the ingest stage to create an index and catalogue that can be used by the search engine. The indexing can be fairly simple using a few key fields: file name, title, author, and keywords. For a large repository, a more sophisticated index will be required. This will avoid the common problem of huge result sets with little relevance to the search criteria. In order to return smaller and more relevant result set, one technique is to use concepts rather than keywords.

Search

Search is an essential facility for any asset management. The user can use the search engine to find content within the repository. Search engines vary from a basic keyword search through to natural language search. Concept searches may well suggest allied content that may be relevant.

Content editing

Many asset management applications include basic video editing facilities. A user can assemble a number of scenes or clips into a contiguous sequence. This assembly of clips generates an edit decision list (EDL). This list can be used later with a non-linear editor to conform the source media at broadcast resolution to finished video content.

Workflow management

One of the big advantages of an asset management is the workflow management. The system provides a platform to automate the business processes. It should have basic features like e-mail alerts. It may include more comprehensive facilities. These can help the project team collaborate and share content.

Task and project management

Much of the use for the digital asset management is for projects to create or re-purpose content. A module for task management can aid the smooth running of a project.

Resource management

Facilities like video ingest will usually have a limited number of encoding ports and associated videotape recorders. A resource management module can manage the allocation of such hardware to a prepared schedule. There may also be the need to manage human resources, like the tape operators.

User management

This module manages the users of the system, with facilities to personalise the web interface, associate with projects, and modify personal configuration settings.

Storage management

The asset management application should offer a number of services to support the storage management. These will include storage networks, hierarchical storage management (HSM) to manage the disk, near-line and offline, and media management for removable and analogue storage.

   The core services of asset management can vary from platform to platform but certain elements will be essential (Figure 6.7).

Load balancing and fault tolerance

Much like a mainframe computer, the application server that runs the asset management is potentially a single point of failure. A successful asset management system is going to become key to the efficient operation of the business, so high availability will be very important. The object broker platforms are usually designed to be distributed across a number of server devices. The load from the users is automatically balanced

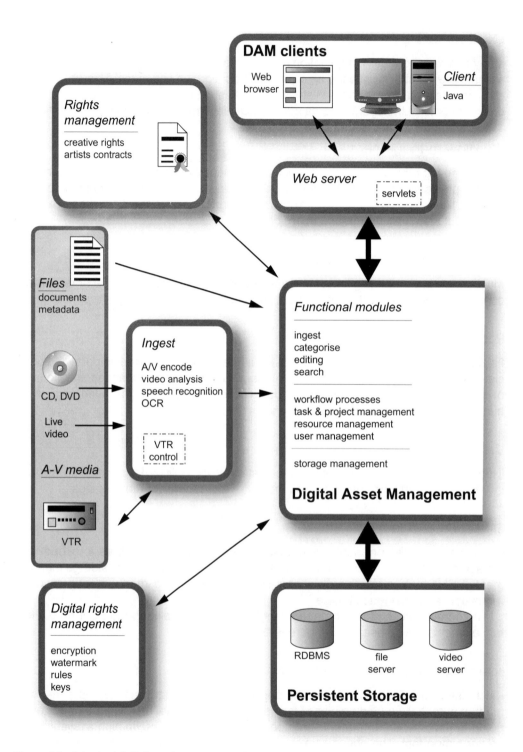

Figure 6.7   A typical digital asset management system.

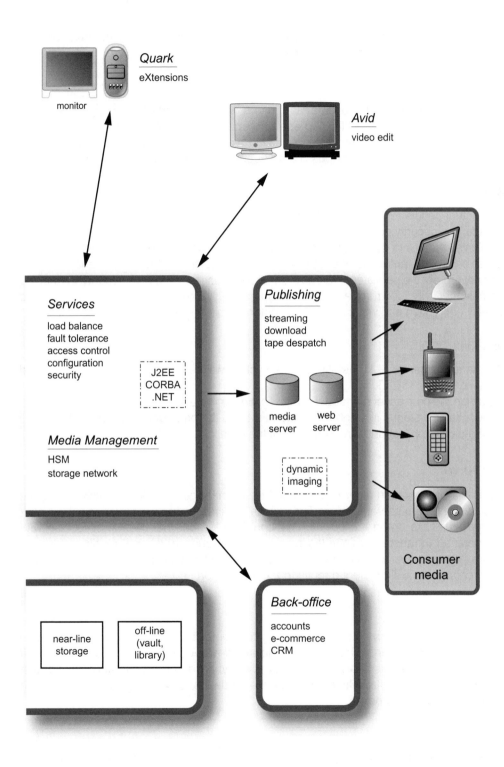

across the servers. In the event of device failure, the load can be rebalanced across the remaining facilities to give fault tolerance.

Access control

Access control is much like a database; users will be allocated a set of privileges to access folders, projects, and files. These privileges may be role based as well as user based. There may also be access to a project team or workgroup. The access control offered should be as flexible as possible to support different corporate structures.

Security

The content assets represent an attractive target for unauthorised access and malicious damage. The security policies to protect the system should be much the same as the existing IT systems within the corporation. Security has to operate at many levels. Although access control will authorise users through the client portals of the asset management, it does not protect the persistent storage against direct access. The total security will include perimeter security, electronic and physical, operating system security, access control, and possibly encryption and watermarking of content within the repository.

Configuration

Just like any other large IT installation, the system will need constant configuration and maintenance.

Outside the core asset management application, there are a number of satellites. Some will be legacy systems, like rights management and the back-office systems. Others will be third-party applications that form part of the complete asset management.

Web server

This is the presentation layer of the digital asset management. It is usually a conventional dynamic web server product. The web server creates the user interface. It will offer the opportunity to brand the pages. This could be for external clients, or for use with departmental intranets. Audio/video previews will require additional media servers to stream the proxy files. Although most users can connect to the system via the web server, craft workstations will connect directly to the application server.

Ingest

This is where some heavy number crunching takes place. For this reason, it takes place on separate workstations. This is where the audio–video content is parsed to make it searchable. The video is analysed to create a storyboard of representative still frames. At the same time, a low-resolution copy can be made that can be used as a proxy of the content for preview purposes.

Speech analysis

The soundtrack of a video clip can be analysed. With varying degrees of success, speech recognition software can extract the meaning of the spoken word. The resulting text transcript will be synchronised to the video and can be used to search and navigate through the clip. Some systems are also able to recognise different speakers and mark up the transcript accordingly.

Scanning and optical character recognition

Content such as paper documents can be scanned, and then read by optical character recognition (OCR) software. This will convert the content into a text file. OCR technology can also be used to read video graphics. An example of this would be the lower-third graphics used for television news broadcasts. These can be decoded and stored as textual data.

File transfer

Much content may already exist in a digital form. Files can be ingested by file transfer protocol (FTP) or other file transfer from clients or partners. An ingest workstation can be used to register the content with the system and to add essential metadata: title, copyright owner, subject, and keywords. Some files may include comprehensive meta-data that can be ingested at the same time and used to populate the data tables.

Digital rights management

Digital rights management (DRM) can be used to protect content from unauthorised access or viewing. It can be used to protect confidentiality or for the delivery of paid-for content. The digital asset management can be used to manage the original encryption, setting the appropriate decryption rules to meet the business requirements.

Publishing

This will possibly be the most non-standard part of any system. The channels for the publishing of content may range from high-definition television and digital cinema, through web delivery of streaming media to the PC, all the way down to lightweight content for wireless applications. Fulfilment may also include physical media, CD-ROMs, DVDs, or videotape.

Third-party applications

The digital asset management can provide search, workflow, and library facilities to many third-party applications within the enterprise.

Video editing

Non-linear editing is the primary application used for video post-production. The asset management can serve the editors as a repository for the raw elements of the production, and for the storage and archiving of finished material.

Desktop publishing

Many asset management products offer powerful links to QuarkXPress, so that the desktop publisher can use the asset repository to store original text and graphics, as well as their finished work.

Back office

There are many possible back-office applications that may be linked to the digital asset management. For example, the workflow management could link to the accounts department to trigger the issuing of invoices. The publishing side of the asset management may need links to e-commerce systems.

Rights management

This is the management of the contracts and agreements with content creators and owners. It is quite separate from digital rights. The rights are vital metadata for those involved in content creation and re-purposing. It would prove very useful for the rights management to exchange metadata with the digital asset management.

Persistent storage

This is the main repository for content, as essence and metadata. The metadata is usually stored in a third-party relational database. Popular products include Oracle and Microsoft SQL Server. A regular file server can be used for content that can be stored in a standard file system like NFS or NTFS. Such content may be documents and image files, or media files: AVI, streaming media, and QuickTime. Video is often stored on specialised video servers, but there are many developments that are allowing video—uncompressed, MPEG, or DV—to be stored on normal file systems.

The persistent storage can be disk based, or any combination of disk, data tape, or optical storage. If removable storage is used, then media management will be needed to track the content. There are many possible architectures for the storage. These include the storage networks (SAN and NAS), hierarchical storage management (HSM), and the basic library systems used to manage tapes on shelves.

Content strata

Content is stored in strata:

- Metadata
- Thumbnails
- Low-resolution preview
- High resolution for production use

The low-resolution preview may have a watermark of an imposed logo to indicate the owner of the content (Figure 6.8).

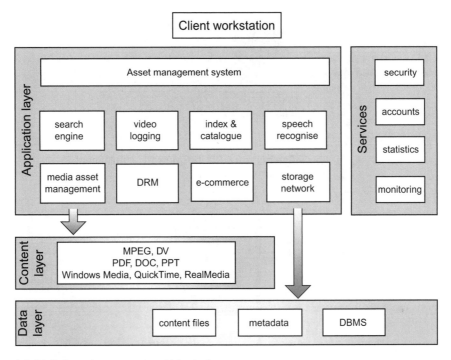

Figure 6.8 Digital asset management block diagram.

Application platform

The asset management system will run on a number of different server devices, although it could all run on one machine that would only be feasible for product demonstrations or small workgroups. To scale to support many users, the functions are separated across different servers. These may even use different operating systems. The database could run on UNIX, the media server could run Windows Media Services for streaming low-resolution video previews (Figure 6.9).

Distributed computing

The smallest asset management application may well be the single-user photo-library. The application, database, and user interface are all rolled up into a single application. Put the photographer into a workgroup, and the application must become distributed. The requirement changes, in that the members of a workgroup want to share files and possibly collaborate on the editing of individual images.

The architecture changes to a workgroup server, and a number of clients that can view files on the server, and check out files for image processing. As the system scales up to large numbers of clients, the asset management database may well reach the limits

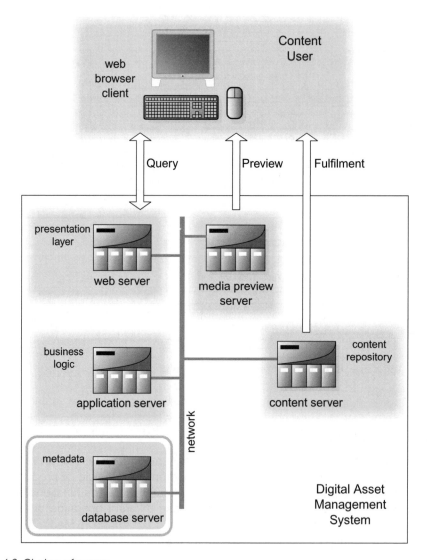

Figure 6.9 Clusters of servers.

of the integral database. To scale the system, the data is broken out and stored on a separate relational database.

No database application is installed on the client; all data queries are performed by the asset management software on the workgroup server. When the client wants to make a query, the command is sent to the server, from where the database query is generated. The result set is then returned to the client. The client is making a remote call on the server to run a function or method; there is no need for the client to load the server application. This is the basis of distributed computing. Quite clearly, it has much in common with the multi-tier model.

In a large asset management system, a request for the metadata on a content file may require a query across a federation of different databases. The digital asset management database may store the core metadata, but other information could be held on a rights management system, or within the accounts department records. The asset management application server can make remote calls for reports from the other systems, then collate and format the information for return to the client. Note that the client does not have any accounting or rights management software loaded. The information is all retrieved through remote function calls.

The client can edit this information and return the dataset, and then the distributed databases are updated. This distribution is not without its problems. Traditional databases retain a persistent connection between the client and the database. The client can lock tables during data updates. The number of connections can be limited. It was not unknown for a potential user to phone round several co-workers to find one that would logoff the database in order to free up a connection.

Web clients are very different in that they are stateless. A connection is made to download a page, and then it is closed. Persistent information about a client has to be maintained by the server using devices like cookies. There is an expectation of constant access to data, with no 'busy tone'. Since most users are not making constant access, the idea of effectively time sharing the connections makes sense.

The communication between the distributed applications is becoming more loosely coupled than the traditional real-time applications like transaction processing. This places a new set of demands upon the software architecture. The communication becomes based more on messages, almost a return to the days before the online database. This stateless messaging has other advantages. A fail-safe system can be put together. If one server fails, the client can simply communicate with another. So the system becomes truly distributed. This makes it very easy to scale a system to the point where it could be distributed across sites in different cities, or even to different continents. It is not without its drawbacks, one issue is the maintenance of data security—protecting the access of data stores to authorised users.

The development of distributed services is leaning towards the technology of extensible markup language (XML) web services. In this architecture each application—media management, rights management, and e-commerce—exposes functionality using Internet protocols. Specifically, these use hypertext transfer protocol (HTTP) as a transport, and XML as the data wrapper. Some vendors have started to adopt web services, and it promises to lower the costs of building complex distributed systems by using shrink-wrap products for much of the infrastructure.

Summary

Most asset management vendors have adopted the multi-tier model for their system architecture. The client can run a local application, or for basic search and preview functions, can be a normal web browser. The metadata is stored in a conventional relational database. The main asset management software runs on an application server.

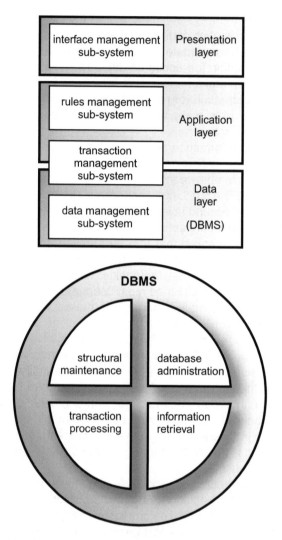

Figure 6.10 System architecture.

This architecture is very flexible; it can scale from a handful of users up to a large enterprise. It also simplifies software maintenance. The DBMS, web server, and web clients are all very familiar products for the IT personnel to manage. The asset management software is typically object oriented, using J2EE or CORBA, so with a suitable application server, it can run on most operating systems, and will feature essential services like fail-over and load balancing that allows large and highly available systems to be assembled (Figure 6.10).

There is a talent pool of DBAs and web server administrators that can be called on to manage the bulk of a multi-tier system. Specialist staff are only required for the application server.

The asset management can be seen as the hub of a wheel. The spokes extend to third-party applications, either to share metadata, or to provide services to the asset management. The business logic integrates all these applications to give the user a federated view of media within the enterprise.

Distributed systems can scale to support a geographically dispersed business. In this application, web services promise new way to design the system architecture. They promise scalable and robust systems, while reducing the cost of ownership.

7 XML

Introduction

Digital markup languages have been around since the standard generalised markup language (SGML) was first published in 1986. Although SGML gained acceptance in certain limited circles, it was not until the development of extensible markup language (XML) that markup was enthusiastically taken up by industries from newspaper publishing to multimedia. XML is a subset of SGML. It has now been adopted as a universal data container that is platform agnostic. XML did not start out this way. Its original application was for documents with unstructured content, mainly for publishing and storage of legal and medical documents. The use of the meta-language as a data container emerged later as the killer application for XML.

The latest software applications for handling rich media may seem a long way from the 35 mm movie, but celluloid has lessons for all. One word sums it up—standards. The movie industry could never have become so successful if every studio had used a different film gauge.

Today, we still see the enterprise made up of a number of software islands. The accounts department may run a client–server system with an Oracle database on a UNIX platform. The marketing department is an Apple Mac house. The rights department may be running SQL Server on Windows 2000. If the applications are linked, the middleware may use CORBA or J2EE.

A digital asset management system has to provide a seamless view of the enterprise; an environment where information and media assets can be created, searched, stored, and traded in an efficient and cost-effective manner.

The soothsayers have proposed XML as a holy grail. They are right and they are wrong. XML provides many answers, but it is only a means of data exchange. Web services provide many of the solutions to the interfacing of dispersed systems. An understanding of web services is useful to see where digital asset management is heading.

Web services take a pragmatic approach. Take a legacy standard like hypertext transfer protocol (HTTP)—it works, it is ubiquitous. Add the cut-down version of SGML, XML. The outcome is the simple object access protocol (SOAP) standard. It has led on to the development of the new standards: universal description, discovery and integration

(UDDI), and web services description language (WSDL). The result is a complete and platform agnostic methodology for connecting services.

Why is all this important for digital asset management? System integration costs have traditionally been a killer for potential projects. The way is clear to assemble a cost-effective system using best-of-breed solutions with a standard interface framework.

Any enterprise-wide asset management system should be made available across the organisation. This negates against the use of specialist client software. The simplest way to give access to all staff is to use the ubiquitous web browser, and then to present the information as hypertext markup language (HTML) pages.

XML

XML has proved to be an essential tool in integrating digital asset management systems. To understand its importance, we have to look back to earlier systems. In all probability, an enterprise-sized system will deploy a number of best-of-breed products integrated to give the whole. This implies that several different application vendors have supplied the components of the system. In the past, each vendor used proprietary ports and interfaces. This meant that the system integrator had to write many software gateways between the different interfaces. Typically, the coding and testing of a single interface could take six man-weeks of expensive human resource. Add in documentation and maintenance, and the total cost of installing a system is going to include large and ongoing fees for professional services, possibly larger than the price of the primary software applications.

The system integrators were not demanding standard interfaces that would have limited technological development. What was needed was a standard framework that could carry any number of proprietary messages. Potentially, the coding time for a new interface could then be reduced from weeks to a few days. Since the acceptance of XML, many industries have developed standard vocabularies; again this simplifies interfacing.

One candidate for the interface was the markup language. The ubiquitous hypertext of the web, HTML, is perhaps the best-known markup language. It is also a subset of the SGML. HTML is a very specific language developed for the exchange of linked text documents over the Internet, so not suited to these new demands.

Markup languages

Anything in a document that is not content is called markup. Before the days of desktop publishing, authors would submit their manuscripts to a typesetter with markup in the margins to indicate any special instructions to the setter. These could be character formatting—boldface or small capitals—or paragraph formatting to define the document layout: bodytext, heading, subheading, or bulleted list.

This markup can be split into two groups: procedural and descriptive. The author may define descriptive or generic markup. This includes instructions about the layout of a document, so the author will indicate headings, footnotes, and sidebars—anything that is not body text.

Procedural markup was the domain of the designer; it defines the appearance of the document. The text was marked up with typeface and font.

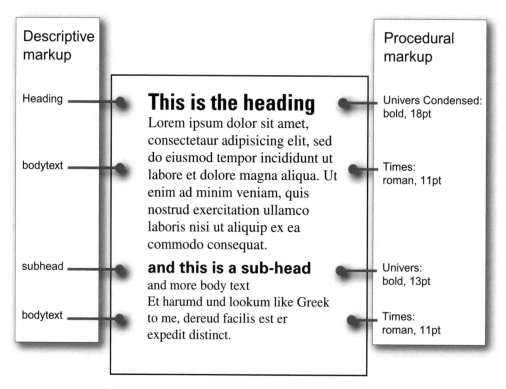

Figure 7.1 Descriptive and procedural markup.

With the word processor, the typesetting markup information is embedded within the document. The word processor allows the author to freely mix descriptive and procedural markup. The very power and flexibility of the word processor initially gave problems for corporate branding. If 10 people produced the same content on a word processor, you could get 10 different versions, all quite different. One may look like a typewritten document stemming from the use of Courier; another may use 10 typefaces. What does the recipient of the document think? Are they all from the same corporation? The way around this was to distribute the corporate style as a document template. This defined the formatting, indents and margins, and the typefaces to use. That way the procedural markup could remain in the domain of the designers in corporate marketing.

A word processor style is often used to define the structure of text, if it is a heading or body text. Character and paragraph formatting are then used for procedural markup. But each style will also have descriptive markup. They two are intertwined. This is not an issue as long as the file is never used outside the host application.

The problems arise when a document is reformatted for desktop publishing or dissemination via the web. The procedural markup is intimately associated with one output channel; with the word processor that is the laser printer (Figure 7.1).

To avoid the endless reformatting of documents, the procedural and descriptive markups should be separated. A style template appropriate to the output channel can then apply the procedural markup. A good analogy has been the development of HTML.

```
<h1>This is the heading</h1>
<p>this is the body text</p>
<h2>and this is a sub-head</h2>
<p>and more body text</p>
```

This is the heading
this is the body text
and this is a sub-head
and more body text

| Markup language (HTML) | Rendered in browser |

Figure 7.2 HTML rendered as formatted text.

Originally, a web page carried all the layout and formatting instructions. Now the HTML carries the text with descriptive markup. The procedural markup is stored as a separate cascading style sheet (CSS). Any number of documents can use the same style sheet, neatly applying the corporate boilerplate to the web page.

SGML

SGML was developed during the 1980s, following on from ideas from the Graphic Communications Association to markup documents with generic or descriptive tags rather than specific tags. These are examples of descriptive tags: *chapter heading* and *sub-heading*. At the same time, another group at IBM who were in the process of automating law offices developed the generalised markup language. Combining many of these original concepts produced the SGML.

The key to SGML was to separate content, structure, and style. An SGML application includes four basic constructs. The first is a declaration of the character set used. So, for example, certain characters could be reserved (like '<' and '>' in HTML). To use these characters in the text, character references have to be substituted. The next is the document type definition (DTD) and doctype, which defines the markup syntax. There may be a specification for the semantics for the markup. Finally, there is a document instance, which includes the content (as text) and the markup, with a reference to the DTD.

SGML was published as an international standard ISO: 8879, in 1986). Although it has been adopted by several large industry sectors, it has never gained wider acceptance, largely stemming from the complexity.

SGML is used with two style languages. The US Department of Defense developed their own output specification (OS). The user can create their own style with a formatting output specification instance (FOSI). Later the ISO developed a complete standard called the document style semantics and specification language (DSSSL).

HTML

HTML is an SGML application. It had modest beginnings; it was used for the exchange of technical documents. The markup was descriptive, and defined the structure of the document. Elements included text, headings, lists, forms, and tables, plus of course the hyperlinks. The browser applied the style, rendering the text in specific typefaces.

Figure 7.2 shows some basic HTML.

The markup is enclosed in brackets, <h1> represents heading level 1, <h2> represents heading level 2, and <p> a normal paragraph. Note each markup has a corresponding closing element </p>, so the content is nested between pairs of elements. The browser reads the markup and renders the text appropriately.

As the use of the web expanded to more applications of a commercial nature, the style became more important, and specifically control over that style. Anyone working in marketing communications is used to having strict control over the look and feel of a document; it has to comply with the corporate style guide. HTML evolved to meet this need by adding a number of additional tags to control procedural markup like font and text colour. The structure was being jumbled with the style.

Once other delivery channels came into use other devices, not just the PC, could render a web page. Perhaps the first was web television. Later hand-held wireless devices became available with displays large enough to display markup files.

Standard-definition television and hand-held devices have a lower display resolution than the PC. They needed a different style. For many good reasons, the style was separated from the structure of the content. The structure stayed with the HTML, but the style was moved into a separate style sheet. A large web site can use the same style sheet for hundreds of pages, that way each page has the same 'look'.

As the design of web pages became more complex, further markup elements were added. These were internationally agreed by the World-Wide Consortium, (W3C) and released as versions of the original standard. Unfortunately, the various web browsers do not render the HTML elements in the same way. To add to the confusion different products supported different and sometimes proprietary tags.

This chaotic situation meant that web designers had to test each page extensively on different browsers, different versions, and different operating systems. So rather than concentrating on the content, an enormous amount of time was wasted on testing. There had to be a better way.

The DTD was hard coded into the browser engine; so if you want to add a new element it was just not possible. Each update to the HTML standard meant the replacement of the web browser with a later release to support the new DTD.

The final version of HTML (4.01) was released in 1999. By that time, coding standards had become very lax, and the browsers very forgiving. But this led to unpredictable results—a more formal standard was needed.

XML

XML is a meta-language that is a form of language used to discuss another language. One example is grammar. This is a meta-language that is used to describe human languages with elements like 'noun' and 'verb'.

XML is a subset of SGML, but retains the freedom to define document structure, unlike the fixed DTD of HTML. An XML document is a data object that contains one or more storage units called entities. An entity contains content; either parsed character data or markup, or unparsed data (which could be binary data like images, MP3 data, or Office files like Word and Excel).

An XML element is bounded by two tags enclosing the text or data content or even further markup. Empty elements need only a single tag, but must be closed with a slash (Figure 7.3).

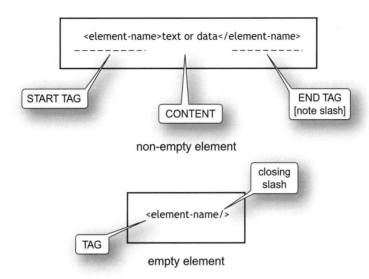

Figure 7.3 Elements and tags.

XML must be well formed, which means it conforms to the XML syntax. That may seem an obvious statement, but HTML documents often contain syntax errors. Web browsers are designed to be forgiving, and will still render a satisfactory page in spite of the errors. Both extensible HTML (XHTML) and XML aim to a more rigorous implementation of the standards.

One reason that XML has been adopted so enthusiastically is the number of associated standards. The DTD has been around since SGML, but new standards include extensible stylesheet language (XSL) for formatting and transforming XML; XML schema for constraining datatypes; and XLink for flexible resource referencing.

Namespaces

When XML is used for unstructured documents, the set of tags can be limited to a similar set used by HTML. These include headings, lists, and tables. As XML is extensible, it can be used with an unlimited number of tags. If we look at asset management applications, the tags include information about rights and ownership, technical information about removable media, and authoring information; the list is endless.

With HTML, the tags are defined by the standard. With an extensible language like XML, anyone can define tags. This is where file interchange becomes a problem. Different groups understand the same tag to have different meanings. Take the word 'title'. This is used very commonly in the field of asset management, but can be understood as follows:

1. As an appellation: Mister, Signorina, Herr, Madame
2. Relating to legal ownership

3. Name of a written work
4. Name of a programme or movie.

A new usage seems to have appeared on web site forms, where 'title' is used as a contraction of 'job title'. If two parties are exchanging an XML document, then they will require a shared markup vocabulary in order to understand the term 'title' in context.

One way around this is to declare a *namespace* for the document. Within a namespace, this polysemy of tags is avoided. A namespace is a collection of names that are used for elements and their attributes. A document may use more than one namespace where document fragments are embedded within other documents. Declaring a namespace avoids collisions between different meaning of an element within the compound file.

Related specifications

Document Type Definition (DTD)

A DTD can be used to define the structure of an XML document. HTML had a fixed DTD, so the necessary information to render and display the document was embedded within the web browser. This has proved to be an inflexible approach, and has one of the many reasons that HTML has been frozen at version 4, and superseded by XHTML. The DTD does not use XML syntax.

The structure of a document does not include data checking, so defining element data as numeric or date format does not form part of the DTD, for this is a separate document describing the semantics that is required. Data typing has long been part of relational database records. To a digital asset management application, this is an important feature to retain. So many metadata frameworks now use XML with a schema.

XML schema

It is standard practice to perform data checks on information being added or changed in a database. Typically, this will be to check that fields contain numeric data, a date, or correct currency formats. In a digital asset management system, a favoured method of data exchange between applications is an XML file. To replicate the data checking of relational database applications, XML needed a vocabulary to define a set of business rules from the data.

Unlike the DTD, the XML schema is an XML application.

Many industry associations are creating schema. One of the advantages of using one of these public schema is that two organisations can validate data to that schema. Therefore, there is no need to write a custom application to check the data structure and content.

XHTML

As XML emerged as the leading markup language, and HTML has reached the end of its life, it was decided to evolve HTML to meet the XML standard. XHTML is the result. XHTML provides the feature set of HTML, but within an XML framework. It is backward compatible with HTML. It conforms to the XML standard, which means that the documents have to be well formed. To be valid, they must also comply with the XHTML DTD.

This new standard eliminates the badly formed code found in many HTML documents, and in the fullness of time will lead to user agents (web browsers) that adhere strictly to these standards.

To cater for the needs of different display devices like personal digital assistants (PDAs), XHTML has been modularised into different functions. For example, a lightweight browser application for battery-powered devices could leave out support for the more complex functions.

XLink

The hyperlink has become familiar to all. It is perhaps this feature that guaranteed the universal adoption of HTML outside its roots in the research community. When XML was developed, naturally the hyperlink was deemed to be very important. The XLink standard builds upon the HTML link, and adds additional functionality. XLink provides for links between resources; that is, any information or services that can be addressed. These could be documents and media files, or result of a query. The resources are addressed through the universal resource identifier (URI).

The XLink can be used for hyperlinking, but it is not limited to that function. Related to XLink are XPath and the XPointer framework. XPath is a language used for addressing internal elements of an XML document through XML trees.

Extensible stylesheet language (XSL)

XSL can be used to transform and format XML documents. Just as CSS are used to format HTML, XSL can be used to format XML. It can also be used to transform XML data into HTML/CSS documents. So it can be very useful for the dynamic generation of web pages for data-driven web servers.

The transformation language XLST is used to convert XML from one tree structure to another; this could be data into a report structure. The output file can then be formatted into a viewable HTML report by XSL-formatting objects.

Simple Object Access Protocol (SOAP)

Traditional business applications require that software is installed upon the user's workstation, the 'thick client'. This is all the more so if there are transactions or if security is important.

Several existing technologies have been leveraged to facilitate remote access to applications. HTTP is used throughout the web, so is an ideal choice for a transport protocol.

These two standards have been combined to give the SOAP:

$$HTTP + XML = SOAP$$

The media object server (MOS) protocol is a real example of XML messaging. This is used by television news for communication between the newsroom computer and the television equipment.

XML in use

These are some examples of applications for XML that have been developed by media industries. They come from the newspaper, television, book publishing, and multimedia businesses. XML is now ubiquitous throughout the electronic media business. It enables the syndicating and aggregation of content, whether a news story or feature. As publishers look to new distribution channels, the PDA and the e-book, it is vital that re-purposing costs are controlled. The use of XML document types and schema is easing the exchange of information between different systems. There are now standard means to convey vital information about intellectual property rights, essential to the rapid turnaround of content. Some of these examples use a DTD, others have adopted an XML schema.

IPTC, NewsML, and NITF

The International Press Telecommunications Council (IPTC) has published a number of different DTDs to support the syndication of news stories. These include NewsML and news industry text format (NITF). NewsML is XML encoding for news packages. This could include text as NITF and JPEG photographs referenced as links. The package can include alternative versions, like different languages or different formats: rich text format or HTML. A NewsML package can define relationships to other news items, like 'see also' or 'for more detail'.

NITF is specifically for encoding the text of the story. NITF includes information about the story, what subjects and events it covers, where and when it was reported, and most important for the editors, why it is newsworthy. It also includes copyright information.

MPEG-7

MPEG-7 uses extensions to the XML schema language to provide rich descriptions for multimedia content. It is described in more detail in Chapter 10, entitled Content Description Standards.

PRISM

Publishing requirements for industry standard metadata (PRISM) is a set of vocabularies to assist the automation of publishing processes. As print moves to encompass electronic publishing, content is becoming every more re-purposed and re-used. Syndication is becoming even more common. The accelerated pace of business dictates that content exchange becomes easier. The slick management of content exchange needs ready access to rights and pricing information. A picture editor with a pressing deadline may want to use a picture as an image library. It is vital that the price for the use, and the rights information is readily available. Magazines and newspapers may well be forced to shoot new pictures rather than use library shots because there is not the time to resolve the rights.

Leaded asset and content management vendors, publishers, and stock libraries, have all contributed to the development of PRISM.

The PRISM shows that metadata is important for additional uses for original content. So as well as a general-purpose description, it includes comprehensive information on intellectual property rights and the use of that property. The metadata can also be embedded within the resource as inline markup.

PRISM uses XML plus additional concepts like namespace. The metadata uses a simplified form of resource description framework (RDF). PRISM uses the 15 Dublin Core Metadata Initiative (DCMI) elements as a starting point for its description of resources, and also adopts the vocabulary.

It can describe content either by a string of characters, or from a controlled vocabulary. These vocabularies can be international standards like the ISO country codes and the Getty thesaurus of geographical names. Users can also adopt their own controlled vocabularies, perhaps based on internal databases.

PRISM describes content by category or genre. There is a controlled vocabulary for the genre. Examples include biography, cartoon, obituary, press release, and transcript. Another vocabulary is used for presentation types: article, homepage, journal, photo, and index.

PRISM allows users of digital publishing assets to syndicate and aggregate content simply by providing a standard framework for resource description. The exchange of content between different parties that may be using different content management systems will benefit from using the common namespaces. It is equally applicable to newspapers and magazines, plus journals, books, and catalogues.

PRISM is based on existing standards, XML, RDF, and Dublin Core, and uses International controlled vocabularies.

MOS protocol

This XML-based communications protocol was developed for use in radio and television newsrooms. MOS is a media object server. This is a source or repository of media objects, which can be video and audio clips, still images like photographs and graphics, or any other media related to the processes of creating television news.

The news process has five steps. The first is to ingest media objects: agency feeds, video footage, location sound, and still photographs. The video and audio encoded onto video servers, and low-resolution copies made for browsing. The next stage is to assemble the story. The journalist can browse the original media objects and put together the story using the newsroom computer. The journalist can add a voice-over as a new media object. The video and audio objects can then be transferred to a non-linear editor for craft editing. The graphics department will also prepare additional objects that will be composited during transmission.

Next the newsroom computer is used to put together all the stories into a running order for the final broadcast. This is sent as a playlist or rundown to the automation system in playout studio.

This workflow used to take place in a number of islands. The newsroom computer, the character generators and stills stores, and the edit bays, were usually from different vendors. The transport of media had traditionally a group of newsroom equipment vendors collaborated to write the MOS protocol. The goal was to interconnect these islands so that all the different systems could be seamlessly integrated. Using the protocol, stories can flow from feed recording, through graphics and editing to transmission and on to archive. At all stages, journalists and editors can monitor the progress of the elements that are finally assembled live for transmission. A system could be integrated without the MOS protocol. It would need custom interface design, a costly exercise to be avoided.

The MOS protocol uses a DTD to define the tags. The protocol can carry rundown information, and metadata about the media objects. This enables a number of operations that are vital to the rapid assembly of stories. The messages fall into two families, one for communication between the news computer and the object servers, the other message family relate to the running order of the stories; been as videotape, a slow process for the newsroom.

As feeds and tape are ingested to the central file repository, basic metadata can be added. The tags include slug, title, description, and file ID. Servers can be queried to find out what media clips are ready to air. During editing new objects are created. Meanwhile, the running order is assembled. A news editor can query a server to see if the final edit is there ready for transmission, similarly the graphics. Finally, the running order is sent to the automation in the transmission area. The media objects referenced in the playlist can be cued to air by the automation, again using the MOS protocol to communicate.

The MOS protocol is a good example of how the use of XML can simplify system integration. A television station can choose the appropriate hardware to build a newsroom, without having to worry about interfacing problems. Not only that, but the MOS protocol gives the news editors all the media information at their fingertips.

Online information exchange (ONIX)

ONIX is another application of XML as a message format. Traditional book publishers used many formats to distribute information about book titles. The rise of the online booksellers has made this information more important. The potential purchaser is unable to browse titles, as they might in a bookshop. You can see the typical information on the Amazon site: title, author, publisher, price and currency, size, and title image. The publishers realised that a standard format for distributing this information would lower their costs. By using XML, the messages can be created inexpensively by even the smallest publisher. Three bodies administer ONIX internationally: the Book Industry Study Group in the USA, EDItEUR in Europe, and the Book Industry Committee in the UK. The standard is published as an XML DTD. This is used to organise and tag data on a title to create the standard message.

XrML

Many digital assets are protected from unauthorised access by digital rights management (DRM). The content is securely encrypted before storage and distribution. Those parties who meet the terms and conditions for access are given a key. This is then used to decode the cipher that was used for the original encryption. Extensible rights markup language (XrML) is a grammar that can be used to specify the rights and conditions for that access. The XrML standard includes a set of XML schema.

Although XML is human readable, the terms and conditions are often confidential. XrML supports encryption of this part of the message, so it cannot be read as plain text.

A licence grants a user the rights to access content if they meet the conditions laid down by the rights holder. One use for XrML is to enable automatic syndication. By supporting a common language to express the rights and conditions for content access, the content aggregators are freed from tie-ins to proprietary DRM systems.

Summary

SGML started out as a way to format electronic documents. XML has become widely accepted for that same function, but new applications have emerged. These can be viewed as three main groups, and all have been adopted by the developers of digital asset management products:

- Electronic documents
- Inter-application messaging
- Data container

XML is now viewed as a universal tool, which can be found in Microsoft Office, DTP products, e-commerce, and web services. It has been adopted by asset management vendors for messaging between software applications, and as a framework for the storage of metadata.

XML has been subject to much marketing hype, the answer to all the problems of interoperability. Used alone, XML does solve one issue of file interchange, in that a standard format is used. But to be XML, the file has only to be well formed. Great syntax, but what of the semantics? As an analogy, consider this sentence from the MIT professor of linguistics, Noam Chomsky: 'Colourless green ideas sleep furiously'. Grammatically it is fine, it just has no meaning. To this end the DTD and XML schema have been developed.

The early adopters of XML soon found that the old disciplines of typed data used with relational databases dramatically reduced the level of errors when adding records to the database. Quite clearly, something similar was demanded for XML. Enter the XML schema. A good example is the content description language, MPEG-7. This is based on XML schema, which restricts valid metadata to the rules of a description-definition language.

Well there is a reason for the hype. XML enables interoperability, so you can build a system from best-of-breed solutions on software and hardware platforms of your choice. The big advantage of using XML is nothing to do with the primary functionality of a digital asset management system. XML is about the little things: interfacing and software maintenance. These two may sound like nuts and bolts, but they usually prove to be the most expensive component in the purchasing, and in evolving the future needs, of an asset management system.

8 Cataloguing and indexing

Introduction

The catalogue and index give a structure to the asset repository. The index is the primary means to retrieve assets from the repository. Without the index, the repository is just another file server. Scientists have always wanted to catalogue as part of their understanding of the natural world. This desire reached a peak during the eighteenth and nineteenth centuries, as collectors scoured the world for new plants, butterflies, and rocks. Anything that could be packaged and returned home was carefully classified and mounted in glass and mahogany display cases. Museums were no longer just collections of fine art, paintings, and sculpture, but encompassed the breadth of human understanding. The science of classifying this myriad of newly discovered species was called taxonomy. To aid the classification hierarchies were developed.

Meanwhile libraries of the written word had long accepted the need for a classification and indexing. The libraries of the religious communities and the lawmakers had well-established systems for cataloguing. If a researcher were looking for information, then the appropriate book could be identified using the catalogue. Once the book was found and retrieved from the shelves, then the relevant section or chapter could be located by a search of the table of contents or the index.

The table of contents provides a logically ordered outline of a book. It has a hierarchical structure based on sections, chapters, and headings. To provide random access to topics or concepts, the index is more useful. The index is a subjectively selected list of keywords that relate to the topics and is sorted alphabetically (Figure 8.1). Many keywords have tens of page links; so to aid the reader qualifiers are used in the form of subentries. A good index should also list synonyms of the keywords. There is a special kind of index called a concordance, which lists all the important words in a book. A search is usually to retrieve information about concepts rather than words.

Basic computer keyword extraction can be used to generate the index for a single document. If this index were extended to cover hundreds of thousands of documents, and then you searched using single keyword you would expect a result set possibly running into millions. How can this be sensibly filtered?

Setting the goals

Choosing an indexing system is intimately related to the use of the digital asset management system. If you have analysed the workflow of content through the organisation,

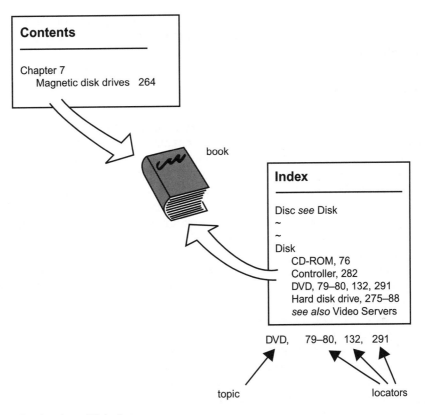

Figure 8.1 The book and its indexes.

different departments have widely varying requirements from a system. But there are common goals. One is to automate repetitive tasks that are costly in human resource. Another is to simply search for wanted information. New paradigms will emerge that were not possible before. New information can be discovered—how do you search for information if you do not know it is there?

These are some of the factors that can influence the choice of the indexing solution:

- Is corporate information structured or unstructured?
- What do you want to do with the information?
- Is it formatted as office documents, images, graphics, or audio and video?
- Is the information arriving in real time, like news feeds?

As time becomes a valuable resource, many corporations want information disseminated immediately. This could be as an aid to public relations. The senior executives of a corporation need to know what the media is saying about them. It could be the stock trader, who is monitoring financial information. So the asset management system has to ingest, filter, and make available the relevant information in a timely fashion. Such processes can be performed manually, but to do this in real time is labour intensive.

Human filtering is subjective, slow, and there is the cost of employment. So many enterprises are looking to computer software to provide answers to the indexing of large volumes of content in real time.

Indexing

The first step when ingesting content into a digital asset management is to generate some form of index. It could be very basic information: file name, author, and file format. To gain the full advantage of digital asset management, a much more comprehensive index is required. This index metadata can then be used for classification and searching. There are well-established techniques for extracting metadata from textual content, but images, video, and audio present more of a challenge. The video or audio content has to be analysed in such a way that data can be extracted in the form of text. That way the metadata can be stored as database fields.

The raw metadata will need pre-processing before an index can be generated. Speech within an audio asset can be analysed and converted to a textual transcript. It is also possible to recognise the voices of different speakers and markup the transcript accordingly. Visual information is much more complex to analyse beyond a simple scene logging. Current techniques offer face recognition, optical character recognition (OCR), and an image signature.

Many of the analysis techniques produce less than perfect results. It is best to combine all the techniques to achieve the highest quality metadata. Some techniques are expensive to apply, so should only be used if really useful. There is not much point in using face recognition if you are indexing a scenic documentary, but if you are working in law enforcement, it would be very useful.

Most indexing needs to operate in real time, especially audio and video (Figure 8.2). This does limit the choices, as some products can only run on a batch basis. It is not

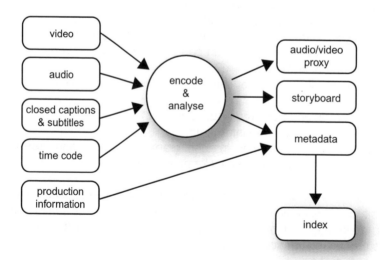

Figure 8.2 Basic audio–video indexing.

practical to play video 10 s at a time, then pause while the processing catches up. For live feeds, like news, it is just not possible to pause. Therefore, any analysis techniques have also to operate in real time.

Index varies in complexity from medium to medium. Content can be split into a number of forms:

- Structured text: databases and spreadsheets
- Unstructured text: word processors documents
- Images: illustrations, drawings, and photographs
- Audio
- Video: film and tape

The first operation is to convert to a digital form. Paper documents can be scanned and processed with an OCR application. Film, stills, or movies can also be scanned into bitmaps or raster image files.

Text indexing

The academic community has a culture of sharing research. Papers carry an abstract, a list of keywords, and references. The business community has different goals. A document is often a means to an end. It may have been written with the expectation that is read once only, then discarded. Typical word processing programs, like Microsoft Word, have comprehensive facilities to save metadata along with a document but there is no obligation to fill out the form (Figure 8.3).

How complete these fields are will depend very much on the author and on corporate policies. It is quite possible that little apart from the author field is filled out (and this is completed automatically by the application). That means that the index will have to be generated by some other process. There are two choices. The first is manual entry by a librarian or archivist. The alternative is to use some form of automation.

Oracle text

Many content and digital asset management systems used the Oracle 9i database as an underlying framework (Figure 8.4). Integrated into the product is a full-text retrieval module called Oracle Text. I am going to use the application as a good example of how a text indexer can operate.

The first stage is a multi-format filter that can convert most office application: word processors, spreadsheets, and presentations including Microsoft Office files and Portable document format (PDF). The files are all converted to a common Hypertext markup language (HTML) format, retaining markup like headings and titles. The next stage is the sectioner. This separates the text from the markup, and can package text into sections: title, body, etc. The text passes to the 'lexer', which filters stopwords and punctuation.

Stopwords are a common concept in document search, if you enter 'What is a stopword' into Google the return page states 'The following words are very common and were not included in your search: '*what*' '*is*' '*a*'. Google ignores common words like pronouns, as well as certain single digits and single letters. Although this improves

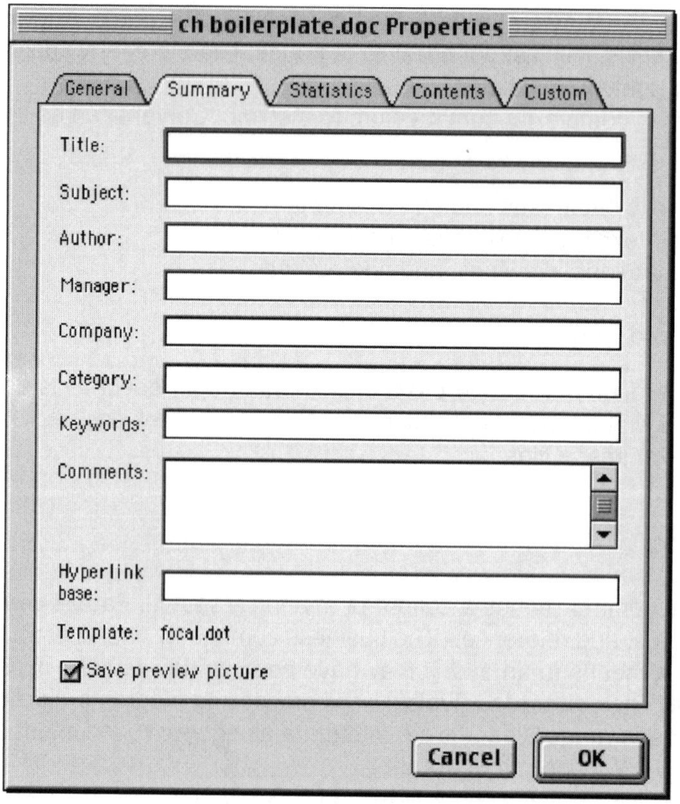

Figure 8.3 Microsoft Word document metadata.

performance, with some search engines the phrase: 'to be or not to be', could be treated as being all stopwords, and would return a null result. In that case, it would have to be treated as a string. The Oracle stopword list can be specified by the user.

The English language is straightforward to section into words, but other languages present more of a challenge. The German language uses compound words, which have to be divided into their component words before indexing.

The output of the lexer is words or tokens. This is turned into an inverted index, so the index is a list of tokens, with each token listing the documents where they occur.

Once documents have been processed, they can be classified and categorised into concepts. As an example, a news agency may want to filter into broad classes like news, sport, lifestyle, and financial. They may want to filter against a thesaurus (or controlled vocabulary) to get a finer-grained categorisation.

Image indexing

The still image is perhaps the most difficult to analyse by a software application. Picture libraries base their core business on selling images from printed or online catalogues.

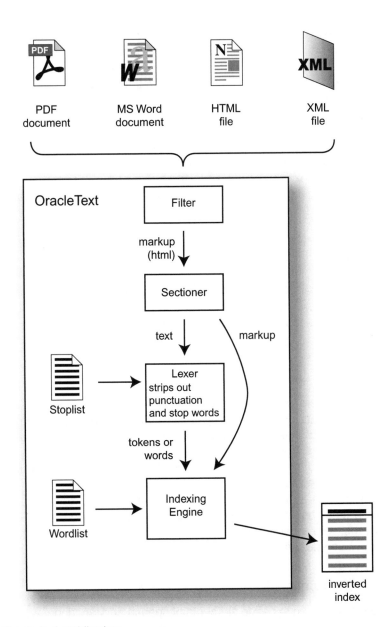

Figure 8.4 Oracle text architecture.

They use skilled cataloguers to manually enter the keywords for each image file. The advent of digital cameras has made it possible to record data at the time of taking; this includes image size (in pixels), compression formats, and other basic image file data. Other information can be recorded, like the camera parameters at the time of taking. Although of possible interest to the photographer, it is not of much use for the end user. Who wants to search for pictures taken at an aperture of *f*/6.3? The user wants descriptive metadata about the content of the image.

There are formal schema for the metadata. One such is the subject reference scheme set up by the International Press Telecommunications Council (IPTC) and the Newspaper Association of America (NAA). It was developed for the categorisation of any news material, text, video, and animation as well as images.

Image attributes

It is possible to search for images by association with an example image, without the need to describe the images in words. The image can be analysed for attributes like colour and saturation, texture and patterns, and these parameters are used as an index. Examples of such indexing are the Dremedia (now Virage) image association filter and IBM's QBIC (query by image content).

Audio indexing

Some basic analysis can be made on an audio signal. Is it music? Is it a silent passage? This can be useful to segment a sound track as an aid to topic or scene recognition. However, the main means of extracting useful metadata from audio is speech-to-text conversion.

Speech analysis

Several speech analysis applications are available for integration into an audio-indexing system. The process is usually referred to as automatic speech recognition (ASR). Telecommunications companies have developed many of the applications for use in automated call centres. The requirements of a general-purpose speech analyser are somewhat different, so the success rate of the different products with your own sound-tracks will need to be evaluated carefully.

If the soundtrack is a trained presenter who is speaking clearly, then the decoding should be excellent. The simplest systems are called *isolated word*. They can only handle single words, with a pause between each word. Normal speech is continuous, so there is no obvious start and finish for each word.

Phonemes and phones

These two terms are used to define elements of speech and language. A phoneme is an atomic unit of sound that that is used to contrast two words within a given language. As an example, the phonemic vowels /ei/ and /ai/ distinguish *tape* from *type*. English has around 40 phonemes, the number depending on regional variations. Typically, English speakers use a repertoire of about 20 vowels and 24 consonants. The number of phonemes varies from language to language.

Continuous speech is made up of elements called phones. A phone is the realisation of a phoneme by a particular speaker using his or her accent and intonation. Even one speaker will use different phones, compare whispering and shouting. The rhythm, stress, and intonation used by a single speaker are called their prosody. Consequently, there is an infinite set of phones. In addition, the preceding and succeeding phones modify the articulation of each phone. Phone represent the sound of speech, and phonemes represent the language.

Therefore, the speech analysis application has to decode the audio input into a sequence of phones. These are then mapped to phonemes and these phonemes are finally converted to text. Many soundtracks have more than one speaker. In a normal dialogue, the speakers will overlap each other. A successful speech analyser has to cope with all these problems.

Some very basic systems can only decode a single speaker's voice. For a digital asset management system, the audio indexing will have to cope with a wide range of speakers. This may be regional accents, or different version of a language: an English person speaking English versus an American speaking English. A system may also need to be multi-lingual. Some systems will only extract keywords from a predefined dictionary.

The speech may be partially masked by a high background noise level. Therefore, a soundtrack like a street interview may not give very good results. A human observer can use binaural hearing to focus on a speaker and exclude ambient noise, the 'cocktail party' effect. The speech analyser does not have this luxury, and can only work on the time-varying spectral characteristics of the soundtrack. Luckily, it is not necessary to decode every word in order to generate metadata. If the transcript is only a partial record of the speech, in all likelihood many of the keywords necessary for an index will still be present.

Hidden Markov modelling

Automatic speech-recognition systems have been under development since the 1960s. By the late 1970s, an IBM mainframe could decode a single sentence in 1 h. The goal of real-time operation with an affordable hardware platform was not realised until around 1990. Successful speech recognition is largely based on statistical techniques, and uses the hidden Markov model (HMM).

Andrei A. Markov was a Russian mathematician who studied around the 1900s in Saint Petersburg. After early work on number theory, he moved on to probability theory. He studied chains of random variables, where a future variable is determined by a present variable. The future variable is independent of the way the present was derived from its predecessors. The observer only sees the input and output of the chain, and the state sequence or chain is hidden.

This work was later developed into the theory of stochastic processes. Around 1960, the work was studied further and was applied to speech processing around 1975 by the James and Jane Baker at Carnegie–Mellon and a team led by F. Jelink at IBM.

The Bakers struck out in a new direction. Earlier research groups were focusing on the context of the original speech. This included what the speaker knew, and what they might say. The Bakers used the statistical relationships of word sequences in normal speech. They constructed a dictionary of phoneme sequences in a word group. They developed an algorithm to decipher a string of spoken words using the probability that the speech matched a word group in their dictionary. This route gave much better results than the contextual systems. The work from those two groups ultimately became to fruition as the products IBM ViaVoice and NaturallySpeaking from Dragon Systems (Dragon is now part of the ScanSoft Group).

The HMM remains at the core of most speech-recognition systems, but has also been applied in many other disciplines, for example in text recognition, image analysis, climatology and in many of the life sciences.

Speaker recognition and identification

Some speech-recognition programs can identify different speakers from their vocal characteristics. We each have frequency profiles and rhythms of speech (the prosody) that can be used to distinguish one speaker from another. The frequency characteristics of speech are a function of the anatomical characteristics of the speaker, including the dimensions of the larynx and throat.

Typical speaker identification operates in several stages. The first is to process the raw audio to detect speech/non-speech boundaries. Structured speech like lectures, presentations, and television news will have a formal structure with distinct boundaries between segments. The next stage is the speech analysis. Each segment can be pro-filed for features of the speech and either matched against a trained profile of a known speaker or marked up as an arbitrarily numbered speaker: 'unknown 1', 'unknown 2' etc. The speaker markup is hyperlinked to the final text transcript using a time reference like the video time code. This means that a transcript of the dialogue between two speakers can be annotated with the names of each speaker.

Speech to text needs a clear soundtrack to get an accurate transcription. The early products were based on systems developed for automated call centres by telecommunication companies. Although these can produce good results with dictated speech, they are not so accurate with the average soundtrack that you may find on a video clip of different speakers.

Video indexing

The primary index for video material is the storyboard. The video-indexing process analyses the video signal and creates a proxy of the content as a storyboard of representative still images or keyframes. This is also called intelligent keyframing.

Keyframes can be extracted in three ways: manually by a trigger from the ingest operator, at fixed time intervals (say every 10 s); or via video analysis to detect segments. In the latter case, the incoming video is analysed for discontinuities that may represent shot or scene changes. A single frame of video that is typical of the segment is grabbed as a bitmap image. Potentially, cuts between different scenes should be easy to detect by a step change in the average luminance level, but flashguns, fireworks, or even fast action easily fools such basic detectors. The analyser should be capable of discriminating between a scene fade and a camera zoom or pan.

Most products include a sensitivity control that can be used to adjust the keyframing to suit the style of the video. A fast action clip will need different settings from a talking head. The sensitivity can be part of a template for the encoder/indexer set up. The goal is to optimise the representation of the story, yet minimise the storage requirements for keyframes.

The keyframe is a thumbnail image, typically 96×72 pixels, with JPEG compression, although there is no reason why it could not be any size up to full-frame video, if storage space allows. It has to be representative of the segment. As an example, if the first frame of a segment were always chosen, what if a fade to black were used as a transition between scenes? The keyframe would be black—not very useful. The video analysis should select a frame from the centre of a sequence of similar frames. The indexers use algorithms to operate on colours, edges, and shapes to pick up differences between successive frames.

Some analysis systems use batch processing. To index from videotape, the system must operate in real time as the video streams from the tape. The application should also run on a low-cost platform, typically a single or dual Pentium workstation.

Face recognition

The security industry has developed a number of solutions that can identify the faces present in a video clip. Some of these products have been integrated into video logging systems. One such is FaceIt from Identix.

The popular method of face recognition is based on eigenfaces. It is used mainly with frontal 'mug-shots' and does not function well in the typical environment of video material that will have varying lighting conditions and different points of view on the subject.

The FaceIt software uses a different approach based on statistical techniques. The founders of the company had been researching how the brain analyses information, specifically how the brain recognises a face in a crowd. Their hypothesis was that the brain focuses on skeletal features of the face, like the size of the eye sockets and their relationship with the nose. From this idea, they developed a way to describe the face as number of facial building elements. They claim to be able to recognise a face to a high precision using between 12 and 40 such elements. The identity is established by the relative positions of these characteristic elements. Each face is represented by a face print that can be stored in a database, and used for matching faces within the video stream.

Face recognition, like speech analysis, needs to be carefully evaluated before purchase. There is much research going on in this area, so performance will no doubt improve with time. The application will have to operate in real time on an affordable workstation.

OCR

Video material often includes captions overlaid by a character generator, typically the lower thirds we see giving the news reporter's name and location. OCR can be used to decode this video information into textual data.

Query by example

The video analyser can generate a data footprint for the colour shapes and textures in the video clip, just as with still images. The movement signature can also be indexed. There has been much research undertaken in the tracking of objects against a cluttered background. One of the results has been the Conditional Density Propagation algorithm, usually abbreviated to *condensation* tracking. The algorithm uses statistical and learning techniques. The simplicity of the algorithm means that the processing requirements are relatively modest. A motion signature as well as the static information can be used to create metadata that can be used for queries of the type, 'find me content that looks like this clip'. One example of such analysis is the Dremedia image association filter (now part of Autonomy's Virage Videologger). This can be useful for editing video; the editor can find a clip, then query for a similar looking clip.

Closed captions (CCs)

Broadcast video material often has CCs. This gives an abbreviated transcript of the soundtrack, so that viewers with impaired hearing can follow a television programme. The textual transcript is embedded in the video stream, hence the qualifier *closed*. Analogue video uses the vertical blanking interval to carry the information, in Europe it is one of the Teletext pages; digital television can use a dedicated data channel. The television receiver decodes the information and renders in as a text box superimposed over the main video display. Subtitles giving a translation of the soundtrack to another language use a similar process. If the original soundtrack is in a foreign language, the translation to the local language may be superimposed over the original video before transmission, this is called *open* captions.

This same CC data can also be used to generate index metadata. The advantage is that the processing is trivial compared with speech analysis. The disadvantage is that only some broadcast video carries CCs. The addition of captions is often the last stage in the workflow during the production processes. Corporate video material is very unlikely to carry the captions.

CCs often carry two chevron markers to indicate a change of speaker: '>>' and three chevrons to indicate story or topic change: '>>>'. This information can be extracted as metadata and used to indicate story segments as an aid to the storyboarding.

The CCs can be used if available, but cannot be relied upon as a primary source of metadata.

Time code

Video and audio metadata are logged against a timeline. The usual time unit for this is video time code. Computers usually count time in millisecond increments from a certain date. Video uses a system that is easier for human to read, and is based upon the basic unit of video, the frame. Since programme tapes rarely exceed 3 h in length, the time code only needs to count up to a maximum duration of 1 day or 24 h. A resolution of one frame is needed. The Society of Motion Picture and Television Engineers (SMPTE) publishs a standard that is used throughout the television industry. This logs each frame in frames, seconds, minutes, and hours.

Edit decision list (EDL)

The edit decision list EDL is a rich source of metadata about the scene structure. Video editing systems can store the list of edits as an EDL. As it carries information about every transition, it can be used to identify individual clips or scenes. The EDL has a *de facto* standard, CMX, but stemming from its age, it is limited in the data it carries. A more recent format that includes compositional data is the Advanced Authoring Format (AAF).

Another rich source of clip-related metadata are the rundowns used for satellite feed recording and by news automation systems. These indicate a sequence in which to transmit the news clips or record the feeds. The rundowns include timing information as well as general metadata about the clips. News is moving towards a standard protocol for metadata information exchange: the Media Object Server protocol or MOS. The rundown information can be transmitted in this format.

Logging audio-visual content

The indexing of text and images is a mature procedure. Systems have been in operation since the 1980s. The metadata for a document or an image is static; it is a single entity referring to the whole. The indexing of video content has presented more of a challenge, partly stemming from the processing power required to analyse the content stream, and partly from the need for a dynamic index.

Two operations are performed when the audio-visual content is ingested. As well as the analysis to extract metadata for the index, a compact file size proxy is generated that can be used as part of the later search and browse for content. With current technology, it is not feasible to make the video asset available for browsing. The files are too large to be kept online, and the bandwidth required for browsing is to great to support more than a handful of users.

The usual approach is to use a hierarchy of proxy representations of the archived content (Figure 8.5):

- Textual metadata
- Storyboard of keyframes
- Low bit-rate streaming video

This means that even the users on a dial-up connection to the digital asset management can browse for content using text descriptions, view the material as a storyboard, and then watch a streamed presentation. They can then order a high-resolution copy for delivery as a tape or by FTP through a system like the TeleStream ClipMail.

The indexing and proxy encoding are generally performed at the same time, but it is not essential. The material can be encoded first, and then indexed later if that suits the workflows.

An audio-visual index is represented as a timeline with a number of parallel channels. The more information that can be indexed, the better the quality of the metadata. A typical logging workstation for a videotape archive will use whatever information is available. Audio and video analysis can be combined with document analysis of productions notes, possibly the original scripts. Much of this is static metadata. Some possible channels of dynamic metadata are shown in Table 8.1.

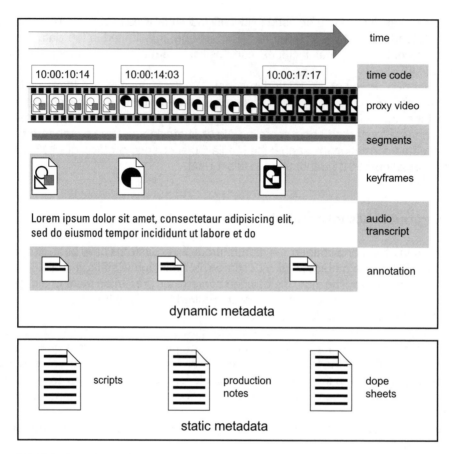

Figure 8.5 Metadata channels on timeline.

Table 8.1 Audio–video metadata channels

Video	Audio	Data
Low-resolution audio–video proxy in MPEG-1 or streaming format		
Thumbnail images representing keyframes	Audio transcript	EDL, rundown
Face recognition	Speaker identification	
In-vision character recognition		
Closed captions, subtitles		
Image attributes	Audio classification	
Time code		

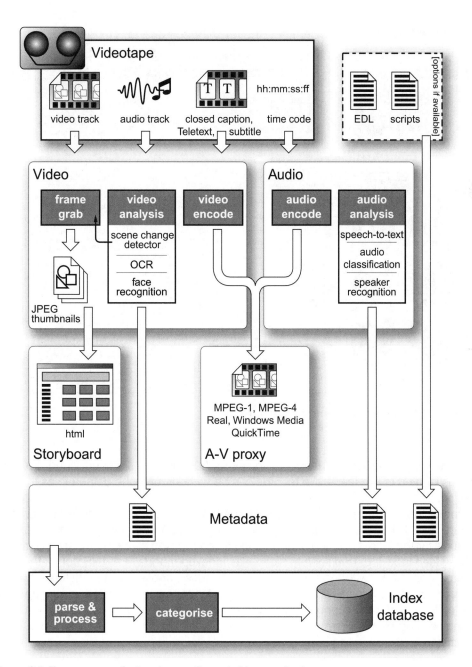

Figure 8.6 The processes for logging audio and video content.

The logging is usually performed on a multi-processor workstation fitted with a video card to offload the video processing from the main CPUs (Figure 8.6). It may be necessary to use different workstations or video and audio to share the processing load, but as PCs are getting ever faster this may no longer be the case. Typical applications

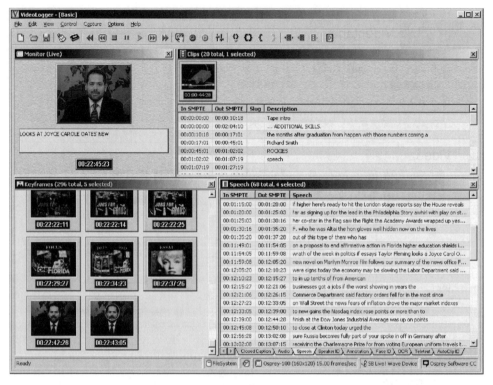

Figure 8.7 VideoLogger user interface: ©Virage Inc.

generate about 1 GByte of metadata for every 50–100 h of encoded video. For continuous logging of live feeds, the records can be written out to the database as they are
created.

One of the most popular indexing systems is Virage's VideoLogger from Autonomy
(Figure 8.7). It has been adopted by many of the leading digital asset management
products for the ingest of video material, and it can be used as a benchmark example of
audio–video indexing. Traditionally, video was indexed manually. A VHS dub of the master tape was made, with the original time code superimposed on the picture—burnt-in
time code. A production assistant would then play the tape and compile a written log of the
time code at each shot change, along with annotations. This could be used to generate
a rough cutting list. This term 'logging' has lived on to describe the process, albeit in an
automated form.

Manual annotation

Although much of this book is about smart systems for managing assets, in many cases the
special capabilities of a human operator to understand the video material is required. The
trained archivist will have many years of experience in tagging material with relevant anno-
tation that will be useful to assist with later searching. Some organisations use controlled

vocabularies to add keywords to the index data channels. That way a user can navigate through a clip using the keywords.

Cataloguing and classification

As you read the marketing collateral for digital asset management products, you will find many different terms used to describe the cataloguing of the content:

- Cataloguing
- Categorisation
- Classification
- Directory
- Ontology
- Taxonomy

Although these terms are often used as if they are interchangeable, they do all have distinct meaning within the context of asset management.

The terms *cataloguing* and *classification* have long been used by librarians. A library catalogue is a list of all the books in alphabetic or some other systematic order. As part of the indexing process, the librarians place documents into subject categories, and give each a class (such as a call number or Dewey Decimal Classification (DDC)) that can be used as an aid to later retrieval.

These terms tend to be used interchangeably with *categorisation*. This is the process of associating a document with one or more subject categories.

A *directory* is an organised set of links, like those on the Yahoo web portal. This gives a view of the site's content as a hierarchy of categories. A directory can cover a single host, a large multi-server site, an intranet, or the web. At each level, the name of the sub-category provides the user with a contextual grouping. As an example, to find videocassette vendors a tree like this has to be followed:

Root > Business and economy > Business to business > Entertainment and media production > Television > Broadcasting equipment > Consumable media

It is quite clear that the user has to have a knowledge of the tree structure to navigate to the required sub-category.

Within the artificial intelligence (AI) community *ontology* is the study of the categories of 'things' within a domain. The word comes from ancient Greek philosophy. It is now used as a logical framework for academic research on the representation of knowledge. An ontology is typically expressed through schema. The relationships of the ontology can be represented graphically through trees, lattices, and Venn diagrams.

Taxonomy is the science of classification. It comes from biology, where it is used to classify species within a hierarchy. Like any classification scheme, biologists have arguments about where various species should be placed in the hierarchy. Modern DNA analysis is helping biologist to refine their taxonomy of living creatures. The concept of the taxonomy has now been extended to include the organisation of any set of information that lies within a defined domain. In informational taxonomies, items can fit into several taxonomic categories.

A *thesaurus* was originally a set of related terms arranged according to their sense, with Roget being the prime example and now the WordNet. Thesauri include synonyms and more complex relationships. These can be broader or narrower terms, related terms, and other forms of words. Latterly it has also become to mean an information retrieval thesaurus. One example is the *Engineering Index Thesaurus* from Elsevier Science (owner of the Focal Press imprint). These thesauri are designed as an aid to find search terms. A thesaurus like *Roget's Thesaurus* is for linguistic understanding.

Taxonomy

As eighteenth century biologists found more and more species, it became necessary to classify the species into groups and hierarchies. Carolus Linnaeas developed a taxonomy of plants and animals. He developed an empirical system that worked up from the individual species. These hierarchies were not new, the Greek philosopher, Porphyry, constructed a semantic network in the third century AD, in his commentary on Aristotle's categories.

The hierarchy that Linnaeas developed is the basis of the current taxonomy of species. The hierarchy divides into ranks: domain, kingdom, class, order, family, genus, and finally species (Figure 8.8).

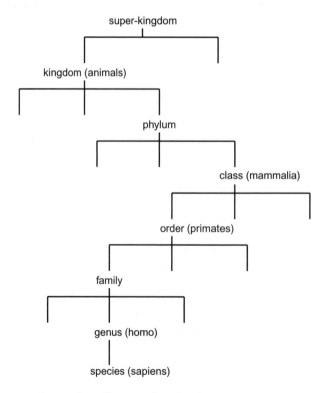

Figure 8.8 The lineage of a species with examples of ranks.

Groups of organisms within one rank are called phyla, taxa, or taxonomic groups. As an example Figure 8.9 shows the taxonomy of the software engineer, and his or her favourite drink.

Taxonomy started as the science of the classification of living organisms. The discipline of taxonomy was adopted by computational linguistics for more general classification tasks. Now the word is used to represent the transformation of classes and categories into hierarchies.

Dewey Decimal Classification (DDC)

For most schoolchildren, perhaps the first classification system we encounter is the Dewey Decimal, as used in the school library. In 1873, a student assistant, Melvil Dewey, working at a college library in upstate New York, conceived the DDC. His hierarchy of classification is based on the decimal system. There are 10 main classes; with each class divided into 10 divisions (Table 8.2). In turn, each division has 10 sections. That means there are a possible 1000 sections, although not all are allocated. Each section can be further subdivided beyond the decimal point to the degree of granularity that is required. A subject can appear in more than one discipline.

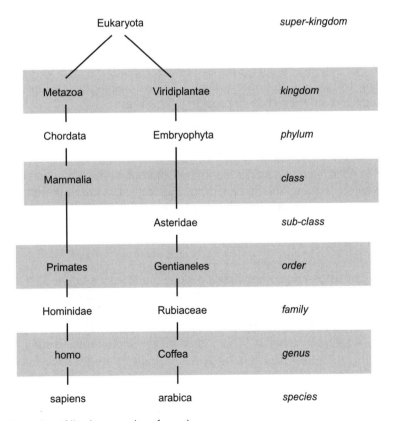

Figure 8.9 Examples of the taxonomies of species.

Table 8.2 DDC main classes

000	Computers, information, and general reference	500	Science
100	Philosophy and psychology	600	Technology
200	Religion	700	Arts and recreation
300	Social sciences	800	Literature
400	Language	900	History and geography

The system does show its age, it was conceived well before electronics or information technology. The, yet to be invented, digital computer has been shoehorned in between 001 Knowledge; 002 the Book; 003 Systems, and 010 Bibliography, viz:

- 004 Data-processing computer science
- 005 Computer programming, programs, and data
- 006 Special computer methods.

In a similar way, the whole of electronics in lumped into 621 as 'Applied Physics'. Older disciplines have a much finer granularity. Perhaps this is a lesson in the design of taxonomies, that they should be extensible. That said it is the most widely used classification system in the world. It has been adopted in 135 countries; the numeric index means that it is language independent. Dewey has been called the father of modern librarianship, not only did he set up the classification hierarchy, but he also spent most of his working life striving to improve libraries. After helping to set up the American Library Association, he served as its president for 2 years.

Hierarchy

A catalogue is not limited to a single hierarchy. Different hierarchies can be used to categorise the same content. This is called polyhierarchy. It allows different views of the same content, tailored to suit different sets of users.

Ontology

Back in days of Aristotle and other Greek philosophers, they searched for a truth about the existence of man. This branch of the science of metaphysics is called ontology. It is the study of the nature of being. The AI community have adopted the term ontology, but with a much narrower meaning. They say that if something 'exists' it can be represented by an abstract schema. This does raise fundamental issues that cannot be satisfactorily answered. There is no absolute truth as to the classification used to construct a schema.

Given an archive of documents, no two archivists will reach a common hierarchy for the classification of that archive. One way around is to have polyhierarchies. But do the end users, making a search, share that same view of the world? To give an example, a production assistant on a video production will look for a programme tape through a hierarchy that possibly runs like this:

Videotapes > [Name of production] > Master tapes > Tape number

The librarian in the tape vault may look this way:

Videotapes > Digibeta > Large cassettes > Tape number

Both classifications are perfectly valid, but represent a different understanding of the world of videotapes. Some in the information research community have suggested avoiding the term 'ontology', but the word does look very impressive in marketing collateral.

Suppliers of smart search systems have advocated that we should avoid classification as a way to search, and focus on conceptual searching using statistically based semantic techniques. That does not mean that classification should be avoided altogether. It has uses for the archivist, and for rapid searching by those who understand the hierarchy.

The classification of documents presents more problems than physical objects. A biologist can classify an object like a flower because it can be considered as a single entity. A document about the ramifications of a regime change in Iraq could be classified under Arab sociology, global oil politics, the relationship between Islam and Christianity, Middle-Eastern history. A wide-ranging article may cover several disciplines, so where is it to be classified? The way around this is to categorise the documents by its primary concept, then link to other concepts in clusters. So a piece on a politician may be linked with an important event that takes place in a certain location; for example, Churchill, World War 2 conference, and Yalta. These three concepts can be linked as a cluster. Searching on the cluster should retrieve all the documents that contain the three concepts. The documents may well be classified under Churchill or World War 2, but the cluster can refer both categories.

That may sound like a Boolean search, but the cluster exists as an entity in the catalogue, so it can be seen by anyone browsing. Contrast a Boolean query, which only creates the cluster at the run-time of the search.

Auto-categorisation

One of the goals of the implementation of a digital asset management is to automate a business and to free the staff resources from costly manual processes. Any corporation that has to ingest large numbers of content files is going to have problems manually allocating files to a location in their corporate taxonomy. The idea of automatically categorising content could offer a solution. Unfortunately, the process of categorisation is not trivial, it requires an understanding of the concepts covered by the item of content. A simple text analysis will produce very poor results.

The starting point for auto-classification is to create a corporate taxonomy. This may already exist; but if it does not, you will not have to start from scratch. Most industries already have templates to start with, and this can be adapted to suit the specifics of your organisation. Once the taxonomy is in place, then one of the automatic categorisation products can then be used to process the documents into the appropriate classes.

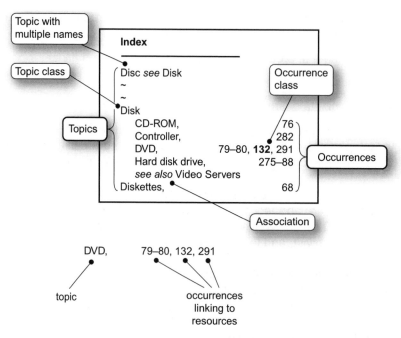

Figure 8.10 Book index with topic map terminology.

Topic maps

Topic maps have been proposed as another approach to the indexing of content. A topic map combines the model of the book index with the semantic network. If the book index is described using the terminology of topic maps, the index entries describe topics, and the page numbers are occurrences of those topics. Topics can be associated using reference '*see* Disk'. Topics can be associated with the reference '*see also*'. A topic may be known by several names: 'disk' and 'disc'. The topics can be split into classes, so the class 'disk', can have sub-topics. Occurrences can also be classified as, for example, a bold page number could refer to the primary entry, and roman font page numbers being used for secondary occurrences (Figure 8.10).

The topic map can be viewed as a number of layers. The resource layer represents the content that is to be mapped into topics. Each file or resource is referenced by a universal resource identifier (URI). The topics are concepts within the resources. Therefore, a collection of topics gives a map of the information resources. Each concept may occur in many of the resources, so the topic is represented by a multi-headed link. A topic may be known by synonyms, so can have multiple names. Similar topics can be related with associations (Figure 8.11). Topics can also be grouped into classes. This is building up much like a semantic network, hence the description as a combination of the book index and network.

Database index

This is a special type of index that is often found in digital asset management systems. Many DBMS products have the facility to index a table. The index is created from a column

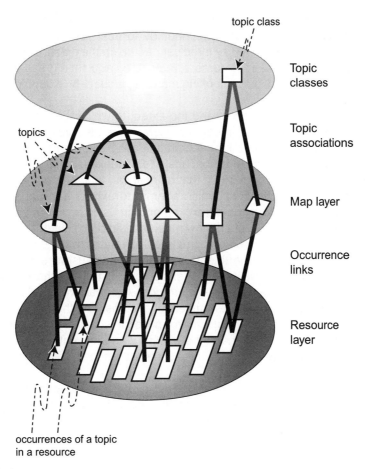

topic class

Topic
classes

topics

Topic
associations

Map layer

Occurrence
links

Resource
layer

occurrences of a topic
in a resource

Figure 8.11 Topic maps.

in the table. To take the book example again, the author column could be used as an index. The index can address records directly. Rather than searching through all the records to find a specific author by a standard structured query language (SQL) query, the index acts as a lookup table directly to the records.

Summary

One of the core features of a digital asset management system is the ability to index the content, to give it metadata. Many of the methods are not new; librarians have developed them over a century or more. To accommodate the special requirement of multimedia content, their ideas have been adapted and extended.

We have to index content so that we can find it at a later date. There are two main types of index, one is as text, and the other is by visual characteristics. Unstructured textual documents and audio can both be processed to extract concepts and keywords. So a human-readable index can be generated. Still images and video present more of a challenge. We cannot expect current technology to describe the images as humans might understand them. We could say a red car parked on the grass. But it could analyse the content by colour layout and textures, a red oblong against a green area. This information could be used to find similar looking material, a query by example, but would not search for 'cars'.

The detail collected for the index, and the extent to which the index is categorised, depends upon many factors. One important factor will be the size of the repository. With text documents, there is a limit to the metadata: it can be keywords or concepts. Video and audio content presents far more options. Most indexing solutions aim to create a textual representation of the content. At that point, it can then be treated as a text document. There are some applications which attempt to extract a visual signature of an image. Such signatures can be compared, rather than using an intermediate text representation. A judgment will be needed; how much should be collected?

Content can be stored in a directory structure that relates to the business. To cite two examples, it could be split by departments, workgroups, and users; or it could be divided by projects. Such a philosophy is just an extension of the structure that may already exist on the company's file servers. Such a system does not scale very well. A large corporation will soon accumulate very large numbers of documents within each directory folder. This directory has become little more than an administrative convenience for the IT department. One option is to abandon the directory and leave it to the asset management to structure the storage. The retrieval of content then relies totally on a search of the metadata.

It may well be more efficient to consider different frameworks for the management of different types of content. Different approaches could be taken for the classification of text documents, images, and multimedia.

9 Search engines

Introduction

We use language to express concepts and ideas. The richness of languages means that there are many different ways to express the same concept. We can use different words in different grammatical constructions, all to express the same concept. Here lies the problem with search; we might express a concept one way. The entry in the index for an occurrence of that concept will not be an exact match. The designers of the index and search applications attempt to solve this difficult problem.

One of the many advantages claimed for digital asset management is the ability to quickly search the content repository to find relevant information. Whether the application lives up to that claim depends very much on the precision and recall abilities of the search engine. Although cataloguing and search are different operations, and undertaken by different users, the two are usually components of the same application. Consequently, the catalogue index is prepared for a specific search engine.

There are two ways to find content. If you are familiar with the taxonomy, you can search through a directory tree until you locate the wanted file. The other way is to use some form of search engine. The first route assumes that you are familiar with the contents of the file. As a repository grows in size this rapidly becomes untenable. Most people can even lose track of files on the local drive on their desktop computer.

Databases have long had the facility to query the data to retrieve records. The simplest search is to enter a string of characters, then search the records for occurrences of that string. The first drawback with this is that the result set can be very large. The second is that you may not know what string the author used. If you are looking for documents on a given subject, it is unlikely that you will know the title. These simple searches may be adequate for a computer user who is searching their local disk, but it does not scale.

If you do not know the title or author of a document, the next step is to use keywords to attempt the location of document. This relies upon the author saving a number of keyword with the document. An alternative is to use a third party like a librarian or archivist to index the document. Both these processes have proved to be inconsistent. The content creators are often reluctant to record good index information, and the separate indexing of documents is labour intensive and subjective. The alternative is to use automatic processes that can attempt objectivity.

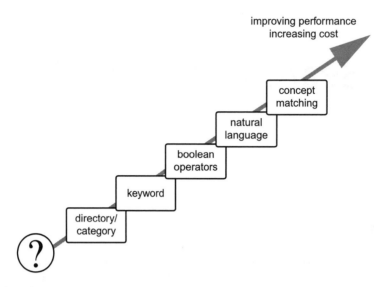

Figure 9.1 Search methods.

To reduce the number of results to a query, operators can be used to qualify the search. The most common are the Boolean operators: AND, OR, and NOT. As the repository grows in size, these basic searches are going to produce far too many results. If you want more accurate and precise results, then a more intelligent search will have to be used. Syntactic and semantic analysis can be used along with concept matching to produce a more relevant result.

A keyword search will tend to produce a very large result set (Figure 9.1). So far I have been describing the search of structured data. The title, author, and keywords are all stored in database columns. Most content is not structured, so the body of a document is ignored in the search.

The alternative is to generate a structured index from the unstructured content. To be useful, the search engine has to produce results that are accurate and relevant. The quality of the metadata will have large effect on the search. This indexing process is very important in ensuring that the result of a search is useful.

The book and libraries

The book publishers and the librarians have been running formal systems to catalogue and reference the printed word for hundreds of years. Their experience, and the systems that they have developed, paved the way for similar cataloguing of multimedia content.

Searching within a book

As a successful application of indexing applied to a large body of text, it is useful to examine the book. There are two ways to navigate a book. The primary means is the contents. This is a logical listing of the chapters and, if used, the section headings. The contents will have entries listing the headings and sub-heading within each chapter.

The other way to find the desired information within the book is to use the index. The index provides an alphabetical listing of the topics rather than the headings, with associated page number references.

The table of contents provides navigation through the author's structure. The index provides random access to the level of passages and paragraphs. The index may also use synonyms to aid the reader.

There are conventions for the compilation of the index. The index normally references by nouns or noun phrases. An index entry may have sub-entries that are semantically or syntactically related. Sub-entries may also be used as sub-divisions where the main entry covers many topics in the book. As an example an entry on disk devices could read:

Disk
  Compact disk (CD)   34
  Digital versatile disk (DVD) 37
  Hard drives   78

An index may often have cross-references to additional entries, *see* and *see also*. Note that the index is not just a collection of keywords, it is a list of occurrences of a concept or topic. If every occurrence of every noun within the text were used to create the index, in all probability, it would be too large and each index would have too many page references. This demonstrates that the way an index is generated is crucial to ensuring its usefulness. A typical index has about three entries per page of text; so that we could have 1000–2000 for a typical volume. The index entries have to be carefully chosen to accurately reflect the significant passages, and to reference those passages by a single noun or phrase.

Searching for a book

A book is just one document. In a large repository of hundreds of thousands of articles, documents and books, the overall index is going to have millions of entries. How is that going to be generated, managed and searched, and produce useful results?

Compare the book with a web portal. Pages about disks drives can be located by drilling down through the category tree:

Home > Computers and Internet > Hardware > Storage > Hard disk drives.

Alternatively, the search form can be used, and hopefully will take the user directly to the same results.

One lesson that can be taken from the example of the book is that there is more than one way to find the required content. The first is the table of contents. This provides a structured and hierarchical view from the top down of the book as chapters. The second is the index, a bottom up and unstructured view of the topics within the text.

When a book is published, it is assigned a unique identifier, the International Standard Book Number (ISBN). The number identifies a specific edition of a specific title in a specific format, so a hardback and softback edition will have different ISBNs. There is another unique identifier for periodicals called the International Standard Serial Number (ISSN). In this context, the word serial refers to a serial publications, which includes journals, newspapers, and newsletters.

If a book is chosen for inclusion for the United States Library of Congress, it will also be assigned a Library of Congress Control Number (LCCN). Note that book will always have an ISBN, but not necessarily an LCCN.

The LCCN encapsulates very little information, just a year and serial number. The ISBN is derived from a group identifier for national, or language groupings of publishers; a publisher identifier; and a unique title number.

Libraries will have a catalogue of books with perhaps 10 record fields per book. As an example, the British Library has an online search for potential lenders. You can search on any of the record fields:

- Author/editor:
- Organisation:
- Title:
- Subject:
- Publisher details:
- ISBN/ISSN:
- Date of publication:

This is an example for a record for a single ISBN:

Title:	The technology of video and audio streaming. Edited by David Austerberry
Joint author/editor:	Austerberry, David
Subject:	Streaming technology (Telecommunications)
Subject:	Web site development
Place of publication:	Oxford
Publisher name:	Focal
Date of publication:	2002
Description:	352p.. ill.. 25cm. pbk
ISBN:	024051694x. m
Shelfmark:	m02/22779

Searching by ISBN will naturally return a single record. Note that the record includes a pointer to the location of the book, the *shelfmark*.

But what if you do not know a likely author's name or title covering a subject of interest? You could search by the subject field. Entering 'web site development' in the subject field returns over 100 items. How do you narrow the search? The full record gives no indication of the content. It is for a beginner, is it for an expert? Does it have a commercial or academic slant? There are no hyperlinks to the publisher, to find further information—you have reached a blind alley.

This example cites the pitfalls of searching. The catalogue has rigorous metadata that enables the content to be traced to a library shelf, but only if you know the title, author, or ISBN. But how do you discover this information. Without prior knowledge of the metadata, you cannot find useful information. Have you ever looked for a business or service in yellow pages and been stymied by the categories that are offered?

The index is not only use for discovery of information. It has also been a tool of censorship. As part of the counter-reformation, in 1559 the Pope Paul IV set up a list of prohibited books, called the Index Librorum. This was an attempt to prevent Catholics from reading the new ideas published in books and pamphlets by Luther and Calvin. There was an associated list of books which could be read as long as certain passages were removed, the Index Expurgatorius.

Text searching

Most searches rely on characteristics of the content being expressed as text, usually in a formal metadata structure. This text description can then be used to build up an index to the content. The primary means of searching is to look for a match between the search keywords and the index. Search engines may process groups of keywords, for example '*moving picture experts group (MPEG)-2, boats, fishing, night*' or can use natural language, '*find me MPEG-2 material about boats fishing at night*'.

There are four main categories of search:

- Keyword
- Boolean query
- Natural language
- Concept matching.

Although keyword searches are simple to implement, they can produce far too many results, perhaps thousands. The index may be ranked by relevance, so that the result set will be ordered by the relevance. Most search engines can use Boolean operators to qualify the search.

With a successful digital asset management system staff should spend less time looking for content than before the system was deployed. This requirement is not going to be met if the result set includes references to tens of thousands of possible media files then. One method of narrowing the search is to drill down through a category tree. So in the example you can select '*Content > Video > People > Occupations > Digital > MPEG-2*' then search for '*fishing, boat, night*'. That way you can avoid spurious results for 'night' or boats that are not used for fishing.

Users of very large collections of assets have benefited from search engines that apply techniques from artificial intelligence (AI). The idea of concept matching has proved to be successful in improving the accuracy of a search. Many of the more sophisticated products use a combination of natural language processing and concept matching. They also support keywords and Boolean operators, and allow category selection. All these techniques can be combined to provide optimum results.

Basic text searching

The keyword search is the basic text search. It has many disadvantages; the first is that it does not take account of the relevance of an index record. The quality of the results can be improved by editing the keywords and their associations (or topics) for each data record, but this is very labour intensive. It is also inconsistent and will vary from person to person, and as a result is subject to misclassification. The classification criteria may change with time. An early newsclip of Bill Clinton was catalogued as 'Clinton with intern'. It was not deemed important to list the names of interns. It was only later that 'Monica Lewinsky' assumed importance as a search criterion. In that case the only way to find such material was to view all clips with interns.

Some tagging schemes expect the author to add all necessary keywords and classifications. Unfortunately, you cannot force content creators to add metadata, so the index is often of poor quality. Classifications like 'general' or 'miscellaneous' abound.

One way around these problems of a large result set is to write Boolean expressions to narrow the search. But this is shifting the onus on search relevance to the user; many people rarely use more than one or two keywords.

Another method is to rank results by popularity. This is great if you are looking for popular material, but with any large content repository, some material will be accessed very rarely. Just because content is not popular it does not mean that it is irrelevant. It may be an obscure reference that leads to the real nuggets of information.

Boolean search operators

Text searches can be improved by entering Boolean qualifiers. Groups of words can be combined by operators such as AND, OR, and NOT. Several expressions can be combined using parentheses to narrow the results. '*George AND Washington*' would return three presidents, as content containing 'George Bush in Washington DC' would be a valid result. To narrow the search, a compound expression could be used: '*George* AND *Washington* NOT (*DC* OR *state* OR *District of Columbia*)'.

Many search engines offer further search operators. There is no standard syntax for the operators; it varies from vendor to vendor. Some common operators are proximity operators, strings, and wildcards.

Proximity operators will return two words within a given distance from each other. For example, to request words up to two words away, 'red *near + 2* car' would return 'red car', and 'red convertible car' but not 'red-haired man driving a car'. The proximity can usually be defined with the search words in any order, or alternatively in the order as the search expression.

To search for a string of words as a phrase or group, the search expression can be enclosed in quotes. This will return results only if they include the character string as specified.

Sometimes you may want to search with wildcard characters. This is useful where a word may have alternative spellings or you want to use a common word root.

Most keyword search excludes frequently occurring words like 'a', 'the'. These are called stop words. Although most exclude 'and' and 'or' some natural language processors can interpret these as Boolean operators.

Word stemming

Word stemming is a technique used by search engines to find different inflections of a word. In linguistics, a more correct description for stemming would be inflectional morphology. Stemming is found more in Latin than modern languages like English.

Word stemming is also used as part of natural language processing, but can be used with a basic keyword search. A stemming algorithm will generate the word stem and return all index entries based on the different inflections of the word. In the absence of stemming, you may have to manually truncate a word to its stem. Wildcards can also be used to pick up words with a common stem.

Similar to the stem is the root word as in *land*: landed, landing, landmark, landlady, and landscape.

Fuzzy searching

Fuzzy searches are tolerant of spelling errors. These errors can occur at source and in the search criteria. One is that the index may have misspellings. This could easily be the case if documents have been scanned and then analysed using optical character recognition. The other reason may be mistyping by the user.

As well as spelling errors, it may also be differences in spellings between versions of a language, English from England versus American English: colour and color, centre and center. These differences occur even more so with proper nouns like peoples names and places.

With a fuzzy search, you can type a close spelling, possibly with wildcards, and the engine will find close matches using a pattern-matching algorithm. The drawback is that they can produce irrelevant results from words with close spelling, but completely different meanings. This is where concept matching is a powerful technique to produce a more relevant result set.

SOUNDEX

This was originally used to search for personal names. Family names have evolved into many spellings, yet still sound the same, 'Smith' and 'Psmythe'. Geneologists developed a coding system to represent surnames by the way they sound. This can be extended for any words, so a SOUNDEX search picks up words that sound like the search entry.

Parametric selection

It is often useful to narrow a search by specifying the basic file parameters that are supported by the operating system. These could be file type, for example MPEG-2 or JPEG files, the creation date of the file, or file sizes.

Tagged search

As more content is formulated using extensible markup language (XML), this structured content can be searched by tags. The user should be given the ability to search by tag. This will make for quicker searching and can lower the processing required by the search engine to the benefit of other users.

Directory search

Another way to produce a more relevant result is to search within a category. Again, the onus is put on the user. This is the same as the search used in a computer file directory.

Directory searching becomes more limited the more branches to the directory tree. It also relies upon the user understanding the chosen hierarchy. It is even possible to use polyhierarchies to reach a given file by different routes. The directory approach can be useful if you are very familiar with the structure, but there is a limit to the usefulness of such trees when accessing very large asset repositories.

Natural language search

The main alternative to the use of keyword searches, possibly enhanced with Boolean and other operators, is to use the natural language search. The user enters their query in plain English rather than a few keywords. The natural language carries many quali-fiers that can be used to narrow a search. Using computational linguistics, a natural lan-guage processor can extract more useful information than would be the case with two or three keywords. This is much easier for many users than to construct a, possibly com-plex, Boolean expression.

The user query is processed in several stages before submission to a conventional search algorithm (Figure 9.2). The first stage is syntactic analysis:

- Tokenise
- Tagger
- Stemming or inflectional morphology
- Noun phrase syntax.

Then the word roots are semantically expanded to include synonyms:

- Semantic network.

The result is a number of concepts that are forwarded to the search for matching with the indices in the catalogue database. The result set is further processed to rank the results according to a relevance rating.

Tokenise

The first stage in natural language processing is to divide the query text into tokens. Any punctuation is stripped along with stopwords. These are very commonly used words that do not contribute to the search; examples are 'a' and 'the'. The stopwords will be substi-tuted by some code to indicate their former presence. This is for use later in proximity searches. Some words are treated as multiple word groups, like 'real estate'.

Tagger

The tokenised words can be tagged as nouns, verbs, etcetera, by a part-of-speech tagger. The Church tagger is the basis for such analysis. A tagger can use rule-based or stochastic techniques to generate the tags. The Hidden Markov model has also been used for speech tagging.

Stemming

Stemming generates the different inflexions of a word. An inflection is a grammat-ical form of a word. Its use varies from language to language and is usually a suffix.

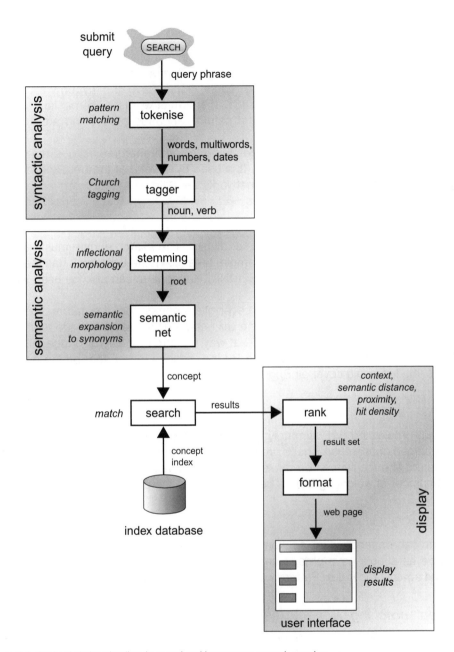

Figure 9.2 Typical data pipeline in a natural language search engine.

Nouns inflect for gender and number, so in English that would be the plural (noun, nouns). In English inflexion is more prevalent with verbs. They inflect for tense, number, and person as in search, searches, searching, and searched. Stemming has to cope with irregular verbs that can inflect as different forms: swim, swam, swum, and swimming.

Stemming is also called inflectional morphology.

Semantic net

A semantic network is like a thesaurus. It generates synonyms and hypernyms for the words. A synonym is a word with a similar sense to the original word; a hypernym is the superordinate of a word. Therefore, a *horse* would have the hypernym *mammal*. Relationships between words can be lexical (the form of words) or semantic (the meaning of words). The relationships used in natural language processing are known as structural semantics.

One popular thesaurus is the WordNet; this is a comprehensive list of synonyms and the other relationships between words. It is used by several of the best-known search engines as the basis of their semantic networks.

Names, personal, and place

Personal names can exit in many forms or aliases. The search engine must be able to cope with the different forms. As an example, take the name Edward; it has the aliases Ed, Eddie, Eddy, Ted, and Teddy. The SOUNDEX algorithm can also be used with personal names.

A thesaurus like WordNet does not cover place names, but the information can be found in a gazetteers. The search engine will need a gazetteer to provide relationships like those between town and country. That way a search for a river bridge in England could return results indexed as London Bridge, bridges in London, bridge over River Thames, the list would cover all English rivers and towns.

Ranking

The input processing will ultimately generate words representing the concept of the search phrase or sentence. These are matched against the index database, and a result set created. The results can be ranked by their calculated relevance. This is generated from a number of weighting factors generated during the preprocessing.

Pattern recognition

The term pattern recognition is taken to mean different operations by different vendors. It can be as simple as a phrase search where the query is treated as a string and matched against the index. Pattern matching is also used for fuzzy searching.

Concept matching

Structured content is represented as fields of data, often complying with a data dictionary. Unstructured content is far more complex. It is often expressions of concepts and ideas, masquerading as words and phrases. It requires an understanding of the underlying concepts to achieve an accurate match between the concepts of the original content and the concept encapsulated by the query. The developments in computational linguistics have been applied to attempt understanding of both the asset library and the query. If that can be achieved, then a match should produce a more precise and relevant result set to the original query.

Problems in natural language

Natural language is very rich. We can express a concept in so many different ways. To solve that many keyword searches use a thesaurus. This can be counterproductive, in that the result set increases rather than decreases as hits from synonyms are added. The same probabilistic techniques that are used for indexing can also be applied to concept extraction.

Some languages use many constructs that can only be understood in context. Some words can function as nouns or verbs, and the meaning can only be gleaned from the context. An example of such a word would be 'set', a group of sets, concrete sets.

Concept matching takes into account the context of the terms in the query. It uses pattern matching to extract a signature of the key concepts.

Bayesian forecasting and statistics

One knowledge management system that has been used in asset management systems is autonomy. They use a number of probabilistic modelling techniques to extract concepts. One technique used is based on Shannon's Information Theory. This has been used in communications theory to model information carried by noisy channels.

Speech and language use redundancy to ensure that ideas can be conveyed in noisy environments and to reinforce understanding. If you compare speech with the written words, speech will often repeat each concept twice, but expressed in different ways. Speakers will often add padding to give themselves time to think. Statistical inference can be used to learn from such noisy data.

Query by example

Another way to search is the query by example. The alternative to submitting a keyword or a natural language query is to submit a sample asset. The engine then finds similar assets. Again, this can be achieved by concept matching.

Thesaurus and WordNet

Many search engines use a thesaurus to aid the search. The thesaurus uses synonyms and antonyms to semantically expand a keyword.

Peter Mark Roget wrote the first English language thesaurus in the first half of the nineteenth century. It was finally published in 1852 after 50 years of work. Before Roget, many lexographers had compiled list of words with their meanings, listed alphabetically. This concept described the signification or the idea that the word is meant to convey. Roget's step was to turn this around and to list words in idiomatic combinations according to the ideas that they expressed.

He ranked synonyms into classes of categories, sub-divided into sections:

1. Abstract relations
2. Space
3. Material world
4. Intellect

5. Volition
6. Sentient and moral powers.

Each category was then divided into topics or heads of signification. Each idea is followed by the opposite or contrasting idea. Note the use of the word 'topic', a term that was to be used later in the technology of topic maps. Although an idea can be accessed through the classification tree, an index is also provided to look up keywords. As an example:

Class I. Abstract relations; I Existence; 1°Abstract; 1. Existence

There, under the possibility of existence, is *ontology*.

Since Roget's time, the thesaurus has been formalised into two International Standards Organisation (ISO) standards: ISO 2788 covers single language thesaurus and ISO 5964 for multi-lingual thesauri. Specialist thesauri have been developed to cover the terms used in the professions. So there are legal and scientific thesauri specifically aimed at using keywords to retrieve records from a database.

WordNet

The WordNet is a computerised dictionary developed by George Miller, a Professor at Princeton. He wanted a dictionary to use as part of his tests to establish how children learn language, but was annoyed by the cost of commercial dictionaries, so out of frustration decided to set up his own. He decided to extend beyond a list of definitions and to show semantic associations with other words. The fruition of his work is the WordNet.

The meaning of a word in WordNet is called its *sense*. A word with several meanings or senses is called *polysemic*. Each different meaning has a set of synonyms called a *synset*. A synonym is another word that means exactly or nearly the same as another. Therefore, a word can have several senses, and each sense has a set of synonyms.

An entry in WordNet gives the following information:

- Definition, sense by sense and then for each sense
- Synonyms
- Antonyms
- Hypernyms and hyponyms
- Meronyms.

Hyponyms (members of a class) are kinds of hypernyms (specific instances).

The original net was American English, but is now available in many other languages including Catalan, Czech, Danish, Dutch, English, French, German, Greek, Italian, Norwegian, Portuguese, Russian, Spanish, and Swedish.

Alternatives to text searching

So far, the search has been text oriented. But digital assets include images, video, and audio. In their raw form, there is no textual information. Still images and video can be analysed to various degrees of success to produce information like the names of faces.

Such technologies have a background in security surveillance. So, although the search is still entered as keywords, the index data is textual information extracted from the images. Similar analysis can be applied to audio, for example speech recognition.

Some indexing systems can generate a description or signature of an image. This could be used to search for a similar image through pattern recognition.

Security

Most corporations will have confidential information in the asset repository. The search engine will need to be able to index all the assets, but the search results should be limited to assets that the user is authorised to view. This means that the search engine has to be intimately linked to the asset management security services. One way to implement this is to use an lightweight directory access protocol (LDAP) server.

How to assess search engines

The choice of a search engine for your digital asset management will be a very important decision. One of the main reasons to use asset management is to make content accessible, easy to find. A poor search engine will severely impair the ready acceptance of the system by corporate users. Some of the most successful systems which used very large archives use AI to attempt to 'understand' the content. For a small repository, the cost of such systems would not be warranted, a basic text search would be perfectly adequate.

The vendors' collateral has to be carefully read. As if to illustrate the problems of concept extraction, different vendors use the same words but with different meanings.

So there is no one solution. I would advocate proper trials on your sample of own repository. It is helpful to see systems already deployed at similar sized businesses to get a feel for their efficacy. Such visits should always be treated with a degree of scepticism. If the business made a bad purchasing decision, they may not want to admit such.

Two factors are key to the search engine performance: recall and precision. Recall measures the proportion of assets that match the criteria that are retrieved. Precision ranks the relevance of the results. Did it find all the right stuff, and did it ignore everything else? The success of the search is very much dependent on the quality of the index.

How good is the index going to be? Is data structured or unstructured? Can users formulate their own structured queries? A multi-national company may need the ability to search content across several languages from criteria in only one of those languages. Some industries have their own controlled vocabularies, gazetteers, and thesauri. These may need to be purchased and linked to the search engine. Is this easy or does it require expensive professional services?

The user interface

Formatting the results

Most search engines will rank the result set by relevance. This information can be extracted in many ways. Most rely on statistics gathered during the search. How many query words were found, how many concepts? What is the semantic distance? The closer the meaning query words to the index, the higher the rating.

One common way is by proximity of keywords. Adjacent words will be rated higher than those at a distance. Concept matching can generate a weighting factor to rank strongly related concepts higher than loosely related concepts.

The keywords and concepts are often highlighted when the user looks at the results. This makes it easy to quickly establish whether the document is relevant. One problem that can arise with documents is that a list of titles is produced, but that is insufficient to describe the contents. A summary is the ideal, but many documents are ingested without one. Some index applications can generate summaries of the document.

The most self-evident search is the image library. The thumbnails show straightaway the relevance of the results. With video content most search engines also display images or frame grabs. The initial view is thumbnails in a storyboard. If a clip looks interesting, then you can watch a low-resolution preview. This proxy is a streaming format like Windows Media, QuickTime, or RealVideo.

Video search

The user interface will vary according to the content. The most complex interface will be for video repositories. This example is the Blue Order Media Archive (Figure 9.3).

Figure 9.3 Media Archive user interface, image courtesy Blue Order.

The interface has three windows: search, results, and file detail. The search form allows the user to set a number of qualifiers: media type (video/audio/image/text), category (sports), time frame (this month), sort parameter (duration), and the size of the result set.

The result set shows the title and duration of the video clips. The large pane shows the video clip as a storyboard.

Summary

It is often cited that knowledge workers waste up to one-quarter of their time searching for information. Basic text searches are useful if you already have key information about the content. If not the simple search can return so many results that it is of very little use. The less you know, the more you will find. Important assets might as well be hidden if you cannot find them.

Search can match words with the index or it can use syntactic and semantic analysis to attempt to derive the concepts behind the query. The quest for more efficient search engines has long taxed researchers in the field of AI. If the engine could understand what you were looking for, then a more successful search would be possible.

The capabilities of a search engine are balanced against speed. It would be great to produce very relevant result sets with long processing times, but the expectation from the user is for a sub-second search time. A typical Google search is around one-tenth of a second, so this sets a benchmark. If an engine takes 10 seconds then many users would consider that too slow. However, the speed for returning the results is not the most important factor. As far as the user is concerned, what really counts is the total time it takes to find the correct information. If it takes half an hour to filter a result set by opening and browsing through documents, then that time has to be factored into the search time. The goal is to get a direct hit in a matter of seconds.

The choice of a search engine is driven by many factors, but the most important is the size of the repository. The more content, the more difficult it will be to find material. Some digital asset management systems have an integral search engine; it is all part of the package. This could well be a big negative when selecting a system. Others allow third party products to be used. In that case the best solution for your business can be chosen.

In view of the many claims made by vendors, it is only really possible to assess the recall and precision with your assets by testing.

One of the more sophisticated features offered by a few search engine products is discovery. The applications include spiders that search for new content as it is ingested. As users make searches, the engines learn a profile of the interests of that user. If new content is ingested that matches the profile, then the user can be alerted.

10 Content description standards

Introduction

Previous chapters have described how content can be indexed, categorised, and searched. Not unnaturally, there have been many proposals to standardise the way that content is described in the index database. Such a move will ease the interoperability between applications.

The complexity of audio-visual content, and the wide range of applications, have led to several frameworks emerging, each focused on one area of use. The moving picture experts group (MPEG) has developed a content description standard for audio-visual content. Another group, called the Dublin Core Metadata Initiative (DCMI), have developed a metadata standard for web resource discovery. These are very general proposals that can be applied to a wide range of content types in many different industries.

There are also industry specific standards. The TV-Anytime Forum has published several specifications for use with television set-top storage devices (the personal video recorder or PVR). For television production, the Society of Motion Picture and Television Engineers (SMPTE) have developed an extensive metadata dictionary, and the European Broadcasting Union (EBU) has been looking at the requirements for metadata to enable programme interchange and archive (Figure 10.1):

- MPEG-7 content description for audio-visual material; ISO/IEC: 15938
- 'DCMI'. Internet Engineering Task Force (IETF): RFC 2413
- TV-Anytime
- SMPTE metadata dictionary
- EBU P/META
- International Press Telecommunications Council (IPTC) for the news industry
- Exchangeable image file format (EXIF) for still photographs.

MPEG-7

MPEG is a working group of ISO/IEC in charge of the development of international standards for compression, decompression, processing, and coded representation of moving pictures, audio, and their combination.

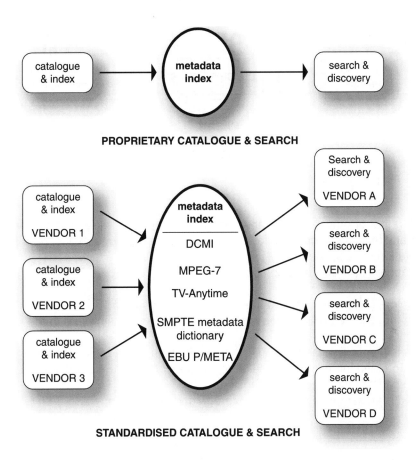

Figure 10.1 Proprietary versus standardised catalogue and search.

They are best known for the very successful MPEG-1 and MPEG-2 standards used for CD-ROMs and television, respectively. MPEG-4, an object-based encoding for audio–video, interactive graphics, and 3-D content is now gaining acceptance. MPEG-7 is a departure from the content encoding, being an interface to describe multimedia content. It sets out to offer solutions to the problems of identifying and managing content.

Many applications have been proposed for MPEG-7, but it is competing with several other description schemes.

The MPEG-7 standard defines a set of tools that can be used to describe audio-visual data content in a multimedia environment. The scope of the MPEG-7 standard is restricted to the description itself, and neither includes the means of generating the description, nor how it is used (Figure 10.2).

MPEG-7 can be used to describe still pictures and graphics, video and audio (including speech), and 3-D models. Although you can use MPEG-7 to describe MPEG-4, the standard is certainly not limited to the description of audio-visual content that has been

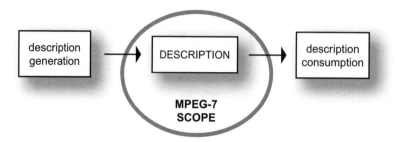

Figure 10.2 The scope of MPEG-7.

encoded to that or other MPEG standards. Its scope is very wide, and can be used to describe any multimedia content: for example a photograph or a movie, both analogue representations of a scene.

The standard has four main components:

- Descriptors (D), these describe the features of the content
- Descriptor schemes (DS) define the relationships and the structure of the descriptors
- Description definition language (DDL) is the language used to define the descriptors and the description schemes; it is an extensible markup language (XML) schema language with extensions
- A coded representation for efficient storage and distribution.

Descriptors

MPEG-7 offers a rich vocabulary for describing content. Still images can have their colour, shape, position, and texture described. Video can be described by the image colour, the motion of the camera (pan, tilt, and zoom), and motion of the subject. Audio descriptions are split into characteristics of the waveform: spectral, timbre, melody, and characteristics of the voice like the spoken content. If you are familiar with MPEG-4, many of these are parameters used in coding (Table 10.1).

MPEG-7 can be expressed as a textual coding based on the XML schema language, where it has to be human readable, or in a compressed binary form called BiM (binary MPEG-7). This latter enables the efficient streaming or storage of the content descriptions (Figure 10.3).

The extensions to the XML schema language were required to support certain necessary features of audio-visual descriptions. These include array and matrix datatypes, and for time and duration elements (Figure 10.4).

Content management

This is descriptive information used to manage the content. The creative and production information is the basic metadata: author, title, genre, and subject. It corresponds to the DCMI elements. Media descriptions correspond to parametric information in the

Table 10.1 Typical MPEG-7 descriptors

Visual	
Basic structures	Grid layout, histogram
Colour	Colour space, dominant colour, colour histogram
Texture	
Shape	Object bounds, region-based shape, 3-D shape descriptor
Motion	Camera motion, object motion, parametric object motion, motion activity, speed, direction, acceleration

Audio	
Timbre	Harmonic structure
Melody	Melodic contour and rhythm
Speech annotation	Lattice of words and phonemes

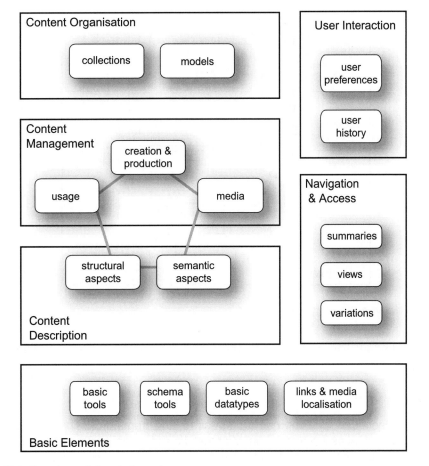

Figure 10.3 Overview of description schemes.

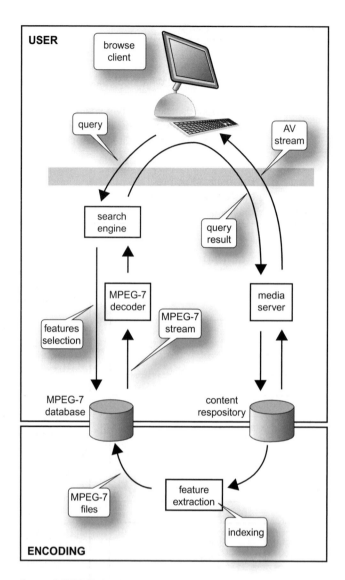

Figure 10.4 Querying an MPEG-7 database.

SMPTE dictionary. This is information about the format and compression of the content instance.

Content descriptions

Content is described by schemes for structure and semantics. The structural tools describe the content as still and moving material, as segments, and frames. The semantic tools describe the meaning of the content, the events, and notions from the real world that are represented by that content.

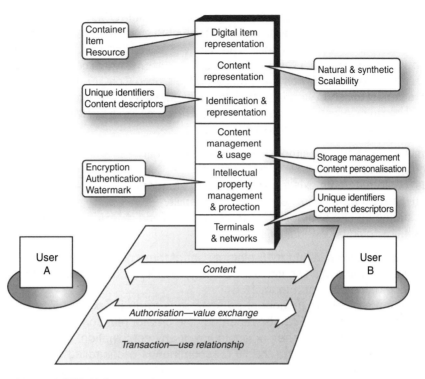

Figure 10.5 The MPEG-21 framework.

Navigation

The navigation schemes include summaries about the content. This is used for discovery and searching.

MPEG-21

MPEG-21 is another standard from under the same umbrella of multimedia interest groups. It is a framework for integrating multimedia resources across a wide range of platforms and services (Figure 10.5). One focus of MPEG-21 is in value exchange, typically the sale of content. Key to this is the management of intellectual property rights. MPEG-21 builds upon the standards of MPEG-4 and MPEG-7. The metadata is extended where necessary to support the framework for value interchange.

MPEG-21 treats all parties as equal users, rather than producer and consumer. This acknowledges that in most cases (excluding piracy) money flows in the opposite direction to the content.

Dublin Core Metadata Initiative (DCMI)

DCMI started with conversations at a WWW conference in 1994. This led to a joint workshop the following year with parties from the US National Center for Supercomputing

Applications (NCSA) and the Online Computer Library Center (OCLC). The OCLC is best-known for owning the copyright of the Dewey Decimal System that is used by most public libraries for the classification of books. The meeting, called the OCLC/NCSA metadata workshop, was held at the OCLC in Dublin, Ohio. The outcome was a core set of semantics for web search and retrieval, from then on called the Dublin Core. Further meetings have refined the project to set up standards for information discovery. The information is called a resource; this can be a web resource, or a physical resource like a book or a map. They had a number of somewhat conflicting goals:

- The metadata should be simple to create and maintain
- It should use commonly understood semantics
- It must conform to both existing and emerging standards
- It should have international scope and applicability
- There should be interoperability among collections and indexing systems
- And last, it should be extensible.

The metadata is formed into a 15-element set of three groups: the first is related to the content or resource, the second to the ownership of the content, and the third relates to an instance of the content (Figure 10.6).

This element set can be thought of as analogous to an index card in a catalogue. Each element is optional and can be repeated. The *creator* of a content resource could be an author, artist, photographer, or illustrator, or any combination. The element *subject* also includes keywords, and the RFC recommends a controlled vocabulary. The *identifier* could be a uniform resource locator (URL) for a web page, or an ISBN for a book. The term coverage has two meanings. The first is spatial, which defines the physical region referred to by the content. This could be by place name, or latitude and longitude. The second is temporal; this indicates the period to which the content refers, either as a period: Byzantine, twentieth century, or as date values.

In many applications, the elements will need to be qualified to refine the semantics. So the basic set of 15 are described as the unqualified elements. Each element is expressed as an attribute-value pair. To maintain interoperability, the qualifiers are chosen from an approved set developed by the Dublin Core community. For example, a date could be date created, date issued, or date valid.

Note that the attribute-value pairs can be put in the metatags of HTML documents, but they are not used for searching by public search engines. This is because there is no control over the content, and the tags are subject to abuse. If you were to use pages indexed by a trusted source like a library, they will then be of use.

In 1998, the metadata element set was published as a request for comment by the IETF (RFC 2413). The Dublin Core metadata for a document can be expressed as an XML application using several different syntactical forms: resource description framework (RDF), DTD, and XML schemas.

TV-Anytime

The TV-Anytime Forum was set up in 1999 to encourage the development of consumer services for television and multimedia using persistent personal storage, often called the PVR. The members of the forum are a global mix of broadcasters and equipment

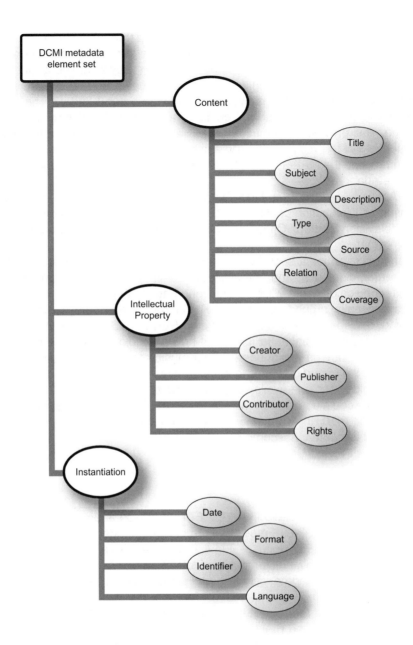

Figure 10.6 DCMI elements.

suppliers. TiVo has established the principles of the PVR, but it is a proprietary environment. The TV-Anytime Forum aims to set up open, thus interoperable, standards that support integrated systems from the content creators, through publishing, to the consumer. The enabler for this technology is the lowering cost of disk drives. A typical PVR on sale in 2002 could record 80 h of programming. Some projections estimate 100 days of storage by 2010—this could replace a large VHS tape library.

The obvious application is for time shifting, but the personal digital recorder (PDR) can potentially deliver far more. One example would be to request content on demand for delivery via broadband Internet, but later viewing on television. The ability to record one television channel while viewing another, and to access content on demand, immediately raises the question 'what is available, and where can I find it?' The consumer user interface is the electronic content guide, analogous to the electronic programme guide (EPG). This provides information for navigation, and more in-depth information about content. All of this relies heavily on a scheme for content description.

TV-Anytime uses the MPEG-7 DDL to describe metadata structure and XML encoding of the metadata.

The TV-Anytime Forum is intended to be agnostic as to the means of content delivery to the consumer. Distribution could be by conventional television systems including the Advanced Television Systems Committee (ATSC) and Digital Video Broadcasting (DVB) or via the Internet.

The standard specifies a security structure that protects the interests of all parties involved: creator, distributor, and unusually the consumer. If the consumer is to adopt interactive technologies, there will be many concerns about privacy.

Some critics have argued that the PDR destroys the business model of linear programming, free-to-air television, funded by advertising. But history has shown that attempts to ignore the potential flexibility that new technology offers the consumer will ultimately fail. The huge growth of peer-to-peer music sharing was encouraged, in part, by the attitude of the record business to the potential for new media distribution models. Once the technology became available, the consumer set the agenda. There is no reason why the same could not happen with video content. To be encouraged to experience the benefits of the PDR, the consumer will demand simple navigation, and the added value of informative content description.

SMPTE metadata

In 1998 the SMPTE, in association with the EBU, released a lengthy report, with very lengthy title: EBU/SMPTE Task Force for Harmonised Standards for the Exchange of Programme Material as Bitstreams – Final Report: Analysis and Results. This has become a required reading for all professional television engineers. The subgroup working on wrappers and metadata established the requirement for a formal metadata dictionary.

The culmination of the further due process has been the SMPTE standard number 335M and the Recommended Practice 210. SMPTE 335M is a metadata dictionary for television and film industry professionals. The spread of elements is very wide, and caters for applications from the military through to entertainment (Figure 10.7).

The dictionary structure defines the format for metadata elements (Table 10.2). Each element has a unique 16-byte numeric reference, or *key*, that is language independent. The actual information is the *value*. For administrative convenience, the elements are grouped into six classes, with two further classes reserved for organisationally registered metadata and one for experimental use. If an element can be expressed in different forms, say binary or XML, each will have a different key.

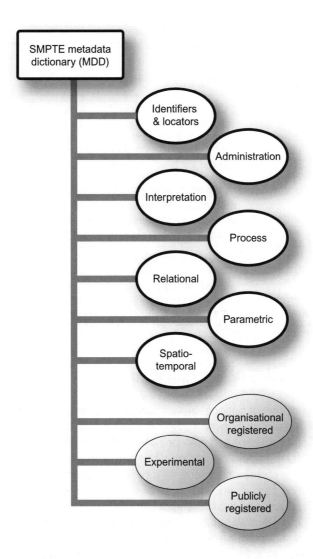

Figure 10.7 SMPTE element classes.

It is intended that the elements are encoded in a compact binary form, as befits the requirements for transport in compressed streams. This is rather different from the human readable, XML, representations of other content description schemes, although it is intended that an XML representation will be supported.

The dictionary is a dynamic document, in that additional elements can be added to the dictionary by applying to the SMPTE registry. The elements are stored and distributed in a key–length–value format.

The SMPTE have developed a data encoding protocol (336M) that uses a key and then variable length data. The key is unique and registered with the SMPTE. By using a common registry, different applications can exchange data.

Table 10.2 SMPTE metadata dictionary element classes

Class	Data elements	Description
1.	Identifiers and locators	GUIDs, UMIDs, ISBN, URL, URI
2.	Administration	Contract and supplier information Episode number
3.	Interpretation	How to interpret the data and content; includes information like the language used and the units: imperial or metric
4.	Parametric	Video parameters: line/field rate, aspect ratio, colorimetry, gamma; similar audio parameters: sample rate, number of channels; compression used; recording tape format; film stock Imager characteristics, focal length, aperture, field of view
5.	Process	Workflow information, versions; editing information
6.	Relational	Information about related objects
7.	Spatio-temporal	Time, date, location coordinates

European Broadcasting Union (EBU) P/META

The EBU is an association of national broadcasters. It has many roles including the nego-tiation of rights for major sports events, the organisation of programme exchanges, and the stimulation of co-productions. It also provides a full range of operational and techni-cal services. The EBU members have a long-standing interest in the management of their valuable programme archives and a long history of programme interchange.

The P/META working group was set up to develop a data model that would enable the exchange of programmes and the transfer of data between content processes and busi-ness workflows. The project was based upon the SMPTE metadata directory. Any add-itional metadata elements can be registered with the SMPTE dictionary.

The remit is narrower than the SMPTE, in that it is, not unnaturally, focussed on the specific needs of national broadcasters. The key goals of the project were as follows:

- Support the identification and recognition of broadcast material
- Define descriptive and editorial information
- Support intellectual property rights management
- Describe how to open and playback content.

The last is very important for archives, as formats come and go over time. The scope of the project covered programme creation (the planning stage before shooting), content distribution, and archiving (Figure 10.8). The delivery to the public is more the scope of TV-Anytime, a body that is cooperating with EBU.

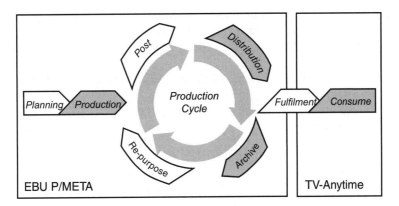

Figure 10.8 P/META scope.

International Press Telecommunications Council (IPTC)

The IPTC is a consortium of news agencies and publishers that was set up to establish telecommunications standards for the interchange of news and multimedia files.

The syndication of stories and pictures by news agencies means that standard vocabularies are needed to ease the sharing of information. Both NewsML and NITF provide for use of an IPTC-managed subject reference system that organises news categories into an extensive three-level hierarchy, and describes types of news articles, such as analysis or opinion. In addition, NewsML features other controlled vocabularies of significance to news publishers. These include the roles of news components, such as 'main' or 'supporting' or 'caption'. It also permits ratings for characteristics such as relevance, priority, and urgency.

News Industry Text Format (NITF)

The NITF describes and identifies news stories. The features include:

- Copyright information, who may republish it, and who it is about
- The subject including who and what the story is about, and where it happened
- When it was reported, issued, and revised and when it can be released.

A very important feature is that it can be used to explain succinctly why the story is newsworthy, based on the editor's analysis of the metadata.

Still image files: Exchangeable Image File Format (EXIF)

There is a standard format for images captured with digital still cameras. The digital still camera image file format standard is called EXIF for Digital Still Cameras. The images are stored on memory cards or microdrives. The file includes a metadata set as well as the image and audio clips. The images are stored with JPEG compression or in a raw form. Audio is stored using the resource interchange file format (RIFF) specification.

The associated metadata can be downloaded to many asset management systems. The metadata is comprehensive, although much is only of interest to the photographer. This is some of the information that can be stored:

- Image data: size image dimensions, bit-depth and compression, and location (GPS coordinates)
- Imaging equipment: make, model, and software version
- Exposure parameters: exposure index, lens aperture, exposure duration, and flash energy.

The standard can also be used to record the artist (photographer), copyright, image title, and the date and time. One potentially useful tag field for an image library, the GPS data, is usually supported by linking the camera to a separate GPS receiver.

Summary

At first site, it looks like another raft of competing standards. But luckily, the different organisations are cooperating to develop a common ground. The standards are also complementary. The SMPTE dictionary is used by other standards. The choice of standard is largely determined by industry sector. There are three main camps: multimedia, broadcasting, and web content.

If your interest is web content or document libraries, then DCMI will be the most likely choice. If you operate within the television post-production industry, then the SMPTE metadata directory, incorporated in the advanced authoring format, is a good choice. For broadcasters wishing to exchange content, then the EBU P/META has much to offer. Vendors of consumer hardware and applications will adopt the TV-Anytime standards for the delivery of metadata to television consumer devices.

For the multimedia sector, MPEG-7 can be used for images, audio, video, and 3-D content. The goals of MPEG-7 are to make the search of multimedia as easy as with text. As the power of computers increases, and as new algorithms are developed, we can expect search engines to be able to retrieve a song, from a whistled stanza, or to identify a criminal from a face captured by a surveillance camera.

The standards offer very different level of detail; the DCMI is a basic set of elements, whereas SMPTE and MPEG-7 have very fine detail. One of the more recent additions to metadata is usage information, including the protection of this information. The usage of content has become valuable information. It assists business with the planning marketing strategies and the optimisation of advertising rates. The consumer also has rights over such information, in order to maintain their privacy. Therefore, although usage information can be harvested as metadata, there is also the facility to protect the access to this information.

If you intend to use any of these content description frameworks, then your digital asset management system must offer compatibility. The main advantage of using these frameworks is the ease with which compliant applications can be used in concert.

11 The presentation tier

Introduction

The presentation tier is the user interface to the asset management system. As such, it makes or breaks an asset management system. The design of the presentation tier ultimately determines the usability of the system. The acceptance and whole-hearted adoption of the system will depend very much upon this usability.

As a user, you will want to undertake a wide-ranging set of tasks. These are just a few:

- Edit index metadata
- Manage authorisations
- Search for content
- Preview content
- Retrieve content for editing
- Archive content
- Manage digital rights.

The presentation tier has two layers: the asset management server and the local client—the users' PC (Figure 11.1). The server can be a normal web server, and the client can be just a standard web browser. The web server accesses the data and content through an application server, where the business logic resides.

Digital asset management is not limited to this architecture; older systems use a client–server model. The ubiquity of the World Wide Web has hastened the migration to a more web-centric design for systems, but some clients still need specialist local applications, so will link directly to the business tier. A typical example is a media logging or ingest station. This application needs to control a videotape recorder, and to encode and index the video and audio.

The advantage of separating the presentation layer from the business logic is that standard web site tools can be used. No special skills are required beyond those needed to run a web site. Much of the functionality is the same as dynamic web site, typical of any large e-commerce portal. This means that the personalisation and branding of the site does not have to be done by the asset management vendor, anyone with web design skills can change the 'look' of the web portal.

The other advantage of using a web-based presentation layer is you do not need any special client applications to be installed, beyond those normally present on desktop

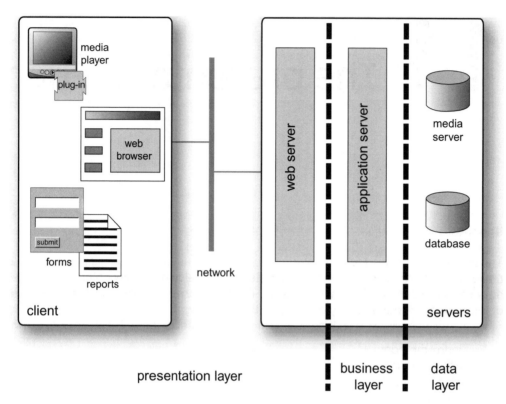

Figure 11.1 The multi-tier model.

PCs: the web browser and its multimedia plug-ins. If the digital asset management is used for video and audio content, then additional facilities, mostly server side, will be required to support the delivery of the multimedia files.

Web browser

This has become the main client for digital asset management. Sometimes a more complex client is needed. As an example an ingest station may need to control a videotape recorder. So a full ingest client application will be installed directly on the workstation, along with any necessary video cards and the control interfaces for the video recorder.

Interactivity

Hypertext markup language (HTML) pages are static, you request a file, and it is transmitted to your browser. This is fine for simple information, but most applications require interaction with the user. There are many ways to implement this. One way is to use server-side scripting. The user responds to a question posed in a form, and on submission of the completed form, a new page is sent. The round trip delay means that this can be very unresponsive. Some intelligence has to be to the client. This is usually implemented by client-side scripts. Again, there are several ways to implement this: JavaScript, Active X controls, and Java applets.

Scripting can be used for interactivity, which is to make a page responsive to user-initiated events, and for dynamic graphics. For asset management applications, the interactivity is the primary requirement.

JavaScript

JavaScript was first supported by Netscape Navigator 2.0. It later became the ISO/IEC standard as ECMA 262, the ECMAScript Language Specification. Like Java, it is an object-oriented programming language. Scripts are simpler than programmes like Java. They use the host environment, the browser engine, for input and output, so it is not computationally self-sufficient. Instead, it is used to expose functionality of the browser to program control.

As an example, HTML can open a hyperlink in a new window, but JavaScript allows the parameters of the new window to be programmed. So the new window may have no chrome—menu bar, address bar, and status—and the window dimensions can be set to certain pixel values. Perhaps the most useful facility is the interaction with the mouse. The browser is aware of the user focus on areas of the screen, either from the mouse, or by tabbing through form fields. The JavaScript can use browser events, like mouse down (click) or mouse up and perform actions in response to these events. This is used for the interactive navigation we are so familiar with, the mouse-over graphics, and fly-out menus.

JavaScript is an interpreted language, and is executed one line at a time by the browser. The core scripting language has extensions for client-side and server-side use. The server-side scripting is less popular, more powerful programming languages are usually used. To summarise, JavaScript is very useful for extending the features of the browser, by exposing functionality to scripted control. For the digital asset management client, this includes the following facilities:

- Validation of forms
- Simple calculations
- Detect browser type and the installed plug-ins
- Animate graphics for navigation: rollovers and new windows.

The first two cut down roundtrips to the server, so make the user interface appear more responsive. The third allows the system to cater for the differences between browser versions. Different HTML can be served to allow for these differences, or appropriate warnings issued. As an example, it may be essential for the user to enable scripting, so the asset management client will operate correctly. JavaScript can detect that the user has disabled scripting, and load a page explaining the need to have scripting enabled. This page could also list instructions as to how turn on scripting. This may seem like a fancy feature, but if it prevents a phone call to the support department that is a real resource saving.

Java

Java applets are compiled programs that are downloaded with HTML files, and then execute on the browser. They can be used for many applications; one example is to play video files within a window without the need for a media player plug-in.

The programmer compiles the Java applets as a program called byte-code, and they are then stored on the web server along with the HTML files. The applets are downloaded by a web page. The browser calls a local Java virtual machine (Java VM) and then executes the Java byte-code. Versions of the Java VM are available that can be run on most operating systems, so the applets can be said to have true cross-platform compatibility.

Many digital asset management products avoid client-side Java because behaviour can be unpredictable with some browsers, or the user may have Java support turned off.

Due to its name, JavaScript is often compared with Java, but they are quite separate languages. They are both object oriented, but Java is class based with formal inher-itance hierarchy. JavaScript can add properties to an object and vary data types dynamically. JavaScript can be embedded within the HTML, whereas Java is in a separate applet. Both languages cannot automatically write to the local hard drive, but applets could contain virus code, so the browser can apply security restrictions to the applets.

Plug-ins

Browsers can render only a limited set of file formats. Early browsers could render HTML as format text, and images were limited to the bitmap formats of GIF for graphics and JPEG for continuous tone pictures. Later another graphics format was incorporated called portable network graphics (PNG). Asset management repositories contain many other formats: text documents, vector graphics, video, and audio files.

Early on in the history of browsers, the concept of the plug-in was developed. Although a browser could launch a separate application to view the alternative file formats, the plug-in allows a seamless viewer experience all within the browser. The plug-in is a dynamic code module that extends the functionality of a browser. It can display the file in a separate window or can draw directly within the HTML page. Each method can be appropriate, depending on the application. For example, a virtual-reality file may need navigation controls (left, right, up, and down), so opening the file in a window complete with navigation buttons can be useful. The chrome surrounding the plug-in window may not suit the corporate branding of a web page, so windowless embedding can be used, with the navigation implemented with buttons designed to match the look of rest of the page.

Plug-in media formats

Perhaps the most popular plug-in is Flash. This is used for displaying dynamic vector graphics. For asset management systems, there are a limited set of essential plug-ins: Acrobat Reader and multimedia players.

Document management

The Adobe Acrobat reader is ubiquitous for viewing all form of documents, from word processor files to full-colour brochures. The documents are converted to the portable document format (PDF), a language based on postscript.

Graphics

Vector graphics are very popular for illustration and animations. Vector art, both static and dynamic or animated, can be saved in Macromedia Flash format (extension .SWF). The graphic file is then displayed in the browser using the Flash plug-in.

Macromedia offers two web players: Shockwave and Flash. Each has a distinct purpose. The Flash player is used for fast loading front-end web applications. It can be used for user interaction, interactive online advertising, and short-to-medium length animations. The Shockwave player is more suited to long-form content. It is popular for games, and for interactive multimedia product demonstrations and training, typically delivered on CD-ROM. The Shockwave player will also play Flash content.

Note that the Flash content is delivered in the Shockwave file format (.SWF). Shockwave content is specifically authored on Macromedia Director, whereas Flash files can be generated by many applications (not just Macromedia). Macromedia has a third plug-in, Authorware, that is used to create interactive e-learning applications.

There is another format for vector graphics that has been developed under the auspices of the World Wide Web Consortium (W3C). This is scalable vector graphics (SVG) and is based on extensible markup language (XML).

Images

Raster or bitmap images do not require a plug-in. If a proxy of the original file is stored in GIF or JPEG format, then the images can be displayed in the basic browser. HTML code defines the display size of image within the window. The browser then scales the image file to fit. Later browsers can open a picture file direct, and scale it to fit the browser window. Since the dimensions of a digital picture may well be 3000 × 2000 pixels, it will not fit the browser window without scaling. Consumers that are exchanging photographs from digital still cameras with friends or their film processing laboratories have driven this requirement.

Audio and video

Multimedia content can also be embedded into a web page. There are several plug-ins that can render the files as audio and video. Apple QuickTime and Real support the standard MPEG-4 format, and the Windows Media player can decode the proprietary Microsoft format.

Note that the plug-ins listed above only support a limited subset of possible file formats. Both users and IT departments are reluctant to install more than a handful of plug-ins, so any other formats are encoded at the ingest stage to a proxy format that can be displayed by the popular plug-ins. A typical example would be word processor files converted to PDF or an MPEG-2 video file converted to a low bit rate MPEG-4 proxy.

Web servers

At its most basic, the web server delivers a file in answer to a request from a browser (Figure 11.2):

- The user asks for a page using a URL
- The web server maps the URL to a file name
- The server reads the file from disk
- The server transmits the HTML file to the browser using HTTP.

This task is trivial; it could be performed with a few lines of code. The problem for the web server designer was to develop an application that can handle many hundreds or thousands of connections concurrently and reliably. This issue has long since been overcome. To achieve this a combination of multiprocessing and multithreading is used. Typical web servers include the open source project, Apache. A digital asset portal could not run just with static web pages, instead pages are dynamically generated using information from the data layer.

Communication between the browser and server uses HTTP over a TCP/IP connection. The first version of HTTP required a separate TCP connection to be negotiated for each browser request. Therefore, a page with many graphic elements needed a TCP connection to be set up for each element, an inefficient process. HTTP 1.1 now maintains a persistent TCP connection during an HTTP session; this cuts down the

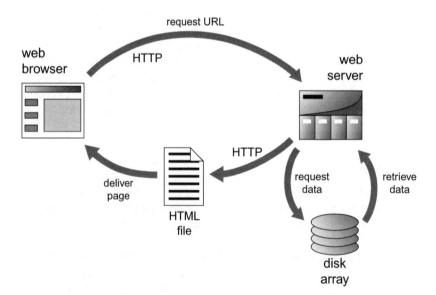

Figure 11.2 Requesting an HTML page.

communications overheads. The digital asset management may use IP addresses for communication, but if URLs are used to access pages then a domain name server (DNS) will also be required to resolve the URLs to the numeric IP addresses.

Only very small installations use one web server device. To give fail-over protection at least two servers are used, each running a web server application.

So the information portal is comprised of a number of physical servers, running a number of services: file transfer protocol (FTP) server, web server, DNS, and media server. Each service usually runs on separate machines for optimum performance and scalability. To apportion the requests across several web servers load balancing is used.

Media server

If you want to view video previews, you may want to operate true streaming. A web server only supports download and play, or a midway process called progressive streaming. To stream video in realtime, you will need a separate media server that runs a service which supports streaming delivery. These applications use feedback from the media player plug-in of the browser to throttle the delivery rate of the streaming file, so that the media data can be viewed as it arrives. Typical examples are Windows Media and RealServer.

Other content, like thumbnail images, is served conventionally by the web server.

WebDAV

Web-based Distributed Authoring and Versioning or webDAV is a set of extensions to HTTP that enables the sharing of content in an authoring environment. A server that supports the webDAV protocol enables the management of file sharing. For example, one person can checkout a file, but any number of workmates can view the file. The first release supported locking (concurrency control), file properties (metadata about the file stored as XML), and namespace manipulation, required when files are moved or copied to other domains. The concurrency control prevents one user overwriting the edits of another user. That is also a core function of an asset management system. Therefore, although there may seem to be a crossover, webDAV is useful, because asset management systems can leverage the technology.

Although developed for web site developers, its use is not limited to HTML pages, but to any resource on a file server like graphics and images. WebDAV is just a protocol, so it is the client and server applications that exploit the information that webDAV can transport.

WebDAV can replace FTP as a transport mechanism for files, which avoids firewall issues, and can use standard high-security HTTP encryption systems.

Security and firewalls

The web server is connected to the Internet, which is an inherently untrusted network. So to decouple the internal, trusted network it will have to be installed in a perimeter network or demilitarised zone (DMZ). This is separated from the internal network by a

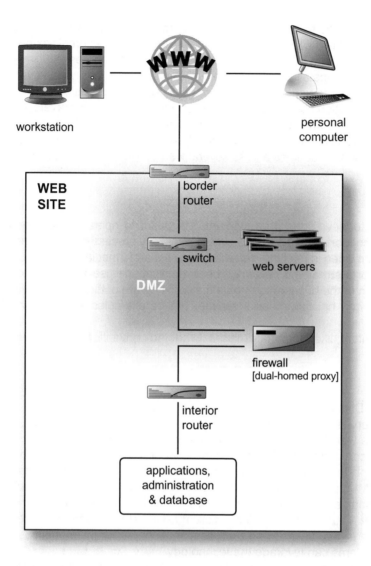

workstation

personal
computer

WEB
SITE

border
router

switch

web servers

DMZ

firewall
[dual-homed proxy]

interior
router

applications,
administration
& database

Figure 11.3 The firewall and DMZ.

firewall. The firewall protects against intruders, and can also filter outgoing traffic
(Figure 11.3).

Dynamic pages

Static web pages alone would not satisfy the requirements of an asset management
system. The highly interactive nature of the user interface means that pages have to be
created on-the-fly from information that has been collated by the business logic from the
backend databases.

The e-commerce sites use dynamic web page generation for two reasons. One is to handle forms and the other is to serve dynamic content using prepared templates. The first dynamic sites used the common gateway interface (CGI) to the datastores. The CGI uses small application programs written in C, Perl, Python, Java, and Visual Basic. It soon became apparent that this was not a very efficient way to run this additional functionality. Each browser request for a CGI program spawned a new process. This adds considerable overhead to a busy server, eventually limiting the number of browsers that can be served concurrently.

To get around this more efficient ways have been developed to serve dynamic pages. One example is based upon Java. Small programs written in Java are called servlets, and represent the server-side equivalent of client applets. The servlets replace the CGI programs. The servlets run on a Java VM and, after the first execution, they are cached. Java server pages provide a simple way to create XML tags and scriptlets that are then compiled into Java servlets. Typical applications are to generate a structured query language (SQL) statement from user input criteria, and then to retrieve and display information from a database formatted for a web page. Java is platform independent, so can run on the same operating system as that chosen for the web server.

There are several other similar technologies: Macromedia's ColdFusion, PHP, and Microsoft Active Server Pages (ASP). Java Server Pages (JSP) have proved popular with asset management vendors because Java technology is also used in the application server for the business logic.

User interface

The design of the user interface is crucial to the wide acceptance of the asset management by the users. It demands special skills from the developers to produce simple yet powerful interfaces within the constraints of HTML. Basic operations like metadata entry can be easily catered for with forms.

Complex form layouts are best avoided with HTML. Even using cascading style sheets, the end result is very fluid. Careful interface design can avoid many of the pitfalls of HTML. Many asset management products avoid browser issues by using a client application.

As part of product evaluation, a web client should be thoroughly tested on all the browsers that are likely to be used. For a digital asset management system that is only used by staff over an intranet, there may only be one flavour of browser.

If the system were to be used with partners, you would have to be brave to stipulate one type of browser. If you imposed Internet Explore 6 because it is used in all your own offices, then that will exclude a small, but an important, proportion. Asset management by its very nature is going to be accessed by creatives. These power users will have strong views about what they want to use on their workstations. Mac users could well have Safari; UNIX and Linux users might use Konqueror, Mozilla, Netscape, or Opera.

Even if there were one browser, the display depends upon the window size and display size. All this puts constraints upon the interface design. The rule is to keep it simple. For the designer, it is a quite a challenge to provide all the features in a simple environment.

Figure 11.4 Main Portfolio window with Portfolio Express in foreground. ©Extensis, Inc.

For specialised applications like ingest, which use Java clients, it may be necessary for the manufacturer to stipulate a certain display resolution, perhaps 1280 × 1024. For web browser applications, such a specification would limit the application.

Since asset management is often used to find files that are to be edited, then a full size window can be a hindrance. The approach taken by companies like Extensis with their Portfolio product is to use a sidebar of thumbnails (Portfolio Express) (Figure 11.4). An image can be dragged directly into an editing application like Photoshop or QuarkXPress using the thumbnail.

Summary

To achieve a good return on investment, any enterprise that is interested in deploying asset management will be looking for an affordable cost per seat. The overheads of managing the user workstations should be minimal. The simplest way to achieve this goal is to use a web browser as the basis of the asset management client. This gives all the well-known advantages of the multi-tier computing model.

Most tasks can be performed from the web browser, but there are more complex tasks that can only be supported with a client application installed on each workstation. These are likely to be ingest workstations, and multimedia edit stations.

There have been many pricing issues surrounding browser access. Traditionally, vendors have priced products like databases by a licence for a given number of connections. Vendors have also had great success selling 'thick' clients. They are a good source of sales revenue to complement the profits from sale of server applications. The new web paradigm may benefit the customer, but does not offer a visible return for the vendor. Many vendors have resisted this move, but ultimately their competitors will offer the facility of a web tier. It must not be forgotten that the slow rollout of digital asset management has largely been a result of the high cost of deployment of the early systems. The rollout of web services to other parts of the enterprise is only going to increase demand for web-based clients.

12 The application server

Introduction

A small-scale asset management application can be designed using the client–server model. Each client includes the presentation and business logic. The server is essentially a database. All inter-process communication between clients takes place via the database using triggers and stored procedures. Although some simple and elegant systems based on this architecture are in use today, such systems do not offer the performance and scalability of a multi-tiered architecture. The limit comes at around 100 clients. At this point, the number of database connections leads to queuing and inefficiency. The other drawback is that any changes to the application logic entail updates to every client.

In Figure 12.1, if client 2 needs to communicate with client 1, then that takes place through data tables. Each client can also access the file and media servers to view or retrieve assets.

The developers of enterprise software applications have long realised that affordable products required a new approach to software design. The monolithic sequential logic of the old main-frame application had many drawbacks. The debacle of the two-digit dates at the turn of the century demonstrated the advantages of object or component-based design. To modify a date component was trivial, to modify date logic embedded in thousands of lines of code was fraught with problems.

The favoured architecture proved to be multi-tier, with an application server based on object-oriented design.

There are a number of compelling reasons why a multi-tier approach, based upon an application server, offers far more flexibility. The business and presentation logic are transferred from the client to a central point like the corporate data centre. This means that the client can be 'thin', possibly a web browser or a lightweight Java client. Although a thin client has many attractions, it is not a reason alone to use a multi-tier approach.

In Figure 12.2, the presentation and business logic has been moved from the clients to a third tier of application servers. These could be a single server for each application: indexing, search, workflow, rights management, or could be clusters of server to give scalability and fault tolerance. The clients communicate with the application servers. These pool the database connections, so all database communication is solely with the application servers. The role of the client is to display information, and for user input.

An enterprise-wide asset management system has a number of requirements that is difficult to implement with the two-tier architecture. Key to asset management is the

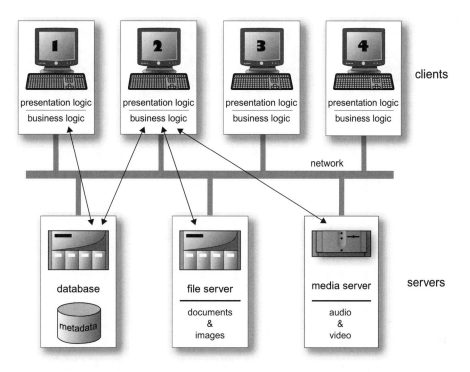

Figure 12.1 The client–server software architecture.

support of many users cooperating in creative content production. This is a list of some of the requirements:

- A distributed, collaborative environment
- Transaction pooling for the database interface
- Scalable and extensible
- Fault tolerant and highly available
- Multiple interfaces to third-party applications.

The pooling of messaging to third-party applications and the database both point away from the client–server model to an application server tier that can host the business logic. This logic can manage and coordinate the distributed systems.

In the drive for more efficient product development, developers split the core application from the services that are common to any application: distributed processing, load balancing, fault tolerance, and database connections. By adopting of-the-shelf frameworks that provide many of the basic services, an application vendor only had to code the new software specific to their product. These supporting services are called middleware.

Middleware

Middleware provides a wide range of essential services that are generic to a distributed system. By using such a framework the vendor is freed from the need to develop these

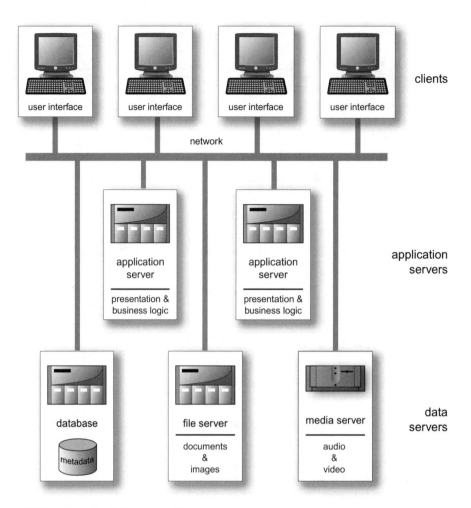

Figure 12.2 The three-tier software architecture.

basic services, so can offer a more competitive end-product. The development cost of the frameworks is spread across hundreds of sales across many markets. To recover the development costs of such services would not be feasible for the much lower sales volume of a niche application like asset management. Therefore, as a customer you can realise cost savings by leveraging technology from the wider world of business computing.

The base service of the middleware is an execution engine to run the business logic of the asset management.

Third-party interfaces

The systems require extensive logic, not just to perform the workflow, storage, and metadata management functions, but also to link to other business systems within the enterprise. Most installations use a best-of-breed selection of four or five products. Together they make up the asset management system.

As an example, many media businesses have an existing product to manage the intellectual property rights of their content. Asset management does not support this functionality, so the two have to be intimately linked to exchange metadata. It is the job of the middleware to seamlessly integrate these separate software applications, and give the user a unified view of the assets, and the rights pertaining to each one.

The middleware that provides the services for the application server can also support distributed computing. That means a large company with several sites can still share the same asset management infrastructure. As an example, this offers possibilities for new business models for groups of television stations—the central-casting paradigm.

Several frameworks can be used for the middleware of a system including J2EE, CORBA, and .NET.

Most vendors have adopted an object-oriented approach to the business logic (Figure 12.3). It has long been the favoured choice for multi-tiered architectures. It offers a number of advantages:

- In the real world we manage objects: documents, photographs, and videotapes
- Improved maintainability of applications
- Reusability of code
- Higher productivity for the software development.

The business logic layer represents the hub of the digital asset management system. This layer interfaces with third-party applications like e-commerce and rights management, and the datastores. By the nature of things, the third-party interface may have to change. They could be replaced with a system from a different vendor, or the vendor may release a new version that has additional features or is not backwards compatible. This could mean the future development of new or revised interfaces. This may need expensive professional services. If an object-oriented approach has been used for the asset management application, then such interface development can be undertaken in isolation from the main business logic, with attendant cost reductions.

Glance through the collateral of any digital asset management application and you will find that they extol the virtues of CORBA, J2EE, and Java. Why should this matter? What is the advantage of using these frameworks?

Object-oriented programming

Object-oriented programming models business processes as objects. This corresponds with our view of the natural world. We can pick up and handle media objects: photographs, CDs, and videocassettes. An object can have a number of states and behaviours. If we choose a real-world example like videotape, it can have a state: format, playing time, and line/field rate. One useful state to know would be cued position of the tape within the cassette. We express this state by the time code. The tape object can also exhibit behaviours: play, fast forward, and rewind. Note that applying a behaviour can change a state. Therefore, if the tape is rewound then stopped, the state of the cue point will have changed. One of the big attractions for digital asset management is that

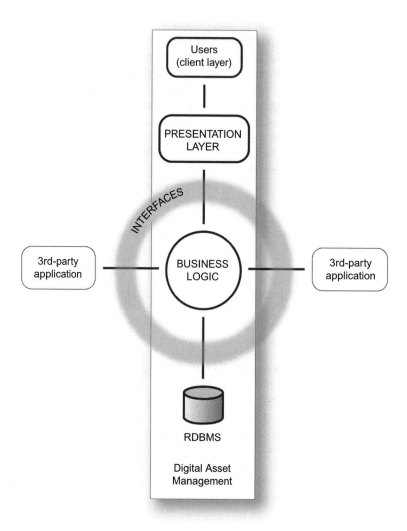

Figure 12.3 Business logic interfaces.

real-world objects and concepts can be modelled in object-oriented programming by software objects.

There are four concepts that are key to object orientation:

- Encapsulation
- Instantiation
- Inheritance
- Polymorphism.

Encapsulation

This really separates object-oriented programming from a sequential program. Conventional software separates the code and the data. Object-oriented programming models a real-world object with a function that can represent the behaviour of the object. The data structures, variables, and procedures are stored together as an object. The public operations of the object are exposed through an interface. The internal function is *encapsulated* from view. Compare the object with a videotape. We can play this through a videotape recorder (VTR), without knowledge of the magnetic patterns on the tape, or how the data compression works.

Instantiation

The state of a software object is maintained in a set of *variables.* Any one state of the object is an *instance.* The case of a videotape could be the tape speed. So there would be a parked instance, a play instance, and a fast wind instance.

Polymorphism

If a program contains polymorphic functions that means it can handle different data types or classes. More specifically, it is the ability to redefine methods for derived classes.

For example, given a base class video media, polymorphism enables the programmer to define different play methods for any number of derived classes, such as videotape and DVDs. Therefore, whatever media an object is, if you apply the play method then it will playback video.

A true object-oriented programming language will support polymorphism.

Methods

The behaviour of the object is expressed with a *method.* An object is represented by data variables and the methods or operations that describe the behaviour.

Consider a television programme as an object. It can be described by its format: film, videotape, and DVD. Videotape could be described by compression format: MPEG-2 or DV. These can be considered as states of the object. One particular state is called an *instance* of that object. To change the state of the programme object you would apply an *instance method.* So to make a Digital Betacam tape from a 35 mm film, there would be a method to take the film to a telecine machine, and dub the film across to videotape.

Normally, the state of an object can only be changed via a method. That means the methods *encapsulate* the object. Objects and classes use interfaces for the implementation of methods (Figure 12.4). An interface is a device that unrelated objects use to interact; it is analogous to a protocol between applications.

Messaging

To continue with the example, to cue a tape to a specific time code value or variable, we have to send it a message. The message would contain the method to perform, in this case *cue*, and the cue point time code—that is the message parameters. The message will also need an address, which tape to cue. This may seem trivial, as a VTR can only hold one tape, but the VTR could be in an automated tape library with possibly hundreds of tapes within the address domain.

In a digital asset management system, there could well be thousands of Betacam tape cassettes. Every tape has the same methods, play, cue, and rewind, but there are

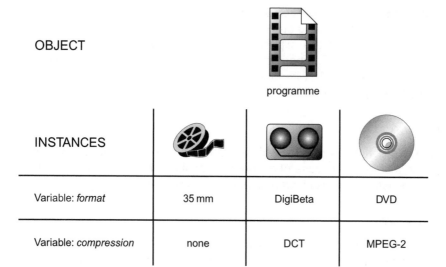

OBJECT

programme

INSTANCES

	35 mm	DigiBeta	DVD
Variable: *format*	35 mm	DigiBeta	DVD
Variable: *compression*	none	DCT	MPEG-2

Figure 12.4 Instances of an object.

Table 12.1 Betacam cassette classes

Classes	Size	Playing time (min)	Format
Beta sub-class	Small, large	5, 10, 20, 30, 60, 90	Betacam oxide
SP sub-class	Small, large	5, 10, 20, 30, 60, 90	Betacam SP
DigiBeta sub-class	Small, large	6, 22, 32, 64, 94, 124, 184	Digital Betacam
SX sub-class	Small, large	6, 22, 32, 64, 94, 124, 184, 194	Betacam SX

sets of values for the states. There are different coating formulations for different video recording formats (SX, SP, etc.), there are two cassette sizes, and there are different playing times. So rather than defining each object from scratch, a prototype object is defined that represents a *class* of objects. A class is a category for objects with similar variables and that responds to the same methods. Object classes can form hierarchies, with sub- and super-classes. In the example of the tape cassettes, the different formats form sub-classes of the class of Betacam tapes. The super-class could be professional videotapes, and itself would have other sub-classes of the DV formats (Table 12.1).

Inheritance

A tape class is a blueprint or prototype that defines the variables: size, playing time, format, and the methods (play, rewind, and record). A sub-class inherits states from the super-class, but can have their own states and behaviours. The principle of inheritance allows programmers to reuse class code in sub-classes.

Why is object-oriented programming useful?

The advantages of object-oriented programming are the ease with which programs can be modified. This stems from the encapsulation of function. The digital asset management can be decomposed into workflow, search, archiving, etc. To take an example, if the search engine is upgraded from keyword search to natural language, this encapsulated object can be changed without impact on other elements of the system.

It is also easier to model the real-world processes of content creation as objects. Another advantage that is often claimed is that objects can be reused (a feature of component-based design), although in practice this does not always happen.

Although the concept has been around for 40 years, there are still programmers that are using sequential code (the functions are in a list). The problems around the millennium caused by programmes with two-character dates underlined the importance of encapsulating functions in objects. To modify a data object that handled the calendar dates in a program was trivial. Modifying sequential programs to change the code for handling dates proved very expensive, not only in coding time, but in the subsequent testing and debugging. Two popular languages for object-oriented programming are Java and C++.

Few asset management systems operate in isolation. They interface with back-office system to share and exchange data. Object-oriented programming offers great advantages when it comes to the development of bespoke interfaces to the disparate systems that will be encountered at different customer installations.

Software components

The need to drive down programming costs, and to allow easy customisation, has driven software developers to adopt components. Rather than writing code from scratch, number of components are put together to provide the necessary function. This means that the systems can be more easily customised to suit the special requirements of each different enterprise. The reusable software objects can be assembled quickly and cost effectively to provide flexible solutions for a wide range of corporate requirements.

Middleware

There are a number of middleware frameworks that can be used to provide the services for object-oriented applications. The most popular for asset management are CORBA and J2EE, with .NET, and component object model (COM) starting to emerge as a contender for products that use the Microsoft platform.

Middleware provides support for objects to interact transparently across distributed platforms. The object framework manages all the potential complexity of intersystem communications and different operating systems.

CORBA

The Common Object Request Broker Architecture or CORBA is an infrastructure for software applications to operate together over distributed computer networks. It is one of a number of standards that have been developed by the Object Management Group

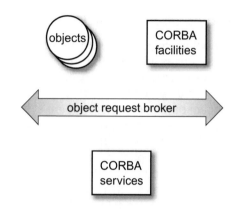

Figure 12.5 Object management architecture.

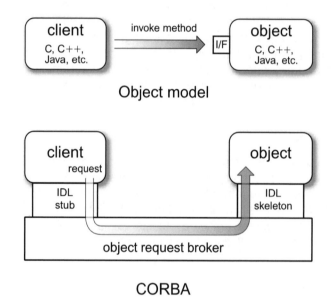

Figure 12.6 CORBA.

(OMG). Together they form an object management architecture (Figure 12.5). One of the goals of the OMG was to develop an architecture that would be independent of programming language, operating system, and platform.

The object management architecture is based around the object request broker (ORB). The group was set up in 1989 to develop a component-based software marketplace by encouraging the development of standards for object-based software. It has 800 members worldwide. One of the OMG standards is the unified modelling language (UML), which is used for the original design of the software system architecture. CORBA is used by leading asset management vendors like Artesia and Blue Order.

CORBA objects can be written in most programming languages, and can be run under nearly all operating systems and on most hardware (Figure 12.6). This portability has

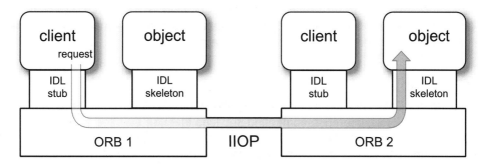

Figure 12.7 Inter-ORB communication using IIOP.

contributed to its success as middleware. A CORBA object encapsulates the functionality and the data. For a client to invoke a method on an object some open interface has to be exposed to broker the invocation. This is the CORBA interface definition language (IDL). This provides the language independence that allows the clients to communicate in a way that is standardised and language agnostic. Each client has a stub that acts as a proxy for the client in the IDL. Similarly, the object has a skeleton proxy.

ORB

As its name implies, the ORB requests between the client and the object. The ORB interface can retrieve references to objects, and can route requests and their responses from the client to the object. To conserve processor resources most object are not running all the time. If an object is called, the ORB will activate the object, then deactivate after the operation. If a dynamic link is made then the invocation can be made at runtime, rather than a static link through the IDL stub.

Inter-ORB communication

In a distributed system, a client may want to invoke an object on another ORB. The OMG has specified a protocol for intercommunication between object brokers: the Internet inter-ORB protocol or IIOP (Figure 12.7). The ORBs manage the remote invocation to give *location transparency*. This means that the client does not know if the object is local or remote. The IIOP implementation of the general inter-ORB protocol uses TCP/IP.

The advantage of using the ORB and IIOP is that the complexity of networks and their protocols is hidden from the business logic.

CORBA services

The object management architecture defines CORBA services. These are a number of facilities that should be expected from the object broker middleware. These manage the lifecycle of an object from creation to destruction, and the persistence if necessary. The services also provide security to control access to objects, asynchronous event management, and multiple transaction models. The standardisation of services makes CORBA application more portable across ORBs from different vendors. There is still great flexibility for the vendors within the specification, so asset management vendors typically offer their products with a limited set of tested middleware.

J2EE

J2EE or Java 2 Enterprise Edition is a specification for a middleware platform. It includes a suite of multi-tiered enterprise computing services that can be used to build complex distributed business applications like asset management. It supports XML data exchange and has a unified security provision. J2EE is maintained by Sun Microsystems but is guided by the large Java developer community. It is supported by more than 25 leading vendors including IBM, BEA systems, and Oracle.

J2EE is part of a family of Java frameworks. The other two are the Java 2 standard edition (J2SE) for desktop applications and the Java 2 micro-edition (J2ME) for wireless and hand-held devices (like third-generation cellphones).

Much like CORBA, the platform provides basic services for messaging, directory services, and transaction processing. At the core of J2EE is enterprise JavaBeans (EJB). These are a server-side components for building object-oriented business applications. The beans run within a container that provides the necessary services to execute the components. EJB supports a scalable, distributed environment for data transactions. The J2EE framework frees the EJB developer to concentrate on the core business logic of the asset management application. There are three types of bean: the session bean for modelling the business logic, the entity bean for object persistence, and the message-driven bean for an asynchronous messaging service. The entity beans represent the real-world digital assets, the programmes and types, the photographs and illustrations. The data for persistent objects is stored in a relational database.

The main components of J2EE that are used for an application server include the following:

- EJB: are reusable server-side components
- Java database connectivity (JDBC) for interfacing to relational databases
- Java naming and directory interface (JNDI) for location transparency
- Remote method invocations, RMI-IIOP
- Java connectivity architecture (JCA) for connecting to legacy applications.

Other services like failover, load balancing and data caching are provided by the platform vendors.

EJB

Enterprise Java Beans (EJB) are reusable software components written in the Java language (Figure 12.8). EJB are similar to the original JavaBeans but have a completely different specification. JavaBeans are software components used to make up complete applications, whereas EJBs are deployable components in their own right. The asset management application will be made up from many components or beans. The business objects, like the asset metadata, appear as proxies for the EJB instance running in the container.

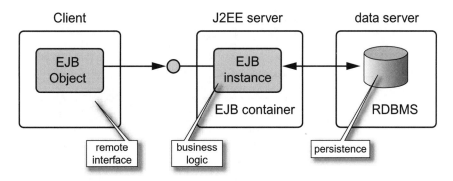

Figure 12.8 The EJB model.

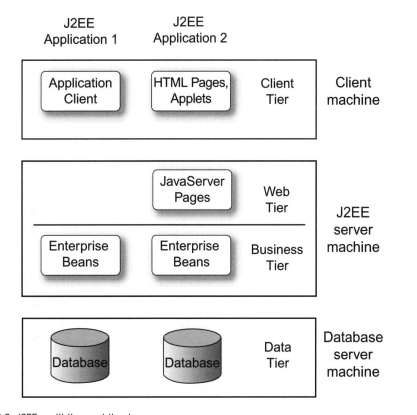

Figure 12.9 J2EE multi-tier architecture.

J2EE multi-tier model

J2EE can be used to build three- or four-tier architectures (Figure 12.9). The fourth tier is added to support thin clients based on a web browser. Where more functionality is needed or a complex GUI, a thick client can interface directly with the bean container using remote method invocations. A thin client should satisfy the user for more basic tasks (like metadata editing or searching).

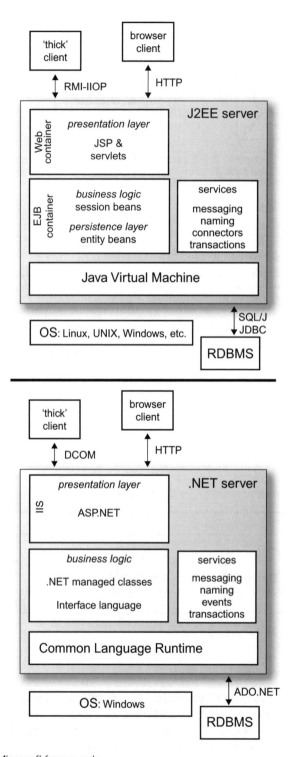

Figure 12.10 J2EE and Microsoft frameworks.

The thick client can be written using Swing or Abstract Windows. The thin client can use Java Applets to increase functionality over the basic HTML/JavaScript capabilities. The J2EE server machine (the application server) uses Servlets and Java server pages for the presentation tier that creates the dynamic web pages and EJB for the business logic. The data tier is a standard database management system (DBMS) like Oracle, IBM DB2, or Microsoft SQL Server (Figure 12.10). The data tier can also be considered to include third-party business systems that exchange information with the asset management. A Java IDL enables connections to CORBA applications.

Microsoft .NET

The .NET is not just an architecture for application servers; it is an all-encompassing solution for the integration of software applications. It can be used with an X-Box through to SQLServer. Unlike the J2EE, a specification, .NET is a suite of products and services, and a software platform. Running throughout .NET are XML web services. XML runs through .NET like blood through arteries. This approach enables loosely coupled applications to communicate using Internet protocols and standards. The .NET can be used by small peer-to-peer workgroups all the way up to large multi-tiered applications with remote thin clients.

The .NET products include 'smart' devices and client software. Typical devices would be games consoles like the X-box, mobile devices, and hand-held PCs. The client software is for the desktop computer. To support the middle-tier, there are a number of servers for running application services, business services, content management, and e-commerce services.

The .NET framework combines the distributed component model of DCOM and XML data services. This chapter focuses on the use of .NET in the application layer of multi-tiered computing.

COM

Microsoft's development of a component-based architecture started back in 1993 with the release of the COM. It allows applications written by different vendors, in different languages to inter-operate across process and network boundaries. The *object* in COM is a piece of compiled code that comprises the component. Access to other components is always via interface pointers stored in a virtual table (vtable). The pointers are binary, so are language independent (Figure 12.11).

In 1996, COM was upgraded to make interprocess communication easier between remote machines. Distributed COM or DCOM makes it easier to split a digital asset management system into multi-tiers, so that the business logic can be separated from the presentation layer. It also facilitates scalability, as components can be run on multi-processor machines or on clusters of machines. DCOM adds provision for network connections between clients and COM components. The network between machines can be any IP connection: LAN or the Internet. DCOM optimises communication to counter the effects of network latency on long distance connections. To use the public Internet, the DCOM can be encapsulated within HTTP to avoid firewall issues.

As a COM object is a binary component, it is reusable across different platforms. Compare this with CORBA objects which are compatible at the source code level, but

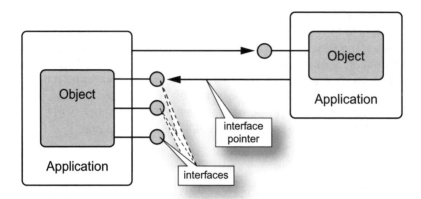

Figure 12.11 COM objects and interfaces.

have to be compiled for each different operating platform. Most implementations of CORBA for simplicity run on a common operating platform.

For .NET, Microsoft has released a new object-oriented language called C#. It combines features from C++ and Java. Microsoft has taken a similar approach to J2EE for the .NET framework. Both are object oriented, and use a four-tier architecture: presentation, business logic, data, and runtime. For the runtime environment, .NET uses the common language runtime engine (also known as the common language infrastructure, CLI). The language used for coding the software components is compiled into the Microsoft intermediate language that runs on the runtime engine. This is analogous to the Java bytecodes and the Java virtual machine (JVM), but the application can be coded in a number of languages including C and Visual Basic.

The .NET applications use the Microsoft host integration server to interconnect with legacy application.

Application servers

The business logic is the lynchpin of the digital asset management system. The reliable operation of your business depends on the smooth running of the object-based software that executes the business logic. The middleware does provide the basic broker service for client to object requests. It also provides much more to give a highly available and reliable service.

The business logic and the necessary services run on the application server. This is usually a cluster of machines in order to provide the necessary performance and fault tolerance.

A web server usually provides the presentation layer. Thick clients can interface directly with the business logic layer. If the presentation layer is ignored, the application server is where the middleware—the business logic—is deployed (Figure 12.12).

The business logic may be interfaced to a number of other software applications. Some may be to legacy systems. Key to the operation of a television station is the sales and traffic system. This is used to sell airtime for the commercials, and to schedule their playout. This system will also be closely integrated with the planning and scheduling of

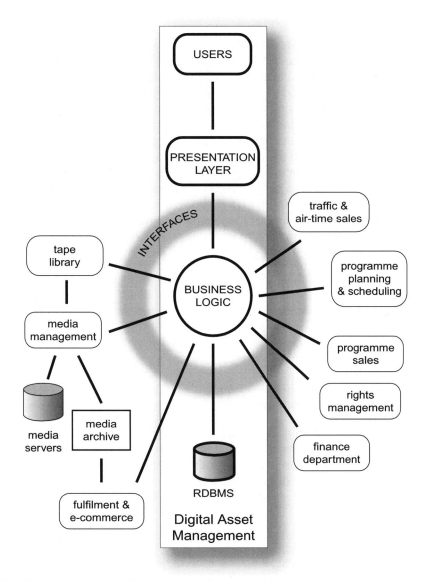

Figure 12.12 Typical interfaces to the business logic for a television station.

programmes. If the station creates programmes, there may well be a program sales and syndication system. Most stations will have a database of the tapes stored in the vault or library.

The older software systems may not have convenient interfaces. Some may use electronic data interchange (EDI) or proprietary interfaces. Some may not have any external interface, so a deal of customisation may well be necessary. Many older systems use a client–server design, based on a relational database. You will need some form of stored procedure that will publish new or changed record out to the digital asset management system.

Electronic Data Interchange (EDI)

The EDI was the first international standard for business-to-business communications. It enabled business software applications to exchange data without the need for human intervention, thus avoiding the rekeying of information. An EDI document comprises groups of data elements called segments. As an example, an element of an invoice would be a line item. A field definition table describes the data segments and their sequence. Each data element is described in a data element dictionary.

EDI can use proprietary and private formats, but generally over 300 approved transaction sets are used to avoid the need to write custom translation programs. If a legacy application has an EDI interface, you need to see if it is a standard, otherwise it will require a custom interface. There is a gradual move to migrate from EDI to XML, specifically to ebXML (electronic business XML).

If you are deploying digital asset management, it may be to take advantage of new business opportunities. To implement these new facilities you may well be purchasing e-commerce systems. In general, these are much easier to interface than the legacy systems.

Business logic functions

- Ingest
- Categorisation
- Media management
- Security, authorisation, and authentication
- Workflow and lifecycle management.

The server will have the runtime services for managing objects and messaging. The application server can manage the database connections intelligently. It could, for example, provide prioritisation of clients, so that real-time clients for encoding or fulfilment have precedence in a queue for resources over non-real-time clients that may just be searching or browsing for information. A straight database connection would not offer these features.

Failover protection

If you are in the media business, the application server becomes a lynchpin of your business. The consequences of a failure of the server will be downtime for the entire business.

Professional services

The most expensive component of any asset management system is often the cost of professional services to code the custom interfaces to other systems within the enterprise. This area stands to benefit most from moves to standardise inter-application communication.

In choosing a complete solution, you should anticipate spending time and resource to pre-empt the inevitable problems that will arise. It is essential to have a prime contractor or project manager to resolve the buck passing that is typical of interface development.

Summary

Asset management demands a distributed collaborative computing environment. This has led vendors to adopt the multi-tiered architecture that is common throughout enterprise software systems. The primary business and process logic of the asset management resides in application servers. These provide a scalable and high performance.

To improve the productivity of the software design teams an object and component-oriented approach has been adopted. Object-oriented design is good for modelling the real-work objects like analogue media assets: film, videotape, photographs, and paper documents. Component-based software can reuse standard components, avoiding the 'reinventing the wheel' syndrome. Object and component-based software decomposes code into self-contained modules. This means that modifications and extensions to functionality can be made without extensive redesign of the entire product.

Common software services migrate to a middleware framework. The potential purchaser of an asset management system is also going to need this framework to run the application server. This includes an execution engine to run the application, an object broker, and a web server. These may be bundled with the asset management product, but are usually separate line items, of not inconsiderate cost.

Middleware is an area that is rapidly maturing as the advantages of the multi-tier approach to computing have been clearly demonstrated.

In some circles, web services are eclipsing technologies like CORBA. They should not be looked upon as alternatives, but as architectures that can co-exist. CORBA's forte is the object-oriented approach whereas web services focus on the business process. Web services provide interfaces between applications that can use object orientation. To use the Internet for application interfaces, CORBA can be wrapped in web services.

J2EE uses one language (Java) and can run on multiple platforms. In contrast, .NET applications can be written in many languages, but they run on a single platform (Microsoft Windows). CORBA is both platform and language agnostic. There have been many arguments as to which is best. Your main decision will be which suite of products will give the best-of-breed solution to your requirements, and will give a return on the investment. The products may be built with CORBA, J2EE, or .NET, and there may be no choice. Unless you have a really compelling reason to choose a platform and architecture, it is the features of the digital asset management product that should be the primary influence. You will probably end up with a mix of operating systems, but that has always been the case. The creatives will want Mac operating system, the data centre may want UNIX, and the general systems will most likely be Microsoft. The introduction of XML web services has eased the integration of disparate systems, so many of the obstacles now belong to the past.

13 Databases

Introduction

Most potential owners of digital asset management systems will already own one or more databases. They are used by office systems for employee records and artists' contracts, and for the sales and traffic management of television commercials. Many media companies use databases to manage rights information. That is ownership of the intellectual property, and the logging of usage of that material. Another database application is the simple index systems for existing libraries of tapes and photographs.

These applications will have either to be closely integrated with, or replaced by, the digital asset management installation. In the former case, should they use the same database management system (DBMS). If you are already using a single database vendor, you will have staff trained and experienced in the maintenance of that product. It makes sense to stick with that vendor, unless there are compelling reasons to run different systems.

At the heart of every asset management system is a database. This is the repository of the metadata and may also be used to store small media files. For reasons of efficiency, the larger media files are stored in separate content servers and referenced by the metadata.

There are several possible architectures for a database:

- Flat file
- Hierarchical
- Network
- Relational
- Object oriented
- Extensible markup language (XML).

The basic table structure of the hierarchical database dates back to the days of mainframe computing. The first designs were static, in that the location of data records was known. This enabled the implementation of high-performance databases with the hardware available. They represent a storage-centric design. The bounded set of fixed length fields was simple to map to blocks for storage on disk or tape. The step change was the development of the dynamic database. In 1970, an IBM researcher, Dr E. F. Codd, described the concept of the relational database. He drew his ideas from the discipline of relational modelling and set theory. This represents information in a logical model. The data is stored sequentially in a flat file and new records appended (with the older hierarchical databases data was inserted into fixed locations). The ordered table view is created dynamically in response to a query. A record in a relational database table does not have a fixed reference, contrast the spreadsheet where each cell has an X–Y coordinate. Instead, a data cell is retrieved by specifying the database and table name, followed by the primary key and column name. To speed this dynamic retrieval with large data tables, indices are used.

IBM enthusiastically adopted the relational model with their DB2 product. They were then followed by Oracle. The design came to dominate the market and the network database, represented by CODASYL, soon died out. The hierarchical database was also to follow into obsolescence. The market has since diverged again into different designs with the advent in the 1980s of the object-based model, and more recently the XML database (with echoes of the old hierarchical database).

As operating systems evolved, and the files were abstracted from the storage blocks, it became possible to add features like variable length data fields to store complex data. We have seen how digital asset management demands much more flexibility for the data repository. Metadata is often stored as key–length–value triplets. Information can be expressed as XML documents. The content essence can be very large binary files. One answer to handle all these different datatypes is the 'universal database'.

Most asset management products use conventional relational databases, although some simple products use flat files to store data in a proprietary format. Oracle, IBM DB2, and Microsoft SQL Server are typical relational database products. Much of the middleware of the asset management is object oriented. File exchange between applications is often in the XML format, so why use a relational database management system (RDBMS)? In terms of efficiency the object database has many attractions.

The great advantage for the relational database is their maturity. They are tried and tested industrial-strength software applications. They can operate 365 days a year, around the clock with very little downtime. They are extensible and scalable. There is a large pool of available staff with the knowledge to administer the databases. While they may not be the state of the art in software engineering, they are a safe house in which to store your valuable asset metadata.

Luckily for the system integrator, the primary suppliers of relational databases have kept pace with developments in software engineering. The first move was to integrate the object-oriented approach with the relational tables to give the 'object-relational' database. This is a hybrid that can store objects, but the underlying structure is relational. Vendors are now adding support for XML files.

The databases that offer relational, object, and XML features could be termed 'universal' databases, and solve many of the problems related to the wide and differing demands of asset management. Most of the big-name vendors now offer such products.

Transactions

The primary interaction between the asset management system and the database is the transaction. This may create a record, change or update a record, or delete a record.

To retain the integrity of the data it is vital that the transaction complies with a number of conditions, usually called ACID:

- *Atomicity:* Each transaction must be either completed or aborted, it is all or nothing.
- *Consistent:* A transaction must leave the database in a consistent state. If a transaction violates the rules, then the transaction should roll back to the former consistent state.
- *Isolated:* A transaction is not available to other transactions until it is committed. If several users attempt to update the same record simultaneously, then the transactions should be performed serially and they should be isolated from each other.
- *Durable:* Once a transaction has been committed in, it should be persistent even if the system fails.

These rules must be obeyed even if the system fails in mid-transaction.

Relational databases

The basic static database is little more than a spreadsheet. All the data is stored in a single 'flat' file. Typical examples are the address books embedded in office software applications (Table 13.1).

The basic unit of the relational database is a two-dimensional table or relation. Note that a relational database is one that is based on *related* sets of information, not on the *relationships* between tables. The entity relationships between tables have led to this misunderstanding. It is perfectly possible to have a database with a single table of relations with no relationships to other tables. For reasons of efficiency, a single table is usually normalised into a number of associated tables.

A typical relation would be that a commercial with a *SpotName*, and a unique *Spot_ID* is stored on a tape number *Tape_ID* in format *Tape_format* and is stored in a *Location*. The relation is made up of attributes: *Tape_format*, *Tape_ID*, etc. These attributes have a domain or datatype. For example, the Spot_ID is four character, numeric, and can have values between 0000 and 9999. An attribute may have a limited set of values, called a domain. For example, there will be a set of shelf numbers within the vault. A record (originally called a tuple) is a statement that has attribute values that match the required attributes for that relation.

Relation values are usually represented as a two-dimensional table (Figure 13.1). The attributes are represented in columns, and the tuples in rows. A collection of relational

Table 13.1 Flat database table

First name	Last name	Company	Town	Post code
John	Smith	Acme Engineering	Newtown	AB1 3CD
Mary	Brown	Vapour Software Supplies	Notre Ville	XY98765
Joe	Soap	Zorro Sabres	Vieuxport	AB12345

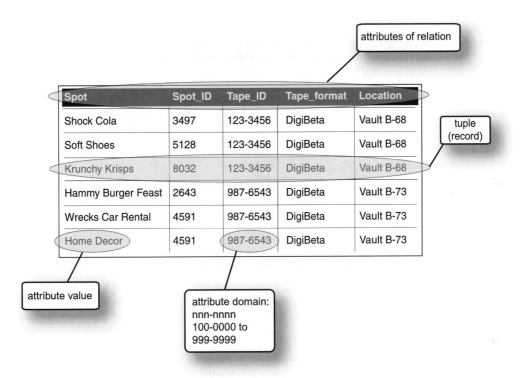

Figure 13.1 Relational variable represented as a table.

variables is called a database. This terminology is rarely used outside the field of relational modelling. Instead, more general terms are used:

- *Relational variable*, usually represented by and called a *table*
- *Attributes*, called *fields* and represented in *columns*
- *Attribute values* are called *field values*
- *Tuples* are represented by *rows* that are called database *records*
- *Domain* refers to the datatype of a column.

The set of columns in a table is called the scheme, so the set of tables is the schema. Records stored in the table can only be identified by the values within the fields. There is no direct system for referencing cells like a spreadsheet. To identify each record, it is given a field that is guaranteed to be unique. This is called the primary key. The key can be composed of more than one field in combination, and the entire record would be a super-key. The primary key can be a unique number formed from the data, like a tape number or for a book the international standard book number (ISBN). These numbers are allocated from a public registry (ISBN) or allocated in some other manner that ensures uniqueness. When automated tape libraries were used for videotape, a bar code was used by the robotics to identify the cassettes. The tape bar codes were pre-printed in sheets of self-adhesive labels, with incrementing numbers for the labels, much like the printing of bank notes or bills. Once a label was peeled off and stuck on a

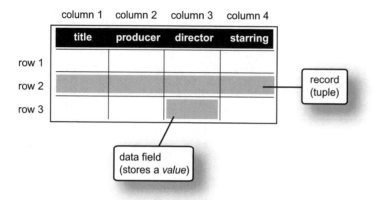

Figure 13.2 Database table.

cassette, then it could not be used again. These are called natural keys. The other way is for the DBMS to automatically allocate a unique number, a surrogate key.

Most databases support the concept of an index. This does allow a record to be directly referenced without the need to query the entire column looking for a matching attribute value (Figure 13.2).

SQL

SQL was devised as a standard means to define and manage the database, and also to access and retrieve data. Most database vendors have developed their own flavour of SQL, with proprietary extensions that add functionality. Unfortunately, this does mean that if a digital asset management product is designed to work with a specific database, then you cannot just substitute an alternative SQL database. It is a standard that is not used as a standard.

The database is designed using the data definition language (DDL). DDL allows you to create or drop (delete) the tables within database or the complete database. Once created, the tables can be altered to add new columns and define the datatype for the columns. In a relational database, there are a limited number of datatypes: character field, date, time, currency, and number (fixed and floating point). These have been added to over the years by evolution of the SQL standard, and also by extensions from vendors. As an example, a datatype called the binary large object or BLOB can carry unstructured data like an image file. This BLOB can be stored and retrieved, but its value cannot be queried like the normal fields.

The data manipulation language (DML) is used to access and manipulate records, specifically to select, insert, update, and delete records. The select statement is used to perform queries. A query results in a temporary table called a view, which forms a sub-set of the information stored within one or more tables. For example, you could return all the spot titles on a given tape number.

The DDL is used by the database designer to construct the schema, whereas DML is used during the normal operation of the asset management system. The user interface, via the application server, initiates the generation of SQL statements (Figure 13.3).

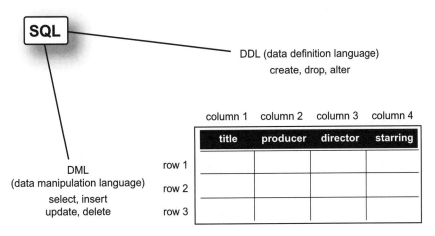

Figure 13.3 SQL.

Multiple tables

The single table has the advantage of simplicity. But as the quantity of data increases, efficiency becomes an issue. Consider a number of tapes containing 30-s commercial spots. Each tape may have a 100 spots, so the information about the tape cassette will have to be repeated in the database for every spot record.

If the tape information were to be held in a different table, the information would only need to be stored once. The spot is then associated to the tape information through the tape ID. The tables are joined through a common column, in this example the Tape_ID.

So one large table with duplicated data and tens of columns is converted into many associated small tables, each with a few columns. The tables are associated through relationships and keys (an example of a key is the Tape_ID) (Figure 13.4). The relationship is implied rather than explicit (e.g. using a URI), in that two tables have identical columns, and matching records imply the relationship, in this example the Tape_ID. The relationships between the table entities are defined in the schema of the database.

This reduction in the stored data using associated tables is referred to as the normalisation of the data. The goal in normalisation is that each piece of data should only be stored once, but for reasons of performance a database rarely meets this goal. There is a set of formal rules for normalisation called forms: 1NF, 2NF, 3NF, and BCNF, where NF is an abbreviation for normal form. There is no one result for a normalisation. It depends how the fields model the model the real-world business objects like tapes and commercials. The goal is to match those objects closely by the table representation.

The user interface will have forms, each field in the form corresponding to one or more fields in the database. The form may present data from many tables, or possibly from a federation of databases. The form could show information from the rights and the media management databases. The user will see a unified view, and does not need to know that the data has several sources. The application server marshals and organises the data to give the seamless view of the asset information.

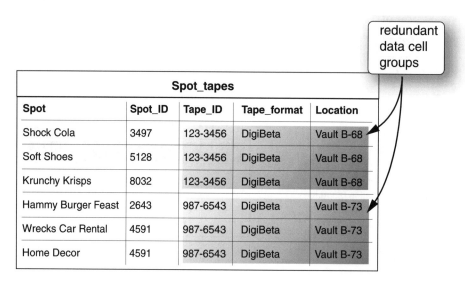

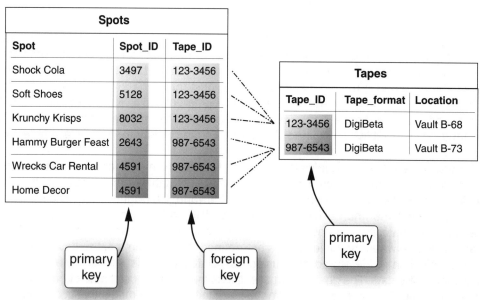

Figure 13.4 Primary and foreign keys.

Conversely, some database fields are never displayed to the users. The application server uses them for control and management functions.

The relational database was developed at a time when system memories were small, under 1 MB. Now the database server will have several gigabytes of RAM, so the emphasis has shifted to performance. The goal now is to minimise the response time to queries. The data-driven user interface demands fast response times. In the interests of performance, a full normalisation may be compromised.

The design of the tables and their associations, or entity relationships, has a large impact on the efficiency of the database. Luckily, the digital asset management system vendor has already carried out most of this work, but it will still be an issue if the system is to be customised for specific applications.

Views

To view information from the database, we usually want to see a virtual table that combines records from a number of tables into virtual records. The normalisation of tables splits the information into many tables, whereas a view combines the information back into a single table. To construct a view, the query retrieves data by joining sets of information from a number of tables.

Database Management System (DBMS)

The DBMS does far more than supporting SQL. Perhaps the most important is to ensure the integrity of a data field during a value update or transaction control. If the operation to change a value were to be interrupted, the transaction could be corrupted, suppose a tape was being checked out from the vault to a user. If the communications between the librarian's terminal and the server were lost, the database could lose the location value of that tape. The tape could be checked out of the library, but the transaction to associate with user may have failed. The tape is in limbo. To avoid this, the DBMS performs a handshaking operation to ensure that the entire transaction is completed before committing the changes to the datastore. If anything goes wrong, it rolls back to the original state, nulling the transaction. The librarian is warned and can take the appropriate action. There should be an operational procedure to temporarily store the information until the database is back on line.

The DBMS control access to the data. It authenticates then authorises users. They are allocated different levels of privileges to read and write the data. The management system also gives isolation between multiple users of the database. Data is locked so that only one user at a time can update information, although many may have concurrent access.

Stored procedures

The end users of the database information do not have to write SQL statements to retrieve or update information. Instead, pre-complied SQL statements are built into the business logic in the application server. This can be tested and debugged at the design stage. A special kind of stored procedure is the trigger. The RDBMS can instigate an SQL procedure when a data event occurs. As an example, an update will be made to the database if a commercial spot is successfully aired at a given date and time. The update can trigger a report to be issued to the airtime sales department. They can then raise an invoice. Many such triggers can also be instigated at the application server.

The database index

Data can be retrieved using a column as an index. This means that the database does not have to scan the entire table for a query, but just the column designated as the index.

A filter can be applied to column and only those rows retrieved. This makes for fast access. Some columns are specified as unique indices, or keys.

Data independence

One of the big advantages of the RDBMS over the static architectures is data independence. The way the data is stored on the physical devices, the disk drives, is independent of the logical view that the user sees. This logical view should also be independent of the table structure. The schema can be changed without changing the view of the data for the user. This means that a user can see a representation of a legacy card index if they so wish, even though the asset management is storing the data in many tables with a very different data representation.

Referential integrity

Within a relational database the referential integrity is maintained if

- the value of each row is unique
- the foreign keys must have a primary key in another table
- the business rules are obeyed.

Object-oriented databases

Relational theory is concerned with knowledge, the vales of cells in the database. Object theory is all about behaviours. Our real-world view of media assets is object based. We often deal with objects that we can handle: a 35 mm slide or a videocassette. The behaviour is an operation; we can *play* a tape. The basic concept of object modelling sits easily with our view of the world.

A software object comprises a set of methods and data representing the state of the object. A method is a function used to implement the behaviour of the object. Contrast this with procedural programming, where the data is stored separately from the functions (code) that perform the operations. The encapsulated object can only be accessed through an interface, which exposes the public operations of the object.

Every object has a unique identity that distinguishes it from every other object (the identifiers are stored in a registry). The relational model has no concept of identity for a record. A record can only be retrieved following a query of the values of all the records in the table.

The values of the parameters of an object are instead stored as values of the attributes or its *state*. Any one state of an object is called an *instance* of the class of objects.

An object is bounded by an encapsulation that hides the private and protected methods and data (state variables) from public view. All communication with the object is via an interface. To examine its state, the object must be viewed through this interface. The operations or methods that the object provides are expressed as behaviours. A videocassette object has behaviours like play and rewind. If you apply one of these behaviours, the state can change, for example the cue point of the tape (expressed as a time code value). Note that we can play a videotape or digital versatile disk (DVD) without understanding how the media player objects works—it is encapsulated. An object has some basic characteristics:

- A unique identity stored in a registry
- It is encapsulated
- It provides behaviours through methods
- At any one time it has a state.

There are some other key concepts to the object model:

- Class and hierarchy
- Inheritance
- Associations
- Polymorphism.

Many objects are similar, and can be grouped into a class, for example all VHS video-cassettes. The class of VHS tapes in turn can belong to a super-class of all videotapes. In this way, the classes can form a hierarchy (Figure 13.5).

The class is a template for the object instances. The object inherits characteristics from its class. Note that the VHS tape object inherits most attributes from the super-class, and the VHS class only has the extended attribute for play speed. This has a domain of normal, long play and extended play. Often the same method appears in several classes. To use an example, we can *play* a tape and *play* a DVD even though the objects are in different classes.

Object can be linked through associations analogous to the relationships in a relational database. Polymorphism means that different data types or classes can be processed in different ways by the method according to the class. The method *play* is polymorphic, in that operation of playing a DVD may be quite different from playing a tape.

Many of these object characteristics are not supported by a relational database, for example: identity, polymorphism, and inheritance.

The object database

An object database is an array of elements or objects. As an object is encapsulated, when that object is retrieved it will have the same code and data that it had at the time it was stored. The database management should control the encapsulation to ensure access only through the object interface.

The relational database is very efficient at handling simple relationships. But the complex many-to-many relationships found in asset management require an intermediate table to store the relationships. In contrast, the object-oriented approach can easily handle complex associations. The pointer references are automatically resolved by the object DBMS, and represented within the database.

There are analogous query languages for object databases. The queries are usually simpler than SQL, as relationships are inherent in the object model, rather than being imposed by the query statement (Table 13.2).

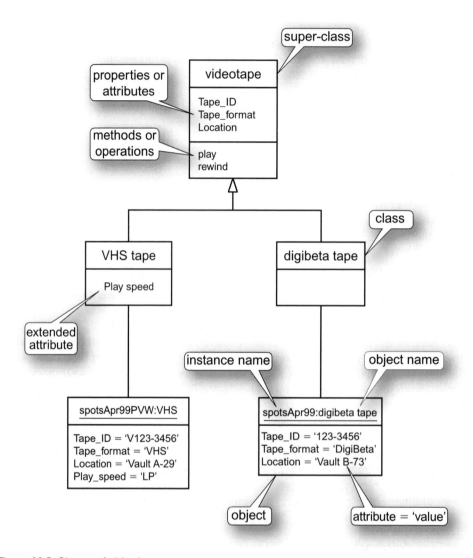

Figure 13.5 Classes of objects.

Object-relational databases

These are relational databases that have been extended to handle object attributes. To support object characteristics, the database has to support additional datatypes beyond the basic character, numeric, and date–time types found in a normal relational database. Some vendors have added support for references to store the object identifier and to allow them to be used as pointers to other objects. This is usually implemented as a foreign key.

The database designer can define tables that approximate to a model of the object classes and hierarchies. Some means must be found to represent inheritance and polymorphism.

**Table 13.2 Relational and object
database-equivalent terms**

Relational	*Object*
Table	Class
Record	Object
Column	Attribute/relationship
Stored procedure	Method
Triggers	Event management
Index	Index

The concept of encapsulating private data and code is not supported except through the general access control of the DBMS.

Limitations

The relational database and object-oriented programming have very different semantics and design approaches. The two require different data models that have to be mapped, adding complexity to the middleware. This adds to design costs, and to the work in software maintenance.

It is possible to store objects in an RDBMS; in fact, most digital asset management products that use an object-oriented approach use the commonly available relational products.

XML databases

The arguments over object versus relational have been running since the 1980s, but now there is another player—the XML database. Asset managements systems make great use of XML, so does the XML database replace the relational? There are two types of XML found in digital asset management. The first is content in an XML format. This is unstructured information, perhaps a text document that is destined to be published in several formats. Although the information is unstructured, the XML file is structured by the document type definition (DTD).

The second type uses XML as a data container, typically used to store the metadata from the digital asset management. This format usually has an associated XML schema, as opposed to the DTD used for unstructured content.

The unstructured XML content can be stored in a conventional file system, just like the rest of the media assets. It is the XML metadata that is the issue. Structured XML with an associated schema can be very easily mapped into a relational database. The choice is between an RDBMS and a 'native' XML database.

A native XML database is not really a low-level database. The data could well be stored in a relational database as a large-character object. The native database is more of a tool for XML applications. The databases store an XML file as a document, and can then

Table 13.3 Relational database design versus UML

RDB	UML	
Entity	Object	
Relationship	Association	Association class
Cardinality	Multiplicity	

retrieve it unchanged. This round-trip integrity is important for some applications, specifically legal and medical documents where the document must not be changed.

The XML database maps the XML into tables as element, attribute, and parsed, character data (PCDATA). If a table were to be accessed using SQL the result would not be very useful, as the records represent a model of the XML document in the data storage domain, and not the business entity domain that the XML represents.

UML

Unified modelling language (UML) is commonly used for the design of databases. This is an alternative to the entity-relationship model (Table 13.3).

Federated databases

Most large enterprises will have a number of databases each for different business applications. Many operations within the digital asset management will need to query more than one of these databases in order to perform a transaction. So, for example, a query about the copyright of a piece of material may require access to the asset management database, and to that of the right management system. The user of the system needs a seamless reply that apparently comes from one source; they are interested in the information, not where it is stored. Similarly, updates should be routed to the appropriate database. This federation is more of a middleware issue than an issue for the DBMS. The business logic performs the federated query and assembles the single response to the original query.

Many large media organisations have 10 or more legacy database systems that may need to communicate with the asset management. Maybe they could be integrated, but the separation of functions give resilience, and the cost of integration may not produce sufficient return in efficiency saving.

The concept of the federated database could also be applied to the object-relational issue. RDBMSs are very robust systems that have been optimised over time to give high performance. To impose object mapping, it may not give the best performance. One way around this is to use a federated system of both relational and object databases. The middleware has available whichever database is most appropriate for the application.

System resilience

As the database is core to the system, careful attention needs to be paid to the design of disaster recovery policies. The database is the vault for the knowledge that enables the management of content assets. It must be protected against the many hazards that could cause corruption or total loss. These hazards can be split into two groups: one is the problems that can occur within a data centre: hardware faults, software bugs, power supply failure; the other is total loss of the centre through fire, earthquake, theft, or even war and terrorism.

Most of the techniques for providing resilience come as part of the database products, such features as replication and high availability. When choosing a DBMS and designing the surrounding architecture, there are many factors to consider:

- Reliability
- Availability
- Scalability and extensibility
- Manageability.

Reliability

This should not really be an issue with a reputable database and hardware platform. The main issues that can affect reliability are usually human ones: misconfiguration or operator error. The usual way to circumvent this is through training and the application of formal operational procedures. There is always the possibility of sabotage, possibly by a disgruntled employee inside the corporate firewall. That is an issue of security.

High availability

The first part of a data resilience strategy is to cope with hardware failure, so that the system remains available to users even in the event of system faults. The data servers can lose hard drives and power supplies. The usual route to counter this is to use a cluster of database processors, with a shared RAID storage sub-system. The cluster allows two servers to run the same database in a fail-over configuration. If one server fails, clients are transparently reconnected to the other database.

The primary security against system failure is the data backup. At regular intervals, a snapshot is taken of the database tables and stored on another disk array or on removable storage like data tape or optical disks. Simple databases have to be shut down to take a backup. The DBMS should also provide tools for management of the backup recovery after an outage. Without such tools, it could take many hours to restore a system.

To provide resilience against a disaster at the primary site you can run a secondary site at a remote location. The two databases are synchronised by a replication link. In the event of the failure of one site, the other continues normal operation.

System design

During the implementation of a digital asset management system, the integrator will have to look at existing forms and reports. This will give them a good idea of the data fields that have been important to supporting the existing business rules. From this analysis, the domains of the datatypes can also be defined. The business rules will define the work-flows and the terms and conditions for trading with partners and customers.

This research on the operational practices cannot be just with management. They will have an overview of the practices, but the fine detail of the data is learnt from the users: librarians, archivists, journalists, authors, illustrators, editors, and accountants.

The asset management schema will need to be aligned with legacy database systems. This will need more work if it is to be a dynamic link rather than a one-time import.

What does all this mean? Why is the database important if the application server wraps it from view by the user? If the digital asset management product uses one of the well-known databases, then there should be no problems.

If it uses some esoteric database product, why is that? Is it to support an object view? Although some database management products may be very good, it is going to be the core of the system. It is the central repository for all the metadata.

So the choice of database should be carefully considered, and if it deviates from the handful of commonly used products then there should be really compelling reasons. Many smaller software vendors have fallen by the wayside, but Oracle, Microsoft, and IBM are here for the long haul. The ideal asset management product supports several vendors. Therefore, you could start with a low-cost solution, and leave open the option to change later to a more powerful product. The choice can also fit with your general IT purchasing strategy and staff skills and experience.

Although many products will operate out of the box, most businesses use proprietary number systems somewhere in the organisation. The system integrator will have to match the user interface and report outputs to your existing business needs. Therefore, the database schema may need customisation to operate within your business environment. This is more likely if the digital asset management has to interface with legacy back-office systems. Much of the schema alignment can be done at the application server level, but some products may still need schema upgrades. These may be done as part of the next product release, or may be custom to your installation. Do not forget that custom upgrades may not be tested to work with future product upgrades, which means that you may not be able to take advantage of new features. The best path is always to persuade the vendor to incorporate your requirements into a formal product upgrade.

Summary

We have what at first site seems strange. Digital asset management uses object-oriented programming and XML, but the predominant database technology is relational. Why is this?

This is where the system design gets conservative. It is all very well to have an innovative application for face recognition used to index video material. If it only works 10 per cent of the time, it can get better as algorithms are improved. However, the asset data is crucial to the integrity of the entire asset management system. It pays to play safe; use a technology that works, can build highly available systems, and has established methods for backup, replication, and disaster recovery. If you choose a popular product, the administration staff will be easy to hire. There is a large pool of talent that can assist with service and support. SQL has become a universally understood language for database professionals, yet SQL relates to tabular databases, and does not support the object model.

Many digital asset management systems use a hybrid approach, with an object-oriented and XML middle tier mapped to a RDBMS. That way you get the advantages of new technologies, but from a trusted datastore. In the 1990, several object-oriented databases products emerged. But there are always questions of vendor viability if you step outside the five or so mainstream relational database vendors. Others may be excellent products, but the world of database administration has to be cautious. It may be better to accept a less than idea technical solution for pragmatic reasons of sound business judgement.

The primary vendors of RDBMSs have incorporated new extensions to handle objects and XML documents. So you can stay with same vendor as legacy back-office systems, yet use the emerging software technologies that are making distributed computing a reality.

The choice of database and configuration will have a marked effect on the performance of the system. During the installation, expect to spend some time tuning the system.

14 Disk storage and media servers

Introduction

The magnetic disk drive is the core technology underlying digital asset management. An array of the disks gives users fast and random access to the content repository. The ever-increasing capacity and read/write speeds of the drives has enabled document storage, then images, and finally video. The capacity has increased to 40,000 times the original in 50 years since the drive was developed. These advances promise to increase apace until the limits imposed by the laws of physics. We will then have to turn to other technologies.

Disk performance is increasing year on year, while the cost falls. This means that ever-larger media libraries can be online to give almost instantaneous access to the content. One only has to look at the video post-production industry to see how the disk has taken over from tape as the medium for editing. Videotape is only used for capture and archiving.

The disk architecture is an important factor in the overall system design. If you were to choose a less than optimum architecture, there will be long latencies for file recall, and also the number of simultaneous clients that can use the system will be limited. These factors are even more important if your archives include video content. This is because of the very large files sizes and the bandwidth required for real-time record and playback.

In a simple asset management system, the content will be stored on a standard computer file server. These are sold for general office use, and may run several applications including central document storage, information database, mail server, shared directory services, and an intranet web server.

These applications have modest requirements. The files are small and there are no time-critical operations. It does not matter if it takes 1 or 10 s to deliver a file to a desktop client.

A larger business will split the applications between different servers. One server may handle the e-mail with an application like Microsoft Exchange. Another may be used to run a database for transaction processing.

In a similar way, the asset management system will dedicate one or more servers solely to the task of delivering asset files. These are called the media servers.

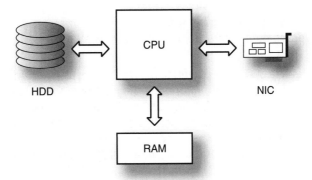

Figure 14.1 Basic server block diagram.

At its most basic, a server comprises a hard disk drive, a central processor with its associated random access memory (RAM), and a network interface card (NIC). Add to that a video card and keyboard for set-up and configuration (Figure 14.1).

The terms used for the components of disk systems' hark back to the days when mainframes represented the ultimate in performance and the multi-gigahertz Pentium was just a dream. The high-speed interface is called the *small* computer system interface (SCSI) and the redundant array of inexpensive (or independent) disks (RAID) uses *inexpensive* disks.

As mentioned before, performance is an issue with media servers. Although the specification of a basic server is ever increasing, if the media server is going to meet the needs of the users, some areas may need special attention to achieve high data transfer rates.

You may have heard broadcasters referring to video servers. Could they be an alternative to the media server? That depends on the application.

Video servers

The video server was originally developed as a temporary store for short effects sequences. As it matured it became possible to use the server to play television commercials (spots) to air. These short clips are typically 30 s in duration, and may be played hundreds or thousands of times. The videotape recorder is not best suited to this short duration and repeated playback. The tape will suffer wear with increasing levels of dropout giving playback errors. Usually visible errors are considered unacceptable for commercial playback, and may even result in a loss of payment. Tape decks are also expensive to run, requiring regular and skilled maintenance. If a disk drive fails, it is just replaced and thrown away.

To drop a disk-based server into the place of a video cassette recorder (VCR) certain facilities are mandatory, but they are not found in a normal file server:

- A real-time operating system for deterministic control
- Guaranteed resources for real-time playback

- Decoder to generate a standard video format
- Decoder locked to the station timing reference
- An encoder to record continuous video to the disk array as files.

A commercial break is cued and played to air with an accuracy of one television frame (40 ms PAL and 33 ms NTSC). Normal operating systems are not deterministic; a commercial could start a frame late. File servers multi-task and apportion resources as needed. If one task is hogging the processor, others will have to wait. This is not acceptable with video. The output stream has to be maintained under all circumstances. Video systems are synchronous. To mix and switch video all the sources have to be locked to a common clock.

The special capabilities of a video server are not a requirement for most digital asset management systems; normal file servers can be used. A video server is only required if you want to stream broadcast-quality video.

Disk drives

The building block of the storage sub-system is the hard disk drive. The first disk drive system was the IBM RAMAC. This used a 24-in. diameter disk and stored 5 MByte. Before the disk, magnetic storage was either tape for linear access, or the drum for random access. Therefore, like the phonograph, magnetic storage started with the cylinder and progressed to a disk. In a period of 50 years, the disk has evolved to the Hitachi microdrive, storing 4 GByte on a 1-in. diameter disk in a 36 $\times$ 44-mm form factor. The popular drives now for storage sub-systems use a 5.25-in. or 3.5-in. form factor.

The first device that pioneered the drive of today was the IBM 3340, commonly known as the Winchester. This used a sealed enclosure to maintain a clean environment for the disk and heads. It stored 30 MBytes.

Disk terminology

The mechanical part of the drive consists of a number of platters mounted on a spindle. The platters rotate at high speeds, between 7000 and 15,000 rpm. The platters carry the magnetic coating. The surface is formatted into concentric tracks. The tracks are divided into small arcs of 512 bytes, called sectors. The vertical group of tracks on different platters at a given radius is called a cylinder. Each platter surface has an associated read/write head that is carried on a moving arm or slider. An actuator moves the slider to position the head above the required track. The head has a special solenoid to write the data to the disk, and a separate sensor to read the magnetic data tracks. The platter motor, the actuator, and the heads are linked to the external interface (SCSI, ATA) by a disk controller. The platters, heads, and actuator, plus the sealed casing, are together called the head-disk assembly (HAD) (Figure 14.2).

Originally, the CPU addressed sectors directly by cylinder number, head, and sector. The disk controllers map the sectors into a logical block address. Consequently, a file is mapped by the file system into blocks, rather than sectors.

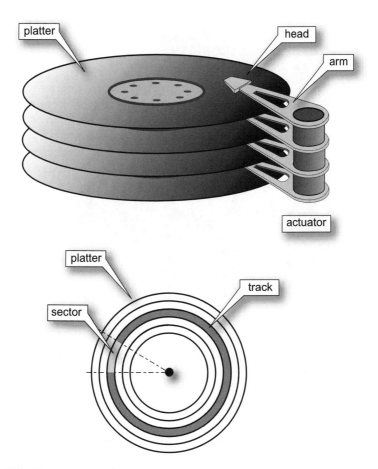

Figure 14.2 Disk drive components.

A disk can be formatted into a number of logical partitions, each containing a volume or group of volumes. The volume is a logical storage unit comprising a collection of directories and files. Note that a volume can span more than one partition (Figure 14.3).

Disk performance

The hard drives have a number of key performance indicators that can be used for selection of the appropriate device for the content repository.

Capacity
This is ever increasing and by 2003 many units could hold more than 100 GBytes of data (Table 14.1). That means about 9 h of television commercials could be stored on a single drive if encoded at 25 Mbit/s.

Figure 14.3 Seagate Cheetah 15k3 drive © Seagate Technology LLC.

Table 14.1 2003 snapshot of typical disk drive performance parameters

Manufacturer/ model	Spindle speed (RPM)	Average seek time (ms)	Capacity (MByte)	Sustained data rate (MByte/s)	Interface
IBM Ultrastar 36Z15	15,000	4.2	36	36–52	Ultra 320 SCSI
IBM Ultrastar 146Z10	10,000	4.7	146	33–66	Ultra 320 SCSI FC-AL
Maxtor Atlas	15,000	3.4 (read)	73	75	Ultra 320 SCSI
Seagate Cheetah 15k.3	15,000	3.6	73	49–75	Ultra 320 SCSI FC-AL

Sustained data rate

This is important for video files. Although drive manufacturers may quote much higher maximum rates, these are only for very small files. For video playback, sustained data rate is the most important parameter.

Spindle speeds

The faster the disks rotate, the higher the data rate that the head can read. The higher speeds will give a better performance all round.

Average seek time

This is the time for the read head to correctly position over the required track. The seek time is essentially wasted time for data transfer, so the shorter the better.

Interface

Most high-performance disks use an ultra SCSI or fibre channel interface.

Disk interfaces

There are several choices for the drive interface. Some of the popular are ATA, SCSI, and FC-AL but there are others like serial storage architecture (SSA). The server uses a host bus adaptor (HBA) to interface between the processor backplane of the host (PCI bus) and the chosen disk interconnection. With a desktop computer, the HBA may be used to connect internal SCSI drives, but the more usual interface is to external drives in an adjacent rack.

AT Attachment (ATA)

This was originally developed for the IBM personal computer (PC) model AT (when that was advanced technology), as the ATA. The original standard is now called ATA-1, to distinguish it from later versions. ATA-6 and -7 are under development. The standard is still the favourite for the internal drives of PCs and represents 90 per cent of the drive market. As the maximum cable length is only 18 in., its use is limited to internal disk drives.

SCSI

The Small Computer System Interface or SCSI is a group of standards for a storage interface architecture (Figure 14.4). It is both a protocol and a physical medium. It has a more flexible bus structure than the ATA standards. Up to 15 devices can be attached to a single bus, as opposed to four with current ATA standards. Apple pioneered its use for the connection of peripherals, media drives, scanners, and CD-ROMs, but it is now universally used for mid-sized disk array where the additional cost of Fibre Channel is not warranted. The standard was soon evolved to support higher data rates. The standards are published by the ISO/IEC.

The standards describe commands, protocols, and interconnections. The commands are not restricted to disk drives. There are command sets for streams (tape drives), media changers (jukeboxes), multimedia devices (DVD), and RAID controllers.

The protocols that can be used for the commands are the SCSI parallel interface (SPI), the IEEE-1394 serial bus protocol (also called FireWire or i-Link), Fibre Channel, SSA, iSCSI, and serial attached SCSI (SAS).

SCSI Parallel Interface (SPI)

The physical layer is often referred to as parallel SCSI to distinguish it from the command sets (Table 14.2). SCSI uses a multiway cable like ATA but the maximum cable length is longer than ATA at 12 m (for low-voltage differential, LVD). Up to 15 devices can be attached to a single bus, as opposed to four with current ATA standards. SCSI can be used to build small arrays of RAID or just a bunch of disks (JBOD) for workstation storage. For larger disk arrays other technologies like Fibre Channel will be required to link large racks together.

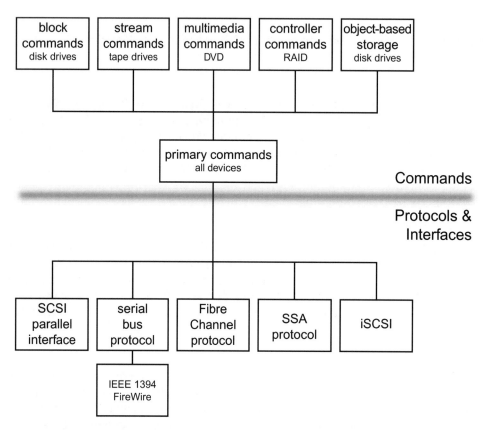

Figure 14.4 SCSI standards architecture.

Table 14.2 SCSI Parallel Interface standards

SCSI parallel interface	Marketing names	Electrical	Bus speed (MHz)	Data rate (MByte/s)	
				8-bit	*16-bit*
SCSI-1		Single-ended	5	5	
SCSI-2 Fast-10		Single-ended, HVD	10	10	20
SCSI-3					
SPI Fast-20	Ultra SCSI	LVD	20	20	40
SPI-2 Fast-40	Ultra 2 SCSI	LVD	40	40	80
SPI-3 Fast-80 (DT)	Ultra 3 Ultra 160	LVD	40 + DT	N/A	160
SPI-4 Fast-160 (DT)	Ultra 320	LVD	80 + DT	N/A	320
SPI-5 Fast-320 (DT)	Ultra 640	LVD	160 + DT	N/A	640

The terms 'fast' and 'wide' are often used. Wide refers to a 16-bit bus rather than 8 bit. This can carry twice the data rate. Fast refers to double transition (DT) clocking, which allows the data rate to be doubled. Ultra means SCSI-3 standard.

A number of different cables and connectors are used for the SPI. These include ribbon, twisted pair shielded and unshielded, and connectors with 50, 68, and 80 pins. The usual configuration for a SCSI system is to link the devices together as a daisy chain or string. The end of the cable remote from the HBA is terminated.

The original electrical standard used unbalanced, single-ended transmission. To improve noise immunity the standard adopted differential transmission, initially at a high-voltage differential (HVD), using 5 V TTL logic levels. SCSI-3 moved to the LVD using a 3 V level that is better suited to chip integration and low-power electronics.

With such a large number of formats, do not expect a SCSI disk to connect to any old SCSI cable. You will have to qualify the SCSI version. The many trade names do not help this potential confusion.

Fibre Channel

Parallel interfaces like ATA and SCSI have a big disadvantage, the maximum cable run is short, and the number of addressable devices is low. So just as the parallel printer port has been replaced with the universal serial bus (USB), serial alternatives are available to replace the SPI.

Fibre Channel is a full-duplex serial connection standard. It can use copper conductors (for low-cost connections over short distances) or optical fibre at distances from 10 m up to 10 km. It supports data rates from 133 Mbit/s up to a proposed 4 Gbit/s. The interface can carry SCSI commands and high-speed protocols like high-performance parallel interface (HIPPI). Three different topologies can be used for interconnection (Figure 14.5):

- Point to point: This can be used with to connect a single drive or to connect a host to a switch or gateway.
- Arbitrated loop: It uses a ring configuration. The data loops through each node. To permit hot plugging of drives, some form of active bypass allows a drive to be hot plugged without disturbing the loop integrity.
- Fabric (switched): The Fibre Channel fabric uses a switch to interconnect the nodes.

SSA

Serial Storage Architecture or SSA is a standard originally proposed by IBM. They were looking for a high-speed serial interconnection to disk storage systems to replace the SPI. It is a full-duplex serial link, using differential-pair copper or optical fibre much like Fibre Channel (Table 14.3).

IEEE-1394

The IEEE-1394 interface is used for directly attached storage for home and small office applications. It is more often marketed under Apple Computer's trademark 'FireWire'. It supports data rates of 400 and 800 Gbit/s, and can address a string of up to 63 devices. The networks can be built with strings and hubs. The copper implementation has

Table 14.3 Comparison of popular drive interfaces

	Fibre Channel	Ultra SCSI and Ultra 2 SCSI	SSA
Cable distance	10 m copper 10 km fibre	1.5 m 12 m with Ultra 2 SCSI	25 m
Variations	One version	See Table 14.2	One version
Data rate (MByte/s)	100, 200	40, 80 with LVDs	80, 160
Address range (devices)	127, with 40 + practical	16	128
Data integrity	CRC	Parity (CRC with Ultra 3 SCSI)	CRC

around 200 mph relative to the surface. The head flies at 50 nm above the surface, so any stray small particle can easily destroy the drive.

Any digital asset management system should have provision to cope with the loss of a drive without losing any of the content. The most basic way would be to use an offline backup, like a streaming tape. This is not going to meet the needs of the users who want a highly available system. The backup has to use additional drives. This implies that there should be redundancy within the array.

RAID

Patterson, Gibson, and Katz first used the acronym RAID for a redundant arrays of inexpensive disks in a conference paper dated 1988. Back then systems used a single large expensive drive (SLED), but now that the capacity of modern small-footprint drives exceeding the old SLEDs, the term 'inexpensive' has since been replaced with 'independent'.

The disk array consists of multiple independent disks organised as a large high-performance logical disk. This gives two benefits. The first is that arrays stripe data across multiple disks. The disks are accessed in parallel, which gives a higher data transfer rates for large data accesses and a higher input/output (I/O) rate for small data accesses. Striping also naturally balances the read/writes across all of the disks. This eliminates hot spots that could saturate a small number of disks while the rest of disks are idle. Striping has proved to be very useful in multimedia applications. If multiple video streams are served from a disk array, a very high data throughput is demanded. Before drive speeds increased, it was not possible to deliver high bandwidth video from a single drive. Striping provided the answer to that problem.

The second advantage is that redundancy can be added to the storage array, so that the loss of one drive does not compromise the integrity of the stored data. If you consider the statistics, the more drives there are in an array, the higher is the chance of one failing. Patterson, Gibson, and Katz defined a number of different configuration for the array, called RAID levels.

data written to drives in sequence

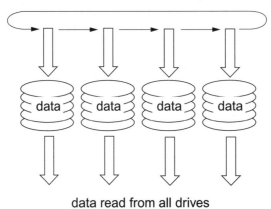

data read from all drives

Figure 14.6 RAID-0: Non-redundant.

RAID-0: Non-redundant

This level is not a true RAID. It is used where a high data throughput is required through data striping. Rather than using the storage space of each drive end to end, the logical space is organised by partitioning each drive into stripes. A stripe can be one sector (512 bytes up to large blocks of several megabytes). The stripes are then interleaved in a round-robin fashion, so that the combined space is composed of stripes from each drive in sequence. The size chosen for the stripes depends upon the application, whether it is the simultaneous I/O of short records, or the sustained throughput of a video file. If short stripes are used for video records, the write naturally distributes the record across the drives. Short database records are given long stripes, so that one record will reside on a single drive. That way other records can be read simultaneously from other drives in the array.

  RAID-0 is used for high-performance applications where fault tolerance is not required (Figure 14.6).

RAID-1: Mirrored

This is a true redundancy with the entire array duplicated or mirrored. It is the most expensive configuration and yet provides no disaster recovery. If you were looking for the ultimate data protection, it would make more sense to mirror across two geographically separate locations. RAID-1 is often used in small systems, replacing a single disk drive with two. With larger arrays, it is double the cost, and other levels offer good protection at a lower cost. It is a popular configuration because it is simple to control (Figure 14.7).

RAID-2: ECC hamming code

RAID-2 provides protection against disk failure, but without the doubling of the number of disks that is required with RAID-1. RAID-2 uses the same principles as the error-correcting code (ECC) used to correct bit errors in semiconductor RAM; this method detects and corrects data errors using Hamming codes. It is more efficient than RAID-1 mirroring in

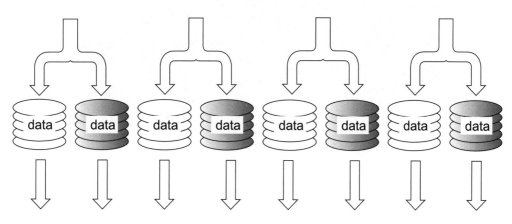

data written to drive in pairs

data read simultaneously from all drives

Figure 14.7 RAID-1: Mirrored.

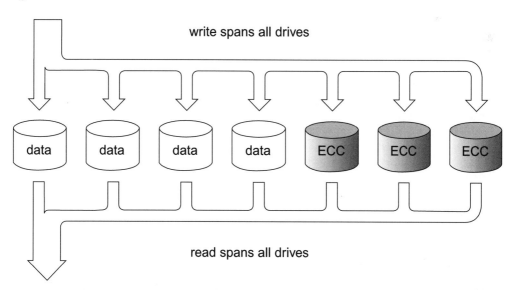

write spans all drives

read spans all drives

Figure 14.8 RAID-2: ECC hamming code.

that fewer drives are needed. Modern drives incorporate internal ECC protection at the sector level, so some hardware RAID products opt for RAID-3 or -5, to get better disk utilisation (Figure 14.8).

The drawback with RAID-3 is that the system is vulnerable to data loss if a drive fails. The original data is rebuilt from the parity information and written to the replacement disk. If a second drive were to fail during this process, the original data cannot be wholly recovered. As an example, the video server products from Leitch use ECC parity with a software RAID control to give full protection against two consecutive drive failures (Figure 14.9).

Figure 14.9 Leitch RAID sub-system. © Leitch Technology Corporation.

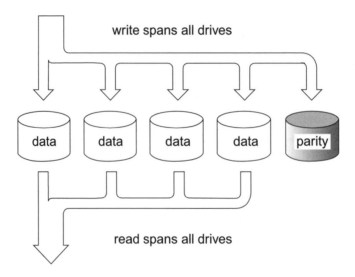

Figure 14.10 RAID-3: Bit-interleaved parity.

RAID-3: Bit-interleaved parity

RAID-3 provides even more efficient disk utilisation than RAID-1 or -2. A single drive stores the parity information, and this is used to reconstruct data in the event of one of the disks failing. As data is written simultaneously across all drives, the write performance is poor when compared to striped configurations like RAID-0. This makes it unsuitable for high data rate video applications (Figure 14.10).

RAID-4: Block-interleaved parity

This is not unlike RAID-3 but uses block interleaving rather than bit level. As every write operation also has to write to the parity disk, this drive becomes a bottleneck. In practice, RAID-4 is not used (Figure 14.11).

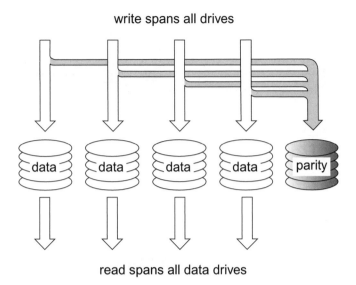

write spans all drives

read spans all data drives

Figure 14.11 RAID-4: Block-interleaved parity.

RAID-5: Block-interleaved distributed parity

Parity data is block interleaved across all drives rather than using a single disk for parity. It protects against the failure of any one drive in an array. It is versatile because the configuration can be tuned by changing the stripe size, to suit the requirements of the application. RAID-5 is not recommended for arrays with more than 14 drives as the risk of data loss increases (Figure 14.12).

RAID-6: P and Q redundancy

Parity can be used to correct any single, self-identifying disk failure. With larger disk arrays, however, it becomes prudent to use stronger ECCs that can tolerate multiple disk failures.

If a disk fails in a parity protected disk array, recovering the contents of the faulty disk requires the success reading of the contents of all other disks. The data restoration may not be possible if an uncorrectable read error is encountered during the recovery. If better data protection is required, then stronger ECCs have to be used. The P and Q scheme uses Reed–Solomon codes and can correct against two disk failures with only two additional disks (Figure 14.13).

There are several other RAID schemes, but in practice 0, 0 + 1, 3, and 5 have proved the most popular, along with some proprietary designs from disk array vendors. There is no single answer as to which RAID level to use. It depends very much upon your priorities for reliability, cost, and performance.

The RAID is run as a logical drive by the RAID controller. This has to perform the basic operations of distributing the redundant information across the drives. It also has to maintain the consistency of the redundant information during concurrent I/O operations

writes data across drives with distributed parity

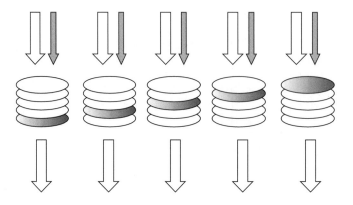

data read simultaneously across all drives

Key

data   P   Q

Figure 14.12 RAID-5: block-interleaved distributed parity.

writes data across drives with double parity

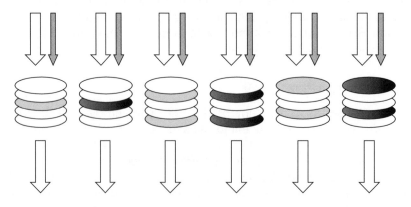

data read simultaneously across all drives

Key

data   P   Q

Figure 14.13 RAID-6: P and Q redundancy.

and through system crashes. If a disk does fail, many controllers can rebuild the original data and rewrite as redundant data back to the array with a replacement disk drive.

RAID only protects against drive failure. If more than one disk fails before the data has been rebuilt, it is likely that data will be lost. A highly available disk array will also need dual RAID controllers and dual power supplies. RAID does not protect against fire or flood, and it does not protect against viruses. It does not remove the need for a regular backup policy.

Some arrays include hot standby drives in the racks. This means that a drive can be immediately allocated as a replacement for a failed drive. The faulty drive can be physically removed at a convenient time, but the system is kept fully operational.

Storage networks

To support the goals of a digital asset management system, the content repository has to be shared among the users. This means that the disk sub-systems have to be linked together as a storage network.

Direct attached storage

The simplest form of disk storage is the directly attached disk (Figure 14.14). This includes the internal drive and any externally connected drives. Desktop computers generally use ATA for the connection to the internal drive. External drives often use the SCSI interface, although serial interconnections are becoming popular, with FireWire and USB 2.0 being typical examples of low-cost solutions for consumer and small office applications.

There are two main storage network architectures: network attached storage and the storage area network. They are rapidly evolving in hybrid solutions that offer the best of both solutions. The storage network system can also integrate the disks with removable

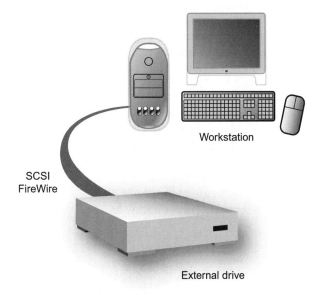

Workstation

SCSI
FireWire

External drive

Figure 14.14 Direct attached storage.

media, both tape and optical, for backup and archive. This is covered in more detail in a later chapter.

Media servers

If your assets include multimedia content, then the digital asset management systems will include media servers. These will include streaming servers for the viewing of the proxy files, and video servers to deliver the primary assets.

Streaming servers

The presentation layer of the asset management uses a standard web server for the user interface. The main audio-visual assets are previewed using low-resolution proxies.

The web server uses hypertext transfer protocol (HTTP) to deliver the pages that are used for searching and general management of the assets. The page files are delivered over the network using TCP/IP as the transport layer. The files are downloaded to the web browser cache as fast as the network allows. TCP incorporates flow control to manage the download rate. There is no pre-determined rate for delivery. TCP will increase the data rate until network packet loss indicates that the network is congested. At this point, the rate backs off. Another constraint is the receive buffer. TCP uses a sliding window of data in transit. The receiver processes packets as they arrive. If data arrives too fast, the receive buffer will overflow. The receiver sends messages to the transmitter to slow down to stop the buffer from filling.

Suppose that you want to stream a video preview file encoded at 100 kbit/s. The TCP transmission could start at 20 kbit/s. The transmitter then ramps up to 200 kbit/s, where network congestion sets the upper limit. Other users come on to the network, the transmission throttles back to 80 kbit/s. At no time has the data rate matched the rate at which the proxy was encoded.

As an analogy, TCP/IP is like driving a car along a six-lane highway, the speed is limited by congestion. What video needs is a train journey that runs to a fixed timetable. This predictable transport is called streaming.

Streaming

If the stream is encoded at 100 kbit/s, it has to be delivered at that rate. One of the functions of transport layer protocol is to regulate the stream rate. But what happens in the example where the network is congested and the best rate is 80 kbit/s? The player runs out of video data and stops.

Another requirement for viewing video is user navigation like a VCR. This means you can play, pause, or rewind the proxy, just like the VCR.

It can be seen that the streaming server needs two additional functions not found in a standard web server:

- Real-time flow control
- Interactive control.

HTTP does support any of this new functionality; so new protocols were developed for streaming media. Under the auspices of the Internet Engineering Task Force (IETF), several new protocols were developed for multimedia real-time file exchange: real-time

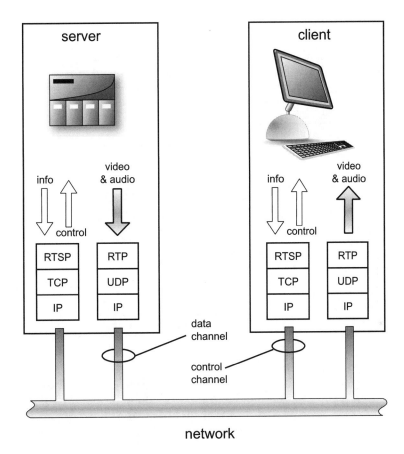

Figure 14.15 The streaming protocol stack.

streaming protocol (RTSP), real-time protocol (RTP), and real-time control protocol (RTCP). There are also a number of proprietary protocols using similar principles like Microsoft's Advanced Streaming Format used by Windows Media.

RTSP is the framework that can be used for the interactive VCR-like control of the playback (PLAY, PAUSE, etc.) (Figure 14.15). It is also used to retrieve the relevant media file from the disk storage array. RTSP can also be used with live webcasting to announce the availability of additional media streams. RTP is used for the media data packets. The RTCP provides feedback from the player to indicate the quality of the stream. It can report packet loss and out-of-order packets. The server can then react to congested network conditions by lowering the video frame rate or gear shifting to file encoded at lower bit rate. Ideally, the real-time media stream is delivered by user datagram protocol (UDP) over IP. The control protocols use TCP/IP for the bi-directional client–server connection.

Video servers

The original video servers were drop-in alternatives for the VTR. As such, they were a self-contained box with video I/O, and a control port. They have evolved since the early days, and have now become more of an interface between the video and storage domains.

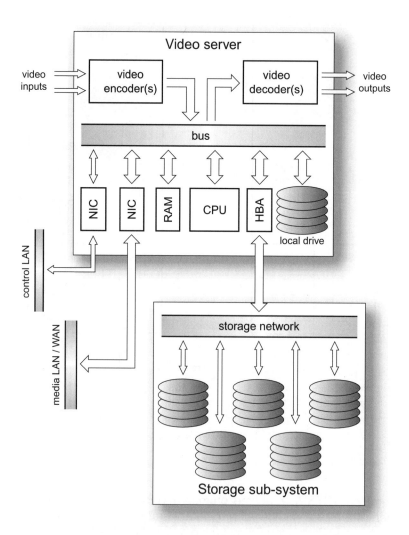

video inputs

video encoder(s)

Video server

video decoder(s)

video outputs

bus

NIC NIC RAM CPU HBA local drive

control LAN

media LAN / WAN

storage network

Storage sub-system

Figure 14.16 Video server architecture.

The video server is similar to a regular file server, but with the addition of a video encoder and decoder. Figure 14.16 shows the block diagram of a typical video server.

Much like a PC, it has a central processor, RAM, and networks interface cards (NIC). The video inputs, either analogue composite (NTSC, PAL) or digital component (601), are compressed to a format by the encoder card like MPEG-2. This data is then stored on the disks in a file structure. The HBA provides a high-performance link to the disk array. Fibre Channel has been the favoured format, but iSCSI would be an alternative. To play the video files, they are transferred to the decoder card, and processed back to regular video.

The video servers support read while write. This means that as soon as the encoder starts writing the video input signal to disk, the decoder can start to read the file.

Figure 14.17 Leitch VR440 video server (© Leitch Technology Corporation).

Therefore, servers can be used for time delay, or in a news application, work can start on a story as soon as it arrives at the television station.

The encoding and decoding must take place at video rate. This means that the processing, busses and disk I/O must all be capable of the maximum data rate to support the video codecs, with headroom for safety. At no time should the decoder ever run out of data, or the video output will fail, usually to black. This is very different from a PC, where the response time just slows down if the resources are insufficient.

So far, the system is no more than a VTR replacement. The difference is that the server has network interconnectivity. The compressed video files, the MPEG-2, can be transferred over an IP network to and from other servers. These could be geographically remote, with the transfer taking place via satellite or over fibre circuits. Unlike the synchronous I/O of video, this file transfer is asynchronous. It can be slower than video rate, or, if the network permits, faster than real time.

Summary

The disk drive is the primary storage medium for the digital asset management system. The ever-falling costs of drive devices has made possible the online storage of large multimedia files. Video assets place high-performance demands on the disk sub-systems. The simultaneous ingest and layout of multiple channels of video requires high-speed networks. Fibre Channel and gigabit Ethernet can support the ingest and playback of multiple channels of high-resolution video.

Video used to be handled separately from computer networks. Dedicated circuits were used to stream video in real time and storage was always on videotape. The new high-performance disk and networks mean that video can be handled as just another digital asset. Video has finally joined documents and images in the file-based digital domain.

Any asset management system for multimedia will need specialised media servers alongside the regular files servers used for the application and database. There are two types in common use: the streaming server and the video server. The audio–video proxies used for searching and preview will need streaming servers. Broadcast resolution assets will need dedicated video servers to meet the special requirements for real-time I/O.

15 Mass storage

Introduction

Magnetic disks are not the only way to store digital media assets. There are many reasons why disk may not be appropriate. First, there may be far too many assets to store on disk arrays. This is highly likely if you are managing video assets. Second, it is astute to keep offline backups of the assets, for security against system failure or to cope with disasters like fire, earthquake, or theft. The third reason is that a permanent archive may be required for business reasons or because legislation requires it. Many industries are obliged to keep permanent records of all files.

Although the price of disk storage is ever falling, there are limits to the size of a disk array. The main alternatives for backup and archives are magnetic tape and optical disks. These can be kept near online in robotic libraries or stored offline on shelves in conventional libraries or vaults.

Data tape

Tape is the traditional data storage medium. Until the development of magnetic disks, tape was the primary storage, but now it has become the main choice for secondary storage: for backup and archiving. Just like the hard drive, IBM pioneered much of the development, but now many vendors are actively marketing tape solutions. Several families of tape drive have emerged. AIT, DLT, and LTO are three of the leading formats. There are several others formats, but they are more suited to small system backup and have neither the performance nor the capacity for the demands of a digital asset management system. Examples of these would be digital audio tape (DAT) and the quarter-inch data cartridge (QIC).

Streaming and start–stop

Data can be written to the tape block by block, a process called start–stop recording. Where large volumes of data have to be written to tape, the alternative is to write data continuously to the tape, not pausing at the inter-record gaps. This is called streaming.

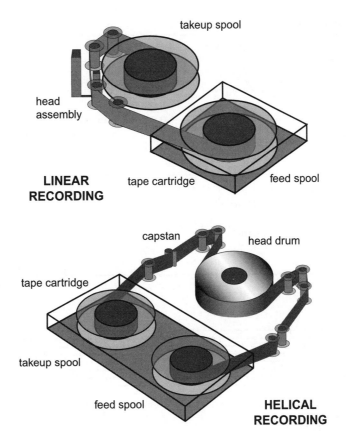

Figure 15.1 *Typical linear and helical tape paths.*

It requires that the disk array and processor sourcing the data can sustain the writing speed of the tape drive. The drive controllers usually cache the files to a local disk before streaming a file. Most families of data tape can operate in either mode.

Linear and helical

There are two ways of recording onto tape. Linear recording uses a stationary head, with the tape moved past at a constant velocity. The alternative is to use head rotating at high speed on a drum and move the tape slowly past the drum. This method records a slant tracks on the tape, and allows very high writing speeds without the need for a high linear tape speed (Figure 15.1).

Most of us have examples of both in the home. The audio cassette (compact cassette) uses linear recording, while the VHS recorder uses a helical scan (Table 15.1).

Linear recording formats

The original open-reel data recorders used linear recording. They recorded nine tracks along the length of the tape. To increase the data capacity serpentine recording is now

Table 15.1 Data tape formats

	Tape width	Form factor	Suppliers
Linear			
3590	½ in	4 in square (3480)	IBM
T9940	½ in	4 in square	StorageTek
T9980	½ in	4 in square Dual spool	StorageTek
LTO Ultrium	½ in		Hewlett-Packard, IBM, and Seagate
DLT, Super DLT	½ in		Quantum
Helical			
Mammoth, Mammoth 2 (M2)	8 mm		Exabyte
AIT	8 mm		Sony, Seagate
SAIT	½ in		Sony
DTF	½ in		Sony

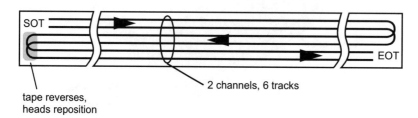

Figure 15.2 Serpentine recording.

used (Figure 15.2). A multi-channel read–write head is used to record four, eight, or sixteen tracks at one pass, but rather than spanning the entire width of the tape the head only covers a fraction. At each end of the tape, the head steps down then records another group of channels in the opposite direction. The tracks are thus recorded in a serpentine fashion, end to end, progressing across the width of the tape.

So serpentine recording enables more tracks from a given number of head channels. The use of narrower tracks means a higher areal density for the data. The second advantage is that by stepping the heads to the appropriate tracks, a file in the middle of a tape can be reached more quickly than searching the entire tape.

If you have a long memory, you may remember the eight-track car audio systems. They used a similar principle with a two-channel head, and four positions to cover the eight tracks. Rather than serpentine recording, it used a continuous tape loop.

Most linear formats now use a single tape reel within a cartridge, although QIC uses a two-reel cassette. The single-reel cartridges have a short leader on the tape, which is extracted from the cartridge and wound onto a take-up spool that forms part of the drive assembly.

IBM 3490 and 3590

IBM launched the 3480 drive in 1984. This used nine tracks on ½-in tape. This paved the way for the evolution of a number of designs, all based upon a 4-in square cartridge housing a single reel sometimes called 'square tape'. This form factor has remained a standard, so the same tape libraries can be used with a number of different formats.

Next, IBM moved to serpentine recording with the introduction of the 3480 (18 tracks). Later, the 3490 with 36 tracks increased the capacity to 800 MByte with a transfer rate of 9 MByte/s.

IBM's next step was the 3590 series, with the same form factor but using a new drive type, so is not backwards compatible. The 3590H, released in 2002, has a capacity of 60 GByte. The transfer rate is 14 MByte/s. The latest design (version H) has 384 tracks recorded as 16 channels (24 passes). It uses metal particle tape and has servo tracks to aid precise head positioning.

StorageTek T9940

StorageTek has proved to be a popular format for multimedia archives. They manufacture a wide range of high-performance tape libraries and drives. The original T9940 tape cartridge had a capacity of 60 GB. The upgraded 9940B holds 200 GByte and supports a transfer rate of 30 MByte/s. The T9940B uses ½-in tape in a single-reel cartridge. It uses 16-channel linear serpentine recording, with a total of 576 tracks covered in 36 passes. It is packaged in the standard 4-in form-factor cartridge.

The other StorageTek tape format is the T9980. Although very popular with mainframes and data centres, it has been designed for access-centric applications, like transaction processing, rather than the high-capacity requirements of multimedia. It uses dual reels still in the square box. The dual reel has a self-contained tape path, so does not need to be threaded. It offers very fast access times.

Digital Linear Tape (DLT)

DLT has proved to be the most popular format for backup and archive in mid-sized data centres. It was developed by the Digital Equipment Corporation, hence the name. The technology is now owned by Quantum who have constantly developed and improved the format.

Super Digital Linear Tape (SDLT)

SDLT is a recent enhancement of the DLT format to improve the performance, yet retain backwards compatibility. The SDLT drives can read regular DLT tapes. A step change in capacity has been achieved using a servomechanism to move the read–write head assembly. The servo that controls the position of the heads uses optical sensing of tracks on the opposite side of the tape from the magnetic coating. This servo enables closer track spacing and higher linear tape speed. The ½-in metal powder tape has 448 tracks read as eight channels, which gives 56 logical tracks (DLT was a four-channel format). As the servo tracks are optical, the tape cartridge can be bulk erased for reuse. The tape is rated for 1 million passes.

The buckle that picks up the tape leader has been redesigned; the older buckle design of DLT could occasionally fail. As the SDLT drives can read the legacy DLT formats, a library can be extended without the need to rerecord all the old cartridges.

Linear Tape Open (LTO)

Many cartridge formats have evolved from legacy formats. Rather than being constrained by earlier technologies, the LTO format was developed as a ground up new design, and the specification was thus released from the restrictions of backwards compatibility. The original consortium of Hewlett-Packard, IBM, and Seagate made the format an open specification. This means that other vendors can take up a licence to manufacture the format. Two versions were originally envisaged: the single-reel *Ultrium* for high-capacity backup and archive requirements, and the dual-reel *Accelis* for data enquiry applications with intensive access. The Accelis has now been dropped.

LTO Ultrium uses serpentine linear recording on ½-in. metal particle tape. There is a roadmap laid down for four generations of development. The first generation allows for 100 GB of uncompressed data. This will be extended, and by the fourth generation (using a thin film tape), a capacity of 800 GByte of uncompressed data and transfer rates up to 160 MByte/s are promised.

The format added a number of enhancements to improve upon existing linear recording technologies:

- More concurrent channels, initially 8 increasing to 16: Legacy formats had only four channels.
- Improved servos for higher track densities: The cartridges are preformatted with five servo tracks. These are used to guide the heads during read and write operations.
- Intelligent data compression: Not a great advantage with compressed multimedia files.
- Cartridge memory: Each cartridge has 32k of semiconductor memory that can be read via a wireless link from the drive. This means, that to speed the access to the relevant portion of the tape, file location information can be read before the tape has been threaded.

Users of LTO are relieved of concerns about single sourcing by having a number of vendors that support the format. When so many technology companies have fallen by the wayside, this is a great comfort when selecting a format to use for long-term archiving.

Helical recording formats

DAT and DSS are used for small system backup but the 4 mm tape formats do not have the capacity for multimedia systems. For the backup and archive of multimedia assets, you have to look to the 8 mm and ½-in. formats. These have been developed from the technology used for videotape recording. There are two leading manufacturers: Exabyte with the Mammoth, and Sony with the AIT and DTF families.

Exabyte Mammoth (M2)

Exabyte tapes have been very popular for backup with multimedia workstations. A typical use is the backup of a non-linear video editor. The disks hold the work in progress, and the tape is used as the repository for the bulk of the material.

The original Exabyte tape was an 8 mm helical design, based on video cassette recorder (VCR) technology. It was launched in 1987, and it used mechanical components from Sony. In 1996, the improved Mammoth was released. This had a more rugged drive, with gentler tape handling and dynamic head cleaning. The tape media was changed from metal particle to an advanced metal evaporated coating. Mammoth 2 (M2) was introduced 3 years later with improved specifications including a Fibre Channel interface. The head drum can read and write four channels, as opposed to two with the original Mammoth, thus increasing the data transfer rates.

Advanced Intelligent Tape (AIT)

Sony developed AIT as a high-performance storage solution for mid-sized archives. Sony has a long experience of tape-drive design, as witnessed by their domination of the broadcast videotape recorder (VTR) market. Their research into the tape-head interface has led to the development of helical recording technology that rivals linear recording in terms of head wear and drive reliability.

SAIT
For users that demanded higher storage capacities Sony has developed a format using 1/2-in. tape that is based on the AIT design. This is called Super AIT or SAIT.

Digital Tape Format (DTF)

The DTF is a development of Sony's Digital Betacam technology that can be used to record data rather than digital video. The associated tape library, the PetaSite, has vast capacity, making it suitable for very large asset management systems. DTF uses ½-in. metal particle tape, and is available in two different cassette sizes (as with Digital Betacam). A Flash memory embedded in the cartridge stores system information to speed up file access. The tape is rated for 20,000 passes.

Format comparison

So how do you choose a format? Originally, linear recording offered a simple tape path, less mechanism to go wrong and long head life. Helical recording offered a higher capacity and fast file access because the tapes were shorter. Now linear has incorporated servo heads to offer high capacities, but with more complexity.

All the advances in servo technology, head design, and tape materials have narrowed the gaps between the technologies in terms of total cost of ownership. That is the data capacity versus storage volume; the cost of the drive, and mean time to failure (maintenance costs). The linear recording tends to give a longer tape life, with up to 1 million passes; helical may be one-fifth of that number.

It may be that your corporation already owns drives in legacy formats, so backwards compatibility may be an issue. The choice of library may also dictate form factor or the tape cartridge.

- Data capacity
- Data transfer rate
- File access time
- Media load time.

Note that all the tape-drive vendors promote the advantages of data compression. Unfortunately, there is little redundancy left in the multimedia data, as graphics, audio, and video files are usually compressed by the codecs before storage. When planning capacities, it is best to use the specifications for uncompressed data, and ignore the compressed parameters. If compression can be used it is a bonus.

Future developments

The different tape manufactures all produce roadmaps of future products releases (Figure 15.3). These plans are just marketing collateral, and should be treated as such. The promised performance parameter are targets, there are no guarantees that they will be achieved, so beware. There is much hype around the question of linear versus helical. Any decision as to a format needs to be taken very carefully, weighing up the total cost of ownership, not just the primary specification.

Tape libraries and auto-loaders

Although tapes can be manually loaded, the full advantages of digital asset management can only be realised with automated tape handling. Television broadcasters used robotic tape libraries to handle material like commercials spots that was played over and over again. The video server has now replaced this application.

The same principles have been used by the data warehousing industry. Companies like StorageTek have been supplying tape libraries for many years. This same robot technology can be used for the backup and archive of multimedia assets. The libraries range from the basic auto-loader with a single drive, up to the big data silos with tens of drives and thousands of cartridges.

Any user of a digital asset management system will see the advantages of an automated tape library (ATL); archive files will be restored within a few minutes. There is no longer the need to wait for a librarian to find a tape cartridge and place it in a drive. For the operator of the system, if the robot is used with a hierarchical storage management system, there will be a much higher drive utilisation than can be achieved with manual loading.

There is a choice of automation. If you have a small library, the auto-loader may have sufficient capacity. The auto-loader has a single drive, so the data transfer rate is limited to the performance of that drive. The ATL has several drives, so the robotic tape handling is shared by the drives. This gives a cost-effective solution while allowing simultaneous access to several cartridges.

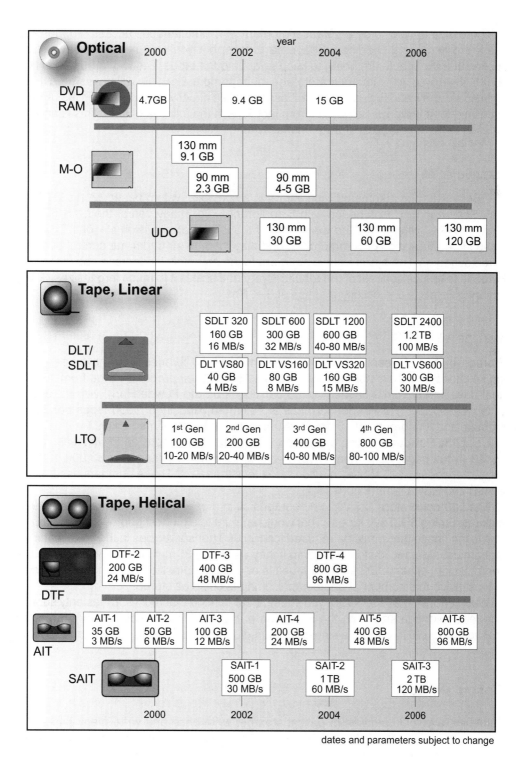

dates and parameters subject to change

Figure 15.3 Roadmap for typical tape and optical media.

There may appear to be a potential problem with simultaneous access. Suppose six users are accessing six different tape cartridges, but you only have five drives. This implies that the robots are going to keep swapping the tapes. The way around this is to control the drives with hierarchical storage management. Each file will be restored to the online disk array, and the users can access their files directly from disk. Files that are not accessed for a while will be purged from the disks in the fullness of time. This is another function of the hierarchical storage management.

Sony PetaSite

The Sony PetaSite automated tape library is a scalable system based on the DTF format. Sony has long experience with tape libraries. For many years, the LMS (Library Management System) was the workhorse of thousands of television stations. The LMS could store thousands of commercials, and play them to air under the control of a prepared schedule. The system could store analogue and digital videotape cassettes. The PetaSite takes the concept of the robotic library and scales it to much larger sizes. A fully optioned PetaSite can occupy a space of 6×6 m.

StorageTek

StorageTek has 30 years experience of automated tape libraries. They have been offering solutions for media storage since the late 1990s. Their products range from the L20 dual-drive library with a capacity of 30 cartridges up the PowderHorn, with its familiar cylindrical shape. The PowderHorn has a maximum capacity of 6000 tapes per library module, and four groups of 20 drives. What is that in terms of media files?

Using the PowderHorn you could store 47 million photographs each with a file size of 25 MB (a full page, $8\frac{1}{2} \times 11$ in, RGB 24-bit, uncompressed image) or 53,000 120-min movies encoded at 25 Mbit/s, in a floor area less than 8 m^2. These numbers assume the 9940B 200 GByte tape (Figure 15.4).

The L20 could store 125,000 photographs all in a space of only four units of a 19-in. rack (assuming SDLT320 tapes). That would amount to a modest photo-library. Compare that to the space that would be required for 150,000 transparencies in the metal cabinets that are usually used to store film, even if they were only 35 mm slides. If you were to use compression, either JPEG for the image file or data compression by the tape drive, then at least twice that number of photographic images could be stored.

When choosing a tape library you should bear in mind that most libraries only support one-tape cartridge size (with the exception of the ADIC multimedia library). It may be that you will have to go with a single-vendor solution if you choose certain tape formats.

Optical storage

There are two main families of optical storage: write once and write many times. The write once is used for archiving. The write many times, or rewritable, can be used for near online storage to extend the capacity of magnetic disk arrays.

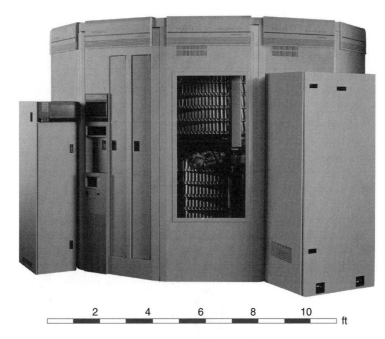

2   4   6   8   10
ft

Figure 15.4 An enterprise-size tape library from StorageTek, the 9310 PowderHorn Tape Library. Courtesy of StorageTek™.

There are a number of different recording technologies. Some are only suited to write-once applications. For rewritable disks, there are two popular technologies: the first is magneto-optical and the second is the phase change that is used by the CD-RW and DVD.

Magneto-Optical (M-O)

The M-O recording format was developed by the data storage industry to replace the microfiche as a removable storage medium that could be used for backup and archive applications. M-O is also rugged and durable compared to magnetic disk and tape alternatives.

The M-O disk uses a property of ferromagnetic materials called the Curie point or temperature. Above that temperature, the material loses its polarisation. The recording layer on the disk has a Curie point of around 300°C. The initial state of the drive is with all the domains aligned in the same direction. A laser is used to heat the surface layer of the disk to above the Curie point. A solenoid produces a magnetic field, which can reverse the polarisation of an individual cell on the surface. As the disk rotates the cell away from the beam, it cools, thus retaining the magnetic orientation. At room temperatures, this is very stable.

To erase data, the magnetic field is reversed to that all cells are aligned to the initial state (Figure 15.5).

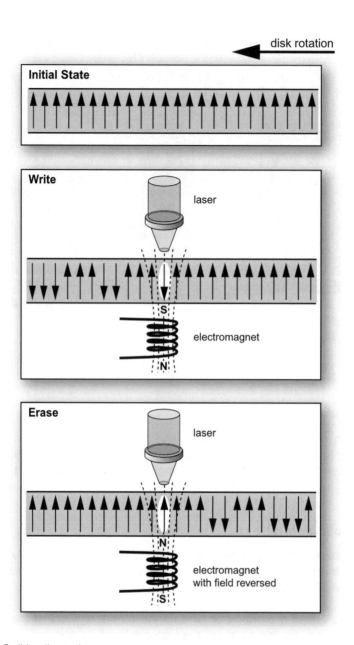

Figure 15.5 M-O disk write and erase.

To read the state of a cell, the laser beam alone is used. The Kerr effect is used to detect the polarisation of the cell. This is where the polarisation axis of light is modified by reflection from a magnetic material (not unlike a liquid crystal display which also uses polarised light). A detector measures the rotation of the polarisation axis to give a value of '0' or '1' for the cell.

The early media could store 640 MByte, with drives storing around 5 GB in 2003. M-O has a very long shelf life, 100 years is normal. This is four times longer than data tape. Therefore, M-O is the main choice for data archives where a very long storage time is demanded. The drive manufacturers pay attention to factors like backwards compatibility, so that older media can be read by today's drives.

Phase change

Although M-O disks are robust and reliable, many applications do not warrant the cost. The consumer industry has spawned the CD and DVD. Both of these formats have been developed as low-cost data stores for computer backup. If these disks are deployed in jukeboxes, they can be used for near offline storage of digital assets.

WORM media

In some industries, here is a legal obligation to maintain a permanent archive of files. The write once read many (WORM) is a special type of M-O media that can be written to only once. This means that the files cannot be overwritten or potential evidence tampered with. There are five different ways to achieve this:

- Ablative
- Bubble forming
- Dye polymer
- Phase change
- M-O continuous composite write once (CCW).

The ablative recording uses a laser to ablate or erode a pit in the platter surface. The bubble-forming disk uses the laser energy to create bubbles in the surface; the dye polymer uses a thermally sensitive dye that changes to a lighter colour when heated by the laser. Phase change uses a laser to change the surface from an amorphous to highly reflective crystalline state. CCW uses M-O recording with write protection from the cassette.

All are read by reflecting a laser off the recorded track. The first four types of recording are read by the change in intensity of the reflection, the last (CCW) by a change in polarisation. The WORM is larger than M-O with a 12-in. glass platter.

Disk file formats

This first standard for the CD-ROM was the standard, ISO 9660. This was created, so the format used for recording on the disk would be independent of the host operating system, thus allowing interchange between say a PC and a Mac. ISO 9660 is a read-only file system.

When read–write media was developed, a new standard was called for. This standard, the ISO/IEC 3346, has the lengthy title '*Volume and File Structure for Write Once and Rewritable Media Using Non-sequential Recording for Information Interchange*'. This is usually referred to as the NSR Standard (Non-Sequential Recording). A consortium of disk vendors has adopted a simpler subset of the standard called the universal

Figure 15.6 Plasmon G-series of optical jukeboxes. © Plasmon

disk format (UDF). It is used for the CD-RW and DVD. It means that computer data and multimedia files can coexist on the same disk and can be read by all popular operating systems: Windows, Mac, and UNIX.

Optical jukebox

Just like the automated tape library, robots have been developed to load disk into the optical drives. Following on from the devices used to play 45 rpm vinyl disks, the robots are called jukeboxes. They have advantages over tape, in that the drives can rapidly access any track, without the delays that tape spooling introduces.

The time to deliver a file includes the time to mount the disk in the drive, plus the time to spin the disk up to speed, then the time for the heads to seek and read back the file sectors. With typical jukeboxes, this is of the order of a few seconds—much faster than the minute or so of with some tape libraries.

Jukeboxes have been developed for CD–DVD media and M-O disks (Figure 15.6).

The jukeboxes are usually supplied with small computer system interface (SCSI)-drives interfaces, and a SCSI port for the robot. An associated server with multiple SCSI hot bus adaptors (HBAs) provides the interface, caching, and transfer management. There are several different ways to interface the jukebox. These include device managers, network-attach managers, volume managers, and hierarchical storage managers (HSM). These are covered in the next chapter.

Emerging technologies

Tape is evolving to higher and higher areal densities. The basic laws of physics do set limits. There comes a point with a very small magnetic domain where their thermal energy can disrupt the magnetic polarisation. This is superparamagnetism. This lower limit on domain size is reached at areal densities of around 8 GByte/in^2. Beyond that point, we have to look for other technologies. One area that is being actively researched is the application of the atomic force microscope (AFM) to data recording.

Another technology is holography. The goal is to store data as 3-dimensional interference patterns in an optical substrate: a crystal cube or a photo-polymer. A laser is used to write and read the pattern. Researchers are promising media with capacities of 100 GByte up to 1 TByte, with read–write rates from 100 to 1000 MByte/s. These figures match requirements for high-definition movie applications.

Historical archives

Most of the storage formats in this chapter have only been around for 20 years or less. Even M-O disks are only rated for 100 years. That is fine if you are storing financial or regulatory documents. There is rarely a need to keep them more than 50 to 70 years. What if you want a real archive: for a local heritage society or government records of a historic nature? We have paper documents that are hundreds of years old, so how are digital assets to be stored? One way is to step back to the document storage solution of the last half of the twentieth century: the microfilm. Although invented in 1839, back at the dawn of photography, it was not used seriously for document storage until the 1920s. Banks started to microfilm cheques as a compact way to store them. Around the 1950s, the microfilm became into common use for long-term document storage. It saved space, and was at the time the ideal way for libraries to keep copies of newspapers and journals.

The introduction of digital assets largely replaced the microfilm as a way of storing documents and line art. But the microfilm has not gone away. How many remember the 8-in. floppy disk? If you had one with valuable data on it, how would you read it? The endless drive for technological innovation often obsoletes storage products after 10 years or so. One solution is to keep copying from an old format to the latest technology. An alternative is to store documents in an analogue form of microfilm. This makes the recovery independent of software or operating systems. By using certified archival film, with controlled processing and storage microfilm can be expected to last 500 years—as long as high-quality rag paper. Of course, it is only suitable for text and drawing, not for audio or video, but it can be a cost-effective solution to very long-term storage of historical documents.

Summary

When you are choosing a mass-storage format, there are many considerations. Whereas a disk array can use the latest technology, with archive storage you have to be careful that the recordings can be read back in 10 or 20 years time. Over time, operating systems and hardware platforms come and go. Any solution should be independent of both. There have been many problems with tape drives becoming obsolete, so that a tape can no longer be played.

Tape storage has kept apace of disk developments, so that the largest tape capacity still exceeds the size of a magnetic disk. Optical media still has modest-storage capacity, so that several disks are needed to backup even a single disk drive. There are advantages with optical systems; the media has at least three times the life of tape.

The choice of a format for a backup and archive does not have to be a unitary one. The best return on investment for the storage may be had through a hybrid approach. Rights contracts and other such documents could be stored on optical WORM; multimedia could be stored on data tape. It may not be cost effective to store standard-resolution video on data tape. If access is infrequent, the cost of withdrawing a tape from a vault, and then making a dub could be much less than the cost of keeping the material near online as a data file.

For long-term storage, any tape format is going to need copying to new media after about 20–30 years. It is a good opportunity to encode lower-resolution copies for search and preview applications as a library is replicated to fresh media. The low-resolution formats use much less space, so can be maintained in an automated tape or optical library, and the high resolution kept on a shelf in a vault.

16 Storage management

Introduction

The concept of shared storage is implied in an asset management system. The shared storage will comprise a number of devices: disks, tape and optical, and a management system to present a unified view to the high-level applications. Shared storage can be viewed in the physical or business domain. The former is about the disk and tape drives that has been covered in the last two chapters. The business view is concerned with return on investment and the total cost of ownership.

Storage management has to provide many facilities to the enterprise in addition to the basic role of a central file repository:

- Fast access
- High throughput
- Wide-area file distribution
- Backup
- Archive
- Disaster recovery.

Fast access is important to the user. If they want to view an asset, they should not have to wait. Few businesses can afford to store all their assets online, so access time has to be a compromise. High throughput may well be an issue if the asset management has to ingest high volumes of video content. A television broadcaster who proves news or sports content may have tens of simultaneous video feeds to be indexed and filed to the repository. This can be testing for the network architecture and storage device technology.

In the enterprise with multiple sites, the storage system will have to extend over wide-area networks (WANs). Issues of latency and cost will restrict what is possible when compared with a single local system.

Backup to cope with loss of files through system failure or operator error is considered essential. Backup allows work to continue after such a failure without the need to restore files from the archive. Backup is usually the work in progress on the servers. The archive is a selection from the working files that are deemed an essential part of an asset (Figure 16.1).

It may be necessary for reasons of government legislation, or for the long-term storage of reusable assets to provide an archive of the central file repository. There are other issues. The world is an uncertain place. We have theft, fire, earthquake, floods,

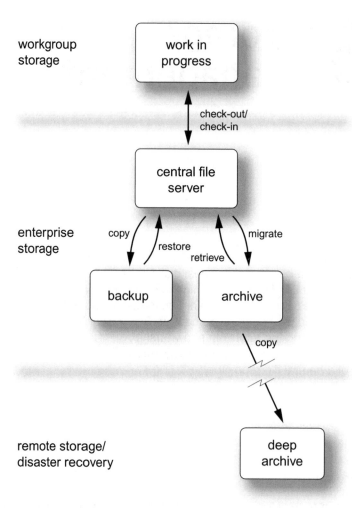

Figure 16.1 Archive and backup.

and wars that could all compromise a data centre. A disaster recovery strategy can also be very important to protect the investment in the digital assets. A copy of the archive can be maintained at a geographically separate location. Backup and archive do overlap in many respects. The disaster recovery can be combined with wide-area distribution, so there are possibilities for cost savings by overlapping these facilities.

Virtualisation

Storage management aims to unify different storage strategies into a seamless 'virtualised' environment. The user should be abstracted from the complexities of storage. Consider a content creator browsing the digital asset management for a video clip. Once the wanted clip is identified, the user should be unaware of the mechanisms that are used to the retrieval of that clip.

Table 16.1 Storage groups

	Media	Access time	Cost per byte
Online	Hard disk RAID systems	Instant	High
Near-line	Magnetic tape in ATL Optical media in jukebox	Seconds to minutes	Medium
Offline	Removable media stored in a vault Library shelves	Hours to days	Low

Often running contrary to this aim is the cost of storage. If the value of an asset is less than the cost of storage, then there is going to be no return on the investment in that asset. Although the design of storage management is ultimately a matter of financial and technical judgement, several architectures lower the overall costs of storage and can improve performance. One is hierarchical storage management (HSM) while another is storage networking.

Many storage systems rely on a vault to store tapes and optical media. These require conventional library software to provide efficient retrieval of content. To realise the investment in a deep archive, you must be able to find and then retrieve that content.

Storage is divided into three main groups: online, near-line, and offline (see Table 16.1).

Much of the searching for assets is a process of elimination. The wanted content may be 10 per cent or less of the original result set. This means that although the metadata should be kept online, the high-resolution content can be stored in the archive, and retrieved on demand. Frequently accessed content can be stored online, this balance between online and offline will be controlled by the media management application or by HSM (Figure 16.2).

Storage networks

If you are storing video media files then the file servers used for general office applications are not going to meet the requirements. The size of video files and the bandwidth required for real-time delivery are both much higher than such basic systems could support. Uncompressed standard-definition video creates about 76 GByte of data per hour of running time with a continuous data rate of 270 Mbit/s.

Storage networks provide the technology that can support high-capacity disk arrays, and attached tape and optical storage. There has been a steady evolution of storage architectures that can handle very large numbers of large files and move the files around at high speed.

Storage can be viewed as a number of layers: application, file, block, and storage device. The digital asset management is the application layer. Between that and the storage devices is the file layer and the block layer.

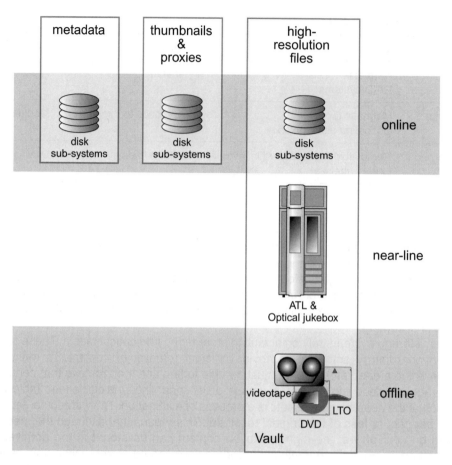

Figure 16.2 The storage matrix.

File layer

The file layer uses file systems like NFS and CIFS to map the files into logical storage block addresses. NFS (Network File System) is an IETF standard used by UNIX systems, and the CIFS (Common Internet File System), also known as SAMBA or SMB, is used by Microsoft Windows. The file system will use a redirector to request or deliver files from remote domains using the local area network.

Block layer

The integrated disk device controllers map the logical block addresses into the physical sectors where the data bytes are stored (Figure 16.3).

The database may map to the file system or directly to the storage partitions (for efficiency with large databases). At the block level, the basic storage blocks can be aggregated to provide redundancy or to increase and decrease block sizes to suit the storage medium. One example is striping a block across several drives. Block aggregation includes RAID, used universally to protect against drive failures.

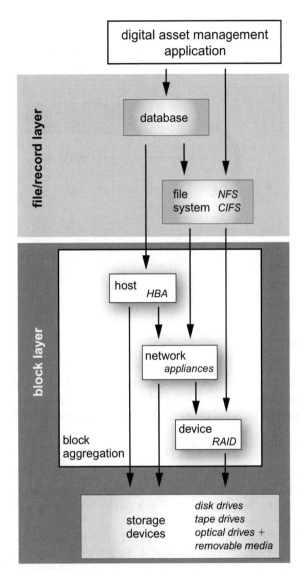

Figure 16.3 Layers of the storage model.

Direct-attached storage

The simplest form of disk storage is the directly attached disk (Figure 16.4). All desktop computers have an internal drive and often use externally connected drives to increase storage capacity. Desktop computers generally use ATA for the connection to the internal drive. External drives often use the small computer system interface (SCSI) interface, although serial interconnections are becoming popular, with USB 2.0 and FireWire being typical examples of low-cost solutions for consumer and small office applications.

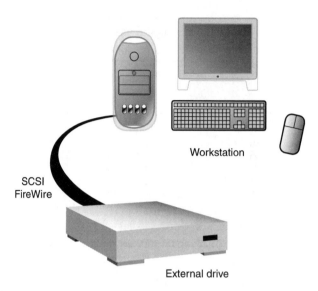

Figure 16.4 Direct-attached storage.

Shared storage

Asset management is all about providing shared access to files in order to support a collaborative workflow. Until the development of gigabit Ethernet, there were two main storage network architectures: NAS and SAN. The distinctions are blurred as the features of each architecture are utilised in a common storage network design.

Network Attached Storage (NAS)

NAS is little more than the traditional workgroup or departmental file server (Figure 16.5). One popular way of extending the storage capacity of a workgroup is to attach a dedicated storage appliance or 'filer' directly to the local network. Files are saved and retrieved using a remote file system like NFS.

The appliance can simultaneously support several file access formats. This feature has made NAS popular with creative users in the media business. Workstations running Apple OS, Unix, and Windows can all share a common file repository, using a single copy of each file. Windows 2000 and XP use the common Internet filing system (CIFS)—formerly known as SMB—whereas UNIX uses the NFS.

One big advantage of the NAS is that it is very easy to install. It can be treated as a black box with an Ethernet connection. The whole setup and configuration should only take about 30 min. A simple tape streamer can be added to the appliance for backups of the data stored on the filer's disk drives.

As the server fills up, further disks can be added to the storage sub-system. The limit will be the data rate that can be supported for the read and write operations. The server will have finite limits determined by the processors, backplane bandwidth, and the network interface card. Once these limits are reached, new servers can be added to form a cluster, but there is no overall file management; it is left to the user to decide

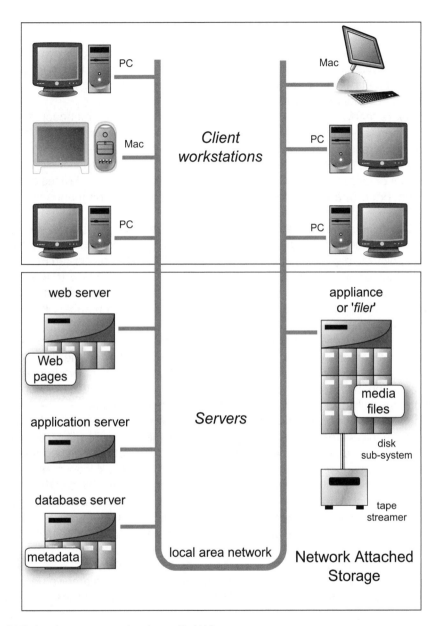

Figure 16.5 Asset management system with NAS.

where to store files. Servers may well be allocated on a departmental basis or application by application; one for images, one for text documents. One of the problems with the NAS is that as a business expands, associated files can end up on different volumes. To get around this, there are several solutions. Some simply replicate files from NAS to another. This is of course wasteful of disk capacity. If NAS filers are to share backup, then the data migration has to share the LAN with the general file traffic.

Storage Attached Network (SAN)

The SAN has its roots in the architecture of the mainframe computer. The processing and storage devices were very large by today's standards, so had to occupy physically separated cabinets. High-speed buses or data channels connected the pool of storage devices to the central processors.

The servers that we use now use several different ways to interconnect storage, but SCSI has been very popular for direct-attached storage. SCSI has many limitations, the maximum cable length is 12 m and the maximum number of devices is 15. Around 1990, Fibre Channel was developed as a high-speed interconnection fabric for storage arrays. Using copper or glass fibre as the physical conductor, it can address devices at distances up to 10 km. Fibre Channel protocol (FCP) allows serial SCSI commands to be carried over the Fibre Channel physical layer.

Fibre Channel provided the opportunity for storage devices to be pooled with common access from a number of hosts. As a point-to-point channel or switched fabric, Fibre Channel provides predictable high data capacity that is not possible with a congested Ethernet LAN.

Although SANs are usually associated with Fibre Channel, they can use any high-speed communication layer for the storage network. One example is gigabit Ethernet. If operated well below the maximum data rate it can provide a comparable performance to a circuit-switched network.

The SAN architecture allows a cluster of network-attached hosts to share the storage sub-system as a pool. This can give a more efficient utilisation of the disk devices. In contrast, the NAS filer will be limited by the throughput of the network interface, the internal bus, and the host bus adaptor. As storage demands increase, further filers are attached to the network, each with a separate storage sub-system.

In general, the block format used by the storage network will be specific to one operating system. If the servers are using different operating systems, then a file will have to be stored in the appropriate block format for each system. The block formats cannot be shared across the different systems. Conversely, if the enterprise uses UNIX and Windows, then generally separate SAN servers will be needed for each operating system. This can make the NAS model more efficient in use of disk space, contrary to the claims for the SAN. The disks can be allocated by the SAN controller into zones, along with a group of hosts. For more granular allocation of the disk space, the disk sub-systems can be partitioned using the SCSI logical unit numbers (LUN). Both zoning and LUN masking do carry an IT management overhead, so there has been a move towards storage virtualisation.

The storage network can also be used to connect backup and archive devices without using precious Ethernet network bandwidth. Tape and optical devices can be directly attached to the storage network. Block-level transfers are used for the data migration and retrieval.

Metadata server (asymmetric pooling)

The metadata server manages the file system mapping to the storage blocks in the disk sub-system. When an application requests a file via the LAN, the metadata server responds to that request with a small file containing metadata referencing the location of the data blocks within the SAN. The application can then retrieve the data directly over the storage network. The use of the metadata server is also known as asymmetric pooling.

SAN storage manager/appliance (symmetric pooling)
The SAN storage manager uses an inline appliance between the host bus adaptors and the storage devices. The architecture is also called in-band or in-the-path virtualisation. The storage manager is a potential bottleneck or the data transfers.

The SAN promised an open system, so that legacy storage could be mixed with new drive arrays. Magnetic and optical disks and tape storage could be mixed in a unified storage system. But the difficulties of managing and controlling disparate products meant that many of the open platform ideals did not come to fruition.

Virtualisation

Virtualisation is a buzzword used to describe a desirable characteristic of a storage network. The storage at block level is abstracted from the host; the logical access is separated from physical access. A system administrator can allocate the resources of a pool of storage devices as virtual disks. Virtualisation allows sensible sharing of precious storage resources. A new storage device can be added as an additional resource, without the necessity to assign it to specific host applications.

One of the advantages claimed for pooling the storage devices is that the IT staff can treat the pooled storage as a single unit, rather than the NAS filers possibly dispersed around a site. Rather than maintaining a number of different disk sub-systems and tape drive attached to different servers, all the backup and volume management can be made from a central console with a unitary view of the storage pool. As the demands for file space increase, new disks can be added to the pool, with no disruption to the NFSs.

SAN/NAS comparison

For many reasons the SAN and NAS are often stood side by side (Figure 16.6). Which is the best? Each has advantages and disadvantages. The buyer of storage really wants the best of each topology (Table 16.2).

Internet protocol-based storage

Many businesses have the expertise to deploy large Ethernet networks, but a wary of embracing other technologies like Fibre Channel. The management of a Fibre Channel SAN requires a new skillset for the IT staff, which may not be readily available.

Now that Ethernet speeds extend to 10 Gbit/s, there have been developments of IP-based storage that can provide alternatives to Fibre Channel SANs, with little loss of performance. The Ethernet switches and routers will be familiar devices to the staff. The same products can be used for the file network and the storage network, with attendant savings in IT resources for maintenance and configuration.

A conventional Ethernet LAN using TCP/IP is a packet-switched network. TCP assembles data into packets, ensures error-free delivery, and then reassembles the packets back into the original files or messages.

In contrast, Fibre Channel is circuit switched. It is designed to support the continuous flow of data that storage device require for optimum data transfer, this is especially so for tape streamers. Every time the data flow runs out, the tape has to stop and backup.

Circuit switching is conventional for telephony. The concept of voice over IP that can use packet-switched networks to save costs is akin to the use of IP-based storage.

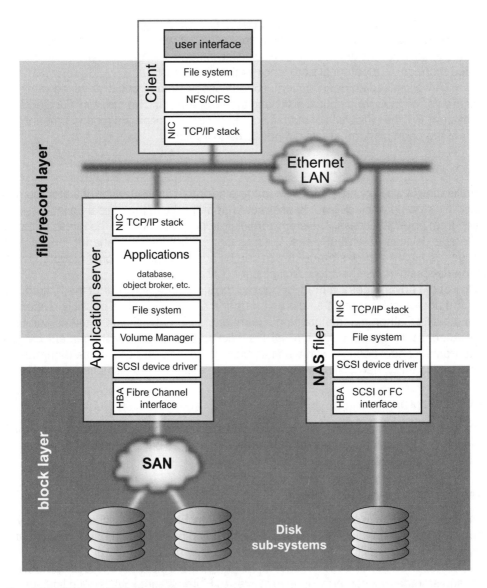

Figure 16.6 SAN and NAS comparison.

Using 1 or 10 Gbit/s Ethernet, the inefficiencies of packet switching can be accepted. By operating at around 33 per cent loading, an Ethernet network can substitute for a circuit-switched channel.

iSCSI
Internet SCSI or iSCSI is transport protocol that allows SCSI block-level commands to be carried over IP networks, rather than the more usual file-level commands. Using

Table 16.2 NAS and SAN comparison

	NAS	SAN	Storage network goal
Performance	Lower	Higher	High
Scalability	Poor	Good	Good
Data sharing	Yes	Rare	Yes
Volume sharing	Rare	Yes	Yes
Backup/archive	Server oriented	Shared	Shared
Management	Simple	Complex	Simple
Cost	Lower	Higher	Low

iSCSI, an SAN can be built from regular Ethernet switches rather than Fibre Channel technology (Figure 16.7).

One of the advantages of using IP is that the storage network can be secured using conventional technologies like secure Internet protocol (IPSec). A Fibre Channel network is essentially open, and relies on physical security. The two can be combined with the Fibre Channel over IP protocol (FC/IP) and IP over Fibre Channel (IPFC).

The iSCSI does not obsolete Fibre Channel, rather it provides an alternative. Fibre Channel is moving to higher data rates, and for raw performance for the streaming of multiple simultaneous video files, it is currently unmatched. The two can also co-exist, with Fibre Channel used for the primary storage networks and IP used for remote storage.

SAN mirroring

There are two forces driving businesses towards the concept of mirroring data to another storage device pool. One is the increasing paranoia about disaster planning that demands a remote backup of the datastores. The other is the increased pace of business. There is sometimes the need for instant recovery, rather than waiting for tape backups to be loaded and the data restored.

An SAN can be mirrored, either via Fibre Channel if the distance between sites is less than 10 km, or by the use of the hybrid protocols, like FCIP where the Fibre Channel storage network can tunnel through a TCP/IP network.

Remote mirroring is an expensive solution, but can be warranted for mission-critical applications. The same concept can still be used to connect disk arrays to remote tape libraries.

Virtual tape storage

Some storage management treats an automated tape library as a virtual drive. If you want to place specific files in a vault as single tapes, such systems are not suitable. They record blocks of a file across more than one tape, wherever there is free space. Removable tapes have to be recorded as physical devices, rather than a virtual store.

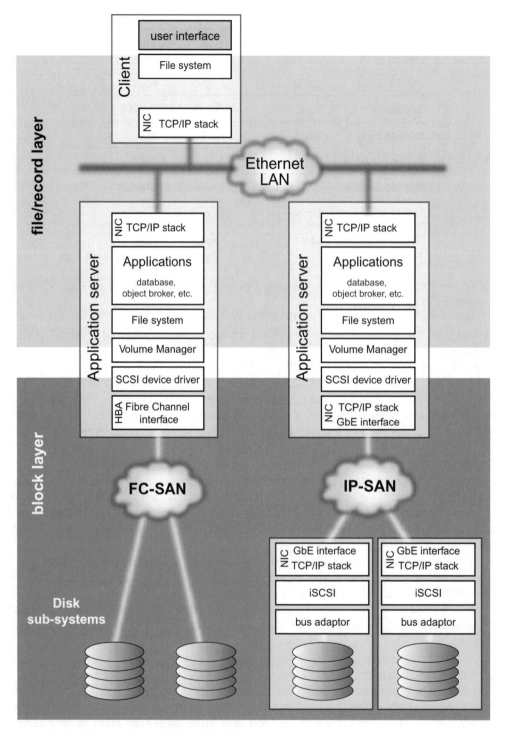

Figure 16.7 Fibre Channel and iSCSI storage networks.

Video servers

Video servers differ from other data servers in that the input and output can be a real-time video signal rather than IP network traffic. The SAN architecture is advantageous for building large video repositories. The video server is essentially a video encoder and decoder. To playback video, the data blocks on the disks are reassembled into a real-time data stream, which is decoded from the compressed form usually used for storage into the uncompressed video signal. High-performance clusters can be built with a Fibre Channel storage network. The LAN is used solely for control data and for non-real-time file transfers.

A typical video server uses a continuous data rate of 25 Mbit/s to playback video in real time. In principal, a Fibre Channel connection could sustain 40 such streams.

Transfer from the disk sub-system to the automated tape library is managed by a robot controller (Figure 16.8). The archive server buffers the block transfers between the disks and the tape streamers. The robot control manages tape loads and unloads.

Hierarchical Storage Management

Hierarchical Storage Management or HSM is the primary means to achieve cost savings in a storage network. It applies business rules to move data across the network. By the use of different storage media, disk, tape, and optical, the time to access assets is trading against the cost of storage. The same storage devices may serve a dual purpose. The low-cost storage may also be used as the backup or archive.

The HSM application may sit between the asset management and the storage network, or may act as a service to the storage network management. It is often called a data mover. As storage networks become more intelligent, the need for a separate application is waning.

HSM has drawbacks. Only the recently used material is available online from the disk sub-system. There will be a latency to retrieve content stored on tape or optical disk. This can be of the order of minutes. In some applications, like a television master control centre operating a live channel of sports or news, there may be the need to access material very rapidly. Some form of prediction should be used to ensure that every file that may be required is restored to the online store.

One way around this enigma is to store a stub of the offline files on the online disk sub-system. The stub can start playback while the remainder of the file is restored. Such up to-the-wire schemes would require very careful capacity planning to ensure that the stub does not expire before the rest of the file arrives. The advantages may be more useful in applications that could stand the potential break in the file delivery.

Wide-area file transfer

New paradigms for media businesses are demanding that media can be shared, not just locally, but across geographically dispersed sites. A typical example is the central-casting model for groups of television stations.

Telecommunications networks were originally set up for telephony, but more than half the traffic is now data. The packet-switched networks used for data and telephony traffic can also be used to distribute media assets. Stemming from the background of telephony,

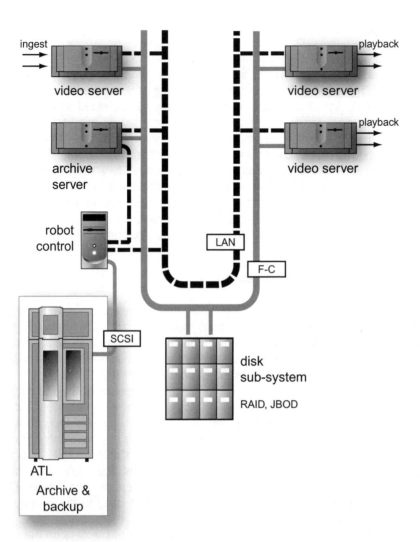

Figure 16.8 Video servers and disk sub-system.

the circuits are constructed in a hierarchy of bit rates. They are designed to carry multiple voice circuits, with the basic unit being 64 kbit/s. General computer data is also carried in a format compatible with this basic unit.

The terms T-1 and ATM are often used as if they were interchangeable, but they are quite different. ATM is a later service that has special features that are useful for real-time video circuits.

T-1 and E-1

The T-1 circuit is the basic digital carrier used in North America. It transmits data at 1.5 Mbit/s in the DS-1 (digital signal) format. The European equivalent is called E-1 and has a data rate of 2 Mbit/s.

Table 16.3 Plesiochronous digital hierarchies

ITU-T standard			ANSI standard		
Signal	Data rate	Channels	Signal	Data rate	Channels
–	–	–	DS-0	64 kbit/s	–
E-1	2.048 Mbit/s	–	DS-1	1.544 Mbit/s	24 × DS-0
E-2	8.45 Mbit/s	4 × E-1	DS-2	6.3 Mbit/s	96 × DS-0
E-3	34 Mbit/s	16 × E-1	DS-3	45 Mbit/s	28 × DS-1
E-4	144 Mbit/s	64 × E-1	–	–	–

US and international standards

There are two main telecommunications standards: ANSI used in North America and parts of the Pacific Rim, and the ITU-T standards used in the rest of the world. The ANSI hierarchy is based on a digital signal (DS-0) of 64 kbit/s (Table 16.3).

Plesiochronous Digital Hierarchy (PDH)

The early digital trunks circuits multiplexed a large number of voice circuits into a single high data rate channel. The systems at the remote ends were not absolutely locked together; instead, each runs off a local reference clock. These clocks were classed as 'plesiochronous'. Plesio- is a Latin word derived from the Greek for 'near', so plesiochronous refers to clocks that are in near synchronism. The early data circuits were asynchronous, the clocks were derived from simple crystal oscillators, which could vary from the nominal by a few parts per million, large receive buffers are used to manage the data flows. In PDH networks, to cope with terminal equipment running on slightly different clocks, extra bits are stuffed into the data stream. This bit stuffing ensures that a slower receiver can keep up with the real payload rate by simply dropping the extra bits.

To extract a single voice circuit from a DS-3, the channel has to be demultiplexed back to DS-1 channels. To build trunks circuits in rings around a country, each city passed would have to demultiplex and remultiplex the data stream to extract a few voice circuits (Figure 16.9).

Synchronous Networks (SONET)

To avoid the multiplexing issues and the overheads of bit stuffing, highly synchronous networks were developed. By referencing terminal equipment to a single caesium standard clock, the synchronism could be ensured to a high degree of accuracy.

The standard uses a byte-interleaved multiplexing scheme. The payload data is held in a fixed structure of frames. At a network terminal, the signals can be added or dropped from the data stream, without the need to process the other traffic.

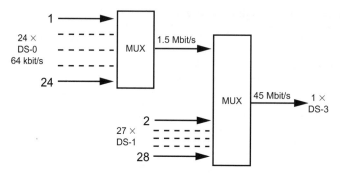

Figure 16.9 Voice circuit multiplexing.

Table 16.4 Synchronous digital hierarchies

Data rate	SDH		SONET	
	Signal	Capacity	Signal	Capacity
51.84 Mbit/s	STM-0	21 × E-1	STS-1, OC-1 or	28 × DS-1 1 × DS-3
155 Mbit/s	STM-1 or	63 × E-1 1 × E-4	STS-3, OC-3 or	84 × DS-1 3 × DS-3
622 Mbit/s	STM-4 or	252 × E-1 4 × E-4	STS-12, OC-12 or	336 × DS-1 12 × DS-3
2.48 Gbit/s	STM-16 or	1008 × E-1 16 × E-4	STS-48, OC-48 or	1344 × DS-1 48 × DS-3

It is rather like a conveyor belt carrying fixed-size containers at a regular spacing. As the belt passes a city, you take away the containers you want, and drop new ones into gaps. The other containers pass unhindered.

The synchronous optical network (SONET) is a subset of the synchronous digital hierarchy (SDH), an ITU-T standard (Table 16.4). The SDH standard can accommodate both ITU and ANSI PDH signals.

Frame relay

So far, I have been describing voice circuits. When a voice circuit is set up, you reserve a bandwidth slot for the duration of the call. If none is available, you get the busy tone. The requirements for data are different. It is the error-free delivery that is important, the available bandwidth is not so important. Data can use the spare capacity as voice traffic changes up and down. Data packets can be dispatched as capacity becomes available. The real-time delivery of video is much like a voice circuit—reserved bandwidth is essential. Video can also be distributed by non-real-time file transfer; in this case, it can be treated like any other data.

Frame relay is a standard for packet-switched networks that operate at layer two—the data link layer of the open systems interconnection (OSI) model. A bi-directional virtual circuit is set up over the network between the two communicating devices. Variable-length data packets are then routed over this virtual circuit. A number of virtual circuits can share a physical link, the link bandwidth is shared dynamically, giving much more efficient use of the link.

This is called opportunistic bandwidth. As there is now a queue of data awaiting available bandwidth, the quality of service (QoS) becomes an issue. The advantage is that the toll rates can be lower than the reserved bandwidth of a voice circuit.

Asynchronous Transfer Mode (ATM)

ATM was developed for high-speed packet transport over optical networks like SONET. ATM uses small fixed-size data cells rather than the large packets of frame relay. Each cell is 53 bytes long, with a payload of 48 bytes. These small cells are more suited to voice and multimedia traffic where low latencies are demanded, so have eagerly adopted by television companies.

Both permanent and switched virtual circuits (PVC and SVC) can be set up. The cell header carries the virtual channel and virtual path identifier that are used to identify connections within the network. ATM is linked to other network layers by the ATM adaptation layer (AAL). The packets are given one of five categories of priority by traffic class:

1. Constant bit rate
2. Real time variable bit rate
3. Non-real-time bit rate
4. Available bit rate
5. Unspecified bandwidth or 'best effort'.

Constant bit rate has the best QoS, with low cell jitter. It can be used for broadcasting video contribution circuits, possibly a 34 or 45 Mbit/s data stream. The variable bit rate real time can be used for standard voice circuits. IP traffic is usually allocated the unspecified bandwidth.

Some characteristics that make ATM particularly attractive for television distribution are the choice of uni- or bi-directional links as the two-way links can be asymmetric (Figure 16.10).

As network traffic increases, the bandwidths grow to the point where optical switching becomes the only cost-effective way to handle the very high data rates of the network backbones. Therefore, the electronic processing of SONET and SDH will fall by the wayside. There is a move to an all-optical infrastructure called photonic networking.

Photonic networking

As IP becomes the standard for data exchange, and voice over IP becomes more used, the overhead over the ATM traffic engineering becomes more of a hindrance.

There are proposals to run IP directly over the dense-wave division multiplexed (DWDM) photonic network. This would greatly simplify the routing of traffic by stripping out two layers, ATM and SONET. To introduce this new concept, the capability of IP routing would have to be extended (Figure 16.11).

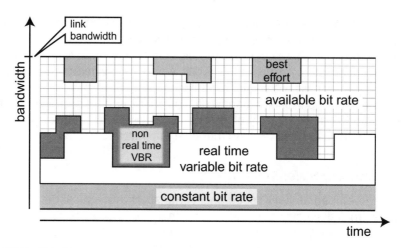

Figure 16.10 ATM traffic classes.

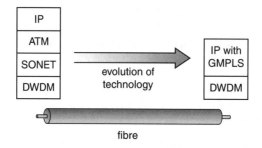

Figure 16.11 The technology migration to photonic routing.

Generalised multi-protocol label switching (GMPLS)

Most of the telecommunications networks have evolved to carry voice traffic and general data packets. Neither of these models is really suited to the streaming of multimedia. IP routing has evolved to use label switching. This can improve the efficiency of network communications. Multi-protocol label switching (MPLS) is a potential technology that can improve the QoS of content delivery, by allowing traffic engineering of packet routing.

Generalised MPLS extends this capability to cover legacy ATM and SONET plant plus the new optical cross-connects, so that potentially IP can be transmitted directly over DWDM.

Satellite

Satellites have long been used for media contribution and distribution links. A typical example is the back haul of news contributions from the field to the network headquarters where fibre or point-to-point microwave links are not available or cannot be used. Satellite is also used for the distribution of network programming, either as a finished channel for cable stations or for syndicated programming. Similarly, commercial spots are distributed by satellite to local stations. Traditionally, these media transfers have been managed manually.

The contribution lies outside the scope of most asset management, but the distribution of content now falls very much under the umbrella of digital asset management.

WAN content transfer

Media management applications often include controllers to manage the transport of media to or from remote sites. These can be a push process for dissemination of content like television commercials, or a pull process where media can be transferred on demand from a client. These applications can be seen in the centralcasting model of television broadcasting, where IP networks act as the disseminators of content, rather than the earlier methods of physical videotape delivery or video via satellite.

Library management

Library management has to provide an organised system for archiving and retrieving removable media. The media has to be kept in a controlled climate, both temperature and humidity, if it is to last for many decades. Tape and film both deteriorate over about 10–30 years. Ultimately they have to be regenerated by copying to a new medium.

Many enterprises use specialist record management companies to provide a long-term archive. These companies provide secure data centres, where the economies of scale should lower costs over a bespoke solution. Some of these systems can act like an extension to the digital asset management. They can provide network access to the digital assets. They index the assets at ingest to the archive, and then provide web-based search to retrieve the assets. In principle, there is no reason why the search could not be integrated with the enterprise system to give a federated search across local and archived content.

Media migration

As media ages and degrades, it eventually becomes necessary to migrate the data to fresh stock, possibly in a later recording format. One well-known example is the dangerous nitrate film that was used before the 1950s. The celluloid (cellulous nitrate) substrate is highly inflammable. It was replaced by cellulose triacetate, but that is not everlasting. The base degrades in a process called the 'vinegar syndrome'. The other problem with film is that fading of the coloured dyes that hold the image. The best way to preserve film is to keep it cool and dry, typically 1–2°C and 25 per cent relative humidity (RH).

Magnetic tape uses a different substrate, so it is not subject to the problems of nitrate and acetate. Polyester is used as the substrate. This is very stable with a life of hundreds of years. The binder is the weak link, this holds the magnetic material and binds it to the substrate and can break down over time. Again tape has to be kept cold and dry: 8°C and 25 per cent RH.

The main problem with the long-term storage of tape is mechanical. Magnetic tape will be physically damaged by constant read–write operations, but may not be an issue with an archive. The tape formats have a relatively short lifetime, 10 years is typical. Will playback equipment in the original format be around 20 or 30 years after recording?

Summary

Storage management is a planned compromise. It balances the value of an asset against the cost of storing that asset. It also has to balance the time to retrieve the asset against the likelihood of it being required. At one extreme, everything is stored on tape, and housed in low-rent area remote from the users. The other extreme is to store every asset on a disk array with a high-speed network linking the users. The usual is some combination. The business decision is where to place the compromise. The sweet spot is constantly shifting. Disk drives have increasing capacity and decreasing cost. A similar evolution is taking place with tape and optical storage. Network bandwidths are increasing. Therefore, a decision made 1 day will not be the optimum 3 months later.

The storage architecture used for the disks is another compromise. The terms NAS and SAN have been very well used in the marketing of storage solutions. The optimum solution for a business could well lie in a hybrid solution. The users want shared access to files. The management would like the best utilisation of the storage hardware. The IT personnel want a system that is easy to administer. The answer is going to be a mix of network storage and a storage network. There have been continual advances in software application that provide the management of the files, volumes, and blocks, so that files can be shared across operating systems and the disk sub-systems.

The first step in planning a storage solution is to analyse the requirements. Is a high data transfer rate needed. How much online capacity is required? If the remote clients are accessing your media servers via a T-3 line, then that probably represents the limiting bottleneck. The T-3 connection has a maximum bandwidth of 5.6 MByte/s, so a very fast Fibre Channel disk array is not going to prove to be a good investment. Make up a list of basic questions:

- What aggregate sustained data rate can the client workstations demand?
- How resilient does the storage need to be? Do you need disaster recovery?
- How available does the system have to be? Will it be a requirement to hot-swap drives?
- What is the level of your IT staff expertise? SANs need special skills.
- Are you dependent on one vendor?
- How does the system scale if the business grows?

Many of the answers will be a trade-off between cost and benefit. A faulty processor can be easily replaced. Lost data can prove to be very expensive to recover.

The storage market is in a constant state of evolution. As networks speeds increase, and disk cost fall, newer solutions can offer higher-performance and lower-maintenance costs than last year's model.

The NAS and SAN should not be looked at as competitors, but as different solutions. The optimum architecture may be to have both systems co-existing. The SAN could store media asset files on disk and tape, and NAS could be used for the asset metadata. As new architectures utilising IP are introduced, the distinctions blur.

17 Document security and digital rights management

Introduction

In the introduction, an asset was described as content with value. Unfortunately, assets of value are also of interest to unauthorised users. This may be a competitor wishing to access confidential corporate information, or it could be the piracy of digital entertainment: music, movies, or games. Some Internet piracy is in the domain of the lone hacker, who treats unauthorised access as a challenge. A bigger problem is piracy for commercial gain. Therefore, digital assets have to be securely wrapped to prevent access to all but authorised users that have been properly authenticated.

Document security and digital rights management (DRM) becomes more of an issue when a digital asset management system is exposed to the Internet through a web server. If a system is deployed entirely within the corporate firewall, the risks will be lower and easier to police.

DRM offers systems that can control access and aid the successful monetisation of content. Like many other issues related to asset management, there are numerous choices to consider when buying a DRM system. In choosing a system, you will have to judge the level of threat; the more secure a system, the more it will cost. With increased security, authorised users will find it more difficult to access the required content. So there is a trade-off between cost, security, and ease of use. Even the most secure systems can be cracked. It only takes one clear copy to be made, then that can be distributed in a flash all around the world.

There are two main facets to rights management; the first is the maintenance of artists and producers' contracts and royalty payments. The second is the secure storage and delivery. The latter is commonly referred to as DRM. The technology allows owners, distributors, and providers of content to deliver content securely to consumers as part of an e-commerce system. DRM can also be used as standalone, to protect confidential information within a corporation and its business partners. At its most basic, a document can be protected against viewing or editing by a password. More sophisticated document security offers support for collaborative workflows.

There is a certain amount of controversy around digital rights systems. Perhaps, the medium with the longest history of rights is the printed book. It is recognised that the intellectual property of the author is protected against unauthorised publication.

Nevertheless, there is also the concept of fair use, without which the public library would not exist. To make a copy of a book using a photocopier is expensive; if there are colour illustrations, the reproduction is poor and usually monochrome, and the result usually lacks an adequate binding. Therefore, it is easier to buy a copy. As we accumulate digital assets, a copy can be made simply at no cost (ignoring the disk space). Fair use—with the attendant risks of illegal copying—becomes difficult to police.

The e-commerce systems already exist to protect the integrity of financial transactions when ordering goods. Traditionally, these goods are physical, and the online transaction merely replaces mail order or telephone order. The goods are then delivered by mail or parcel service. When the goods are digital media, not only does the transaction have to be secure, but the goods also have to be protected against unauthorised access.

Authentication and trust

Consider a person going to the local store to make a purchase. The storeowner will recognise that person by their gait as they walked in, their physical appearance, and by their voice. They have already authenticated the customer as a trusted customer. The customer pays by cheque; the storeowner hands over the goods. The keywords here are authentication and trust.

The same customer now travels to an out-of-town store. The checkout assistant does not know the customer, so refuses the cheque. The customer has the option of paying by charge or credit card. The card is authenticated then the transaction authorised by the terminal. The store trusts the credit card company to pay them for the goods. The customer walks out of the store with the goods—everyone is happy.

As retail transactions become globalised, the opportunities for fraud escalate. The mail order/telephone order sector has procedures in place to authenticate customers. Most will only ship goods to the address where the payment card is registered. Card suppliers have added extra digits to the card number that are not printed as part of the embossed number, or carried in the magnetic strip. This can be used during a phone transaction to confirm that the purchaser has the actual card in their possession, and not an impression.

The usage contract

Digital commerce is based on the usage contract. The content provider and the user agree a contract, possibly involving the payment of fees. Then the user receives the right to use the content (Figure 17.1).

As the user views the content, usage reports are returned to the content provider.

Conditional access—the television model

Television is funded by advertising, subscription, or in case of state-controlled networks, from government taxation. A limited number of channels also offer pay-per-view, primarily for movies and for major sporting events. Channels funded by advertising, sponsorship, or taxation can be broadcast free-to-air or 'open'. Subscription-based channels and pay-per-view use encryption to protect content against unauthorised viewing—this is called conditional access.

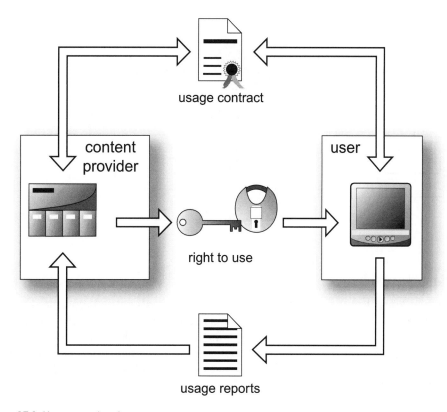

Figure 17.1 Usage contract.

Conditional access

The television broadcasters have chosen closed systems of conditional access to protect subscription and pay-per-view channels. The receivers or set-top boxes use smart cards and possibly a phone back channel as part of the authorisation procedures.

Assets delivered via the Internet are usually viewed on personal computers (PCs). These users have great resistance to add-ons, software dongles, and other additional hardware, so other methods have to be used to authenticate consumers.

The value chain

Content and payment form a cycle (Figure 17.2). The content is delivered for use by the consumer. The consumer then pays the intellectual property owner for the content, usually through the publishers.

The DRM system ensures secure delivery of the content in accordance with business rules defined by the contracts. The monies collected are then apportioned by the contracts management application to the relevant parties.

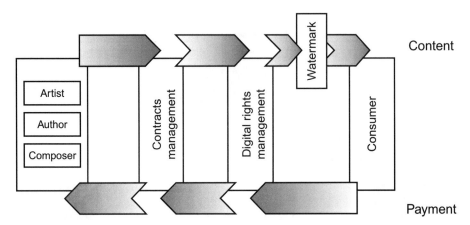

Figure 17.2 The payment cycle.

Content distribution

Although an artist can sell work directly to the consumer, most content is sold through a conventional distribution chain. A DRM system should support the classic supply chain: content creator, publisher, aggregator or portal, distributor, retailer, and finally the consumer.

The DRM should also support traditional product marketing tools like promotional offers and viral marketing. Finally, the methods of payment have to be flexible, all the way from subscriptions through to micro-payments and electronic purses.

Document security

Document security provides answers to many issues that arise when we move from paper to digital documents. A paper document, like a formal letter or contract, carries a signature that is used to authenticate the document. In the case of a contract or treaty, it could also carry a seal, and details of witnesses to the signatures. All these measures are used to ensure that this is an original document, so it cannot be repudiated or the content changed.

More difficult is to ensure the document is read only by the indented recipients. In the past, this could only be through trust of the bearer and recipient, and through physical security—the locked filing cabinet or safe. The sub-miniature spy camera, and later the photocopier, have both been used for unauthorised access to documents. If a document is to be delivered through insecure channels, the content can be encrypted or concealed (through secret writing).

These examples illustrate many of the techniques that have now been adopted for digital documents.

- Digital signatures
- Encryption
- Secure file servers.

The digital signature can be used to authenticate a document. Encryption ensures that the document cannot be read by anyone without the correct authorisation. Secure file servers provide access control to the document repository.

There are many solutions on the market. Some will only work with specific document formats, like Microsoft Office (Word and Excel) or Adobe Acrobat. Others are dependent upon proprietary features of an operating system, like the encrypted file system of Microsoft Windows 2000 and XP. All documents can be stored in an encrypted form, and only viewed by users or groups with permission set as with the main operating system. In some circumstances, a user may not want the operating system administrator to have access. In this case, a shared secret key should be used to allow decryption of the document.

Even if a user has correct access to a document, the author may want control over that access:

- Can it be copied via the clipboard?
- Can it be printed?
- Can it be edited?

It many circumstances you may want other users to be able to view a document, but not change it or even print it. Take the example of a report. You may want to sell a printed copy, but make the report available for free viewing. If printing is forbidden, then you will also want to bar the copying to the clipboard so that the text cannot be pasted into a fresh document and then printed. Such features are all supported by Adobe Acrobat, a very popular format for general document distribution.

DRM

DRM is the use of computer technology to regulate the authorised use of digital media content, and to manage the consequences of such use, for example a payment.

A DRM system encrypts the content so that distribution can be controlled in accordance with the agreed rights and their terms and conditions. To this end, it wraps prices and business rules around the content to enable the payment transaction (Figure 17.3).

For the transaction, the DRM is tightly integrated with the chosen e-commerce systems. An Internet content provider may want to manage, deliver, and sell documents (financial reports, analysis), images (photo library), or multimedia assets. Most DRM systems are designed to protect some or all of these different media formats. The initial developments in DRM were for documents. Not all these systems can handle multimedia files. Encryption tends to be at file level. This works fine where the asset is downloaded before viewing. For a file that is delivered by streaming, the encryption has to be implemented at packet level. Without this, the media playback cannot start immediately.

This, plus the intimate connection required to the player, has led naturally to many multimedia DRM solutions being proprietary to the codec format. The MPEG-4 format has a standard intellectual property management interface, so will potentially offer a more open environment.

Why do we need DRM?

Digital content is subject to many forms of piracy:

- Illegal copying
- Loss of data integrity—tampering with content
- Peer-to-peer distribution.

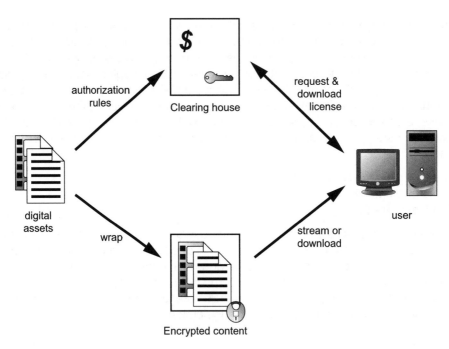

Figure 17.3 Exchanging the licence.

Perhaps the most notorious example of peer-to-peer distribution was the case of Napster. The use of e-commerce for the trading of online assets needs secure DRM. Electronic distribution removes the manufacturing costs of physical media, and can simplify distribution. Within the corporate networks, it can protect valuable and confidential information. For a fee-based distance-learning project, it ensures protection of intellectual property.

Piracy protection

Two methods are used to fight piracy; one is *encryption* and the other is *watermarking*. Encryption gives the primary protection. Should the encryption be compromised, watermarking enables the tracing of the possible sources of the piracy.

Business models

The DRM has to be very flexible to accommodate the many different ways a consumer can purchase the content. There are many business models for monetising online content.

Usage

There are several ways to sell content. There is rental or outright sale. The rental may have qualifiers applied; it could be for fixed period or for a certain number of plays. Then there is the video-on-demand model where a payment is for each viewing of the clip.

Delivery

The delivery of content can be as a download or stream. The download might be for music files to be used by a portable player or a personal digital assistant (PDA). Streaming could be for ephemeral content that it only watched once. A third possibility is to archive the file, while it is streaming, for repeat viewing. If it is possible to download content to portable players, security is potentially compromised. Microsoft has developed an interface that allows content to be downloaded securely from the Windows Media player to portable audio devices that support the secure digital music initiative (SDMI) standard.

Promotion

DRM enables many forms of product promotion. The first is to let the viewer see a preview. This may be the edited highlights or the first few minutes of the clip. The preview may be at a lower resolution than the main clip. Other forms of promotion may be special offers—'pass this on to five friends and get a free play'.

Payment

The traditional method for mail order payment is by credit or charge card. This is not a good method for very small transactions; it may only cost 10 cents to listen to a single music track. Therefore, other methods have to be used that have a lower-cost overhead for such low-value transactions.

Subscriptions, long popular with print media, are another method of collecting payments. They are more suited to a service rather than pay-per-view. Subscriptions are usually prepaid. An alternative for business-to-business transactions would be to bill in retrospect. Account payments can support a fixed rate service or pay-per-view.

For the business-selling content to the consumer, the prepaid purse or micro-payments are the alternative. With the purse, the customer buys credit from the clearinghouse. This credit is stored securely in the DRM client. The value is decremented as content is viewed. Micro-payments are aggregated by the clearinghouse into larger transactions that can be made at monthly intervals.

Business rules

The business model will dictate a set of business rules. The DRM client uses the rules to gain access to the content. The terms and conditions can change with time, so the licence issuer must be able to change the rules or revoke a licence. This may be necessary for legal or business reasons, or the content may become outdated or inappropriate. A good DRM system should allow the revocation of content even after it has been downloaded.

Wrapping

This is the process of securing the content and associating with the content the business rules to enable unwrapping by the media player (Figure 17.4). The processes are not necessarily concurrent. Encryption may be performed at the same time as the media is encoded, and the business rules added later.

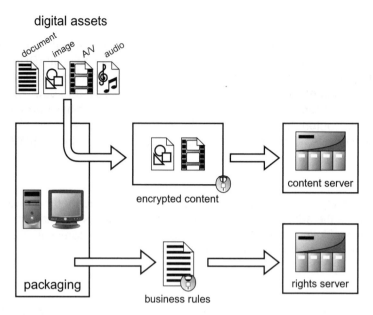

Figure 17.4 Wrapping the content.

Most assets are delivered by some form of file transfer. They are delivered to the local drive before consumption. The alternative is to stream the content. This is used for audio-visual assets. The data is rendered as it arrives, and there is no local copy kept of the data.

There are two different points where content files can be encrypted. The first is before asset is placed on the content server. The second is to encrypt on-the-fly, as the content is delivered to the consumer. The latter is the model that has been used by conditional access systems for pay-per-view television.

Pre-encryption and on-the-fly

Pre-encryption systems usually package the asset file as a whole, rather than packet by packet. For live audio-visual content, there is less choice of DRM, only a limited number of products support live encryption. To meet this need, a different form of encryption has been developed, where the processing takes place at the point of delivery. This on-the-fly encryption has a second advantage that a new key is generated for each stream. Pre-encryption generates a single key for the file at the time of wrapping. If the key is compromised, then all copies of the file can be opened.

On-the-fly encryption can be an additional application running on the streaming server, but this will lower the number of streams a given server can deliver, typically by 30 per cent. The alternative is to use a bridge or router at the output port of the streaming server that can perform the encryption. This allows the use of a standard media server (Table 17.1).

Unwrapping

The final user or the consumer wants to view and listen to the content. To decrypt the content, first user has to obtain authorisation. This authorisation, suitably modified by the business rules, initiates the decryption of the content (Figure 17.5).

Table 17.1 Pre-encrypted files versus on-the-fly encoding

	Pros	*Cons*
Pre-encryption	Content is secure on the server No serving overheads	Single key per file
On-the-fly	Can be used for live Webcasts New key per stream	Additional server-side processing Content can be compromised on the streaming server

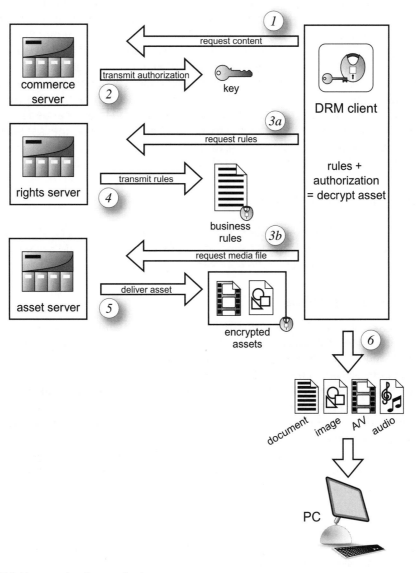

Figure 17.5 Unwrapping the content.

This typical sequence is followed by the DRM client:

1. The first step is to send a request for the asset and, if necessary, undertake a financial transaction
2. If the client has credit, the commerce server transmits the authorisation key
3. The DRM client requests the business rules from the rights server and the asset file from the asset server
4. The rights server forwards the business rules
5. The asset server delivers the content
6. The DRM client allows access to the content according to the business rules.

The exact sequence varies from product to product. Note that the business rules can be downloaded each time and are separate from the content. This allows the content owner to change the rules at any time without the necessity to re-encrypt the asset file. A movie might be initially available on a pay-per-view basis, then at a later date released for outright sale. The publisher may want to add or withdraw special offers.

This division between the product, and the promotional wrapper, gives the retailer of virtual products greater freedom than the vendor of physical merchandise (where the offer could be printed on the packaging). It also allows pricing to be changed in real time, much like the street vendor, or an airline trying to fill empty seats at the last minute.

The authorisation can be issued in several ways. It could be from a subscriber management system (long used by pay television) or it could be an e-commerce system.

The rights management parties

If you are using DRM to protect traded assets, then there are several parties in any content transaction. Each is looking for a different set of features in a DRM system. The final choice has to satisfy all parties if the commercial model is to be successful.

Content creators/publishers

Online content can take many forms. The first focus was on music distribution, a consequence of the Napster debacle. The distribution of video content is very much tied in to satisfactory security, much like the delayed release of the DVD. Live events are an area where pay-per-view could be applied.

The target devices are not just PCs; they could be wireless PDAs or portable music players. Content will have to be re-purposed for the requirements of each device. Content aimed at the PDA requires careful design to be compelling within the limits of a small display area.

If you are protecting streaming media, then you may be locked to a vendor. Two of the popular streaming architectures already include DRM systems (Real and Windows Media). If you want to support several streaming architectures, you may end up having to interface with more than one DRM system.

Commerce

When you are selecting a DRM system, you need to look at the features on offer. Does it support cross-selling? An important factor is the transaction costs for micro-payments.

Can you make retrospective changes to the business rules? This allows price changes for downloaded content that already resides on the customer's PC. Is it possible to revoke access to content?

Reseller

The reseller could be a retail web store, or a content portal, aggregating content from several suppliers. The content could be sold on through several stages, before the final purchase by the end consumer. A distributor may buy content from many creators and sell on to the consumer. The distributor will want to set up the business rules for the trading of content. He may want to add further rules, add his own margin, and then add special offers. The DRM systems should support modification and additions to the business rules by trusted partners in the value chain.

Consumer/user

The end user first gains authorisation from the clearinghouse or data centre. Then he or she is free to open and view the encrypted content. Now a consumer may want to preview content before making the decision to buy. This purchase may be outright, or could be for a fixed period rental. Consumers are often encouraged to forward media to friends—a process known as viral marketing. The DRM system has to support secure super-distribution for this personal recommendation to operate.

Payment and usage information is passed back to clearinghouse. An electronic purse can store small cache of credit within the media player. This avoids the need to clear every transaction. DRM systems should have means to silently report tampering back to the data centre.

Super-distribution

Super-distribution is commonly used in viral marketing. This is where customers pass content to friends, perhaps in the belief that it is a 'cool' shared secret. Content that is passed from user to user has to have persistent protection after copying. Therefore, each user will have to make an individual transaction to gain authorisation to use the content.

Issues for the user

So far, I have considered the providers' issues. The choice of DRM is also an issue for the consumer. If the system is too complex, there are thousands of other web sites out there, only a click away. Another major issue is payment security. Customers have to trust the supplier with their credit card details. The consequence of this fear is that reputable traders can lose potential business. There are steps being taken to counteract these fears where trusted third parties act as brokers for online transactions.

A good DRM system should be transparent to the end users. The acquisition of the software executables should be automatic, and not require manual intervention from the user. Browsers now include rights management pre-installed. The second is that the financial transactions must be simple and secure.

Most DRM systems allocate the licence to a node, and not the user. Some attributes of the PC are used as part of the key. For example, the file may be locked to an IP address. If you want to move protected media between a desktop PC and a laptop, this may require a nodeless DRM. Note that this is not copying, the content is moved to the portable machine, and then moved back to the desktop.

Clearinghouses

Subscriptions could be managed by a web site database. All that is required is secure authorisation and usage statistics. If the consumer pays for content, the clearinghouses will process the micro-payments from consumers and pass payments to the content providers. An electronic purse may hold a small local cache of credit.

Financial clearinghouse
A facility that receives financial transaction records, resolves the transactions, and makes the required payments to the value chain participants and value chain delegates.

Usage clearinghouse
This facility gathers reports and statistics of how DRM protected media is used by consumers and by other participants in the value chain. It resolves the requirements for usage reporting, and provides reports to specified recipients.

Third-party revenues
The DRM supplier has two possible sources of revenue, a fee for each transaction or by a licence for a fixed period (typically annual). The clearinghouses usually charge per transaction.

System integration

The digital asset management system can provide the business logic to integrate the DRM with back-office systems. These include e-commerce systems, contracts management, and the clearinghouse.

Contracts management

Most DRM systems produce comprehensive statistics and reports of consumer usage. To apportion payments to the relevant parties, the DRM operator may well need other software products, specifically a contracts management package. These products are outside the scope of this book. Good examples can be found in *System* 7 from Jaguar Consulting and *iRights* from Ness. These products have modules for the following functions:

- To manage contracts with artists
- To acquire content from production companies

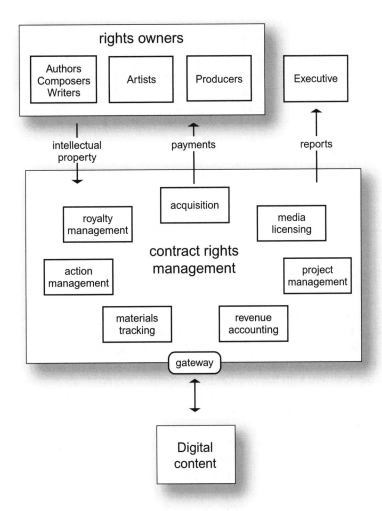

Figure 17.6 Contract rights.

- To track the usage of content
- To distribute royalties to artists.

The contracts management application often sits at the hub of the business revenue streams. A gateway links to the asset management and from there to the DRM (Figure 17.6).

Encryption

Cryptography has two uses within DRM. The first is to encrypt content for confidentiality or protection of the owner's rights. The second is for the protection of the certificates that are used for authentication and for access control (authorisation).

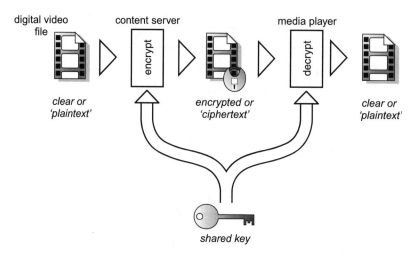

Figure 17.7 The secret, shared encryption key.

There are two families of cryptography: shared secret and public/private key. A shared secret key (also called a symmetric) uses the same key to encrypt the content and then to decrypt it at the receiving end (Figure 17.7). In cryptography, the clear file is called *plaintext* and the encrypted version is called *ciphertext*. The scrambled ciphertext can only feasibly be decoded with the key. One way to crack the encryption is to try many different keys until the correct one is chanced upon. The more characters in the key, the longer it will take on average to find the key. This cracking can be made more difficult by changing the key at certain intervals. Shared key encryption is efficient and suited to large files—just like media files. An example of a shared secret is a personal identification number or PIN used to withdraw cash with an automated teller machine. The PIN is used to verify the physical credit card. The PIN is a secret shared by the bank computer and the authorised holder of the card.

The standard for shared secret cryptography is the data encryption standard (DES) algorithm.

The problem with a secret key is the secure distribution from one party to the other. Different methods can be used to deliver the key; one is the secure courier and another is the telephone callback. One party phones the other and says 'call me back'. The other party calls back to an unlisted phone number, now the original party has authenticated they have the wanted party, and can divulge the key.

The courier is not a viable option for e-commerce systems. Pay-per-view conditional access uses a smartcard in the set-top box, plus a phone link to connect to the box. Each box is uniquely accessible, so can be shut down by the subscriber management centre. The PC is a much more open system than the proprietary hardware in the set-top box. There is also consumer resistance to the use of a smartcard, although such systems exist.

The alternative is an electronic version of the telephone callback. This uses the digital signature security standard or DSS. Once the rights server has authenticated the client from the digital signature, then the secret key can be exchanged.

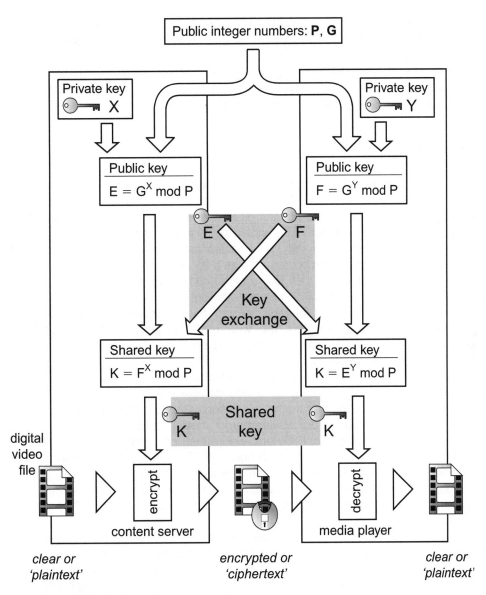

Public integer numbers: **P, G**

Private key
X

Private key
Y

Public key

$E = G^X \bmod P$

Public key

$F = G^Y \bmod P$

E

F

Key
exchange

Shared key

$K = F^X \bmod P$

Shared key

$K = E^Y \bmod P$

K

Shared
key

K

digital
video
file

encrypt

decrypt

content server

media player

clear or
'plaintext'

encrypted or
'ciphertext'

clear or
'plaintext'

Figure 17.8 The Diffie–Hellman key agreement.

One algorithm that has proved popular is the Diffie–Hellman key exchange. It starts with two publicly available integers, P and G. Each party, the rights server and the client generate private keys, X and Y. The Diffie–Hellman algorithm is then used to generate public keys, E and F, which the two parties exchange. Each party then uses the other's public key, their own private key, and the public number P to generate a common number. This common number K is now a secret shared by both parties. Note that at no time has this shared secret key been exchanged over the Internet (Figure 17.8).

This description is somewhat simplified, the full description can be found in the IETF RFC 2631: Diffie–Hellman Key Agreement Method. This shared key can then be used to encrypt the media file.

Note that the Diffie–Hellman key agreement can be intercepted by a man-in-the-middle attack, as there is no authentication between the two parties. Such authentication could involve the prior exchange of digital signatures.

Watermarking

In the digital domain, watermarking embeds a persistent signature that identifies the source of the content or the client copy. The latter is often called fingerprinting. For a content provider to trace the sources of piracy, two clues are necessary. The first is a means of identifying the owner of the stolen content, and the second is a trace of the client that compromised the security. These clues can be introduced as a watermark to identify the owner of the stolen content and as a fingerprint to identify the instance that was copied. The fingerprint is akin to the serial number of the copy. If a clear copy is found, the fingerprint identifies the copy that was compromised.

Originally, a watermark is a faint imprint from the mould used to make high-quality paper. We are all familiar with the use of watermarks in bank notes. In his application, the watermark is part of a number of measures used to indicate that the note is genuine, rather than a counterfeit—to authenticate the note.

A watermark can be highly visible, like an embossed logo. This is often used for pre-view copies of still images or video, where its role is partly to brand the content. Something subtler is needed for the full-resolution content, just like the watermark on a piece of paper or bill. Invisible digital watermarks should not be visible, but are extracted or detected by a software agent. Watermarking does not have to be visual; there are schemes that embed a watermark in an audio file. This uses similar auditory masking processes to those exploited by audio-compression schemes.

Automatic web spiders can continuously search the web looking for open (unencrypted) content that carries invisible watermarks. A typical example is the MarcSpider from DigiMarc.

Persistent watermarks should usually survive copying to be effective. The copies may be compressed using codecs like JPEG or MPEG. There may be intermediate analogue copies. The watermark should survive all this signal processing. There are other watermarking schemes where the mark is deliberately made very fragile. It should not survive the copying process, so if it is missing that content can be identified as a copy. This is very much the analogue of the bank note. The lack of the watermark would indicate a counterfeit.

Unlike data encryption, watermarks can be embedded in the waveform rather than the data. This can be used for images, audio, and video. Spread spectrum techniques can be used to add data in the time domain. These can be thought of as time-delayed echoes. These can be recovered by cepstrum analysis. If video and audio is compressed by a codec like MPEG, the coding thresholds can be modulated with the watermark data.

Watermarks are no panacea. They can be defeated, just as encryption can be broken. They form part of an environment where the theft of digital assets is made more difficult and the culprits can be traced more easily.

Security

Before setting up a secure media distribution system, it is a good idea to look at your goals. What are you trying to protect, and how do you want to spend on security? The security analysis splits into three areas:

1. The content
2. The monetary transaction
3. The server infrastructure.

DRM gives protection of the content, and often includes the monetary transaction. The transaction can use mature technologies from the e-commerce arena. The third area, the server infrastructure, is covered by normal enterprise level computer security (outside the scope of this book). The infrastructure should be protected for several reasons. One is the value of the content asset library; another is that attack could compromise the brand of the publisher, aggregator, or retailer. This attack could be from denial of service or loss of data integrity.

Hackers present many threats to a business. It could be through unauthorised access to confidential information, or loss of data integrity, where the hacker alters the content, possibly to embarrass the content owner by substituting inappropriate material.

The threats

Although cracking of the encryption may appear to be a common threat, it is difficult and can take a very long time. The more usual threat is theft of the keys.

Some licences are valid for a short time period; one method that has been employed to fool such licences is to change the computers date and time. A good DRM plug-in should be resistant to such manipulation.

Video and audio content can be copied once in the analogue domain. The wires to the loud speakers and the VGA connections to the computer monitor are both easy access points to make analogue copies of audio–video content. It is difficult to prevent such attacks, just as it is difficult to stop somebody sitting in a movie theatre with a camcorder.

Third-party audit

Before investing a considerable sum in a DRM product, find out how secure it really is. Ask to see third-party audits, or instigate your own.

Caveats

No encryption is proof against determined efforts to crack:

- DRM makes piracy difficult, but does not prevent it
- Other methods of defence of property rights will be necessary
- Watermarking aids tracing of stolen content
- Some level of theft is inevitable and should be included in the cost of sales.

XrML

As asset management usually comprises a number of software products, communicating through data exchange, there is a need to express the content rights and the rules for access in a portable format through the content lifecycle. That means that information can be passed from one application to another without the need to develop custom interfaces. The extensible rights markup language (XrML) is one such grammar.

XrML was developed at the Xerox Palo Alto Research Center in the late 1990s as the Digital Rights Property language. The original meta-language was changed to XML in 1999 and renamed. It has now been adopted by leading software developers and publishing houses as a common rights language for digital resources, both content and services.

The core concepts of XrML are as follows:

- Principal
- Right
- Licence
- Grant
- Resource
- Condition.

The *principal* is the party who is granting or exercising the rights. The *right* details what action a principal may undertake using a resource. As an example, you may be granted the right to view a movie once only, or you may be given the right to print an electronic document.

The *licence* is a set of grants and it identifies the principal who issued the licence. The *grant* gives the authorisation upon a principal. The rights expression is authenticated by a digital signature. A *resource* can be digital content: an e-book, a digital image file, or a video clip. It can also be a service like an e-commerce service or a piece of information like an address that is owned by a principal. The *condition* specifies the terms and conditions of the licence. This could be a rental agreement or the terms for outright purchase.

XrML has been used for the basis of the MPEG Rights Expression Language, part of the MPEG-21 standard.

Examples of DRM products

There are many different approaches to DRM. As an example, InterTrust has focused on developing patented intellectual property for DRM systems (Figure 17.9). Other companies, like Microsoft, have developed proprietary products that are specific to the Windows architecture. A number of companies sell general-purpose products for the encryption of document or image files, often with roots in document security.

This section gives a number of typical examples of DRM products. The first, DMDSecure, is an end-to-end framework that utilises third-party products to encrypt the content, so that rights can be enforced.

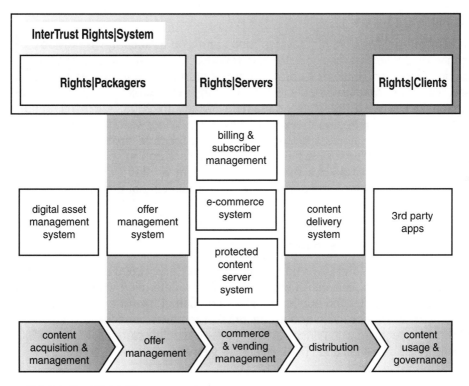

Figure 17.9 InterTrust Rights Management.

Digital Media Distribution Secure (DMDSecure)

DMDSecure is a server-side framework to build a complete rights management solution. It does not include technology for encryption, but uses third parties like Microsoft and Adobe. The product abstracts the management and control functions from the underlying protection mechanisms. Suppose that you wanted to protect both RealVideo and Windows Media content using two different DRM schemes, DMD allows the system to be managed in a unified manner.

The DMDSecure solution is designed for a wide range of delivery channels: IP/Web to the PC and wireless for mobile applications. Content can be live or delivered on demand. DMDSecure uses XrML to exchange information with the third parties.

SealedMedia

SealedMedia is a flexible solution for the secure distribution of files via networks or on removable media: CD-ROMS or random access memory (RAM) cards. It can encrypt Microsoft Office files, PDFs, image files (JPEG, PNG, and GIF), and audio-visual files (QuickTime, MPEG-1, and MPEG-4). Each file is wrapped with instruction for the client to communicate with a licence server to retrieve the key. Like most systems, it requires a network connection for the transaction.

Microsoft

In recent years, Microsoft has devoted much attention to security. To provide stronger security for documents and for streaming media, Microsoft has two solutions. Their initial focus was on solutions to protect digital entertainment in the form of audio and video files. The Windows Media Rights Manager can protect audio-visual content encoded in the Windows Media streaming format. In 2003, Microsoft announced Windows Rights Management Services. Much like Windows Media, a central rights management server stores licences that control access to protected files. Windows 2000 and XP both offer flexible file security and access control, but only on the corporate network. There is always the constant problem of staff burning copies of files to CD-ROM. Network security and access control lists cannot protect files outside the corporate firewall.

Windows Rights Management

This is a new service, and forms part of the Windows Server 2003 product. It allows content creators to wrap files with a set of rules. These determine who can view, edit, or print the file. The protection applies whether the content is online (on a corporate network or via the Web) or offline (on a local drive or removable media).

Although integrated with Windows, Microsoft will supply a plug-in for Internet Explorer to allow protected e-mail and HTML files to be viewed.

Windows Media Rights Manager 9

Microsoft's Windows Media Rights Manager provides a secure end-to-digital media e-commerce solution for Windows Media. This solution enables both application service providers and Internet content providers to manage, deliver, and sell streaming media. It supports download-and-play and conventional streaming.

The Windows Media Rights Manager system is designed to work with third-party credit card software that is compatible with MS Site Server 3.0. The Windows Media Rights Manager allows the publisher to set up the rules for the transaction. The player then uses these rules to open the encrypted content (Figure 17.10).

Flexible business models

New licensing rights have been introduced with Windows Media Rights Manager 9 to help enhance the creation of new, innovative business models.

Licences are issued independently of the actual media files. This provides flexibility for the business model and allows wider distribution of content. The Rights Manager checks for the consumer's licence every time a media clip is played. If the user does not have a valid licence, they are directed back to the registration web page.

As the licences and media files are stored separately from the media, the licensing terms can be changed without the need to encrypt the media file again and then redistribute to the client.

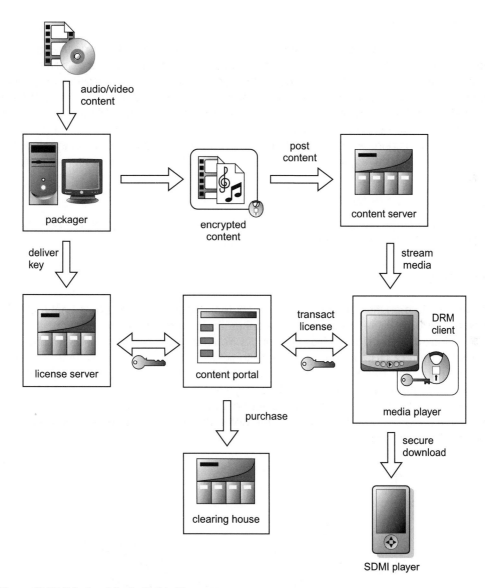

Figure 17.10 Window Media Rights Manager.

Windows Media Rights Manager supports rental or subscription business models. Limited play previews allow the potential purchase to look before they buy.

Windows Media Rights Manager can pre-deliver licences. This helps to remove the consumers' resistance to the acquisition and playing of secure media files. On feature is silent licensing, which means that a content provider may 'silently' deliver the licence to the consumer, without the need for the consumer to intervene.

Secure audio path

One area where content can be stolen is within the user's PC. If the clear audio data passing between the DRM client and the sound card driver is intercepting, then the content can easily be diverted and saved to the disk. To prevent this Windows Media has a feature called the secure audio path (supported by Windows ME and XP). The DRM is embedded in the operating system kernel. Before decryption, the DRM kernel component verifies that the path to the sound card driver is valid and authenticated. If any unauthorised plug-ins exist, then the decryption is barred. This prevents plug-ins on the sound card from copying the audio data. Microsoft certifies valid drivers for security.

Controlled transfer to SDMI portable devices

Windows Media Device Manager permits the secure transfer of protected media files to SDMI portable devices or the removable media for those devices.

Summary

If you want to monetise content, then that content has to be protected against theft. For media producers, the Internet has become the home shoplifting network. Certain groups look upon music as a free commodity. You may have confidential corporate information to protect. DRM can provide you with solutions. DRM can be expense to license and operate. You need to define your goals for content protection. Identify possible threats. A cost-benefit analysis would be very sensible.

The level of security that you use is very much a compromise. Strong security does not come cheap. You need to balance the potential loss of revenue against the cost of the DRM solution (Figure 17.11).

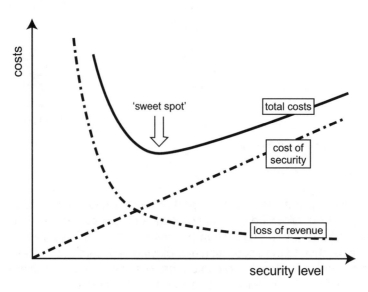

Figure 17.11 Finding the sweet spot.

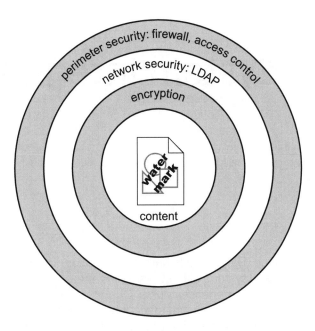

Figure 17.12 Circles of security.

Traditional text file DRM packages the entire file into a secure container. To stream, the encryption has to be in chunks, so that the player can render the file immediately. Securing the client is quite a challenge, so most DRM systems have means of identifying tampering that could compromise the security.

The best systems employ a number of means to protect assets against unauthorised access. When assets are within the asset repository, they can be protected by physical means like access control for the building. Once in the building, the standard network security provides password-controlled authentication. Once logged into the network, the files can be encrypted with a DRM product to provide further protection. If an unauthorised user penetrates these three layers, then the watermark can be used for forensic tracing of the leak (Figure 17.12).

If assets are accessed remotely, or are sold, rented, or syndicated, then the physical and network security are stripped away. Encryption and watermarking become the primary means to discourage theft.

A successful rights management deployment will require constant vigilance against efforts to compromise the system. To justify the expense of DRM, proper auditing and monitoring is required. Never take the word of a vendor that their system cannot be cracked. There is a large community constantly probing for weaknesses in asset protection systems.

18 System integration

Introduction

This is make or break time. The products have been chosen. The next stage is to install a highly complex software system without disrupting the smooth running of the business. This is an area where experience counts. One route is to use the services of one of the major IT consultancies to project manage the integration of the system.

Like any enterprise-scale software installation, the integration of digital asset management needs expert planning and implementation (Figure 18.1). The integration has two components. The first is the installation of the application. This can be managed just like any other new software purchase. The other component is the ingest of content and metadata into the repository. This can be a very manual process, and may need a temporary team of contractors, as few enterprises are likely to have spare staff available without shutting down part of the business. During the ingest, the content can be indexed as an aid to the later cataloguing and search:

- Install and integrate the application
- Ingest the content
- Index the content
- Integrate with the back-office applications.

As asset management systems are complex, with many connections to other applications, the integration can involve a deal of customisation. The cost of the professional services for this task can be considerable. Some systems can have a ratio as high as 5:1 for price of essential professional services versus the licensing fees or purchase price of the basic product. Broadly, the cost of digital asset management divides into four: the product, the platform for the product, the system integration, and any required customisation.

Just as the case with any corporate database deployment, the business processes and workflows have to be carefully analysed before the detailed system design can take place. Many companies like to run a pilot project, perhaps using one workgroup to assess the product in a real application. This is going to use human resources and investment. If successful, it should ease the roll-out of asset management across the enterprise, with potential cost savings.

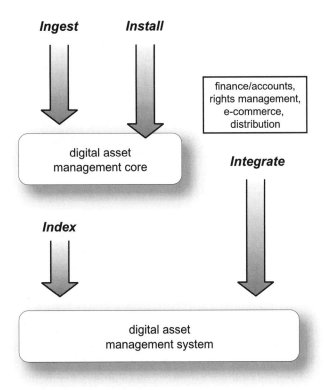

Figure 18.1 The implementation of asset management.

IT department

The corporate IT staff will need continuing involvement in the project, right from the start through to final operation. They may have to integrate with existing databases and web servers. They operate the corporate network security, the perimeter firewalls, and any virtual private networks to remote sites. It is vital that they buy in the project from the outset. Some IT staff are suspicious of multimedia content using corporate networks, it interferes with a smooth running and secure system. They may have to be diplomatically reminded that they are there to provide a service, and not a means to an end.

Issues to consider

Customer surveys consistently come up with a number of issues, it is useful to look at these as part of the planning. The first is price of asset management products. Obviously, customers always want to pay less. But underlying this is the need to get a return on investment. High prices are going to be a real barrier to any project. Another common bugbear is the amount of customisation needed. Again, this is partly a price issue. It would be great if the product provided everything you need out of the box. Inevitably, a certain degree of customisation will be needed. These professional services tend to be expensive.

One reason for the customisation is that many features of digital asset management products have often evolved to meet the specific needs of one customer. Many vendors have only sold around 10 systems. Consequently, the product features fit a narrow set of customers. Since every business is different, and the range of requirements is very wide, it is unlikely that a system will fit your requirements without an element of customisation.

Many customers feel that not only is too much customisation needed, but also it is not flexible enough to fully meet their needs. They also view that the customisation takes too long. Obviously, the vendors will need reassuring, but it is up to the project manager to agree costs and timescales during the vendor negotiations.

User interface

The user interface is very important if the digital asset management is to gain acceptance with the users. How does it inter-operate with your creative applications? Whether you are using Quark, Photoshop and Illustrator, Avid, or Adobe Premier, your chosen asset management must integrate with the tools that you are using for content creation and finishing if the investment is going to prove worthwhile.

Connectors to third-party applications

Many third-party applications will need to exchange data with the asset management. It could be the systems to manage artists contracts and property rights. This data exchange will allow a federated view of all the information about an asset without the need for separate interfaces. The content ingest modules may need to link to resource management products like Xytech or ScheduALL (both software systems to manage technical resources and the operators' schedules in video production facilities). That way, a busy ingest operation with many channels of encoding can properly manage the scheduling of the logging hardware, tape decks and the operators.

The asset management may also need to back-office systems like accounting and management information systems.

The first question to ask is 'can the third-party application be interfaced?'. Most products are now adopting open systems, but older product may need extensive software coding to provide facilities for data exchange. That cost has to be factored into the total project costs.

Legacy content

The digitisation of legacy content can be considered as part of the system integration, or it can be treated as an entirely separate exercise. Much depends on how the business case for the investment has been put together. Digitisation is often justified solely because the archives are decaying, so it is an issue of preserve it or lose it. Asset management is all about improving efficiency and lowering costs, and it should not be considered solely as a system for a digitisation project.

The business case may also be about providing the infrastructure to enable new business opportunities that can leverage the value of the archive. The two projects, archive preservation and lowering costs, are often interrelated, but still treated as separate tasks.

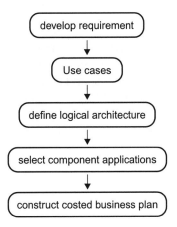

Figure 18.2 Typical planning flow.

Planning

The first stage in the planning cycle is to draw up the request for a proposal (RFP). This will need to define the scope of the project and the corporate workflows. This may require detailed workflow analysis to identify what actually happens throughout the content creation, production, and delivery.

On receipt of the proposals, it should be possible to hone the system architecture and to start evaluating the product offerings in detail. Reference customers may give you useful information, but do not forget that people will rarely admit if they bought the wrong product, but will put on a brave face. Once the vendor's pitch, the references, and the result of the product evaluation have been analysed and filtered, then you can start price negotiation. Most products have close competitors that can be used to leverage a good deal. Some products can be sold as an annual licence rather than an outright sale or perpetual licence. This can cap the upfront cost but does, of course, cost more in the long run (Figure 18.2).

The other alternative is to outsource to a service provider. This can be a good route for the smaller company. You can get all the advantages of enterprise databases like Oracle and a J2EE multi-tier architecture all for a monthly fee. The high entry level for purchasing such a system outright may not give return on investment for the small- and medium-size enterprise with a modest asset library.

Will the network take it?

If your asset management is handling video content, then the demands on the corporate network will be high. The bandwidths required for video will dwarf the needs of mail and document sharing. Modern network technology, like gigabit Ethernet, can easily cope, but an aging 10baseT network is not going to fit the bill. If the network requires a major upgrade, then that must be factored into the return on investment equations.

Some IT departments are very protective of the network, the less it is used the more they like it. They will need to be won round to the exciting possibilities that asset management brings to the enterprise, and their key role in the implementation.

Project management

Asset management is a large complex system that will impact on many areas of an enterprise. It is vital that the deployment is properly managed to avoid unnecessary disruption to the general business processes, and to the IT infrastructure.

There are several theories about project management with names like 'Work Breakdown Structure'. The project is divided into bounded pieces of work, all arranged in a hierarchy. Each work chunk is allocated as a task to a member of the integration team.

The first step before the start of the system integration is to agree the requirements and deliverables.

Resource management

Any project of this nature is going to need internal staff resource as well as the contractors employed by the system integrator. It is essential that the contractors can get inside knowledge of legacy systems and the IT infrastructure. This means that internal staff must be made available; therefore, they should have time allocated for liaison as part of their day-to-day duties. If they are too busy with fulltime tasks, then the system integration is going to be delayed through lack of knowledge of our system. Before the integration starts, it should be agreed who is going to be made available to assist with the integration; these internal 'champions' will be key to a smooth integration.

The system integrator will manage their own resources from a pool, and their timescales should fit their available resource. The management problems arise if there are overruns. Essential contractors may not be available, thus extending the delay.

Both the task scheduling and resource allocation can be managed using software tools like Microsoft Project. Such products can produce comprehensive reports for the project managers and for the client to monitor the progress.

Risk management

Life is uncertain; many external or internal events can place at risk the successful completion of a project on time and to budget. As examples, the late delivery of computer hardware or hold-ups in the building work at your data centre. Another risk is unforeseen problems in interfacing to legacy applications. A good project manager will exercise management of the inevitable risks in large software deployments and proactively anticipate possible problems. It is also possible to insure against risks.

Cost control

There is a natural tendency in any project for the costs to creep upwards. Cost control monitors spending against the planned projections. Any departures from the plan can be managed with sufficient warning. The problem that often occurs is an overrun on the time taken over a task. To bring a project back on target, the project manager may have to make compromises with the integration team or the client.

Purchasing

Once the bids for a project have been received, then you may want to negotiate the price or terms with the vendors. Some system integrators can handle this task as part of the project. This should also include delivery schedules and maintenance contracts.

System design

There are a number of separate components to the system design, each of a very different nature:

- Network
- Storage
- Ingest audio–video, document, and image scanning
- Client terminals
- Fulfilment and distribution.

Installation

The main installation is no different from any other large IT project. Where digital asset management differs is in the modules for ingest and fulfilment. If the system is going to be used to manage audio–video content, then video engineering expertise will be needed for the ingest modules.

Testing

The final commissioning of the digital asset management will need thorough testing because of the complexity of the different systems that make up the asset management. Once all the elements have been tested, commissioning should prove that the installation meets the requirements agreed in the original contract.

Loading the system

Once it is established that the primary components are all operating correctly, then the asset management is loaded with the content. Apart from the content, there is metadata, which is probably coming from several sources. This could be from a card index, or from legacy databases. The records from external databases may be imported as a one-time operation, or it may be an interactive operation through a data link.

The card index will have to be typed into a computer database. There are specialist contractors who can arrange the keyboard entry of a large card index into a database. Similar labour-intensive operations, like document scanning and film transfer to videotape, can all be handled by such contractors.

As the content is ingested, the system can be carefully monitored to check all is well. Once some content is in the asset management repository, then trial operations can be made to check the end-to-end workflow is all operative. This includes ingest, searching, retrieval, and fulfilment.

At this stage, the connections to external applications can be tested. This will need special precautions to ensure the external data is not corrupted.

Once the entire system is tested to ensure it conforms to the original requirement, the iterative process of tuning can begin. It is most likely that operational procedures may need to be optimised. Any modifications or upgrades must be managed as a new project. Any feature creeping during the original installation will lead to cost and project duration overruns.

Training

Once the system has been installed, one of the most important operations is the formal training of staff. Without this, the acceptance of the system can be compromised. The return on investment for digital asset management partly stems from efficiency gains. This is very dependent on a complete buy-in by the staff. Good training will explain the benefits of the system.

Training falls into three programmes:

- Maintenance for the IT staff
- System operation for staff handling media (ingest, storage)
- General use (authors, publishers).

The enterprise IT personnel will be familiar with the hardware, database, and networks, but there may be new technologies to manage: Fibre Channel and application servers. If the digital asset management uses a multi-tier architecture, it could be the first deployment of application server middleware. If the storage network is based on Fibre Channel, this requires specialist knowledge. A network engineer who is familiar with Ethernet may not have that knowledge. He would need further training, on Fibre Channel configuration and the management of the storage network.

Most asset management systems use familiar security procedures that any competent IT staff should be able to manage.

Internationalisation

One decision that should be made right at the start of a project is the issue of language. Is the system to run in a single language? Will other languages be rolled out later, or will it be multi-lingual from the start? If there are any plans to use more than one language, then that should be built into the design. It is easy to add languages if the system is designed that way from the start. It can be very difficult to patch multiple languages in at a later date.

If you are planning to use only languages with the Latin character set, then there should be no great issues. If all the applications use Unicode, then other character sets can be used like Greek or Cyrillic for Russian. All these languages have the same directionality; that is they are read left to right. There are other languages, like the Semitic languages, which is read right to left. To set Arabic text, it requires bi-directional support for characters; text runs right to left, and numbers run left to right.

The design of the user interface becomes more complex if right to left or bi-directional script is to be supported as well as left to right. Other scripts are not character based. Ideographic languages, like Japanese and Chinese, use glyphs to represent entire words or phonetic elements.

All these should be carefully considered before purchase of the system. It impacts not just the user interface, but also the way that the metadata records are stored in the database.

Planning for disaster

One of the primary reasons to purchase asset management is to make your content available throughout the enterprise. This all-pervading nature of the application means that it becomes the key infrastructure for all content-related operations. Therefore, the system has to be highly available.

To run the digital asset management with 24/7 availability, the system should be designed to minimise disruption during downtime. Downtime can be planned—new hardware installation, software upgrades—or unplanned, equipment failure, human error, or disaster.

Planned downtime includes routine operations like database backup and security management. There will also be periodic maintenance for schema upgrades, software patches, and network reconfiguration. If the system needs to be scaled up, then there will be new deployments of servers and software applications. Unplanned downtime can be from software failures, hardware failures (processors, power supplies, disks, or network cabling), and human error (accidental operator error or intentional sabotage). Finally, there is disaster: power failure, fire, flood, or even bombing.

A typical breakdown of unplanned downtime is 40 per cent human errors, 40 per cent process errors, and 20 per cent product faults. Human errors can occur with any task that requires human intervention. You can reduce these errors with proper training and formal procedures. Process errors result from poor planning, design, or documented procedures.

Product errors are covered below under software and hardware failure. The simplest means of protecting against downtime is by deploying dual systems, and by avoiding single points of failure. Planned downtime for the database is well catered for in the design of Oracle. If other databases management systems are used, then you will need to check the product specifications in detail.

The main concern in system design is for unplanned downtime, so I shall consider each point in more detail.

Software failure

Although any of the software can fail, the database is the most fundamental to the asset management. It is used for the persistent storage of the metadata and control information. If you have chosen the Oracle database, it has a feature called FastStart Recovery. This enables the database to be brought back online rapidly after an error condition. If you have chosen another vendor, then you will have to check for support of similar facilities.

Hardware failure

Processor failure includes power supplies, memory, CPU, or even bus failure. The servers should all have dual hot-plugged power supplies, so that faulty supplies can be exchanged without shutting down. Memory or bus failure can be protected against by use of server clusters. This requires that application server middleware can apportion the primary applications across the cluster.

Peripheral failure includes disk drives and their controllers, plus archive storage: DVD/CD-ROM and tape. Protection against disk failure is provided by redundancy or RAID. The array chosen should allow hot plugging of disks plus automatic rebuild of data. The disk storage systems that store the content can be backed by tape or optical disk.

Human error

This can take two forms: operator error or deliberate sabotage. Recovery from operator error usually requires a restart of the application, using a set recovery procedure. Sabotage can take many forms. Firewalls will provide perimeter protection, but much confidential information is removed by staff. Encryption should be considered for sensitive information stored within the media repository.

Disaster

The most likely form of disaster is loss of the main power supply. Resilience against more critical disasters can be avoided by siting the system in two locations. Uninterruptible power supplies (UPSs) can provide short-term protection against power glitches and provide power for a long-enough period for servers to be shut down gracefully. Power conditioning will protect computers from spikes caused by switching of air-conditioning plant that may share the same power supply. Long periods of power failure will require the provision of a standby generator. The only way to protect against fire, flood, and bombing is to replicate the content and metadata at two sites remote from each other. Data backups can be stored at a third site for additional protection.

Summary

A successful integration of the asset management system is a precursor to the efficiency gains promised for the installation. In many ways, it is not different from any other enterprise-scale software installation. The ingest of unstructured data, whether documents or multimedia content, does add to the complexity, and may demand craft skills outside the usual IT knowledge required for the software applications.

The skills required from the project manager are no different from any other project. There is an element of diplomacy required. The personnel involved in content creation tends to be fiercely independent and can be resistant to change. Their ready acceptance of the project is vital to its success, they stand to gain most. With asset management, they can concentrate on the creative side of their work, with the former time-consuming and repetitive tasks now automated.

Perhaps the most difficult investment decision is how much to spend on disaster planning. What will happen to you revenue flow if the system is down for days or even weeks?

Many asset management vendors offer systems integration services, or you can choose you own. Beware of consultants that promise to do everything that you want—'no problem'. It is just not possible, and it will surely end up being *your* problem. Can their track record justify such statements?

19 Digital asset management products

Introduction

Digital asset management products fall into many categories by application and by function. Some have been developed to manage documents, some images, and some for video content. The content management products have been designed to explicitly handle the assets that are served from web sites. Many products have been enhanced, so that they can handle any form of digital content. In general, the more all-compassing the product, the higher the cost.

The driver for the general-purpose product is the rapid adoption of multiple channel distribution of information and content. As an example, a brand manager will need to control document templates, marketing collateral, images (product shots and logos), television and radio commercials, web pages, and now information for wireless devices: the third-generation phones and personal digital assistants (PDAs). Another example is a training department. Again, they use the full gamut of asset types: manuals and guides, images and illustrations, CD-ROMs with training movies, and now DVDs and streaming media.

Digital asset management helps to merge these different asset formats, so that they can be managed as a whole, with no regard for their format. Just as a distance-learning product combines video, audio, PowerPoint slides, and text into a web page, the control of a multimedia content repository can be implemented with digital asset management.

Document management

Document management is a mature product area. There have been systems in use since the 1980s. The users have tended to be large corporations especially those obliged to maintain proper archives (like pharmaceutical companies). The leading products in this area are Documentum and FileNet.

Documentum

Documentum started out in document management in 1990. They have successfully made the transition to enterprise content management. They now offer products for all areas of asset management including web content, video, and unstructured information. They have over 2500 customers worldwide, mostly major corporations across the full gamut of industry sectors. Through the acquisition of Bulldog, they gained a full digital asset management capability. In 2003, Documentum 5 was the latest version of their enterprise content management platform.

For more information: www.documentum.com

FileNet

Founded in 1982, FileNet has grown to be the largest supplier of document management solutions. Their products can be used to improve the efficiency of business processes through the management of information, whether as documents or in the form of images and audio–video content. As befits their background in document management, the FileNet F8 product has strong support for the capture and ingest of paper documents using scanners and OCRs.

FileNet has moved on from a purely document management company into enterprise content management with strong support for business processes and workflow.

The F8 product focuses on connectivity, both with internal systems and with external organisations through XML, SOAP, and enterprise application integration (EAI). This aims to replace the conventional information interchange between suppliers and customers by interactive data interchange.

For more information: www.filenet.com

Image libraries

Unlike document management, which has tended to be focused on the enterprise user, image library products can be purchased at all price points from $50 to over a million. Image libraries need some form of asset management as the images can only be sorted and retrieved by viewing thumbnails. In the same way colour transparencies have always been carefully filed in plastic wallets and selected using a lightbox. Many image library products are based on this very model.

Photographers and stock libraries have always had to use formal systems for filing transparencies and negatives. Their businesses depend upon the swift retrieval of the right images from ten of thousands of possible shots.

Professional photographers file material by client and shoot. Image libraries use classification and keyword descriptions. These following products are listed by library size and capabilities, rather than alphabetical order.

iView MediaPro

iView is aimed at creative professionals with a large digital image or music library. iView MediaPro was originally developed as a set of software tools to assist the production of multimedia CD-ROMs. It was distributed as shareware, but is now sold as a fully supported product. It can be used for media management, cataloguing, and slideshow applications.

For the content creator, using iView MediaPro may be their first brush with digital asset management. It supports all the popular file formats. These include bitmap and vector images, DTP files (QuarkXPress and InDesign), audio, and audio–video formats like Flash, QuickTime and MPEG-1. Like much larger systems, it supports comprehensive metadata including EXIF data from digital cameras and the IPTC fields (news publishers metadata).

For more information: www.iview-multimedia.com

Extensis Portfolio

Extensis sells a number of different tools for creative professionals in the publishing sector. These include font management, pre-flight checks for desktop publishing, and software plug-ins for QuarkXPress and Adobe Photoshop. The asset management product is Portfolio 6. It is aimed at graphic designers, photographers, image libraries, and service bureaux.

The Portfolio catalogue sits on the operating system folder structure. Non-Portfolio users can access content using the conventional file manager. Content thumbnails are viewed in a floating palette and can be simply dragged into application like QuarkXPress. Image libraries can be published directly to the web or to CD catalogues. Larger systems can use an Oracle or Microsoft SQL Server database to store asset metadata.

For more information: www.extensis.com

Canto Cumulus

Cumulus is a modular asset management for digital images and multimedia assets. Cumulus can be used by single users, like digital photographers, a workgroup, or for an entire enterprise. Cumulus provides a virtual view of the assets in user-defined categories. The assets can be stored anywhere within the OS file system.

Searching for assets can be via the category directory structure or through a search of the metadata fields.

The workgroup edition uses a client–server architecture. The larger enterprise edition can use an Oracle database, with web browser clients. It can reference assets outside the local domain via uniform resource locators URLs. It has an API that can be used for automating repetitive tasks. The product can be used to catalogue PDFs and QuarkXPress files right down to page level. In both cases, the document text can be directly searched from Cumulus.

An option allows assets to be very easily published to the web. This can be used to publish asset catalogues online.

For more information: www.canto.com

FotoWare

FotoWare has a range of modular products for image libraries, advertising agencies, and print media publishers.

The entry-level product is FotoStation 4.5. This is aimed at photographers with digital image libraries and interfaces to digital cameras and scanners. For the larger system, the asset management is made from a number of FotoWare modules.

The FotoWare system is built from a number of modules. FotoStation Pro can be used to ingest images and enter metadata: title, caption, keywords, etc. It also offers image editing, and can interface with Photoshop where a more extensive manipulation is needed. The pictures are then exported to the archive. An index manager provides search facilities. For very large libraries with millions of images, the search engines can be linked together in a cluster. The user can make a federated search across all the indices simultaneously.

To support the publishing workflows, FotoWare has a colour profile engine called the Color Factory. This can process batches of images, for jobs like conversion from RGB to CMYK space. It has full support for ICC colour profiles. The engine can also perform image manipulation like unsharp masking and dust removal.

The Norwegian software company has been selling digital asset management solution for image archives since 1994. They have over 400 large FotoWare systems deployed across Europe. Most customers are newspaper groups and picture libraries.

For more information: www.fotoware.com

MediaBin

MediaBin is an enterprise scale digital asset management product that is now focused on the brand asset function. MediaBin started out in the digital imaging business in 1987. The products have since been adopted by large enterprises for the management of corporate photographic libraries, marketing collateral, and web site resources. The product can handle image assets, MS Office files, and video assets.

MediaBin has pioneered the concept of dynamic imaging. Images can be re-purposed in real time for delivery as different file formats. This means one file needs to be stored in the image repository. If a low-resolution copy is required for a PowerPoint presentation or a web page it can be generated on the fly from a high-resolution master. Photoshop images can be viewed as layers, then specified layers rendered as a new file. This can be used for multi-lingual collateral, where different language text layers are all stored as a single Photoshop file.

For more information: www.medibin.com

eMotion

eMotion has strong roots in the image library business. It was formed in 2000 by the merger of two companies, Picture Network International (PNI) and Cinebase. PNI was founded in 1992 as a developer of media asset management software called MediaQuest. As a service provider, they ran PictureQuest, an online repository for stock photographs. PNI was purchased by Kodak in 1997 and held until the merger with Cinebase. The Cinebase product, CreativePartner, was developed as a workflow tool for agencies handling large number of creative assets.

eMotion has since been developed into an enterprise scale solution for rich media assets. The product remains very much suited to the collaborative workflows typical of media agencies and television broadcasters. One of its strengths is the powerful natural language search engine. The integrated range of products called MediaPartner uses a multi-tiered architecture based on C++ core code with XML interfaces for links to back-office applications.

For more information: www.emotion.com

Web content management

Many products have been developed to manage the thousands of assets that are needed to build and maintain large web sites. Some have remained in the web development sector; others have expanded to become more general enterprise content management applications. Generally, the vendors offer modules for support of workflow processes and personalised portal development, either for customers or for the staff and partners.

BroadVision

BroadVision's focus is on portal development. A portal is not just a web site for content delivery. A portal is a key to collaboration between the enterprise and its suppliers and customers. BroadVision can be used to build unified portals, personalised, so that the business user can access relevant information from a single point of access. This can replace the maintenance of a public-facing web site, an intranet to provide staff with information, and an extranet for collaboration with suppliers, clients, and customers.
  For more information: www.broadvision.com

Gauss

Gauss has been providing document management solutions since 1983. The current product, VIP Enterprise 8, is an enterprise content management application spanning both document and web content management. Like most products of this nature, it is multi-tiered J2EE architecture with XML interfaces to external applications. The product is modular, with components to support workflow processes, content management, document management, and portal management. The latter can be used to build personalised intra- and extranets, as well as customer-facing web sites.
  For more information: www.gaussvip.com

Interwoven

Interwoven was founded in 1995, and has grown rapidly to become one of the leading suppliers of enterprise content management solutions. The core product is the content management module, TeamSite. Other modules provide support for metadata management and content distribution. Interwoven partners with MediaBin provide enhanced rich media asset management solutions. Interwoven provides a complete solution for brand management, e-commerce, and enterprise portal development.
  For more information: www.interwoven.com

Vignette

Vignette is a leader in portal and web content management solutions. Vignette V7 is more than web content management. It can also handle unstructured and transactional data, so that it can be used for enterprise-wide document, content, and digital asset management. Vignette also includes services that can be used to support workflow management.

The portals services can be used to set the business rules for personalisation of pages. Vignette includes analysis service that can be used to track the interaction of users with the web content. This can be used as an aid to site design improvements or just for gathering statistics about users interests.

For more information: www.vignette.com

Kitsite

This is a good example of an alternative approach to the large products like Vignette. Kitsite is a London-based team of developers that has created a power content management system with the emphasis on usability. It provides a full toolkit for controlling the workflow to create dynamic web sites. It can be used for the initial design, and later to add content on a day-to-day basis to predesigned templates.

It is designed for use by editorial staff, without the need for great technical knowledge. The client uses a web browser, so can be deployed almost anywhere. The user interface has been carefully designed to give a fast loading page for responsive interaction with the database. Like most products in this arena, it uses the Java platform with an Oracle database. It makes extensive use of XML and extensible stylesheet language (XLST) and has a SOAP API for access by external applications.

For more information: www.kitsite.com

Video asset libraries

One of the first digital asset management products was the Media360 from Informix. That product has since gone; it was a casualty of the turbulence in the marketplace after the turn of the century. Many of the remaining vendors are now leaner and are refocused on corporate application rather than the media sector.

These are some of the leading vendors that provide solutions for large video libraries. Many are not limited to video assets, but can be used for images and documents. They are listed in alphabetical order.

Artesia

Artesia was one of the first companies to develop a comprehensive digital asset management solution using a multi-tiered architecture. An early customer was General Motors. Perhaps, as the best-known example of digital asset management deployment, the General Motors project created a digital archive for the corporation's communications and marketing collateral library. The archive included 3 million still images, 2000 movie films, and 10,000 video masters.

By digitising this archive, the General Motors library could make the images and video clips more accessible, not only internally, but also to outside agencies and partners. Video content can now be retrieved without any need for the services of a librarian.

The Artesia TEAMS system is written in Java and runs on CORBA middleware services. Extensive facilities are provided to link to external application with XML. Artesia has interface modules to EMC and Sony for mass storage of assets and Virage for automatic logging of video assets. The usual client is a web browser, but Artesia also has a special client for the Apple Mac. Acknowledging that most creative professionals use this platform, Artesia provides a fully featured client that integrates with QuarkXPress, so that TEAMS can support an integrated workflow in publishing applications.

For more information: www.artesia.com

Documentum digital asset management

The Documentum video asset management solution started out as the Toronto-based Bulldog. The company was acquired by Documentum in 2001. The acquisition gave Documentum the ability to offer the capability for brand resource and content management for a much wider range of assets outside the realms of conventional documents and web assets. Like most video asset products, the primary files are represented by lower-resolution proxies generated by indexing applications like the Virage VideoLogger.

For more information: www.documentum.com

Blue Order

Blue Order has both workgroup and enterprise level media management applications. Blue Order is a Tecmath company and is based in Germany. The Media Archive product was first developed for television applications. The product has a distributed architecture that uses CORBA for interprocess communication and XML for content exchange.

Blue Order interfaces with many popular broadcasting applications. For mass storage system, they partner with ADIC, EMC, and StorageTek. It can be used with non-linear editing systems from Quantel and Avid. One application that makes good use of asset management is television news, Blue Order can interface to Associated Press' ENPS newsroom computer system.

The Blue Order media management is in use at some of the Europe's leading broadcasters, including Kirch Media, Bertelsmann MediaSystems, and SWR in Germany, ORF in Austria, and SVT in Sweden.

For more information: www.blue-order.com

IBM and Ancept

IBM has multiple approaches to the provision of digital asset management solutions. They have two different products tailored for different market sectors, plus they can be found as infrastructure in solutions offered by partners.

For the high-end broadcast market, IBM has the Media Production Suite. This is the basis of the system deployed at CNN for the management of their news archive. The Media Production Suite can use the IBM general parallel file system (GPFS).

This is a shared disk file system that can scale to very large computing clusters like the ASCI White at the Lawrence Livermore laboratory. This super-computer, with 8192 processors and 6 TB of RAM, is used to maintain the US nuclear weapons stockpile. GPFS allows such large clusters to share disks without the bottlenecks of file locking protocols that a conventional file system would exhibit.

Such a highly parallel design is needed for an asset management system that can support the needs of a major broadcaster. As an example, during normal course of their work the broadcaster could easily have 1000 users that all want simultaneous access to view video proxies. The IBM VideoCharger is designed to serve such large numbers of concurrent video streams from the disk storage array.

For more general enterprise content management, IBM partners with Ancept to offer a complete solution. The Ancept Media Server provides the user interface and business logic and is optimised to handle video assets. IBM provides the infrastructure using the content manager for low-level business logic, the security, messaging and workflow elements, and then underlying the entire system is the IBM DB2 database.

For more information: www.ibm.com

Search and retrieval

Some vendors have focused on the application of statistical processing technologies to intelligently index and classify content. These products can be used as search engines for digital asset management systems.

Convera

Convera's RetrievalWare is one of the most powerful search and categorisation applications. RetrievalWare is designed for the text search of very large document libraries, but Convera also has another product, Screening Room, that can be used to index, re-purpose, and publish video content.

The RetrievalWare product finds application wherever very large number of unstructured documents has to be indexed, categorised, and finally, searched. The product can be used for intelligence gathering as well as more conventional knowledge management.

The RetrievalWare search engine uses semantic and pattern recognition techniques to extract concepts from digital content. The semantic network technology uses natural language processing, including syntactical analysis and word morphology. The product leverages the content of dictionaries and controlled vocabularies or thesauri. The end result is a high precision and recall.

RetrievalWare can be used as an add-on search engine to media management applications that may lack a powerful search facility.

Screening Room extends the capabilities of the RetrievalWare to video assets. It includes modules to index, manage, re-purpose, and publish video content. The capture module can index video into storyboards of thumbnails images, convert speech to text, and decode closed captions. The re-purpose module allows the user to retrieve and assemble video clips into a rough-cut version using the storyboard. This can be exported as an edit decision list (EDL) to finish the broadcast resolution content on a non-linear editor.

For more information: www.convera.com

Fulfilment

The content management applications tend to focus on assets delivered through a web portal. With rich media applications, there is often the need to deliver digital copies of the original asset. As an example, a video library may use streaming media proxies to preview content, but if an asset is to be used, then typically an MPEG-2 version is required. This can be delivered by file transfer over wide-band network, or alternatively burnt to DVD or recorded on videotape.

This follows the traditional model for video production. Video facilities have much legacy equipment that supports the transfer of assets as physical media (videotape), and is still favoured by a large sector of the production community. Even in 2003, most video productions still use one of Betacam formats, analogue and digital, or DVCPro for programme interchange. As the Material eXchange Format (MXF) becomes more used, the file transfer may become the norm. The DVD is a useful medium for delivery, either to the consumer, or for business applications like training.

As an example, Sony has used their MAV video servers as an intermediary between robotic data tape silos and the video domain. The video server acts as a file buffer and decoder. Compressed video files are transferred from data tape to the server in non-real time. This may be a high-speed transfer at many times of the video playback rate. Once the file copy resides on the video server, it can be played out through a decoder as uncompressed video in real time. Such video can be used for live transmissions or copied onto a regular videotape. The server is acting as a buffer between the file and streaming domains.

Summary

No one selecting an asset management solution can complain about lack of choice. There are products available at all price points for the single user up to enterprise scale. There are niche application and end-to-end solutions. Some products are aimed at specific industry sectors like broadcasting or publishing, others are more general purpose. Many of the products are designed for enterprise portal development to enable business-to-business collaboration and commerce. As such, they lie outside the scope of digital asset management. They are included because they use digital asset management for the operations of content cataloguing, storage, and distribution.

This chapter represents a snapshot of the market in 2003. The large number of products launches and the slow take up in many areas of business has resulted in a high churn of companies. Some have risen fast and then fallen back to a small size. Others have gone altogether. Some of the most well-known names have made great strides, attracting customers and retaining profitability.

I have by no means listed all the vendors. It is a representative sample that illustrates many of the features and facilities that asset management products can offer.

The products tend to fall into customer groups. Some vendors have focused on general corporate users, some provide products aimed at image libraries, others specialise in products for the television community.

Often it can be a problem choosing a product. Many are very similar in features and facilities. How do you make that final decision between like products? Obviously, cost is a major issue. However, vendors should be willing to cut a deal to match a competitor. Other differentiators can be the support services; can you get a good quality response 24 h a day? Are associated costs the same and does one vendor use an application server that will require you to recruit new staff? Once all these issues are factored together, you should arrive at a clear leader.

The adoption of new technologies is allowing prices to become more attractive. The case for the purchase of an asset management is becoming more compelling.

20 Applications

Introduction

This chapter describes some typical digital asset management systems. It starts with a web content management solution to demonstrate the principles of these applications and the benefits that they offer. The next system is a digital asset management system that was developed for a web site that makes historic newsreels available to the public. The third is a large archive project for a television news organisation. These three demonstrate the range that asset management covers. The first is an extranet web site, the second makes video content available online, and the third illustrates the improvements in operational efficiency when a video library is made available from the desktop throughout a corporation.

Guardian Newspapers

Newspapers and magazines rely on advertising for their main revenue, with the subscription or whole price at to the news distributor making a small contribution. To a publisher, the advertising sales department is a primary revenue generator for the business. To attract advertisers, the publisher needs a 'shopfront'. A potential advertiser will want to see comprehensive information about the title they may want to use. They will want to see the audited circulation figures and the demographic profiles of the readership. They will also want to see the rate card—what it is going to cost. There is a host of other information including upcoming features, editorial contacts, and classified advertising details. If they decide to advertise, they will want the mechanical specifications. Traditionally, this information is supplied as a printed media pack, supplemented by mail outs and e-mails.

   Guardian Newspapers is one of the leading publishers in the UK. It is part of the Guardian Media Group and produces *The Guardian*, *The Observer* (a Sunday paper), and a very successful web site, *Guardian Unlimited* (Figure 20.1). This combination of two media, and weekly versus daily advertising, means that there is a large amount of information that a potential advertiser may want to view before embarking on a campaign. With such a successful web site, it was only natural that Guardian Newspapers should consider a web portal to give advertisers easy access to all the information needed. The use of a portal can also reduce the demands on sales staff answering enquiries for basic

Figure 20.1 GNL advertising information site. © Guardian Newspapers Limited.

information. Guardian Newspapers already had a large content management system managed by their IT staff, but one of the requirements for this new departmental site was to avoid increasing the load on the corporate IT department. The decision was made to use an outsourced solution that could be maintained and updated by non-technical users.

The product chosen was Kitsite. This uses a web interface to update content, so there is no need to install any software on the desktop clients, save for a web browser.

The advertising information site uses the same look and feel as the primary *Guardian Unlimited* site, so, although hosted separately from the main site, the Guardian brand is seamlessly maintained across all web presence. The information for the advertisers takes several forms, from editorial copy, with tables and images to PDF for more detailed information. Much of this information was mailed out, so every update demanded a new mailing. In the rapidly changing world of newspaper publishing, the ability to change information daily means that the advertising campaigns can align to events.

The site design started out with a modest site of 30–50 pages. It has grown to several hundred pages without increasing the complexity of the site management.

This web content management project demonstrates several aspects of digital asset management in general. The first is that operational efficiency is improved. Many

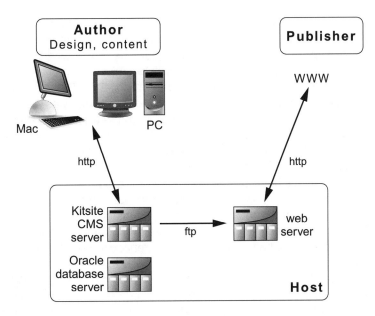

Figure 20.2 Kitsite content management block diagram.

time-consuming phone calls to the staff are eliminated, as potential customers can easily access the information that they need. The second is that projects can be outsourced, so that internal IT resources are not over-burdened. The third is that by selection of the appropriate product means that a complex portal can be updated by regular staff without the need for skilled web designers and developers.

The Kitsite content management is optimised for web-based users that access the hosted facilities via the Internet (Figure 20.2). The user interface has been carefully designed to meet high standards of usability, essential with non-technical users and fast loading pages, so that the site can be used with slow dial-up connections and congested networks. Kitsite can be used for the original design of the site templates as well as the day-to-day content updates. It can also import templates designed in applications like Macromedia's Dreamweaver. The product uses the Java platform with persistent data stored in an Oracle database. Each new page is output as a static page to the web server. This gives a fast loading site for the customers; dynamic sites can often suffer from delays as the database is queried to retrieve the content.

British Pathe

In the days before we watched news footage on television, the only way that the public could see the news in moving pictures was the cinema newsreel. This was a short compilation of four or five news stories from the previous week. The films were silent and ran for around 5 min, with brief titles introducing each item. Later, sound was introduced and the running time was extended to around 10 min. The last development to the newsreel was the use of colour film. New reels were released twice a week. For about 70 years, between the invention of cinematography and the universal penetration of television into the home, the newsreel was the primary vehicle for topical moving pictures.

British Pathe is one of the oldest media companies in the world. Its roots lie in its founder, Charles Pathé. He pioneered the development of the moving image in 1890s Paris. By 1920, an offshoot in London started to produce the Pathe Gazette newsreel. After the Great War, they started to produce magazine programmes as well. These covered entertainment, culture, and women's issues. The cinema newsreel was killed off by colour television and production stopped in 1970. By that date, British Pathe had built up a library of 90,000 short-film clips. This amounted to a total of 3500 h of film negative, in black and white, and later material in colour.

This library has always been available to television producers for use in programmes and commercials. The library was run using traditional manual processes. A comprehensive card index cross-referenced every item by subject. The index was classified into a number of categories to ease the search: location, sport, transport, and people, represent some of the categories. One-half a million cards referenced the 90,000 clips. The card index was also copied to microfiche.

This process was all manual; most searches used skilled archivists at Pathe. A production assistant could call up with a request for content related to a topic. The archivist would then suggest suitable film clips that cover that topic or event. If that suited the needs of the production, then a copy could be dubbed and despatched to the production office.

The library is a valuable historical record of the first half of the twentieth century. The first step to improving the exploitation of this asset was to migrate the index to a computer database.

The next stage was the transfer of the film to Digital Betacam. This move was going to make distribution much easier. British Pathe then decided to make the material available to a much wider audience with the use of the Internet and streaming video compression. This new access meant that schools could use the Pathe library as part of a local studies course. The general public could access items of personal interest; maybe they had appeared in old clips, or new relatives and friends in the old newsreels.

A digital asset management system is used to host the archive and to provide the search and fulfilment facilities.

Although the material is encoded in a streaming format (Windows Media), the delivery is by download-and-play. The data rate is too high to stream over dial-up connections, but, as the clips are only around 2–3 min long, they only take 10 min to download. The decision not to stream means that a standard web server can be used, rather than a special media server. The clips can also be ordered on VHS tape.

British Pathe is owned by the Daily Mail and General Trust Group.

Metadata

The card index did not carry much information; it was used mainly to locate the film canister number. When the material was logged onto the original database, the opportunity was taken to provide detailed descriptions of each clip. With the silent films, there were often captions that gave a description. The cameramen also made out a 'dope sheet' that gave information about each clip: the location, key people appearing in the clip, and what was happening. At the editorial stage, when the clips were put together into the

Table 20.1 British Pathe Database fields

Subject metadata	Film metadata	Tape metadata
Title	Canister number	Tape number
Summary	Duration	Time code in
Description	Length in feet	Time code out
Issue date	Sound/silent	
Year and decade	Music cue information	
Description		
Keywords		
Cataloguer's name		

finished newsreel, there would also have been a shot list. This may give further information about the clip. Where this information survives, it forms a valuable source of descriptive metadata. From the cataloguer's description, a number of keywords were extracted. This is a partial list of the database fields (Table 20.1).

The web portal offers a search by keyword, and can be restricted to a decade (the 1940s) or to a specific year.

Digital asset management

Pathe had the content and all the metadata necessary to make it searchable. All that was needed was a digital asset management system. The system chosen was Imagen from Cambridge Imaging Systems. Pathe wanted to store video master files on disk as well as the Digital Betacam master tapes. The disk files are encoded as MPEG-2 at a data rate of 5 Mbit/s. These can be used to make consumer-quality copies on VHS without the need to load them aster tapes.

Pathe chose to make the Internet video clips available at two resolutions: 128 kbit/s for preview and 512 kbit/s for fulfilment. The files are transcoded to SIF resolution (384 × 288 pixels) and in Windows Media format with the intention to add Apple QuickTime later. At the same time as the transcoding, a copyright watermark is keyed into the video (Figure 20.3).

It was decided to also offer clips to the public on videotape (VHS format). A decoding workstation was specified that could produce tapes directly from the MPEG-2 files.

The Imagen system includes four encoding stations, three transcoders and a decoder. The system can be expanded to meet future increases in demand. The ingest processes are set up as a batch; so all the clips on one tape can be ingested in a single sequence. During the earlier tape digitisation exercise, all the clips had their in and out time codes recorded in the database. This makes setting up the record list for ingest very easy.

At the encoding stage, the digital asset management system creates the thumbnails for the search pages that are used on the web portal. The metadata is stored in a reverse

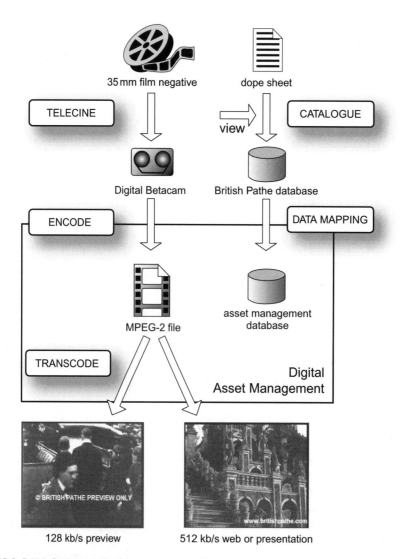

35 mm film negative   dope sheet

TELECINE

view CATALOGUE

Digital Betacam British Pathe database

ENCODE   DATA MAPPING

MPEG-2 file asset management database

TRANSCODE

Digital Asset Management

128 kb/s preview 512 kb/s web or presentation

Figure 20.3 British Pathe media flow.

indexed flat-file database. The Pathe web portal is a conventional dynamic site, with an e-commerce component to handle the purchasing transactions. The public uses the site via a search engine. They can type a keyword or keywords, and the engine returns a list of all clips that are referenced by those words (Figure 20.4).

The Pathe project has brought two benefits. The first is the ability to search and preview the archive from the desktop. The second is to offer the content for preview and sale via the Internet to the public. As a result, a valuable historical asset can be accessed by all, not just a small group of television producers.

The site has proved very popular since the day it opened. It has been designed, so that there is no single point of failure and it demonstrates what can be achieved with a

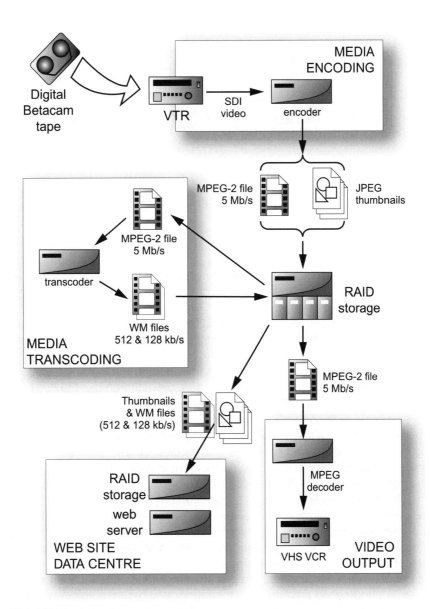

Figure 20.4 British Pathe system components.

simple yet elegant solution. The site is robust, with redundant web server locations, and can be easily expanded, either to handle extra video formats or to serve more users.

CNN archive project

The Cable News Network (CNN) is one of the world's best-known news broadcasters. It is based in Atlanta. Georgia, and is an AOL Time Warner Company. The Archive Project

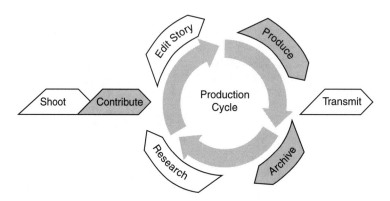

Figure 20.5 Television news workflow.

is the fruition of an ambitious plan to build an online library of their news archive. The project is being implemented by the installation of a digital asset management system from IBM, with mass storage by Sony Electronics.

For CNN, digitisation brings three benefits. Their news archive will be preserved, it enables new opportunities for content distribution, and it will improve the efficiency of the existing news operation.

Television news organisations have been early adopter of disk-based video storage (Figure 20.5). For the fast pace of news production, disk storage has the two big advantages of random access for editing and content sharing for collaborative workflows. Neither are possible with conventional videotape. Tape is a linear medium, and for production personnel to share the news material, copies have to be made. In contrast, disk storage gives the journalists and editors simultaneous access to the same material. Disk also has the added bonus of immediacy. As material arrives from the news feeds, it can be viewed immediately as it is being recorded.

Like much content creation, news is a combination of a linear flow from shooting to transmission and a circular flow, where the content is archived then re-purposed and re-used. As news often places current events in a historic perspective, the archive is vital to the production process. It can be used for research and as a contribution to a news story—the process of re-use and re-purposing.

Creating television news is more than just shooting video material, then editing it into a video clip. The journalists have to write their story and record a voice-over. The news producer has to put all the stories into a running order for the newscast. The anchors need scripts for their presentation. Character generator pages are prepared for the lower third captions and titles that are keyed over the stories. All this information flow is handled by a newsroom computer system. CNN use the Avid iNEWS newsroom computer. This contains valuable metadata that will also be stored in the archive, all referenced to the relevant video material.

Mediasource

The technologists at CNN have pioneered many aspects of digital asset management in the television environment. These asset management projects have been used on live news, and were not just pilot studies carried out in isolation. CNN have an ongoing technology plan to digitise their entire news operation. The goal is to reduce the time to air and to lower the production costs. The first project was called Mediasource. This is used for the ingest of incoming news feeds from the CNN bureaux and agencies.

CNN receives about 250 h of video material per day. Right around the clock, news video arrives by satellite to the headquarters in Atlanta. The feeds are encoded and indexed by a bank of Virage VideoLoggers. These loggers create browse-resolution copies of the incoming material and intelligently segment the video into storyboards of keyframes or thumbnails. The browse video and thumbnails are stored in an SGI Studio Central asset management system. From there, the journalists and news producers can simultaneously browse content from the same workstations they are using to access the newsroom computer.

The archive project

Once a story has passed the disk-based daily production, it was archived on videotape. If a journalist needed news footage from the archive, either to research the background for a story or to incorporate into a fresh story, then a production assistant would have to locate the tape, and then ship that videotape to the relevant bureau. Quite clearly, this puts a big delay in archive retrieval, and with a fast-breaking story it rather excludes the use of the archive.

The archive project will make browse-quality video of the archive available in just the same way as the Mediasource. A journalist can search and browse the archive. If a clip looks useful, then he or she can immediately view a browse proxy of the clip. If they like the clip, then they can retrieve the standard-resolution file to a local video server and edit it into their story.

The digital asset management provides facilities to search the archive online and then retrieve the video, without the need for staff to retrieve tapes, duplicate tapes, or ship tapes.

IBM media production suite

The digital asset management is based on the IBM content manager. This application runs on the IBM DB2 universal database. More general information on the content manager can be found in Chapter 19, entitled Digital Asset Management Products.

Newly ingested material is reviewed and keywords can be added to the clip metadata. CNN uses a controlled vocabulary customised for the special needs of a news organisation.

Sony PetaSite

The Sony PetaSite is a modular automated tape library system. It is based around the digital tape format (DTF) tape cassette. This uses half-inch tape and helical scanning.

The library is supplied as a number of different consoles for drives and cassette storage. Thy can be connected together to make very large libraries. The capacity ranges from 130 to 56,158 tape cassettes. Each DTF-2 tape can store up to 200 GB of data, so the maximum capacity is 11.2 TByte.

For MPEG-2 video recorded at a data rate of 25 Mbit/s, a fully configured PetaSite could store just under 1 million hours capacity. Sony predicts that the tape capacity will double for DTF-3 cassettes, and then double again to 800 GByte for the DTF-4.

The library is controlled by Sony's PetaServe HSM software. This application virtualises the hard drive cache and the tapes, so that the user can treat the library as a very large disk array. 'Live' files are kept on disk, and inactive files are automatically migrated to data tape. If a file is recalled that is not on the disk array, then it is restored from the data tape. If a file is required for transmission or editing, it can be transferred via a LAN to a Sony video server and then played out in real time as conventional video.

MXF

CNN has purchased a number of different video server products from different manufacturers. Until recently to transfer files between systems, they were streamed as live video. The development of the Media Exchange Format (MXF) will circumvent the vendor lock-in of proprietary server file formats. In the future, CNN will be able to transfer video as files from one make of server to another. The advantages of this, combined with the digital archive, will mean than file-based news production at CNN can become a reality.

Summary

Companies from newspaper publishers to television news can all benefit from the management of content as a digital asset. The lowering of storage cost and the increased power of computer processors have both helped to make digital asset management not only a viable proposition, but an essential tool for the sensible management of large content repositories.

The choice of an asset management system has often been complex. It a compromise between cost and performance that must meet the original demand for a return on investment. The system has to not only mould seamlessly into existing workflows, but must enable new operational practices.

The range of products now available offers something for every price point. There are specialist products for niche areas, media encoding, and search, and there are core products for file and workflow management. Digital asset management is steadily being adopted across the full gamut of business and industry. It is providing new opportunities for selling and syndicating assets. It can streamline workflows and improve the efficiency of knowledge workers. Some products are more suited to the project team or workgroup. Others can be adopted across a corporation for applications like brand management.

Digital asset management promises to bring changes to businesses from the smallest craft content creators through to the largest of enterprises. Just as digital processing has transformed desktop publishing and general office communications, the digital management of assets is going to change the way content is used and re-used.

Abbreviations

These are some of the abbreviations and acronyms used in the text:

AAC	Advanced Audio Coding (MPEG)
AAF	Advanced Authoring Format
AES	Audio Engineering Society
AI	Artificial Intelligence
AIFF	Audio Interchange File Format
AIT	Advanced Intelligent Tape (Sony)
ANN	Artificial Neural Network
ASCII	American Standard Code for Information Interchange
ASP	Active Server Page (Microsoft)
ASR	Automatic Speech Recognition
ATA	Advanced Technology Attachment
ATL	Automated Tape Library
ATM	Asynchronous Transfer Mode
AVI	Audio Video Interleaved
BLOB	Binary Large Object
BWF	Broadcast WAVE format
CAD	Computer-Aided Design
CCD	Charge Coupled Device
CCW	Continuous Composite Write-once (M-O)
CELP	Code-book Excited Linear Prediction
CGI	Common Gateway Interface
CIE	Commission Internationale d'Eclairage
CIFS	Common Internet File System
CLI	Common Language Infrastructure (.NET)
CMYK	Cyan, Magenta, Yellow, and blacK
COM	Component Object Model (Microsoft)
CORBA	Common Object Resource Broker Architecture
CSS	Cascading Style Sheets
DAM	Digital Asset Management
DAVIC	Digital Audio-Visual Council
DBMS	DataBase Management System

DCM	Digital Content Management
DCMI	Dublin Core Metadata Initiative
DDC	Dewey Decimal Classification
DDL	Data Definition Language (SQL); Description Definition Language (MPEG-7)
DES	Data Encryption Standard
DLT	Digital Linear Tape
DML	Data Manipulation Language
DMZ	Demilitarised Zone
DRM	Digital Rights Management
DS	Description Scheme
DTF	Digital Tape Format (Sony)
DTD	Document Type Definition
DTH	Direct To Home (satellite television)
DTP	Desk Top Publishing
DV	Digital Video
DVB	Digital Video Broadcasting
DVD	Digital Versatile Disk
DWDM	Dense-Wave Division Multiplexed
EAI	Enterprise Application Integration
EBU	European Broadcasting Union
ECM	Enterprise Content Management
ECMA	European Computer Manufacturers Association
EDI	Electronic Data Interchange
EDL	Edit Decision List
EJB	Enterprise Java Beans (Sun)
EPG	Electronic Programme Guide
EPS	Encapsulated PostScript
EXIF	EXchangeable Image File format
FC/IP	Fibre Channel over Internet Protocol
FTP	File Transfer Protocol
GbE	Gigabit Ethernet
GIF	Graphic Interchange Format
GMPLS	Generalised Multi-Protocol Label Switching
GPS	Global Positioning System
HBA	Host Bus Adaptor
HMM	Hidden Markov Model
HSM	Hierarchical Storage Management
HTML	HyperText Markup Language
HTTP	HyperText Transfer Protocol
HVD	High Voltage Differential
IDL	Interface Definition Language (CORBA)
IEC	International Electrotechnical Commission
IEEE	Institute of Electrical and Electronics Engineers

IETF	Internet Engineering Task Force
IIOP	Internet Inter-ORB Protocol
IP	Internet Protocol, Intellectual Property
IPFC	IP over Fibre Channel
IPSec	Secure Internet Protocol (IETF)
IPTC	International Press Telecommunications Council
ISBN	International Standard Book Number
iSCSI	Internet SCSI (small computer system interface)
ISO	International Standards Organisation
ISSN	International Standard Serial Number
iTV	Interactive Television
J2EE	Java 2 Enterprise Edition (Sun)
JBOD	Just a Bunch Of Disks
JDBC	Java DataBase Connectivity
JFIF	JPEG File Interchange Format
JPEG	Joint Photographic Experts Group
JVM	Java Virtual Machine
KLV	Key–Length–Value
LAN	Local Area Network
LCCN	Library of Congress Control Number
LPC	Linear Predictive Coding
LTO	Linear Tape Open
LVD	Low Voltage Differential
LZW	Lemple–Zif–Welch
MAM	Media Asset Management
MDCT	Modified Discrete Cosine Transform
M-O	Magneto-Optical
MOS	Media Object Server
MPEG	Moving Picture Experts Group
MXF	Material eXchange Format
NAA	Newspaper Association of America
NAS	Network Attached Storage
NCSA	(US) National Center for Supercomputing Applications
NFS	Network File System (IETF)
NIC	Network Interface Card
NITF	News Industry Text Format
NLP	Natural Language Processing
NTFS	New Technology File System (Microsoft)
NTSC	National Television Standard Committee
OCLC	Online Computer Library Center
OCR	Optical Character Recognition, Optical Character Reader
ODBC	Open DataBase Connectivity
OLE	Object Linking and Embedding (Microsoft)

OMG	Object Management Group
ORB	Object Request Broker (CORBA)
PAL	Phase Alternation Line
PCDATA	Parsed, Character Data
PDA	Personal Digital Assistant
PDF	Portable Document Format
PDH	Plesiochronous Digital Hierarchy
PDL	Page Description Language
PDR	Personal Digital Recorder (TV-Anytime)
PHP	PHP Hypertext Preprocessor
PICS	Platform for Internet Content Selection
PNG	Portable Network Graphics
ppi	pixels per inch
PQMF	Pseudo-Quadrature Mirror Filter
PRISM	Publishing Requirements for Industry Standard Metadata
QIC	Quarter-Inch Cartridge
RAID	Redundant Array of Inexpensive (or Independent) Disks
RDF	Resource Description Framework
RDBMS	Relational DataBase Management System
RFC	Request For Comment
RFP	Request For Proposal
RFQ	Request For Quotation
RH	Relative Humidity
RIP	Raster Image Processor
ROI	Return On Investment
RTCP	Real Time Control Protocol
RTF	Rich Text Format (Microsoft)
RTP	Real Time Protocol
RTSP	Real Time Streaming Protocol
SAN	Storage Area Network
SCSI	Small Computer System Interface
SD	Standard Definition (television)
SDH	Synchronous Digital Hierarchy
SGML	Standard Generalised Markup Language
SMPTE	Society of Motion Picture and Television Engineers
SOAP	Simple Object Access Protocol
SONET	Synchronous Optical Network
SQL	Structured Query Language (ess que el)
SVG	Scalable Vector Graphics
TCP	Transmission Control Protocol
TIFF	Tagged Image File Format
UDDI	Universal Description, Discovery, and Integration
UDF	Universal Disk Format (CD, DVD)

UID	Unique Identifier
UML	Unified Modelling Language
URI	Universal Resource Identifier
VCR	Video Cassette Recorder
VPN	Virtual Private Network
VTR	VideoTape Recorder
W3C	World Wide Web Consortium
WAVE	Waveform Audio (Microsoft)
WCM	Web Content Management
WebDAV	Web-based Distributed Authoring and Versioning
WORM	Write Once Read Many
WSDL	Web Services Description Language
XHTML	eXtensible HyperText Markup Language
XML	eXtensible Markup Language
XLST	eXtensible Stylesheet Language
XrML	eXtensible rights Markup Language
XSL	eXtensible Stylesheet Language

Index

 **Focal Press**   **www.focalpress.com**

Join Focal Press online
As a member you will enjoy the following benefits:

- browse our full list of books available
- view sample chapters
- order securely online

Focal eNews
Register for eNews, the regular email service from Focal Press, to receive:

- advance news of our latest publications
- exclusive articles written by our authors
- related event information
- free sample chapters
- information about special offers

Go to www.focalpress.com to register and the eNews bulletin will soon be arriving on your desktop!

If you require any further information about the eNews or www.focalpress.com please contact:

USA
Tricia Geswell
Email: t.geswell@elsevier.com
Tel: +1 781 313 4739

Europe and rest of world
Lucy Lomas-Walker
Email: l.lomas@elsevier.com
Tel: +44 (0) 1865 314438

Catalogue
For information on all Focal Press titles, our full catalogue is available online at www.focalpress.com, alternatively you can contact us for a free printed version:

USA
Email: c.degon@elsevier.com
Tel: +1 781 313 4721

Europe and rest of world
Email: j.blackford@elsevier.com
Tel: +44 (0) 1865 314220

Potential authors
If you have an idea for a book, please get in touch:

USA
editors@focalpress.com

Europe and rest of world
ge.kennedy@elsevier.com